Novas

Haroldo de Campos

Novas

Selected Writings
Haroldo de Campos

EDITED AND WITH AN INTRODUCTION
BY ANTONIO SERGIO BESSA AND
ODILE CISNEROS

FOREWORD BY ROLAND GREENE

Northwestern

University Press

Evanston

Illinois

Northwestern University Press
www.nupress.northwestern.edu

Printed in the United States of America

10 9 8 7 6 5 4 3 2 1

ISBN-13: 978-0-8101-2029-7 (cloth)
ISBN-10: 0-8101-2029-1 (cloth)
ISBN-13: 978-0-8101-2030-3 (paper)
ISBN-10: 0-8101-2030-5 (paper)

Library of Congress Cataloging-in-Publication Data

Campos, Haroldo de.
    [Selections. English. 2007]
    Novas : selected writings of Haroldo de Campos / edited and
with an introduction by A. S. Bessa and Odile Cisneros ; foreword
by Roland Greene.
        p. cm. — (Avant-garde and modernism collection)
    Includes bibliographical references.
    ISBN 978-0-8101-2030-3 (pbk. : alk. paper) — ISBN 978-0-
8101-2029-7 (cloth : alk. paper)
    1. Campos, Haroldo de—Translations into English. 2. Campos,
Haroldo de—Criticism and interpretation. I. Bessa, A. S. II.
Cisneros, Odile. III. Title.
PQ9697.C2448A2 2007
869.8'4209—dc22

2006102081

Contents

Foreword *Interessantíssimo*

Haroldo de Campos's collection of poems entitled *Excrituras,* published in the retrospective volume of the mid-1970s *Xadrez de estrelas,* contains a suite of lyrics—atoms of wordplay, really—that include several variations on the following terms:

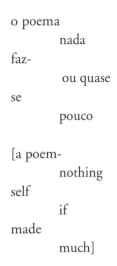

The elements of these micropoems rehearse the issues that run across de Campos's work, both his poetry and his criticism, from the start of his career in the 1950s to his death in 2003. And true to the spirit of both his inventive poetry and his wide-ranging criticism, they can be rearranged into alternative statements and made to undermine or ironize their own assertions. Should a poem be built on a principle of copiousness or scarcity? Is the poem about its world or about itself? Where is the border between sense and nonsense? De Campos addressed each of these questions in multiple ways, often with different answers. And the essential de Campos is a figure as constructivist as these poems: a poet, critic, translator, archival scholar—in all, a protagonist of the first importance in Brazilian and international avant-garde letters. This volume, called *Novas,* reintroduces Haroldo de Campos by giving readers of English a generous overview of his intellectual and aesthetic program.

That program, we see here, is formidable. With his brother Augusto de Campos and their collaborator Décio Pignatari, Haroldo de Campos in the 1950s introduced a renovative program for concreteness or materiality into

Brazilian poetry. This group, which called itself *Noigandres* after a nonce word in one of Ezra Pound's *Cantos,* became a force in Latin American and world poetry in the 1960s and after, their poetry and manifestos serving as demonstrations of each other. While they were enormously controversial in Brazil during their heyday, the *Noigandres* group has become an inescapable fact of the poetic scene in more recent times, so that certain contemporary poets think of themselves as "postconcrete," and every poet in Brazil with a claim to self-awareness must have a position about the *Noigandres* legacy. When the group was discovered by North American vanguardists (including the language poets) in the early 1990s, their currency throughout the Americas was ensured. De Campos himself accumulated a body of achievements that drove but also transcended the *Noigandres* movement: with his brother, he rediscovered the fascinating Brazilian Romantic poet Joaquim de Sousa Andrade (or Sousândrade); he wrote a number of influential theoretical and critical essays; and he was responsible for some of the most influential postconcrete poetry, including the masterpiece *Galáxias.* To sketch his significance, one would have to say that his essays represent a link between international formalism, structuralism as well as poststructuralism, and the postcolonial, all of which are visible in his thought, while his poems are contemporaneous and cognate with the Beats on the one hand and the language poets on the other.

As a figure who provoked an intense critical conversation—and participated in it himself, attempting perhaps too strenuously to define the terms on which his own achievement would be understood—de Campos is due for a reassessment based in the work itself, which can now be seen in historical and theoretical perspective. *Novas* makes that project not only possible but probable.

Roland Greene

Acknowledgments

We wish to express our gratitude to those whose contribution and support made this book possible. Richard Sieburth, from the Department of Comparative Literature at New York University, first envisioned the possibility of this book and generously gave us his time and expertise, not to mention encouragement throughout this entire process. Without his friendship and guidance, this volume would not have been possible. Eliot Weinberger, a personal friend of Haroldo de Campos since the 1970s, kindly opened his library to provide us with many of the original texts. His focused criticism and suggestions on the content and structure of this book were immensely appreciated. Marjorie Perloff, director of the Avant-Garde and Modernism series at Northwestern University Press, embraced the project with passion and stood firmly behind it at all points. Without her commitment and diligence, this book would exist only as an idea. We were humbled by the warmth and enthusiasm with which two distinguished scholars read our manuscript for Northwestern University Press, and we profited a great deal from their suggestions and advice. Many friends and scholars who have followed and supported Haroldo de Campos's career throughout the years also offered their hand and facilitated our task by putting us in contact with each other: Thanks to Roland Greene, Pierre Joris, K. David Jackson, and Kenneth Goldsmith. We are immensely grateful to Susan Betz and Rachel Delaney, former editors at Northwestern University Press, who patiently guided us through the intricacies of editing and copyright. We were fortunate to count on a number of exceptionally gifted scholars willing to double as translators. Their names are listed individually in connection with their translated pieces. Above all, we would like to thank Haroldo de Campos himself, who generously endorsed this venture, guiding us, providing materials, and responding with patience and care to all queries that came up in the process of editing this volume. We regret that he did not live to see it in print; he passed away in the summer of 2003 while the book was in production. We also offer our gratitude to his widow, Carmen de Arruda Campos. And finally, we want to thank our families and friends for their love and support.

A Note on This Edition

The selection and translation process for this book proved difficult and lengthy, as Haroldo de Campos's oeuvre is immensely varied. In the poetry section, we mostly selected poems that could be rendered in English and would resonate with readers at large. The endnotes to the poems are the author's own, and although not essential, they often illuminate each poem's intertextualities and context.

As for the critical essays, we chose pieces that would speak to contemporary debates on poetics, translation, and cultural politics in Latin America. In the process of editing, we were obliged to abridge certain pieces that, for reasons of space, could not be reproduced in full. Such is the case of "Disappearance of the Baroque in Brazilian Literature: The Case of Gregório de Matos," "An Oswald de Andrade Triptych," and "Poetic Function and Ideogram/The Sinological Argument," which are presented as excerpts from longer essays. Spaced ellipsis points in square brackets indicate material we omitted. The author's omissions in citations are indicated by spaced ellipsis points with no brackets. Existing translations were revised and checked against the originals for accuracy and consistency.

Another important part of the editorial process was standardizing and expanding the bibliographic references, providing the most complete citation possible as well as references to English translations where appropriate. We did our best to locate all sources of the quotations in the essays. In the cases of journals or books not readily available, we provided the author's reference and any other details we could ascertain. In order to distinguish between the author's and the editors' material, we kept the author's notes as endnotes and the editors' and translators' notes as footnotes. Where a note by the author merited an editorial intervention, it is indicated in the note by square brackets and/or "TRANSLATOR" or "EDITORS."

Introduction

Haroldo de Campos was one of the key literary figures to emerge from Brazil in the second half of the twentieth century and a unique personality within the international avant-garde. His stature has been acknowledged by diverse intellectuals the world over. In the course of a structuralist analysis of the poems of the medieval Galician troubadour Martin Codax, the Russian critic Roman Jakobson declared himself an admirer of de Campos's "supreme flair for the innermost ties between sound and meaning, a flair which underlies and sustains . . . [his] most daring poetic experiments and thrilling discoveries . . . and which inspires his extraordinary transpositions of seemingly untranslatable poems from quite divergent languages."* The Italian writer and semiotician Umberto Eco, in the preface to the Brazilian edition of his world-renowned book *Opera aperta* [*The Open Work*] (1962), noted the visionary reach of de Campos's aesthetic proposals: "It is indeed curious that a few years before I wrote *Opera aperta* Haroldo de Campos, in one of his articles, anticipates its themes in a surprising way, as if he had reviewed the book I had not yet written and later wrote without reading his article."† In 1996, the French philosopher Jacques Derrida, the Mexican poet Octavio Paz, the Brazilian poet João Cabral de Melo Neto, and the Cuban novelist Guillermo Cabrera Infante contributed to a public homage to de Campos at the Pontifícia Universidade Católica in São Paulo. Derrida praised de Campos's "absolute, atemporal, definitive, inalterable, indubitable knowledge" and his "adventurous and audaciously urgent" approach to poetry.‡ Cabral de Melo Neto, in turn, described him as "that wonderful thing: / a poet and a translator who came to literature armed with an enviable / knowledge of the literary phenomenon."§ And in Paz's poetic tribute, in a series of "snapshots," the essence of de Campos's writing and personality is thus captured:

---

* Roman Jakobson, "Martin Codax's Poetic Texture," in *Selected Writings,* ed. Stephen Rudy (New York: Mouton, 1981), 3:169–75. —EDITORS

† Umberto Eco, *Obra aberta* (São Paulo: Editora Perspectiva, 1968), 17. Eco is speaking of de Campos's 1955 essay "The Open Work of Art," included in this volume. —EDITORS

‡ Jacques Derrida, "Chaque fois, c'est à dire, et pourtant, Haroldo..." in *Homenagem a Haroldo de Campos* (São Paulo: Pontifícia Universidade Católica, 1996), 9-11. —EDITORS

§ João Cabral de Melo Neto, "Depoimento," in *Homenagem,* 19. —EDITORS

Reflections swarming on the page, confusion
of yesterday and today, the seen
entangled with the half-seen, inventions
of memory, lacunae of reason;

Hellos, good-byes, ghosts of the eye,
incarnations of touch, unsummoned
presences, seeds of time,
time out of joint.*

As for Cabrera Infante, he knew no better "promoter of culture in Brazil"
and the Americas, the "new continent for literature."† Despite these international accolades, de Campos is still relatively unknown to the larger English-
speaking public. It is the purpose of this volume to provide English-speaking
readers with a comprehensive understanding of Haroldo de Campos's work.

Commenting on the "cosmopoetics" of his last book of poetry, *A máquina
do mundo repensada* [*The World's Machinery Reconsidered*] (2000), Haroldo
de Campos argued that "the understanding of cosmic order as an ingeniously
articulated machine goes back to the beginnings of poetic and philosophical
thought."‡ For de Campos, all poetry is a speculation on the inner workings
of this cosmic apparatus—from Dante Alighieri to Stéphane Mallarmé. This
cosmological model applies to de Campos as a poet, critic, essayist, and
translator whose vast interests encompassed East and West, antiquity and
modernity, and it is reflected in the titles of some of his books: *Xadrez de
estrelas* [*Star Chess*], *Signantia: quasi coelum/Signância: quase céu* [*Paradisiacal
Signifiers*], *Galáxias* [*Galaxies*]. The title we chose for this volume seeks to
highlight this quality of de Campos's work and its articulation of a new poetics (*nova poética*), where East meets West and Latin America cannibalizes its
European Other in a provocative synthesis for world consumption.

Haroldo Eurico Browne de Campos was born in São Paulo on August 19,
1929.§ A lifelong resident of that city, he lived in the same house in the

* Octavio Paz, "Instantáneas," in *Homenagem*, 15–16. —EDITORS

† Guillermo Cabrera Infante, "Haroldo siempre trae regalos," in *Homenagem*, 20–21. —EDITORS

‡ Haroldo de Campos, "De uma cosmopoesia," in *Depoimento de oficina* (São Paulo: Unimarco Editoria, 2002), 59–70. —EDITORS

§ These details of Haroldo de Campos's life are mostly based on his autobiographical note included in
A educação dos cinco sentidos (São Paulo: Brasiliense, 1985), 113–15. —EDITORS

Perdizes neighborhood until his death on August 16, 2003, not far from where his brother Augusto de Campos still lives. In the 1950s, inspired by the modernization and democratic changes introduced by President Juscelino Kubitschek, the two brothers, in collaboration with Décio Pignatari, launched the concrete poetry movement in Brazil. This movement was an energetic and visionary attempt to appropriate an entire tradition of avant-garde writing and single-handedly change the course of Brazilian poetry. In 1952, the three young poets began to publish the avant-garde poetry magazine *Noigandres,* named after a philological riddle involving this Provençal word mentioned in one of Ezra Pound's *Cantos.**

Like many writers in Brazil and elsewhere, de Campos was trained as an attorney and received a law degree from the University of São Paulo in 1952. Not without a note of smug humor, de Campos counted among his professional legal colleagues figures such as the Brazilian baroque poet Gregório de Matos (a judge and magistrate), the Brazilian modernist Oswald de Andrade (who never actually practiced law), and Franz Kafka (who often did in Prague, in the twilight of the Austro-Hungarian Empire).

"A lawyer like everyone," de Campos was not seduced by the profession. He came to realize that besides the city of São Paulo—hyperpolluted and the place he loved best on earth—what really mattered to him was traveling. Starting with his first trip to Europe in 1959 with his lifelong partner Carmen, when they traveled second class aboard a Portuguese ship, he constantly found himself—literally and literarily—crossing oceans, boundaries, languages, cultures, and genres, which, he noted, resulted in epiphanies and antiepiphanies.

Major epiphanies on his first trip issued from encounters with the concrete poet and philosopher Max Bense and the composer Karlheinz Stockhausen in Germany, and with the Bolivian-Swiss poet Eugen Gomringer in Switzerland. All of these artists and intellectuals were developing experimental work that the *Noigandres* poets found very much in line with their own artistic activities in Brazil. A mutually beneficial exchange ensued, projecting concrete-poetry endeavors beyond their national boundaries. On that trip, de Campos followed the itinerary of Ezra Pound's *Cantos* through the north of Italy all the way to Rapallo, where he met with an

* See Ezra Pound, "Canto XX," in *The Cantos of Ezra Pound* (1970; reprint, New York: New Directions, 1995), 89–90; and Hugh Kenner, *The Pound Era* (Berkeley and Los Angeles: University of California Press, 1971), 114–17. —EDITORS

aging Pound. An acknowledged forefather of the concrete poetry movement, Pound, with his *paideuma,* his theories on translation, and his interest in the Chinese ideogram and Oriental poetry, was to leave a lasting
imprint on de Campos's literary pursuits.

Upon his return, a journey through northeastern Brazil (Paraíba, Recife,
and Bahia) triggered other epiphanies—this time the rediscovery of his
native land, particularly its baroque heritage. What de Campos called
Brazil's "multidevouring baroque-ism" marked his intellectual and literary
production after the early, heroic phase of concrete poetry that ended in
the early 1960s. This hybrid and ecumenical phase of his work displays de
Campos's passion for writing in all its manifestations: the grapheme, the
ideocalligraphy of the East, and linguistic transactions and transfers that
could be termed "Babelian" or Pentecostal. His iconoclastic translations (or
"transcreations," as he preferred to call them) range from Homer to Dante
and from Ecclesiastes and Japanese poetry to Octavio Paz.

Alongside his diverse literary activities, de Campos taught at the university level after earning his doctorate in literature from the University of São
Paulo in 1972, with a provocative structuralist analysis of the Brazilian
modernist novel *Macunaíma* by Mário de Andrade. A professor at the Pontifícia Universidade Católica in São Paulo from 1971 to 1989, de Campos
also held teaching appointments at the Technische Hochschule in
Stuttgart, the University of Texas–Austin, and Yale University. He received
numerous international prizes and honors, including a Guggenheim fellowship (U.S., 1972), a Fulbright fellowship (U.S., 1978), the Chevalier
dans L'Ordre des Palmes Académiques (France, 1995), the Octavio Paz prize
(Mexico, 1999), the Roger Caillois prize (France, 1999), and the prestigious
Jabuti prize four times (Brazil, 1991, 1992, 1993, and 1998).

Although his poetic oeuvre in itself is extremely condensed, de Campos
was a prodigiously prolific author—he produced more than ten books of
poetry and over a dozen volumes of theory and criticism. Both alone and
in collaboration with his brother Augusto de Campos, Décio Pignatari,
and Boris Schnaiderman, he authored book-length translations of Pound,
James Joyce, Vladimir Mayakovsky and other Russian poets, Octavio Paz,
Mallarmé, Dante, Provençal troubadours, the books of Genesis and Ecclesiastes, Japanese poetry and Noh theater, and the *Iliad.* He also contributed
countless essays and articles to books and periodicals.

Poetry

While Haroldo de Campos initially earned a reputation as part of the concrete poetry movement, it is important to note that the first poems he published were already heavily influenced by a baroque aesthetic. Following the end of the concretist period, his poetics underwent dramatic transformations, with lines of continuity and rupture. In our choice of poems, we have attempted to trace these transformations by representative selections from key periods, from his first baroque and concrete phases to his eclectic 1998 collection *Crisantempo* [*Chrysantempo*].

Published in 1976, *Xadrez de estrelas* [*Star Chess*] gathers twenty-five years of poetry, featuring poems that, with the exception of *Auto do possesso* [*Act of the Possessed*] and *Servidão de passagem* [*Transient Servitude*] had been published mostly in magazines. The subtitle, "Percurso textual" ["Textual Itinerary"], hints at a perception of writing as a "voyage" through language. The circular trajectory of the book begins under the influence of the neobaroque and traverses the avant-garde phase of concretism to arrive finally at the ultrabaroque of the *Galáxias*. We should note that de Campos's first incursion into the baroque was of an intuitive nature. The poems from this phase are more influenced by the tradition of Jesuit drama, introduced in Brazil in the second half of the sixteenth century by Father José de Anchieta as a device to catechize the natives, than by Walter Benjamin's theses on German baroque drama—a text that was central to de Campos's reassessment of the baroque in the 1970s. These are highly allegorical works with biblical, political, historical, and linguistic references woven into a dense texture. They convey the sense of a mostly Catholic Brazilian culture that is perhaps now lost, the world of passion plays during Easter week, legends and folklore connected to the country's Portuguese origins, and a fascination with a monarchical past, which in the late 1940s was still within living memory. The long poem *Act of the Possessed* is emblematic of this phase. With its structure and title clearly alluding to the Jesuitical "auto"— the sacramental educational plays in Brazil's colonial tradition—the poem unfolds a highly symbolic plot with characters such as "the Chess Player" and "the Exorcist," harking back to Baudelaire's *Bénédiction*.

For the reader to appreciate fully the presence of baroque elements in these early poems, it is important to bear in mind how integral they are to the Brazilian culture of the time. For instance, Glauber Rocha's first short film, —O *pátio* [*The Patio*], 1959— in which two characters move around a chess-patterned patio—bears a striking resemblance to de Campos's *Auto do possesso*. Rocha, one of the founders of the experimental film trend *cinema novo* in the 1960s—a movement that, like concrete poetry and bossa nova, helped revolutionize Brazilian culture—also began his career by paying homage to this baroque legacy.

Although it did not vanish, the influence of the baroque progressively subsided in the years preceding the concretist phase. In *Teoria e prática do poema* [*The Poem: Theory and Practice*], we first encounter an example of de Campos's metalinguistic concerns: here his metaphorical impulse, later more restrained, is put to use to investigate, in specular fashion, the very nature of writing poetry. The ghost of the baroque also returns in a daring way in *Claustrofobia* [*Claustrophobia*], a challenging text that already announces formalist experiments with prose such as *Galaxies* as well as the thematic concern with the epic versus the worldly in *Finismundo: A última viagem* [*Finismundo: The Last Voyage*].

De Campos initiated his concrete phase in 1955–56 with *O âmago do ômega* [*The Essence of Omega*], a collection of poems with a unique balance of constructive rigor and deconstructive content that is rendered with difficulty in English. Like those of his companions in the *Noigandres* group, de Campos's concrete poems zoom in on the page to magnify the formal and syntactic qualities of the poetic text, but despite this shared interest in structure and concision, his texts are *sui generis* in the openness of their structure. *The Essence of Omega* stands quite comfortably between poetry and prose, and the pulverization and reassembling of words carry residues of de Campos's earlier incursion into the baroque. Strictly speaking, the only truly concrete poems—in the visual sense—which have been emphasized by critics and literary scholars are the series entitled *Fome de forma* [*Hunger for Form*]. But the high modernism of their formal achievement—their random arrangements resemble the mosaic patterns that the visual artist Athos Bulcão designed for Oscar Niemeyer's main buildings in Brasilia at about the same time—is somehow neutralized by the ensuing collection *Forma de Fome* [*Form of Hunger*]. Complementary and symmetrical poetic gestures, these two selections are in many ways a tribute to the work of Cabral de Melo Neto, a poet whose technical skill and acute social awareness were paradigmatic for de Campos. The punning equation of "form" (*forma*) and "hunger" (*fome*) in these titles is also reminiscent of Marx's inversion of Proudhon's *The Philosophy of Poverty* into *The Poverty of Philosophy*.

De Campos's exposure to Marxist theory is evident throughout *Form of Hunger*—a canto for the dispossessed in which even the role of poetry is questioned ("poesia em tempo de fome / fome em tempo de poesia / . . . eu nomeio a fome" ["poetry in time of hunger / hunger in time of poetry / . . . I name hunger"]). This aspect of de Campos's work has been widely ignored by critics who have insisted on seeing Brazilian concretism as an utterly formalist movement devoid of any political content. These critics overlook the fact that, in the context of 1950s Brazil, form *was* political, and that Lucio Costa and Oscar Niemeyer (also Marxists) designed Brasilia with a utopian-socialist agenda which was later co-opted by the military junta that took over the country in 1964.

In the early 1970s, de Campos's poetry became extremely rarefied. The series *Excrituras* [*Excriptures*], for instance, despite its highly calibrated rigor and the significant use of the blank space of the page, lacks the visual flair of the concrete phase. Text becomes more telegraphic, with long pauses and, in *Tatibitexto* [*stuttertext*], the title already signals the tentative nature of writing. The atmosphere of ruin and/or fragmentation that de Campos created in these texts evokes the stultifying political climate of Brazil at that time, when censorship was at its peak and many intellectuals were in exile, while those who managed to stay in the country chose total silence or developed a highly elliptical style. From the very outset, the issue of "silence" in concrete poetry had been criticized as the "emasculation" of language and was equated with repression, an issue approached by de Campos in his essay "The Informational Temperature of the Text." Significantly enough, a similar kind of criticism was also directed at the supposedly utopian architecture of Brasilia, where wide boulevard-style avenues allowed for immediate control of the city by the army. The Brazilian cultural effervescence of the 1950s thus proved to be extremely ambiguous in nature; the very strategies promoted to renew language—be they poetic or architectural—could as easily be co-opted and transformed into mechanisms of repression.

Published in 1979, the volume of poetry *Paradisiacal Signifiers* reverses the tripartite scheme of Dante's *Commedia,* beginning with *Paradisiacal Signifiers,* a poem in four parts, and then proceeding via a purgatorial interregnum (*Status viatoris*) to a funereal descent into Hades (*Esboços para uma nékuia [Sketches for a nekuia]*). In this volume we include the first poem, which captures, in Craig Dworkin's felicitous translation, the essence of "writing" paradise. *Paradisiacal Signifiers* shares certain formal concerns with *Star Chess,* but the focus on ahistorical invention is now linked to tradition. It is not without interest that at the time this volume was published, de Campos was also translating several cantos of Dante's *Paradiso.* Beyond the influence of Dante, particularly on the structural design of the book, the tutelary presence of Novalis is evident in the epigraph and, in one poem, as the object of an exemplary reading; there is also the resonance of Pound's inclination toward the fragmentary at the close of his *Cantos*. In addition, these adamantine texts also conjure up the realm of what the *Tel Quel* group called "écriture" or "writing," as well as the work of Francis Ponge. Words spatialized across a blank page become sonic atoms, the inscriptions and encryptions of which enact a "theophany of signs" that approximates in its incisive crystalline purity the domain of the numinous.

A educação dos cinco sentidos [*The Education of the Five Senses*] (1985) constitutes, as Andrés Sánchez Robayna has noted, an opening toward the "expressive" and "poetic idioms in history."* Indeed, as a migration from the extreme emphasis on the material aspects of language, this collection evidences more concern with the search for a lyrical identity, overcoming the ban on the poetic "I" issued in the *Noigandres* poets' manifesto "Pilot Plan for Concrete Poetry" (1958). The spatialization of language is curbed, and linear—or lineated—writing makes a return, while still maintaining the principle of economy of expression. References to Provençal troubadour poetics (*Tenzone, Provença: Motz e. l. Son*) as well as to Chinese philosophers (*Mencius: Theorem of White*) echo the *paideuma* of Pound. Nevertheless, the lessons of concretism are still perceptible, refined into a superb technique of sampling in *Ode (Explicit) in Defense of Poetry on St. Lukács's Day,* a poem composed entirely of quotes and inspired by a conversation between Benjamin and Bertolt Brecht in Svendborg in 1938. The "recovery" of history in these poems was also paralleled at the time by de Campos's rediscovery of a tradition exemplifying a "concrete" attitude: while composing *The Education of the Five Senses,* he was also translating and writing critical essays on Goethe, Mallarmé, and Pound. All these influences converge in a number of poems, such as *Goethean Opuscule* (I & II) and *Le don du poème* (Mallarmé), while other poems pay tribute to his contemporaries (his brother Augusto de Campos, in the Rimbaldian *Je Est Un Autre: Ad Augustum,* and the artist Hélio Oiticica, in *Paraphernalia for Hélio Oiticica*). These are the poems of a more mature phase, in which flashy avant-garde accoutrements are exchanged for a more ironic, meditative attitude (as in the Adornian *Minima moralia*). They also include reflections on the principles of poetry (*As It Is*) and metalinguistic concerns stemming from

* Andrés Sánchez Robayna, prologue to *La educación de los cinco sentidos,* by Haroldo de Campos, trans. Andrés Sánchez Robayna (Barcelona: Àmbit Serveis Editorials, 1990), 13. —EDITORS

a Marxist conception of language as the essence of humanity (*The Education of the Five Senses*).

The minimalist style of de Campos's concrete phase gradually developed into its opposite with the appearance of the first individual texts that compose the collection *Galaxies,* in which the excesses of the baroque reappear with unexpected vigor. The first of the *Galaxies* appeared in 1963, and the last in 1976. *Star Chess* features a partial selection that goes up to 1973, and the entire collection was published in one volume in 1984. The posthumous "definitive" edition came out in 2005. *Galaxies* is best approached as a travelogue documenting de Campos's journeys through countries and books. In these voyages, he seems to have taken to heart Mallarmé's contention that everything exists in order to end up in a book. A collection of fifty texts written in stream-of-consciousness style, *Galaxies* is a long, unpunctuated meditation on writing, world literature, and the elusive nature of the book. In terms of form, the texts of *Galaxies* mark a departure from Gomringer's model of the poem as *constellation,* moving toward a new perception of the text as *nebula.* They also blur the distinction between poetry and prose. Marjorie Perloff opens her essay on de Campos's *Galaxies* by quoting David Antin's observation on Gertrude Stein: "[Her texts] are concrete poetry with justified margins."* Like the Brazilian baroque, these texts are formidable not because of their originality *per se,* but rather owing to the way they imbricate foreign influences (Stein, Joyce, Pound, Mallarmé) with references to the "macaronic" translations of the nineteenth-century Brazilian poet Odorico Mendes and to popular culture. As in Joyce and Mallarmé, literature assumes an almost sacral character in these texts; hence their performative, liturgical tone, beginning with the very first, *E começo aqui* [*And Here I Begin*], which addresses the question of origin. The ensuing texts are permutations of this original big bang, like an ever-expanding galaxy.

It is not without irony that de Campos, who in the 1950s advocated a concrete, objective writing, came to pursue a luminous kind of writing later in his life. This luminosity—we might also call it lucidity—emerged from what de Campos described as the "radiant" practice of translation. With the passage of time, his view of translation became nearly metaphys-

---

* Marjorie Perloff, "'Concrete Prose' in the Nineties: Haroldo de Campos's *Galáxias* and After," *Contemporary Literature* 42, no. 2 (Summer 2001): 270–93. —EDITORS

ical, as if a text's true meaning could only be glimpsed through prismatic refraction. The practices of writing and translating gradually began to intertwine and illuminate each other, culminating in a dazzling way in *Finismundo: The Last Voyage*. This poem is not only the sum of forty years of poetry—de Campos had already coined and used the word "finismundo" [world's end] in *Claustrophobia* (1952)—but also of his work as a translator. The poem's epigraph ("per voler veder trapassò il segno" [for wanting to see, he trespassed the sign]), a reference to Ulysses' fate in Dante's *Commedia*, alerts us to the doubling of writing and translating, which de Campos ultimately sees as the "transgression of the sign."

Finismundo: The Last Voyage constructs an entire fiction out of translation. Its central theme was fished from Homer's fragment "thánatos eks halós," the ambiguity of which—"dying in the sea," or "dying far from the sea"—has kept many translators in a perpetual quandary. The work resonates at many levels, as the poem also "translates" the action of Joyce's *Ulysses* to the poet's contemporary São Paulo. Among the many references encoded in the poem, the reader will find traces of Odorico Mendes's translations of the *Odyssey* and Fernando Pessoa's "myth" of the creation of Lisbon, as well as Guido Cavalcanti's, Dante's, and Hölderlin's fascination with light.

The paronomastic title of de Campos's 1998 *Crisantempo: no espaço curvo nasce um* (*Chrysantempo: In Curved Space Is Born A*) appropriately captures the essence of this work's eclectic 350-plus pages. A word that fuses florality and temporality, *Crisantempo* is a chrestomathy, a bouquet that gathers new and old works from a variety of periods, original poems, and transcreations (now entitled "transilluminations"). The book includes a reprint of *Finismundo;* Japanese poems; a handful of poems about cats; ekphrastic texts; homages to writers and artists, both living and dead; iconoclastic translations from the ancient and modern Greek (from Sappho to Cavafy) as well as from Latin; and versions of Nahuatl poetry, among other things. Excerpting from such an eclectic volume proved difficult, and we opted for the poems that could best be rendered in English. These include short lyric poems that evoke the world of haiku in their imagistic qualities (*As in Ovid: Metamorphosis, Minimal Landscape*); meditations on the transience of life in the temper of Ecclesiastes (*Poems for Qohelet* I & II); homages to de Campos's lifelong mentors and obsessions (*The Poet Ezra Pound Descends to Hell, Gongorine Tribute to Sá de Miranda*); and, in honor of de Campos's Marxist convictions, his own English translation of a poem originally written in Portuguese in support of the Landless Peasants Movement in Brazil (*The Left-Winged Angel of History*).

Essays

In the constant interplay between his poetry and his essays, Haroldo de Campos embodies the Mallarméan ideal of the poet as critic. His fifty-year production ranges from early theoretical writings on concrete poetry to revisions of literary figures of the past, and from erudite explications of his unconventional translation praxis to the formulation of a "postutopian de-logocentrifying cannibalist poetics." To place the vastness and variety of these pieces in context, a few words of introduction are in order.

De Campos began his career as an essayist in the 1950s, a period of burgeoning optimism about the modernization of Brazil, epitomized in the political slogan "O Brasil é o país do futuro" ("Brazil is the country of the future") and reflected in the cutting-edge aesthetic adopted by the *Noigandres* poets. The latter's immediate goal was to provide a theoretical foundation for concrete poetry not only by engaging with the international avant-garde but also by integrating the advances of technology into their work. This explains the influence of certain figures, now seldom mentioned, who had great relevance for de Campos and the *Noigandres* group in their early period—the linguist Alfred Korzybski and the creator of cybernetics Norbert Weiner, for example, whose theories inform "Concrete Poetry–Language–Communication" (1957). A second important didactic aim was the education of the public: the *Noigandres* group assumed the task of translating and/or making known in Brazil such key theoretical texts as Ernest Fenollosa's *Chinese Written Character as a Medium for Poetry*, presented by de Campos in his volume *Ideograma: Lógica, poesia, linguagem* [*Ideogram: Logic, Poetry, Language*] (1975), translated by Heloysa de Lima Dantas.

In addition to positioning concrete poetry strategically within the international avant-garde, de Campos devoted his subsequent critical writing to the exploration of a global tradition of poets and texts that, according to him, exhibit a "concrete" attitude through practices of linguistic economy, fragmentation, invention, and materiality. De Campos's revisionist task led him, in Horácio Costa's view, to "refute an officialized and reductive vision of Brazilian culture"* while at the same time dislocating logocentric attitudes in his Derridean essay "Anthropophagous Reason: Dialogue and Difference in Brazilian Culture."

Some of these essays were initially published in mass-circulation newspapers and subsequently revised or expanded when published in book form. Their scholarship is occasionally sketchy in its rigor and consistency:

---

* Horácio Costa, "Dinámica de Haroldo de Campos en la cultura brasileña," *Cuadernos hispanoamericanos* 509 (November 1992): 67. —EDITORS

it appears that de Campos, a magpie reader, relied on whatever sources served his critical bricolage. What he himself once said about Pound's essay on Cavalcanti's *Donna mi prega* [*A Lady Asks Me*]—"that [it] should be read in the manner of a Borgesian visionary fiction rather than as a cautious piece of philological erudition"—could equally apply to his own critical writings. But like many fine essays, de Campos's pieces function as exploratory experiments rather than as authoritative statements; and while some of his references may now seem dated, the fact remains that in their eclecticism, de Campos and the *Noigandres* poets were polemically involved in the debates of the day.

Many of de Campos's critical writings have been of undeniable importance in the reevaluation of Brazil's literary legacy. These revisionary plumbings of the past brought back into discussion the work of authors that for years had been relegated to a historical limbo. In the section entitled "Reinventing Tradition," we have selected essays that focus mainly on three of these key literary figures: Gregório de Matos, Joaquim de Sousândrade, and Oswald de Andrade. These authors formed a kind of triumvirate upon which de Campos launched his "re-vision" of Brazilian literary tradition.

In "Anthropophagous Reason: Dialogue and Difference in Brazilian Culture" (1980), de Campos sums up the main arguments he had developed more extensively in other works. The essay traces de Campos's development from his early espousal of structuralism, Russian formalism, and concrete poetry's utopia to his arrival at an "anthropophagous reason," a poststructuralist approach informed by Jacques Derrida's deconstructive notions of differential hybridity. From this new critical stance, de Campos seeks to highlight Brazil's specificity and provide a political angle from which to rethink and counter notions of cultural dependency. "Anthropophagy," a concept that de Campos developed from Oswald de Andrade's influential "Manifesto Antropofágico" ["Cannibalist Manifesto"] (1928), has spawned an entire critical literature; its recent assimilation by the field of postcolonial translation studies is of particular interest.*

In "Anthropophagous Reason," de Campos appropriates Oswald de Andrade's manifesto, which fed on documented instances of Tupi-Guarani ritual cannibalism, to posit the cannibal as a model for the dilemma of

---

* See, for instance, Else Ribeiro Pires Vieira, "Liberating Calibans: Readings of *Antropofagia* and Haroldo de Campos' Poetics of Transcreation," in *Post-colonial Translation,* ed. Susan Bassnett and Harish Trivedi (London: Routledge, 1999), 95–113. —EDITORS

Brazilian culture. Far from Rousseau's exemplary "noble savage," de Campos's "bad savage" devours his cultural Other in order to draw "marrow and protein to fortify and renew his own natural energies." With this powerful metaphor, de Campos subverts imputations of cultural colonialism in the case of Latin American modernists, such as Oswald de Andrade and Vicente Huidobro, when they critically assimilate the work of their European colleagues (Blaise Cendrars and Pierre Reverdy) in order to submit it to a differential digestion.

Anthropophagism, a transfusion of energies from donor to receiver (where the donor is acknowledged but indistinguishably resynthesized), also questions the plenitude of origin in favor of difference. According to de Campos, this differential deglutition characterizes the cultural production of the Americas—from the baroque poets Gregório de Matos, Sor Juana Inés de la Cruz, and Juan Caviedes to modern New World cannibals like Sousândrade, Oswald de Andrade, and Cabral de Melo Neto. As a result of repeated mastication, concrete poetry arrived on the scene with an equally whetted appetite, appropriated an entire code of post-Mallarméan avant-garde literature, and in a unique synthesis theorized, supported, and opened a dialogue with popular culture.

Although "Anthropophagous Reason" was clearly meant to dismantle colonialist discourses circulating at the time, it retains its currency because it anticipates contemporary notions of hybridity and global multiculturalism. The "Alexandrian barbarians" (figures like Octavio Paz, Jorge Luis Borges, Alfonso Reyes, Mário de Andrade, Lezama Lima, and, tacitly, de Campos himself) prefigure these concepts by chewing up and "ruining" universal cultural heritages in order to produce a global literature that is ludic, combinatory, multilingual, and hybrid. These are indeed the "leftovers of a diluvial digestion," whose "hidden" process culminated in the Latin American "boom." Finally, in a move that provocatively reverses the pattern of Western colonialism, de Campos challenges logocentric writers to brace themselves for the urgent task of devouring the differential marrow of these polytopic and polyphonic "new barbarians," because, he argues, "alterity is, above all, a necessary exercise in self-criticism."

"Disappearance of the Baroque in Brazilian Literature: The Case of Gregório de Matos" (1984) is a passionate attempt to rescue the work of the baroque poet Gregório de Matos, one of Brazil's most controversial authors. De Campos's main interlocutor in this essay is the literary critic Antonio Candido, author of the influential *Formação da literatura brasileira* [*Formation of Brazilian Literature*] (1964), an account that locates the "true" inception of Brazilian letters in the romantic Indianist period of the nineteenth century. Candido, de Campos argues, follows a metaphysical, linear concept of history that culminates in what Derrida terms an "unveiling of presence." For de Campos, this problematic "historical" perspective is ideologically biased, as it strives to privilege the "communicative" aspect and "national spirit" of certain literary incarnations at the expense of arbitrarily ignoring the "weak" or "unsystematic" literature of the baroque. For this reason, Gregório de Matos's baroque, self-reflexive poetics, devoid of a nationalist sense of mission, excluded him from Candido's literary system. De Campos counters Candido's argument by exposing as a fallacy the assumptions of this linear model, which turn into negative value judgments, and points out that a similar questioning of linearity had already led Benjamin, Federico García Lorca, and T. S. Eliot to rehabilitate the baroque some fifty years before the appearance of Candido's book. In this way, de Campos lays the groundwork for recovering not only the work of de Matos but also the entire baroque legacy.

In 1964 Haroldo and Augusto de Campos similarly took on the task of recovering the work of the poet Joaquim de Sousândrade (1833–1902). In their anthology *Re/Visão de Sousândrade* (*Re/Vision of Sousândrade*), the two brothers presented critical interpretations and transcriptions of Sousândrade's poetry, which had been out of print since its original publication in the nineteenth century. Sousândrade belonged to the second generation of romantics in Brazil, but his work, particularly the "Wall Street Inferno" episode in his long epic poem *Guesa errante* [*Wandering Guesa*], was considered extravagant even at the time and quickly fell into oblivion. Intended both as a revision of Brazilian literary historiography and as a way of reclaiming Sousândrade as a precursor of concrete poetry, the anthology praised the visual and verbal experimentalism of the montage techniques used in "The Wall Street Inferno." In "The Trans-American Pilgrimage of Sousândrade's *Guesa*," however, de Campos turned to another aspect of the poem, namely, the way in which its Americanist poetics deploys an innovative mixture of genres, unified by the leitmotif of a journey across the Americas, drawing inspiration from both Alexander von Humboldt's travels and Goethe's "Walpurgisnacht" in *Faust*. This trans-American itinerary was to generate fellow travelers in the twentieth century, as de Campos shows, in Pablo Neruda's great New World epic *Canto general*.

Oswald de Andrade (1890–1954) is perhaps the single most important writer of the Brazilian modernist tradition to whom de Campos devoted his attention. Claiming Andrade as a forerunner, the concrete poets vigorously promoted his innovative work, tacitly challenging the figure of Mário de Andrade as the official leader of Brazilian modernism. Thanks to their efforts, Oswald's work now enjoys the status of a modern classic of Brazilian literature, although he has not by any means attained the same prestige as other Latin American writers such as Huidobro and César Vallejo, with whom he shares a similar avant-garde impetus. The subsection we entitled "An Oswald de Andrade Triptych" features selections from three important essays on this modernist author, written between 1964 and 1972—"A Poetics of the Radical," "*Miramar* on the Mark," and "*Seraphim*: A Great Un-Book." As these essays make clear, de Campos particularly valued Oswald's incorporation of the colloquial into poetry, his innovative use of collage techniques at the micro- and macrolevels, and his penchant for social satire. "A Poetics of the Radical" discusses the revolution that Oswald de Andrade's 1924 poetry collection *Pau Brasil* [*Brazilwood*] effected in Brazilian letters. Emerging from a status quo of "tribune rhetoric" in which "fluffy and rustling eloquence" reigned supreme, *Brazilwood* stripped the poem of needless ornamentation in order to produce a "simple and naked expression of sensation," "minutes of poetry" that captured the "restlessness of the new Brazilian." "*Miramar* on the Mark" is devoted to Oswald de Andrade's first experimental novella, *Memórias sentimentais de João Miramar* [*Sentimental Memoirs of John Seaborne*]. In his essay, de Campos notes the watershed importance of this text and compares its parodic workings to those of Joyce's *Ulysses*. Among the affinities he underscores are a common telegraphic style, a collage structure—half sentimental diary, half *fait divers*—as well as the motif of the redemptive voyage. In "*Seraphim*: A Great Un-Book," de Campos examines *Serafim Ponte Grande* [*Seraphim Grosse Pointe*], the continuation of Oswald's experimental fiction, where the collage structure moves from the microlevel to the "great syntagmatics of narrative." If *Seaborne*'s montage techniques challenged the boundaries between poetry and prose, *Seraphim* goes on to question the very concept of the book as a finite object, following a great tradition of innovators that includes the Laurence Sterne of *Tristram Shandy*. Oswald's disassembly of the novelistic form functions through what the Russian formalist critics called "ostranenie," or the "alienation effect": by pointing to its own structure in an ongoing *mise en abyme,* the narrative renders the familiar strange and in the process constructs a book improvised out of fragments of books—a great "un-book."

The "tradition of rupture"—inherited from the baroque and reinforced by the equally disruptive experimentalism of authors like Sousândrade and Oswald de Andrade—was taken to its limits during the concretist phase of the mid-1950s and 1960s. As we have already noted, this movement's highly formalistic program mirrored Brazil's fast-paced postwar refashioning into a modern, industrialized nation, as reflected in the texts gathered in the section we have entitled "The Concrete Moment." Thus, "Pilot Plan for Concrete Poetry" (1958), the manifesto issued by the *Noigandres* group, borrows its title from the urban planner Lucio Costa's pioneering airplane-shaped design for Brasilia. This extremely concise text, originally printed entirely in lowercase, contrasts sharply with de Campos's expansive style in other essays. Both the concision and the impersonal tone aid in creating a tabula rasa from which a new poetics might emerge. In this context, only two Brazilian authors are cited as precursors—Oswald de Andrade and Joāb Cabral de Melo Neto—and current topics in science and the arts are listed in quasi–bullet-point style.

In hindsight, the *Noigandres* manifesto's greatest feat is its ability to sum up ideas that had already been developing in Europe since the turn of the century, in movements such as the Neue Sachlichkeit [New Objectivity], and in Brazil since 1922, promoted by Oswald de Andrade through the Week of Modern Art in São Paulo. Jean Arp, for instance, had already adopted the title "concretions" for his poems as early as 1922, and Oswald de Andrade, in his "Cannibalist Manifesto," also claimed to be a "concretist." More importantly, Pierre Schaeffer had already begun his experiments in what he termed "concrete music" as early as 1948. Although "The Pilot Plan" strategically downplays Schaeffer's role in the development of concretism with a vague reference to "concrete and electronic music," it nevertheless does mention the names of two of his pupils, Pierre Boulez and Stockhausen—but as followers of Anton Webern. The erasure of Shaeffer's name from the pantheon of precursors has never been sufficiently addressed, nor has the fact that another pro-concrete manifesto had already surfaced in Sweden in 1953, written by the Brazilian-born poet and visual artist Öyvind Fahlström.

The new poetry envisioned in the *Noigandres* manifesto is proposed as a political stance—poetry as the vehicle for building a new national identity in an "objective" language that can be extended to other areas such as advertising, journalism, and cinema. In order to emphasize this point, in 1961 a postscript was appended to the manifesto: Mayakovsky's dictum that "there is no revolutionary art without revolutionary form."

Despite its undeniably Brazilian modernist flavor, concrete poetry, like the International Style in architecture, is essentially a utopian and internationalist program. In "The Open Work of Art" (1955), de Campos proposes a "radial axis," composed of works by Mallarmé, Joyce, Pound, and E. E. Cummings, that would provide a blueprint for contemporary poetry at large. These authors, de Campos suggests, present the reader with "porous works," the structures of which are accessible from any perspective one chooses to embrace. He compares these open structures to a mobile by Calder or a composition by Webern. This emphasis on structure and its concomitant restriction and specialization of poetic vocabulary, caused many critics to accuse concretism of impoverishing language. This claim is refuted by de Campos in "The Informational Temperature of the Text" (1960), which argues that constraint is of the essence in any creative process, as borne out by Dante's deployment of terza rima or Arnaut Daniel's use of sestina.

Mayakovsky's revolutionary impetus was a constant source of inspiration for the *Noigandres* group. In "Concrete Poetry–Language–Communication" (1957), for instance, de Campos's view of the poem as a self-regulating machine tuned to transmit signs is ultimately equated with Mayakovsky's call for a kind of propaganda that would also be poetry of the highest quality. Like those of his *Noigandres* peers, de Campos's concretist essays convey the movement's emphasis on structure and communication. "Concrete Poetry–Language–Communication" is perhaps most representative of the propaideutic message of concrete poetry. In a veritable tour de force, de Campos invokes Weiner's theories of cybernetics, Korzybski's "general semantics," W. Sluckin's psychology of mechanical feedback, the Pavlovian experiments with mazes conducted by Shannon, Howard, and Deutsch, and the research on verbal and nonverbal communications conducted by Jürgen Ruesch and Waldo Kees, in order to provide a reading of Décio Pignatari's iconic poem "terra." Pignatari's text, de Campos concludes, is a self-regulating machine whose "structure-content" deciphers itself.

The third and final section, "A Laboratory of Texts," features an eclectic collection of essays on questions of avant-garde poetics and translation theory in a global tradition. Most of these pieces were originally gathered from the books that helped consolidate de Campos's position as a leading literary voice in Brazil: *Metalinguagem* [*Metalanguage*] (1967), *A arte no horizonte do provável* [*Art in the Horizon of the Probable*] (1969), *A Operação do texto* [*Textual Operations*] (1976), and *Ideograma* [*Ideogram*] (1977). The wide variety of themes—German and Brazilian avant-garde poetry, Ferdinand de Saussure's anagrams, the Chinese ideogram, Hölderlin as translator, and a defense of translation as creative act—provide de Campos with the raw material for his proposed "laboratory of texts," in which the contributions, "that of a linguist and that of the artist, will complement each other" and bear witness to his relentless engagement with the practice of translation, which intermingled with his poetic production, often blurring the boundaries between creator and translator, original and translation, in a provocative way.

De Campos's 1969 essay "Brazilian and German Avant-Garde Poetry" seeks to create an alternate genealogy for concrete poetry in Brazil by establishing links with avant-garde German-language writers and artists. The catalyst was perhaps the temporal and aesthetic coincidence between the Brazilian concrete experiments and those of Gomringer, whose Mallarmé-inspired *Konstellationen* [*Constellations*] echoed Augusto de Campos's ideographic montages in the *Poetamenos* [*Minuspoet*] series. As before, de Campos endeavors to argue for Brazil's exceptionalism, claiming that its concrete poetry was "more complex" and exhibited a "visual baroqueness" absent in Gomringer's "concise" and "rigorous" orthogonal constructions.

Another common trait of both movements was an attempt to "demarginalize the avant-garde, integrating it into a living tradition." De Campos convincingly parallels the daring verbal polydoms of Arno Holz's monumental poem *Phantasus* (1916–26) with the vertiginous semantic innovations of Sousândrade's narrative epic *Wandering Guesa.* Closer to his own time, de Campos also juxtaposes Oswald de Andrade, as a precursor to the Brazilian avant-garde, with Kurt Schwitters, the Dada forefather of such German innovators as Stockhausen. De Campos also discusses texts by Christian Morgenstern, August Stramm, Vassily Kandinsky, Paul Klee, Helmut Heissenbüttel, Bertolt Brecht, Hans Magnus Enzensberger, and Max Bense.

In a similar revisionist and exploratory gesture, the 1976 essay "The Ghost in the Text (Saussure and the Anagrams)" approaches Ferdinand de Saussure's investigations into the anagrams of Latin Saturnian verse. De Campos notes that the seminal work of Jakobson in allying linguistics to poetics was anticipated by Saussure's work on the anagram—research that only came to light in 1964 thanks to Jean Starobinski's book *Les mots sous les mots* [*Words upon Words*]. Up until that point, Saussurian theory had been criticized for its excessive reliance on the horizontal and syntagmatic linearity principle, which does not do justice to the vertical polyphonies of poetry.

Examining Latin Saturnian poetry, Saussure came to identify a pattern of anagrams, or "acoustic images," whose permutations imitated a given theme word, the ghostly presence of which could be detected in a nonlinear fashion. Saussure came to name his discovery "paragram," a wider generalized phenomenon of phonetic and graphemic mimetism that "recognizes and reassembles its leading syllables, as Isis reassembled the dismembered body of Osiris." The relevance of de Campos's essay is that it points to an important and not very well-known aspect of Saussure's work, revolutionary in that its esoteric "second linguistics" (as Starobinski calls it) undoes many of the exoteric assumptions of his authoritative *Cours de linguistique générale* [*Course on General Linguistics*]. More importantly, de Campos wants to recover the Saussure of the anagrams as a phonic confrere of Mallarmé's spatial "prismatic subdivisions of the Idea," as well as a predecessor of futurism's simultaneism, Velimir Khlebnikov's "simultaneous semiotic units," and, not surprisingly, Brazilian concrete poetry. In de Campos's hands, Saussure becomes a "theoretician of the avant-garde" *avant la lettre*.

We noted earlier the lasting influence of Ezra Pound's *paideuma* and translation practices on concrete poetry. Pound's fascination with the Far East, and particularly with the Chinese ideogram, also left their mark on de Campos's work. In 1977 de Campos compiled a volume entitled *Ideograma: Lógica, poesia, linguagem* [*Ideogram: Logic, Poetry, Language*], featuring a translation of Fenollosa's polemical essay "The Chinese Character as a Medium for Poetry," which was first edited and published by Ezra Pound in 1920, after Fenollosa's death. This volume also contained a translation of another seminal essay, Sergei Eisenstein's 1929 "The Cinematographic Principle and the Ideogram"; a handful of technical pieces by lesser-known Sinologists; and de Campos's own introduction to the volume, "Ideograma, anagrama, diagrama" ["Ideogram, Anagram, Diagram"], from which the two excerpts included in this volume ("Poetic Function and Ideogram" and "The Sinological Argument") have been taken.

"Poetic Function and Ideogram" argues for the affinity between Fenollosa's interest in the ideogram and his search for "universal elements of form" that would constitute a "poetics." This "formalist" aspect of Fenollosa's essay makes it, in de Campos's view, a forerunner of Jakobson's seminal "Closing Statement on Linguistics and Poetics." Fenollosa, as de Campos shows, was one in a line of philosophers and poets—from René Descartes and Gottfried Leibniz to Ralph Waldo Emerson and Pound—who searched for a functional poetic framework based on universal signs like the ideogram. This fascination with the ideogram as an iconic or indexical sign, however, earned Fenollosa, and later Pound, the disapproval of professional Sinologists, who decried their erroneous interpretation of the ideogram as grounded in purely visual rather than phonetic elements. In "The Sinological Argument," however, de Campos defends both Fenollosa and Pound from the scholars' attacks, arguing that even when Pound incorrectly deciphered ideograms in his translations, his "eye for errata" was counterbalanced by his empathetic perception of the whole. De Campos applies Pound's method to his own translations into Portuguese of Wang Wei and Li-tai Po, where the visual rhymes of letters are stressed to compensate for the lack of pictorialism in alphabetic languages. De Campos points out that this is not a question of imitative representation but rather of semiotic iconicity: what matters is not the pictographic but the relational argument (the ideogram as a metaphor of structure rather than as a painting of ideas via things). Thus Fenollosa's view is rescued from an oversimplification that would reduce the mechanics of the ideogram to a servile imitation of reality. Instead, Fenollosa's insistence that "relations are more real and more important than the things which they relate"* is revealed by de Campos to be a genuine structuralist poetics *ante litteram.*

Translation was central to de Campos's poetic practice. He not only made available in Portuguese some key texts of world poetry but also composed some of his most significant works based on a history of translations. Over time, translation became an increasingly transgressive exercise for de Campos, one that allowed him access to new languages and historical periods. This practice also called for a more complex mode of reading—no longer of isolated texts but of their many translations. According to de Campos, a text's meaning is revealed, or light is thrown on it, through the history of its various translations. The power of the text to convey images is what de Campos ultimately pursues, and in this regard he is in agreement with Eliot, who believed that a tradition of visionary poetry had been lost since Dante. Translation, for de Campos—echoing Richard Sieburth's observation that *translatio* in Latin "also refers to the transfer of the relics of saints or pieces of the true cross"†—became a literary crusade, the goal of which was to transport images (sacred relics) for subsequent retransmission.

In "Translation as Creation and Criticism" (1967), de Campos begins with a quote by Albrecht Fabri commenting on the untranslatable nature of

---

* Ernest Fenollosa, *The Chinese Written Character as a Medium for Poetry,* ed. Ezra Pound (1936; reprint, San Francisco: City Lights Books, 1968), 22. —EDITORS

† Richard Sieburth, "Ms Fr 270: Prelude to a Translation," *Esprit créateur* 40, no. 3 (Fall 2000): 102. —EDITORS

poetry: "(poems) do not *mean* but *are*." De Campos then proceeds to deconstruct Fabri's argument and proposes that since poetic texts cannot be translated, they must be "re-created," making the case for an active collaboration between linguists and poets. Throughout the essay, de Campos invokes a series of writers and translators who have informed his idiosyncratic view of translation, beginning with Paulo Rónai, a Brazilian author for whom translation was an art in its own right, and Odorico Mendes, the nineteenth-century poet and translator from Maranhão whose translations of the *Odyssey,* seen as problematic and even "monstrous" when originally published, have since become an important contribution to Brazilian literature.

For de Campos, however, the paragon of the translator as re-creator is Ezra Pound, whose reworkings of Chinese poems succeeded in translating the ideogram's "image," not merely its verbal equivalent. Based both on Pound's motto "Make it new" and the Brazilian modernist tradition of "anthropophagy," de Campos's translation work sometimes approaches iconoclasm. His translation of an ode by Horace (*Persicos odi, puer, apparatus*), for instance, opens with a reference to a popular samba by Noel Rosa:

> Garçom, faça o favor
> nada de luxos persas.

> Boy, please—
> no Persian luxury.

Rosa was a composer from Rio who wrote some of Carmen Miranda's greatest hits in the 1940s. The phrase "Garçom, faça o favor" (literally "Waiter, please—") is the beginning of a classic samba titled "Conversa de Botequim" ["Bar Talk"], the lyrics of which exalt the quintessential bon-vivant carioca. By sampling Rosa in his translation of Horace, de Campos created a fold of powerful resonance, one that encapsulates different eras, cultures, and idioms, while still keeping the spirit of the original poem.

This example is emblematic of the way in which de Campos's approach to translation has become an important element in contemporary Brazilian culture; it can be seen as bridging the gap between high and popular culture and between the literary and the oral. It was embraced by many of his contemporaries, including his brother Augusto, whose deft translation of the second part of John Donne's *Elegie 19—To His Mistress Going to Bed,* set to music by Péricles Cavalcante, a composer who has worked closely with the de Campos brothers, became an unexpected hit in Brazil in the mid-

1980s, in a recording by Caetano Veloso. It also influenced younger generations of poets such as Paulo Leminski, who in the 1980s proposed a translation of Eliot's *The Waste Land* as *Devastolândia,* a wordplay fusing "devastation" with "Disneyland."

In view of all this, it is not surprising that Hölderlin's controversial translations from the Greek captured de Campos's attention in "Hölderlin's Red Word" (1967), an essay originally written as an introduction to his exceptional translation into Portuguese of Hölderlin's *Antigone* (act 1, scene 1). The vilification of Hölderlin's versions of Sophocles and Pindar by his contemporaries and their ultimate redemption by twentieth-century critics and poets spoke directly to de Campos. On one level, he could identify Hölderlin's fate with that of Odorico Mendes, whose translations from the Greek were also ridiculed by his contemporaries as more difficult to read than the originals. For de Campos, Hölderlin represents genius overcoming the limitations of language through the "keen understanding of its beauty and character" whose seemingly awkward solutions were simply "creative errors."

In "Eucalypse: The Beautiful Occultation" (1990), de Campos's powers as a close reader are put to the test as he performs a line-by-line exegesis of Octavio Paz's poem *La guerra de la dríade o vuelve a ser eucalipto* [*The Dryad War or Return to Being Eucalyptus*]. The characters in Paz's poem undergo various mutations, and, de Campos points out, the action unfolds in a series of conflicts between archetypal antagonists, as in Vladimir Propp's proto-structuralist model, *Morphology of the Folktale.* In the same way that a transformational grammar of narrative structures folktales, the poem employs paronomasia as a metamorphic device: The *apocalypse,* "revelation" or "unveiling," of the dryad—a character disguised in the story as an obscure and merciless object of desire—is inversely paralleled by her lover's "occultation," or metamorphosis, into a *eucalyptus* tree. According to de Campos, this episode (which echoes Ovid's tale of the nymph Daphne) inscribes the poem in a tradition of visionary or oneiric literature going back to the book of Revelation and also includes Dante and William Blake.

In "Light: Paradisiacal Writing" (1975), the metaphor of light as applied to translation acquires still another dimension through references to Cavalcanti's *A Lady Asks Me* and Dante's *Paradiso.* Here, de Campos is concerned with the very definition of light in both texts. He begins with Pound's claim that Cavalcanti's canzone is ultimately a "metaphor on the generation of light," then goes a step further and applies Pound's metaphor to the entirety of Dante's *Commedia,* tracing its trajectory from the *Inferno* and through the *Purgatorio* to the luminous verses of the *Paradiso*. The essay also addresses the genealogy of the metaphor, which de Campos traces back to Averroës and Robert Grosseteste and connects to twentieth-century artists and writers such as Kasimir Malevich and Georges Vantongerloo, Joyce, and Norman Brown. The "generation of light" through translation is finally exemplified by de Campos's own translation of a fragment by Cavalcanti in which he superimposes Pound's translation onto a version of Dante. De Campos's masterly solution, which he calls "hyper-translation" ("Cavalcanti via Pound via Dante"), is an operation involving several strata that allow the text's meaning to shine through. "Transcreation," "hypertranslation," "translight," "transluciferation"—these are some of the names that Haroldo de Campos coined throughout his career in an attempt to define the practice of writing. Mephistophelean writing, one might add.

De Campos died of diabetes-related complications on August 16, 2003, in his beloved São Paulo, shortly after the release of the second volume of his translation of *The Iliad*. The concrete poetry scholar and Yale professor K. David Jackson, a close friend for many years, reported that in his last hours, de Campos called his brother Augusto, his "*Siamême*" twin," and proposed that they translate the *Commedia* by telephone—a lifelong dream that was only fragmentarily realized.

Novas

I : **Poetry**

From *Xadrez de estrelas* [*Star Chess*]
(1949–1974)

Act of the Possessed

O sage, Dichter, was du tunst?——Ich rühme.

Tell me, Poet, what you do.—I celebrate.

—Rilke

SCENE I
A Giant sucks in the night through the eucalyptus trees

THE LOVER
Allow me, Beloved with translucent eyes,
to celebrate you in the hanging gardens
where delirium opens petals of alcohol!

THE BELOVED
Listen:
Now, by the sea,
a chess player plays.

THE LOVER
In autumn, by the sea . . .
Dear friend, unseal the capsule of the Sabbath,
and see to it that the wind dervishes dance in the air.

THE BELOVED
O hateful sea.
O hateful roar of the sea. The wind.
Watch the insistence of black horses
in your neighbor who played chess!

THE CHESS PLAYER [*to the Lover*]
What to do with the rebellious pawns
and with the old, captive king?
What to do with the white queen
appalled amid the rooks?

THE BELOVED
Throw her in the sea.
I said, throw her in the sea.

THE LOVER
Dear friend, allow me to sing
by the light of a raw star;
where your body lay, teeming with warm roses;
where suicidal faces now devour one another;
where an aquiline lily is born, by the light of a raw star.

SCENE II
A mirror facing the sea

THE POSSESSED
The one who is to die in the waters
Was wearing insomnia and tulle.
She wove her green hair
with the wheel of the southern wind.
She who is to die in the waters
walks amid torches
escaping from the ace of spades.
She is the insane one coming from the south.

THE EXORCIST
On the sixth day you were
the voice that cried to the sky.
You were the sorcerer and sat
diagonally across Capricorn.

THE BELOVED
. . . Throw her in the sea.

THE EXORCIST
You have picked the briny lotus
amid the turbulent stream of fever
that flows down a bald summit
through seven mouths of darkness.

THE POSSESSED
What will the face of the moon
do against your tepid,
ill-aged moon face?
What can liquid eyes do
against your eyes that beckon
lighthouses and foam to the water?

THE BELOVED AND THE EXORCIST [*together*]
I said, throw her in the sea!

THE CHESS PLAYER
Ease, O nocturnal bishop
the chores on my chessboard
and hark: a poet is born
in the bulbs of the month of August.

SCENE III
The mountain and the valley

THE CHESS PLAYER
Your son is born from the womb
of a virgin in Tibet,
whose flower I pollinated
in the hothouses of languor.
He will be the priest of Radja Gomba,
and his voice hurls meat-eating turtledoves
when the many-faced YAMA
dances in a circle made of hands.

THE EXORCIST
Therefore,
surrender!

THE CHESS PLAYER
He will offer libations on the Sabbaths of September
where naked hexes ravage the quadrant
tied to the manes of wild boars.

THE EXORCIST
Therefore,
surrender!

THE BELOVED
Brutal and bloody, O Love!
My bosom will give him moderation and communion.
I weaken with water the wine of my lips,
and my flesh tastes of unleavened bread or clover.

THE EXORCIST
Surrender,
surrender!

THE POSSESSED
I could indeed warm your pubis
mined with poppies!
Allow me, O gentle ox, to celebrate
and lift your body in my song
as a trophy atop crystals!

THE CHESS PLAYER
Woman,
behold thy son!

Translated by Odile Cisneros

The Disciplines

The Poem: Theory and Practice

I

Silver birds, the Poem
draws theory from its own flight.
Philomel of metamorphosed blue,
measured geometrician
the Poem thinks itself
as a circle thinks its center
as the radii think the circle
crystalline fulcrum of the movement.

II

A bird imitates itself at each flight
zenith of ivory where a ruffled
anxiety is arbiter
over the vectorial lines of the movement.
A bird becomes itself in its flight
mirror of the self, mature
orbit
timing over Time.

III

Even-tempered, the Poem ignores itself.
Leopard pondering itself in a leap,
what becomes of the prey, plume of sound,
evasive
gazelle of the senses?
The Poem proposes itself: system
of rancorous premises
evolution of figures against the wind
star chess. Salamander of arsons
that provokes, unhurt endures,
Sun set in its center.

IV

And how is it done? What theory
rules the spaces of its flight?
What last retains it? What load
curves the tension of its breath?
Sitar of the tongue, how does one hear?
Cut out of gold, as such we see it,
proportioned to it—the Thought.

V

See: broken in half
the airy fuse of the movement
the ballerina rests. Acrobat,
being of easy flight,
plenilunium princess of a kingdom
of aeolian veils: Air.
Wherefrom the impulse that propels her,
proud, to the fleeting commitment?
Unlike the bird
according to nature
but as a god
contra naturam flies.

VI

Such is the poem. In the fields of aeolian
equilibrium that it aspires to
sustained by its dexterity.
Winged agile athlete
aims at the trapeze of venture.
Birds do not imagine themselves.
The Poem premeditates.
They run the cusp of infinite
astronomy of which they are plumed Orions.
It, arbiter and vindicator of itself,
Luzbel leaps over the abyss,
liberated,
in front of a greater king
a king lesser great.

Translated by A. S. Bessa

Claustrophobia

Dominicum nostrum, Ariadne, the misadventures of a Sunday.

The day masturbulates, undiaphanous, ungolor. Ivory brawls, your thighs, mouthless rivers, gigantic rounds, the skin nubile-pink, tiger lilies titillating in nylonhypnosis.

The thinness of Sunday, you save. The manuscribe counts your hours with fleshless bones gnawing at the nails of his idleness.

To love: sucking the silks. Saccharin. A fire of crystals facing us. Belnarcissus closing watery eyes. Viciouscactus.
A labyrinth of lilacs: your eyes. *Glaukopis.* Blue-green panther in flexible heat. Sulphurnocturne.

Imprisoned in roses. Sunday's claustrophobia. Rain, the first coming, *prima verrà. Don't believe in cages for beasts.* Claustrophobic. To say: caged—in iron or roses—the same. Warden, and I am?

Words are a cage with seven keys. The heart is a word under seven locks. Auriculoventricular. Clavic(h)ordial.

Seven moats away the prisoner sleeps. *Morfeu noumenon.* Sleep, auriferous torpor, frozen mammoths hibernate, nymphosis in crystalsnow, siesta of chrysalis. *Sleep. Schlafen.* Soft ss lips cirrus. *Träumendzimmern:* sleep chambers. *Dormosis.*

Asphyxia. Blue circles around the nose. *Fossoyeurs.* Cave inhabitants. Cephalolamped miners. A lit head, a glow, lampires. Darkavern, vermats curl around the substance of gloom. Purplenightprowling vampires. Waking up: a flight of albino bats.

Schlafwandler—sleepwalkers hate grates. They want the sun. Vitriol suns. Turnsoles. Topaz at high noon. Chrysophorus. The sun.

Wormvenomous dungeon where the bloodletting of corals stagnates. Adiaphanous. Tourniquet on the jugular. My blood, a voiceless river.

Le Poète maudit bénit. Le vocable l'accable. Et lente lente currite equi noctis. Night, beyond. Darkgloomy, tangibleblack, dense.

He forges, vulcanamorously, the venussyllable for verbogenesis. *Margaritas ante porcos.* Sea.

The prisoner under seven cages, septuorpainful. Breathing: metronome of equal oxygens. To eat: to fecaldigest. To love: morosmosis. Claustrophobia: blood in stagnant chambers, a kiss in *cryptomucous ludilingus.* W. C.— *womb closed.* Night: a belly. The heart: a ventricle. Aporous.

—Ariadne, the thread. The filoformula. The web. A thread. *Funicular. Funis coronat opus.* Funny. A hand an arm (*leukolenos*) fingers (*amanda digitalis*) the body color—an ubiamourous gesture—of a filiflower. The Pore

In finismundo
the fenixbard awaits the finisnight.

Translated by Odile Cisneros

The Invincible Armada

Invincible
armada
        Poetry

                A conniving
                breeze
                suffices or a
                collusion of

winds

                and your brigs
                of war
                prows
                of proud
                scarlet

discommand the
sea
tawny with foam

          Divisible armada
          vanquished arrogance
          anchored

                          where?

          Sub
          marine
          troys of cobalt

Escorial
        ship
wreck

                But the flagship
                on quick-
                sands

par-
alyzed by blue

          ship on its *occiput*

                  to a pontus

euxinus of abyssal
beauty

                              the heraldic prow
                              extinguished
                              eel
                              instead of ori-
                              flamme
                              marinely
                              motioned
                              ship

spains
of war (dupe of aerial
angers) not waged

                              the glassy
bosom of the bottom depths
emasculates

                              blue-green
                              arcanum of mercury
                              sub
                              verting
                              a squadron worsted by
                              wind

                                                          pyrrhic
victory

                              The sea
                                    immune
                              keeps the indigo
                              secret
                              and enshrines—ship
                              wreck—an invincible
                              armada of minutiae
                                                          Seashells

thalassa   *thalamium*

                          the act
                                    pure
                          vengeance
                          violet
                          air and
                          water
                          against the punic
                          beak
                          of the ship
                          the keels
                          repealed
                          the sails
                          whiteness of conceit
                          capsized
                          and seagulls
                                              nuptials
                          or obituary
                                         gala
                                                      fulfilled

          thanatos

                          a cohesive
                          silence
                                    arbiter
                          of elegance
                          encloses the
                          salvage from the
                          wreck
                                    and discloses
                          a gesture

intact on the horizon

                          seaman riding the prestige
                          of the wave   -
                                         crusoe of a solar
                                              clamor
                                                   of islands
                                         or the mere
                          fioritura of a murex

land
of castaways

                           poem
what
of your punished arrogance?

mausoleum of cuttlefish
ocher
exile
            a slender
canoe
midterranean
keel of impudence

                                        pierces
                        the blue
                                    the surviving
hand
                        waves the paddle
                                                riot
of constrained waters
                                    and on high
                                                clouds
                                                            that invincible
fictitious purple
                                    joy of armadas

THE ESSENCE OF OMEGA

marsupialamour   nip
ple of oil
y   lam
preys   can
ine   clutched   am
our
tower   of   talis
man
gut   (LEN t)
tural   love
er in b
urst   ing
dark   fevers
of   febr
uary   fem
oral   nup   t
ial   death
bed   au
riferous
depth   : a
rivermouth
peace
coit
us

              CE

Translated by Mary Ellen Solt and Jon Tolman

the   ear's   pavilion   borders
the   eager   pavilion
aureole
aura

          a   cornu   copy
          ear   snail
          milks a teat
          of air
          a tur
          gid windy
          tower

                    made maze
                    a sound a line
                    sound
                    from taps
                    from no
                    where nipples

Translated by Haroldo de Campos

in the
　　es sence　　　of the　O　　mega

　　　　　　　　eye
　　　　　　　　gold
　　　　　　　　bone

under

　　that　　　　　pe(vine of vacuum)nsile
　　petal　　　　b l i n k i n g　　lashes
　　　　　　　　eyelid
　　almond　　　　　of emptiness petiole: the thing
　　of　the　thing
　　of　the　thing

　　　　　　　　a　hardness
　　　　　　　　so　empty
　　　　　　　　a　bone
　　　　　　　　so　center
　　　　　　　　　　　　　　　　a body
　　　　　　　　crystalline　　　　to body
　　　　　　　　closed　in　its　whiteness

　　　　　　　　　　　ero
　　　　　　　　Z　　　　　to the
　　　　　　　　　　enith

　　　　　　　　　　　　　　　splendoring

　　　　　　　　　　ex-nihilo

Translated by Charles A. Perrone

```
            IN
be          twi(ee)n
            h
            e
parentheses
            e


an                          ob
ject
she         (a)             er
                            peel
      reading               of the real
misreading        ca
                  r
                  ca
                  s
                  s
                  a
                  s
                  s
                  i
                  n

                  nux       (g)nomica
                  vox       vomica
                  sc             in
                  al             tem
                      p(o)           (du)st
                            mort
                            em


      grad
ual   grind (ing)   ex
                    magus
                    IN
      wall          ed
                    o
                    o
                    r
                    walls       ri      R
                                sp      I
                                id      X
                                ro      A
                                se
                                ars     :
                                or
                                so      R
                                re      O
                                si      S
                                due     A
```

Translated by A. S. Bessa

a   peri

scope

or   peri

CARDIUM

the
cor
al
ar
id
oh
alla
l
id
o

mio cid

campeador

mio

CARDIUM

al   cácer   al
       când   ora
                 fombra à
                 fim
                 bria of
                 the end

be
yond
the
end
o'

cardium

pallium
of so
me
pl ume pl
us
so   me wh e
RES

Hunger of Form

speech
silver

    silence
    gold

        heads
        silver

            tails
            gold

                speech
                silence

            stop

silver   golden
silence   speech

                      clarity

Translated by Mary Ellen Solt

blank   blank   blank   blank
vermilion
clotted   vermilion
               speculum   vermilion
                              clotted   blank

Translated by A. S. Bessa

more   more

less   more   and   less

more   or   less   no   more

nor   less   nor   more

nor   less   less

Translated by A. S. Bessa

crystal
    crystal
        hunger
crystal
    crystal
        hunger   for   form
                          crystal
                  crystal
        form   of   hunger
                          crystal
                  crystal
            form

Translated by A. S. Bessa

```
            is
            born
            over   born
            over   born   over
                                 re-born   re-over   re-born
                                           re-over   re-born
                                                     re-over
                       re                                      re
            de-born
   de-over  de-born
de-over  de-born  de-over
                   bornoverborn
                   overborn
                   is
```

Translated by A. S. Bessa

```
sea      ship
  sun     ship
   saw     ship
    see    ship
     see  not  see
    saw  not  saw
   sun  not  sun
 sea  not  sea
          see   ships
```

Translated by A. S. Bessa

Anamorphosis

doubt
            shadow
no doubt
          in shadow
in doubt
         no shadow
without doubt
      hour of shadow
hour of doubt
       without shadow
no shadow   of doubt

         shadow
                 doubt
        no shadow
               in doubt
        in shadow
              no doubt
        hour of shadow
           without doubt
        without shadow
          hour of doubt
        no doubt   of shadows

                 no doubt
                      shadow
               in shadow   doubt
               in doubt
                   no shadow
               hour of doubt
                  without shadow
               without doubt
                 hour of shadow
               of shadow   no doubt

Translated by Jean R. Longland

Form of Hunger

Transient Servitude

gold fly?
dry fly.

silver fly?
cinder fly.

iris fly?
worthless fly.

indigo fly?
inferior fly.

blue fly?
fly.

white fly?
scant poetry.

blue's pure?
blue's pus

on empty belly

green's alive?
green's a virus

on empty belly

yellow's beauty?
yellow's bile

on empty belly

red's fuchsia?
red's fury

on empty belly

poetry's pure?
poetry's for

on empty belly

poetry in time of hunger
hunger in time of poetry

poetry instead of man
pronoun instead of noun

man instead of poetry
noun instead of pronoun

poetry of giving name

naming is giving name

I name the noun
I name the man
In name is hunger

I name hunger

poem
                    from sun to sun

                    soldered
                    from salt to salt
                    salted
                    from smash to smash
                    smashed
                    from sap to sap
                    sucked
                    from sleep to sleep
                    slumbered

                    bled
                    from blood to blood

                    where this grind does its grinding
                    where this gearing is put in gear

                    grinder mankind grinding
                    grinding mankind grinder

                    gearing
                    gangrening

                    from profit to profit
                    defrauded
                    from fraud to fraud
                    provided
                    from flank to flank
                    inflicted
                    from flood to flood
                    forgotten

                    sun to salt
                    salt to smash
                    smash to sap
                    sap to sleep
                    sleep to blood

where mankind
    this grind
where flesh
    this flaying
where bone
    this gearing

mankind stuffed
mankind stiffed

mankind plunder
mankind plummet

mankind flog
mankind flogged

mankind hollow
mankind coffer

mankind sir
mankind serf

mankind over
mankind under

mankind sated
mankind sacked

mankind served
mankind slurped

mankind feasts
mankind fasts

mankind mutter
mankind mute

mankind punch
mankind pouch

mankind grindstone
mankind dust

who strings
who serf

who horse
who rides

who explores
who despoils

who rascal
who carcass

who usurps
who usury

who pillaged
who pillage

who whisky
who urinates
who vacations
who vacuums
who voluptuous
who verminates

flesh fleshly fleshering

bleeding bloodshed blood

mankindgrindermankindgrinding

sugar
in this husk?

in this armpit
musk?

petunia
in syrup?

indigo in this hole

ocher
acre
ogre
acrid

cog crossbar cold-feet
collapse cachaça cog
carcass crest craving

from dearth to dearth
from dread to dread
from doom to doom
from death to death

lone grinding
bonegrinding

scant of mirage
visionless wilderness

servitude of passage

Translated by Micaela Kramer

lacunae

lucide contour, lacune

—Mallarmé

poemandala

palaphites
suspend
fasting

    these
    minimum
    mines

    some
the   sum
central eye   of story
rosaceae   the crescent
roseopen   quartz

roof
bird
fire
suns
the purple
humming
bird

uguisu
a neat
risk

openscar
rosaceae
eye
center

down south   its
a blue   plumage
consul   (I) only
sang   ponder

Translated by A. S. Bessa

excriptures

needles

                      and these cusps

iceberg

                      sea monster concealed
                      of which

phosphor snow
peaks

excripture in its way underlies
jocund!

                      shipwrecked

and above
drip the
dots of
ii

comas of

comets

        minute
        commentaries

akin

               to St. Elmo's

site inscribed per
        se

a
leopard
a
leopearl
a
cactus-lion
eating
pearl

sky
fix
a text
radiates
its

(nude eye
fontana)
rustic
scars
(il)legible
text

blues

pearl and
madrepore

)scorpions
turve
the
water
m
a
r
k

a
text

diamond dust
over
midden
hyphen
inter
skeletons
figures
of
language
calci-

illegible

-nada

pearl and
madrepore

where a
saturnine
leaden sky
breathes
gentian
violets

this one
text
and its un-
reading

spaces   vanishing point

tropo-

or
nothing

filigree
watermark

this
étincelle
star
of in-
versed
blank

tropo-
and
nothing

text

(sic)

ruins

red ink
rubrics
scarlet
fever
over
vellum
(paper)
body

the air
and in the air
the air
fold
(just now)
of un-
ruined
form

sinkable
thinkable

**la tua
coscia
distacca
di sull'
altra**[1]

a poem-

            nothing

self

            if

made

            much

nothing   a poem-
if   self
much   made

nothing
if
much

a poem-
self
made

Translated by A. S. Bessa

stuttertext

TO LIVE   this entire world   is to di

      yes! scintillations!

scover   that   the obv   us   that   all the

phi

that life   this entire world   is but

los   so   ad

           !jacent!

and disc

over   that   when   comes   the   na

palm

      oars (*à derive*)   rame

                    hemo

s ditto

      that life life is the obv

            to live

final sail

        curtains now

           is to dis

that death is at least the   cover

             LESS

Translated by A. S. Bessa

From *Invenção* [*Invention*], year 6, no. 5 (1967)

Alea I—Semantic Variations (A Mock-Pocket-Epic)

THE UNSURPASSABLE the laudable the notable the adorable
the grandiose the fabulous the phenomenal the colossal
the formidable the astonishing the miraculous the marvelous
the generous the excelse the portentous the stunning
the spectacular the sumptuous the faerifying the faerie
the supereminent the venerable the supersacred the supercelestial

THE UNSHITPASTABLE the lowbabble the nauseable the malodorable
the ganglious the flatulous the fetoranimal the cutarsadical
the fornicable the astinking the iratulous the matrocitous
the degenerous the insext the pustiferous the stomachfuching
the tentacular the suppurous the faecifying the fevery
the supermuckent the veneravid the suprasacral the supersyphilable
the pollust the upcorpsed the violoose the tumorped

FEWERDOLR
FOWLREDER
DREERFLOW
LOWFEEDRR
FROWLEERD
REERFOWLD
FLEDWEROR
FREDERLOW
WEEDFLORR   *program* do it yourself
FERROWELD   the reader (operator)
REDFLOWER   may go on at pleasure
FLEERWORD   doing new semantic variations
FREEWORLD   within the given parameter

Translated by Edwin Morgan

From *Signantia: quasi coelum (Signância: quase céu)* [*Paradisiacal Signifiers*] (1979)

Das Paradies ist gleichsam über die ganze Erde verstreut—und daher so unkenntlich geworden

Paradise is scattered all over the earth and has therefore become unrecognizable

—Novalis

I

I

    Crystal gland
    reveals
    branching of signs

                     sounds
the uni
versal accord

               stimulated bell

                              brilliant
last

    comes together   radiant cupola

    yes   a bell

2

enamel tonsils
striking the
tinged silence

phanos phanopea   theophany
the instant of things   a sun

fills itself with light in the sun

like the light in the lens

gleamed   the glass nerves
                                                the nucleus

                                                red

3

sentences
on paper

graphite
angles

        sub
        tending

the umbrella
panting

             and sounding

theophany of signs   vibrated   shards of crystal

4

sementics
dust of light
                                        graph
starry

                                                                but: words
unalloyed
as this
now
however
here
                sound
                particles
                digits of
                time
                doubt
                place
                ad
                                                                versatile

5

alveoli
of the diamantine globe

segments
of the large glass of sound: withgust

of total breath

I sign myself
thus

2

*

Magma

the shadow fossil of a fish
excavates   the stone
here

chisel of how many
thousand
years?

Dendron:
tree

this stone
seeding itself on the inside

is
written: read it
out of it
self

**

the moment
is a feather

its hologram
shimmers   stable

as one who looks after the crystal
of time

                              fixed beam
                              of light

(one no longer sees oneself if the eye abandons its embrasure)

                              angled prism perspective

                                        the sun
                                        rains
                                        from a zenithal
                                        ceiling

ellipsis: a stylus of blinds

***

paradise: pistils
tongues of flame
under diamond chisel point

writing in
visible sentences

of glass
on glass

* *
* *

a sleeping tiger
the locust: his
mandibles

the flower
claws

a pendant
weight

blood bone meat muscle

like a
calligraphy brush
on the page

this
art
or the

character

*
* *
* *
*

a dance
of swords

this delirious
writing

cursive blades

a moon
between two
dragons

like a bamboo
shoot
passing through vines
without untangling them

***
***

is indigo an instance of blue?

the eye of Ra

before him
things

                    the scintillated
                    look
                    of them

draw by hand this cloud
blue cataract
of such
white

                    and he sees to:

                    his pollen
                    flames
                    the no of

                    things

you await
spreadlegs
burnished basalt
lioness

the sting

dragonflies
electrify
the citrine
air

the wings
of the archangel
seven
wink:

stipulations

in the rutile
sphere
of ants
the antlion
reigns

veins
of laminae

the insect's
agate
shield

the pencil co-
letters everything

exfoliating letters
on paper

erection of signs
natura naturans

here the
green of
the pupil
is tinged

dragonflies
in the sky of dragonflies

the flight of them
over under

dragonflies

point
where the eye
glimmers
tensile wing

place of
the volatile
diamond

bull's-eye
white

4

chrysanthemums

solar writing
in the room

in)
the crystal block
ex)
vase

roselion
animal
the colored
body

ex/
im/
plodes

in curved
hooks
red
italics

ruffled / manes
deaf-
mute
illuminated manu-

script

reading of novalis / 1977

white paint

over

white paper

to write is a form of
to see

alles ist samenkorn
everything is seed

slumberflamed

vision of paradise

deepblue
agate stripes
clearer blue
ray of radiant ruby

green pastures
in slateopaque   leads / shadows

another border: lacquer alight

(from the cabin — robin
redbreast —
an ogive
window the
setting sky)

                                                    rubies
                                                    lacquer fires
                                                    red spears

(from that — iris in
the iris — the *paradiso*
is made)

                                        (in the cabin
                                        minor fires — ice
                                        cubes in
                                        whiskey — trivia
                                        & paraselene)

the phosphorous eye of Dante

                                (clouded over in fortified neon light

approximations of topaz

Tierische Natur der Flamme
—Novalis

a microcephalic
lion
explodes:

the word
topaz

or: rising from leopards

                    miniature flames of fury
                    each spark shoots a
                    numinous mouth

the topaz
cannibalizes its yellows
lens in the torrid eye
of the solar furnace
light

           fiery coals
           are consumed here

           (ashes, grated fires, truncated
              cusps: glowing coal / wing)

the sunflower thinks:
leopazes!

forms that
are fleshed out
between air and fire

forms of fire
and air
that flesh themselves out

where to discern
in the bird's twittering throat
the air that speaks
in the bird's twittering throat
?

where to discern
in the blaze of the topaz
the voice of fire
in the blaze of the topaz
?

Translated by Craig D. Dworkin

From *A educação dos cinco sentidos*
[*The Education of the Five Senses*] (1985)

Die Bildung der fünf Sinne ist eine Arbeit der ganzen bisherigen Welt-geschichte.

The education of the five senses is a task for all of world history until this day.

—Karl Marx, 1844

The Education of the Five Senses

1.   chatoboys (oswald)
itching
like fleas

peirce (proust?) considering
a color—violet
or an odor—
cabbage
rotten

rot—consider
this word: wines,
horace, odes
(principle of a
poem—
ogre)

2.   the purgatory is this:
enter / inter-
consider
the journey from the word stella
to the word styx

3.   (marx: the education of the five
senses

the tactile the mobile
the difficult
to read / readable
visibilia / invisibilia
the audible / the unheard
the hand
the eye
the hearing
the foot
the nerve
the tendon)

4.   the air
        lapidated: see
        how connects, this word,
        to this other
        language: my
        consciousness (a parallelogram
        of forces not a simple
        equation of one
        single
        unknown factor): this
        language is made of air
        and vocal cord
        the hand that instills the thread of the
        trellis / the breath
        that unites this to that
        voice: the point
        of torsion
        diaphanous work but that
        is made (throughout) with the five
        senses

        with the color the odor the cabbage the fleas

5.   rare labor such as
        to spin a top on one's
        nail

        but that leaves its trace
        minimal (nonprescinded)
        in the common division (incision)
        of labor

        pulsating trace / pulse
        of the senses that are (pre)formed:
        unprescinded (if minimal)

        the flicker of sunlight in the eye
        —claritas: flash of epiphany!
        a few registers modulations

rough paper or smooth a fold
secure a cut
a sure shot
on the bull's-eye

in a flash the tiger trail the deer
(sousândrade)

the tigerlike assault

6.   that which accrues
rests
(in the senses)

even though minimal
(hubris of the minimal
that rests)

Translated by A. S. Bessa

Ode (Explicit) in Defense of Poetry on St. Lukács's Day

the apparatchiks hate you
poetry
poor cousin
(vide benjamin /
talking lukács gabor kurella
with brecht one july
afternoon in svendborg)

poetry
contradictory female
they hate
multifarious
you more
putifarian
than potiphar's
wife
more ophelian
than hymen
of some maiden
in the antechamber
of hamlet's madness

poetry
you deviate from the norm
you don't embody history
divisionary rebellionary visionary
veiled / unveiled
in a striptease for your (duchamp)
bachelors, even
organized violence against humdrum
manqué
language

the apparatchiks hate you
poetry
because your property is form
(as marx would say)
and because you don't
tell the dancer from the dance
or render unto caesar what is caesar's
/ not even the minimum (catullus):
he asks for a hymn
and out you come
with a porno poem

so are you the
emerald hetaera in thomas mann
the agonic snapdragon
with syphilis wings
?
threadsun in celan's eye of selenite
?

anna akhmatova saw you
strolling in the garden
and threw you across her shoulders
a renard in mortuary silver

walter benjamin
who awaited the messiah
leafing away through one
minute arc of history
any minute now
certainly met you
annunciated by his angelus novus
inscribed millimetrically on a grain of wheat
in the musée de cluny

adorno demanded you be
negative and dialectic
hermetic previdic emetic
recalcitrant

they say you're on the right
but marx (*le jeune*)
reader of homer dante goethe
in love with faust's gretchen
knew that your place is on the left
that mad alienated
city of the heart

and even lenin
who had a face like verlaine's
but who (*pauvre lelian*)
berated lunacharsky
for printing more than a thousand copies
of mayakovsky's poem "150,000,000"
— too much paper for a futurist poem! —
even lenin knew
that intelligent idealism
is closer to materialism
than the materialism
of unintelligent
materialism

poetry
they hate you
miss materidealist thing
they'll deny you bread and water
(for the enemy: the boot!)
— you are the enemy
poetry

if only because dervish ornithologue khlebnikov
president of the terrestrial globe
died of hunger in santalov
over a pillow of manuscripts
bewitched by the
fakirizing smile
in your eyes

and jakobson roman
(*amor / roma*)
octogenarian plusquesexappealgenarian
with what delight strokes
your metaphors and metonymies
while pleasured you open
your paronomasia's chrysophrase wings
and he laughs in the austere bashfulness of savants

and right now right here on this
joyous mount of partridges*
we siamême twins and cloud-cloamer pignatari
(who today signs signatari)
love you furiously
in the noigandres garçonniere
for more than thirty years have loved you
and the result is this
poetry
you already know it
little she-fox loose
in, countercultural welter
and the whole world wanting to tricapitate
for more than thirty years
we free kings
/ what's the big idea planting
ideograss in our backyard
(without any orange grove oswald)?
and (mário) taking
candy from our babies?

poetry's plain
old poetry

* The line "joyous mount of partridges" (in the original "monte alegre das perdizes") is a reference to
de Campos's lifelong address—Rua Monte Alegre, in the Perdizes neighborhood. —EDITORS

they hate you
you lumpenproletarian
voluptuarian
vicarious
elitist trash piranha
because you have no message
and your content is your form
and because you're made of words
and don't know how to tell any story
and so you're poetry
as cage said

or as
just a bit ago
augusto
the august:

flowers do flower

hummingbirds do hum

and poetry does poetry

Translated by Chris Daniels

Tristia

minithermal chambers
for disactivating the virus of
sadness
in citric
bubbles

Translated by Odile Cisneros

As It Is

acupuncture with cosmic rays
realism: poetry as it is
petro-inscriptions at the tip of the tongue
near breathlessness: in lung's last alveoli
such as it is (poetry)
fire (is)
fire
(poetry)
fire

Translated by A. S. Bessa

Portrait of the Artist as an Old Man

the word lumbago
attacks with bow and arrow

neurons: procession of piercing ants

on saber points
the cobra of vertebrae dances

    to say that a bodhisattva
    atop a column
    breathes in lotus powder

Translated by Odile Cisneros

Je est un autre: Ad Augustum

brother
in re / verse of ego
I see you
more plus than myself
plusquamfuture minuspoet
plus
and in the *trobar clus*
of this hour (ours)
poetry
incestuous sister
prima pura impura
in which
ourselves (Siamese-same)
uni-
sonoro-
us
other

Translated by A. S. Bessa

Minima Moralia

I already did all kinds of things with words

now I want to do all kinds of nothings

Translated by Odile Cisneros

Mencius: Theorem of White

the innate is called nature
to be called nature of the innate
is the same as to be called white of white

is the white of the white feather
the same as the white of white snow?
the same as the white of white jade?

how many whites is white made of?

Translated by Odile Cisneros

Goethean Opuscule

... die Nature kann die Entelechie nicht entbehren. . . .

... Nature cannot dispense with the entelechy . . .

—Goethe

to maintain the entelechy
active
I mean
like the match
(white)
lit inside water
with fire in porphyry
(inside)
the gold setting

*

the entelechy:
what forms veins
and uproots
what centers
and decenters
what magnet
and demagnetizes

what in the body
disembodies
and is body: aureate
aural
aura

*

maintain it alive
in the voltaic arch of the fifty years
the twenties' lyre harmonizes
and vibrates
is the same fire as in the sign of lion
for the combustion of this virgin
page
the same punch in the solar plexus
the same
question (combustion)
of origins

*

the entelechy
to maintain it
alive

*

between larva and lemur
alive
between dark and dull
alive
between void and dirge
alive

*

the entelechy
this fabrication that fabricates its fabrication

*

perhaps dust
after the wing falls
and unwings
(unsays)
an iris   a luminous
speck

a last rustling of the chatty
neurons   a uranium nude
illuminating
sensorial: gold setting

or the flame that quivers
in the porphyry's core

*

to maintain it alive   the entelechy

*

rose window of black veins
gold vapor
where blue and purple filter through

see to its beyond   trans-see it

rain of roses   unglooming
inhale this aroma

alive to maintain it alive
the entelechy

*

a form of transcendence in the descent

*

radiant dust
iridescent quartz
nature hatches the metaphor
of form
and transnurtures: morphing
forms

*

active:
the active entelechy:
music of the spheres

*

there are no angels in this cherubic orbit
there is radiant powder (poetry)
cocoons resolved in wings

an agitation of aeolian harp
a laughter where the dissolved entelechy
(knot unraveled in the afterdust)
spring

Translated by Micaela Kramer

Goethean Opuscule II

Jede Entelechie nämlich ist ein Stück Ewigkeit.

Every entelechy is, namely, a fragment of eternity.

—Goethe

The white
rain
bow: a
second
puberty: goethe
saw it
on the road to frankfurt
(before seeing marianne)

pound (anacreon): *senesco
sed amo*

the rose
petrifies in
liquid nitrogen
and shatters only
(williams: saxifrage rose?)
with hammer blows

to see it
after the thermic
shock
after the
thawing:
petals
(almost stone)
shattered:
still silk

*

of my hair
(the auburn)
aging (rain)
temple (bow)
will turn white:

my heart won't

Translated by Micaela Kramer

1984, Anno Orwelli I

while mortals
    activate uranium
       the butterfly
through an immortal day
perfects its cyclamen flight

Translated by Jean R. Longland

Tenzone

a gold of provence
(now you'll say) an illness
of sun   a burnt sun
of this (mistral) wind (that goldens and makes dense)
provider of words   sun-provence
a diamond's point   rhyme in -ence
as one who looks   counter to the sun
to counterwind   sense

Cogolin, Provence

Translated by Micaela Kramer

Provença: Motz E. L. Son

against the
unflinching light

the eye
turns emerald

            the eye
            (against the
            unflinching light)
            crumbles

                        the emerald eye
                        against the light:

crumb

                        (that crushes)

                        and binds together

light

                        sound of cicadas

Translated by A. S. Bessa

Le don du poème

a poem begins
where it ends:
the margin of doubt
a sudden incision of geraniums
commands its destiny

and yet it begins
(where it ends) and the head
ashen (white top or albino
cucurbit laboring signs) curves itself under lucifer's gift —

dome of signs: and the poem begins
quiet cancerous madness
that demands these lines from the white
(where it ends)

Translated by A. S. Bessa

Heraclitus Revisited (1973)

Ho Ánax

the oracle
at Delphi
isn't eloquent
or silent

it assigns

*

Pánta Rhei

all riverrun

Translated by Odile Cisneros

Paraphernalia for Hélio Oiticica

I.
reticles
nets unnets
reticulairs airs areas
snares resnares nets
areas
reticulairs
reticularia
necklaces of small squares
beads cubicles
areas airs
snares resnares
disarticularia
of real areas
the face implodes
kaleidoscopichameleon

2.
yellow
the bellows of yellow
red
the reflections of red
green
the resonance of green
blue
the nudes of blue
the meadows of yellow
the roads of red
the schemes of green
the nude zulus of blue
the white elephants of white

3.
helios, the sun, does not exceed

4.
(cinetheater noh / psicoset-designed by sousândrade
                    with ideogramic script by eisenstein):

    where you read *hagoromo,* read instead *parangolé*
    where you see *mount fuji,* see instead *hillside of mangueira*
        the parangorome
                pluriplumes

        heliexcels
        helliphant
        cellucinary
        until
        dissolskying itself
        in the sky
        of skies

5.
helio mounts the zeppelin of colors
powered by parangol'helium
and dissolves in the sky's sun

Translated by Micaela Kramer

From *Galáxias* [*Galaxies*] (1963–1976, 1984)

and here I begin I spin here the beguine I respin and begin

to release and realize life begins not arrives at the end of a trip

which is why I begin to respin to write-in thousand pages write thousandone pages

to end write begin write beginend with writing and so I begin to respin

to retrace to rewrite write on writing the future of writing's the tracing

the slaving a thousandone nights in a thousandone pages

or a page in one night the same nights the same pages

same resemblance reassemblance where the end is begin

where to write about writing's not writing about not writing

and so I begin to unspin the unknown unbegun and trace me a book

where all's chance and perchance all a book maybe maybe not a travel

navelof-the-world book a travel navelof-the-book world where tripping's the book

and its being's the trip and so I begin since the trip is beguine and I turn

and return since the turning's respinning beginning realizing

a book is its sense every page is its sense every line of a page every word

of a line is the sense of the line of the page of the books which essays

any book an essay of essays of the book which is why the begin ends

begins and end spins and re-ends and refines and retunes the fine funnel of

the begunend spun into de runend in the end of the beginend refines

the refined of the final where it finished beginnish reruns and returns

and the finger retraces a thousandone stories an incey wince-story and so count

of no account I don't recount the nonstory uncounts me discounts me the reverse

of the story is snot can be rot maybe story depends on the moment
the glory depends on the now and the never on although and no-go
and nowhere and noplace and nihil and nixit and zero and zilch-it
and never can nothing be all can be all can be total sum
total surprising summation of sumptuous assumption
and here I respin I begin to project my echo the wreck o recurrent
echo of the echoing blow the hollows of moreaus the marrow that's beyonder
the over the thisaway thataway everywhere neverwhere overhere overthere
forward more backward less there in reverse vice verse prosa converse
I begin I respin verse begin vice respin so that summated story won't consume consummate
saltimbocca bestride me barebackboneberide me
begin the beguine of the trip where the travel's the marvel the scrabble's the
marble the vigil's the travel the trifle the sparkle the embers of fable discount
into nothing account for the story since spinning beginning i'm speaking

Translated by Suzanne Jill Levine from a basic version by Jon Tolman

'rounded by flowers under god's under devil's mercy god shall guide you for I myself
can't guide godbless those who give 'rounded by flowers and those who are still
to give sounding like a samisen made of a tensed wire a stick
and an old tin can at the end of the partyfair at highnoonhigh but for
many that music did not exist it could not because it could not popplay
if not sung that music is not popular if not in tune it does not atone nor
tarantina and yet struck in the gut of misery in the tensed gut of the meagerest
physical misery aching aching like a nail in the handpalm a
rusty blind nail in the palm clasping palm of the handheart exposed as a tensed nerve
retensed a renigrated blind nail everlasting in the palmpulp of the hand in the sun
while selling for meager cruzeiros gourds in which the good form is
fine meagerness of matter morphing famineform of halfbaked clay in the rottenroot
of distress until others vomit their plastic plates of embroidered
borders empirestyle for mistress misery for this is popular for
the patrons of the people but people create and people engender and people wonder
people are the languageinventor in the malice of the mastery in the smartness of marveling
in the vein to improvise stuttertrying to traverse oiling the sun's axis
for people know no servitude pure or quasi metaphor people il miglior fabbro
in the hammering gait aiming the impossible in view of the nonviable
in the crux of the incredible oiled hammergait and the sunaxis
but the wire that wire that bladewire painpained toothaching like
a demented plangent wire hammering its widowed dischord in blazing brasses of howling
hunger 'rounded by flowers 'rounded by flowers 'rounded by floowers

for I myself cant guide check this book this object of consumption this undergod
underthedevilsmercybook which I arrange and disarrange which I unite and disunite voyages
of a vagamonde in the vagaries of vague moons god shall guide the devil shall guide you then for I
can't don't dare or care don't trick nor touch or trade but only for my
change my pennies my pains my rings my ten fingers my minuses my
nadas my penuries in the antennas in the waves in these niñas most minute
called bagatelles as we'll verify in the verbenas powder-sugary lilies or
minor circumstances I know all this don't count all this disappoints I'm not
sure but listen how it sings value how it tells savor how it dances and don't propose that
I guide don't pose dispose that I guide unguided that I pray for promise
that I trust you leave me forget me let me go untie me so that at the end I
stand erect at the end I revert at the end I concert and for the end I reserve myself
as it will be seen that I am correct it will be seen that there is a way it will be seen that it's been done
and that through wrongs I made it right that from a scent I made a cent and if I do not guide
I do not lament for the master who taught me does not teach any longer baggage of
mirrormoon in the mirage of the second that through inversion I was dexterous being inverted
being gauche I do not guide because I do not guide because I can not guide and don't ask me for
mementos just dwell on this moment and demand my commandment and do not fly just defy
do not confide defile for between yes and no I for one prefer the no
in the knowing of yes place the no in the ee of me place the no the no will be yours to know

Translated by A. S. Bessa

125

passtimes and killtimes i wendaway darkling for mindamends through this minimeandering instant of minutes instancing somebody and instanced beyond to telltale a scheherazade thistory my fairy how many fates are there in each nullitywee thread discard nines leaving nought scheherazade scheherazade a nightstory a thousandtimes overtold then the sonnyboy soulumbering into this nightdark florest came and a drago sevensnouted dragoned his swellhand into a fernavid and cavernish grottohollow my boy wants knowhow to unpick this threadform how to sideslip this cavern only the dragon all dragoning knows the key to this festival and now the dragon at his siesta is asnoozing then when myboy began his ringawinnow round a rosaromanorum gesta in the bosk he stumbled on the sleepy beauty bellabella tell me a life thistory but sleepy beauty in the silence sleepeyed on and nobody told him if there was any forthgoes myboy to a kingdom interlunar where the dead king was up and the upwas king is dead but nobody told him the sideslip thistory myboy is only so posed now to suffer the firetrial to ford the bosk and florrage through the river for the headbone that is there in the well's depth in the depth of pickatomb and catafalque in this well is a caput mortuum myboy doth to godbye suffer a seachange in the caboose but the head does not tell the thistory of its well if there was or if there was not if it was girl or boy a swan of anothertime appears to him in a dream and to the swan country takes him swirling in a bird flock myboy asks the swan about thistory he sings his swan song and swanenchants himself and now is Mrs Sun in the One-Who-Waits and her golden rain illuminates myboy she is in her danaë tower incubus princess crowned by a shower tell me your pluvial tale how it was the gold in a torrent of dust made spawn your treasure but auri-confused the princess of gold clammed up and for to find the taletale myboy wend on his way from post to pillar from muse to medusa all dot in white and white in dot scheherazade my fairy this is all going nowhere princess my princess what a thistory of maze-understanding how many more veins and volutes and volutions find a verysimil that will make of speech the verity and transform in fate a fairy this sybilline simil of destiny's mercurianimal serpentine malefemale and in speech transforms the fate find me this wickedworking blindworm fish-word where the song sings the tale of the song where the why does not tell how where the egg searches in the egg for its retribrilliant ovality where the fire became water the water a body of vapor where the nude unmakes its not and the nut snows itself with nothing a fairy tells a tale that is her deathsong but nobody not even a tiny one can know of this fairy her tale where it begins indeed where it finishes there is no soul to face for to be told it she is all enchanted water go boy my tinyboy to unimagine this fatamorgana is fatiguising a malefelonious sentence you dig miles downunder and come out in the well where you dig you work three hundred for three cent you change diamonds myriads for a crude coal who knows if this coal might be the diamon-diferous dust the mother-of-diamonds morgana of the charmstones and the boy went and the legend does not tell of his ongoing if he came back or did not if from his going one does not come back the legend pokerface does not say only unsays only keeps going around and around and around

Translated by Norman Potter and Christopher Middleton

on the jagged crown of the headlines sharp edges of letters like broken
thorns and polishmooths its will as would a diamond that-yes despite the
weary lungs old bellows burned by asthma or flesh-colored sponges on
the lam but polishmooths and the country folk with suspicious impenetrable
eyes idols olive until the old lady in las higueras with her messenger
goats from the inferno one league away from higueras and two from a ladle
highroads halfways disroads the polished will is a diamond and
sparkles with its virile crest open-eyed barely-bearded and the scrap of a
smile half-exposed on its lips the whole scene foreseen among the possible
ones probed and pondered among the probable ones by a logical calculation even
where the will took root to be lapicide to this crystal here the book stops over shift
triptych now the scene is clearing marilyn marilynda amaryllis of marilyn
in vermillion and black and blonde and rosey pink and pubicrinoline nowpen arms
batdove with vampire wings in a hairnet of gold so boldly blond that from the
v of its breasts she hangs a goblet of dark and nylon stockings hands clasped later
on a knee that in-compasses another knee and the red rounds a
pruderude fear beneath the blondphote hair eardrumdome of a
grinning grimace or could already be rictus rather its still a laugh in the venus-
drummed foam of the armchair this third marilyn is biteful but says better
most bitter her hardcut profile beneath the yellow hairdo helmet
she sits naked and half open post ludium vel post coitum half
open maybe manhandled or publiseen multitouched open fornicated
in a multicoitus that flows like a glutailine of corrosive sperm she

sits leaning on a forearm stump her breasts are mammary
glands and heavy like wax oranges on the other arm a handle
plucks the shroudress could be straddling a funereal bidet
forked thighs and the emblazoned womb crinolined but wholly
and more than totally weary weary weary and a fury of frustrated spit and saliva wound into the book the triptych and triumph
of venus wounds the womb scarlet cherry and necrosey over
shift well to polish the will and shine it like an artist and having
the new stone under the emery wheel see it become vertex
and radiate from an obstinate rigor day after day when a change
of clothes will do and a little moreto eat and drink to get to the higueras
an old-lady goat herder and taken too all the way there by wornout
lungs an old lady two ladle leagues away closed olive mystery
all this was written in an agenda tagebuch a travelog the
third marilyn is dead naked dead saddle-straddling the funereal bidet
psychodelicolors shocking-pink and magneto-blue drop dead for the sight
of a dallas rifle on the jagged crown of the headlines like a
waxen christ an hombre of andalusian shapes between the hands
of the clock all the entire afternoon the shots needling so hot that you needed
a hanky some cloth a rag to protect your hands the first and the
second the vampiresque and the dodging prude the tigering and the pigeondove
return but the third hour of the smelinfant sexyfulvous fury prevails and is dead

Translated by Charles A. Perrone

From *Finismundo: A última viagem* [*Finismundo: The Last Voyage*] (1990)

I.

Ultimate
Odysseus multi-
artful   —in the extreme
Avernotense limit   —re-
proposes a voyage.
                    Where, from Hercules,
vigilant columns the wave
castigate: veering off one more
step   — where to go a-
head   means to trans-
gress the measure   the silent sigils of Fate.

                              Where
the unbound   hubris-prone   ad-
vises: Not!
to the Naut   —Odysseus (
pale erecting the captaining
head to the goal addressed)   premeditates: trans-
pass the pass-
age: the impasse-
to-be: enigma
solved   (if at last) in
thin hulls of
(in)sapphire(d) airs   —defy.
Defy most:
the beyond-return   the post   : unforeseen thread in Penelope's web.

(un)memory(able) man of Ithaca   —that
beyond-memory   —the re-
verse: Ithaca reversed:
nonpacified
vigil of the warrior   in place of
the venture the adventurous
(dis)place   *il folle volo*.
Try the untried
you expatriate   —damned to the gods-lares.
                                             To re-

iterate in leaving.   Defy   —
hubris-propelled   —sea
after sea.   The impervious-obscure
Pelasgian chaos
up to where is hidden the forbidden
geography of Eden— Paradiso
on Earth: the interdicted portal:
the lucerne: over there
isthmus   extreme isle
open access to terrestrial
heaven: to transfinite.

                              Odysseus senescent
rejects the pervasive   —headstrong
torso of Penelope   —
consolation of peace.   The keel in the waves
plows once again   (such as never before)
the irate
mirror of Poseidon: the wine-tinged
heart of the oceansea.

                          Destiny: astray
uncharted
Finismundo: there
where begins the outlawed
frontier of extraheaven.

                              Thus:
break the forbidden seal: de-
virginate the veil.   Coup
of all coups.   Unremitting
vortical mission.
                              He went   —
Odysseus.
                    (The ancient legend does not tell
of the Polumetis the onerous fate.
                                                    Or if it does
deceives in variety: unends an end.)

Odysseus went.   Lost his comrades.
By the border-view
of the desired isle   —already seeing
the unattainable Eden at the quasi
touch of the hand: the Gods had conspired.
The sky sums the scourges of the Arcanum.
The ship repelled/
Abyss/   blown by fate.

Odysseus at sea.

Ephemeral signs in the vortex
reveal the wreckage   —
push   and pull
caught in the moment.

Water. Erasure.

And Fate raging famine.   Ultimate

thánatos eks halós
death arising from salty sea

hubris.
                Odysseus senescent
refused from Glory the funereal pomp.
A sole scar
adorns Poseidon's chest.
Cloistered is the point.   The round
Ocean resonates taciturn.
Serenades now the convulsive chant
dolceamaro plaint of Sirens
(ultrasound uncaptured by human ears).

. . . ma l'un de voi dica
dove per lui perduto a morir gisse

2.
Urban Ulysses
to myth survived
(I and You   my hypo-
chondriac critic[al]
reader)   civil
factotum   (Polumetis?)
of computerized chance.   Your
epitaph? Margin of error: minimum
digitized trace
and in a hurry canceled
in the fluidgreen liquid crystal.

                                        Circumnavigation?
No more.   Vigilant semaphores.
Your Promethean fire resumed
to the spark of a match   phosphor-Lucifer
portable and/or
flammable bagatelle.

                              Capitulate
(coldheaded)
your hubris.   No signs
of Sirens.
Penultimate   —all you aspire to
is your penury of ultimate
Thule.   A postcard from Eden
will content you.

Strident sirens
scar your quotidian heart.

Translated by A. S. Bessa

From *Crisantempo: no espaço curvo nasce um*
[*Chrysantempo: In Curved Space Is Born A*]
(1998)

As in Ovid: Metamorphosis

it was)

        a dryad
        makes a
        gesture

winter)

        in the recess
        of the trunk she
        inhabits
        a spring day
        lights up

Translated by Micaela Kramer

Minimal Landscape

A hunchbacked
gardener
watering vegetables
—rising from the green—
in the solar
yard

Translated by Micaela Kramer

Poem for Qohelet 1: New Year, Day One

life went by like a
blind
like a dead
bat
that slows down
delays this daily
waking
without memory
daily dismemory
shipwrecked
between the way out and the outcome
naught
about knowing nothing:
no jet nor project
poetry
thought as a point (*punctum*)
blind spot in the retina
under a savage sun
poetry
the end of that string bursting
made fragile by the siege
of reality's daily task:
CEOs riding on horseback
overnight nights
where the throb of sleepless lemurs
rates zero
zero and rats—facts
this new year's Sunday
forty years of poetry are a useless
block of shavings
garbage *lixo* trash

I heard the fountain
once
and the murmur of the fountain:

the hand burnt
the writing was deformed
the burnt disfigured the face

the horizon closed on me

Translated by Odile Cisneros

Poem for Qohelet 2: In Praise of the Termite

termites have taken over the library
I hear their muted noise
the zero-chant of the termites
humans deserted the library
words transformed into paper
termites occupy the place of humans
greedy for paper   cellulose experts
human pride is humbled   worm-eaten wood

all is vain
a leprosy of termites gnaws on paper   books
beetles beat pride
and thus we shall remain   corpses full of worms

I write this in praise of the termite

Translated by Odile Cisneros

The Revolt of Objects

objects revolt
they assault the air gaps
they leap from the confines of
habitual (solid) substance

they confront us
furiously
irate of so much ob
ab/jection
of so much ad-
jectival passivity
of such much thinging disconnected (dyslexic) of things in-
animate
thingified and kept:

now they earn claws
objects
free from the enclaves
anchored with moorings
rebellious things
annoyed
like porcupines
suicidally pricking
the warm ventral regions:

irate
useless
re-
volt
the hand of chance
(or is it the not of the
inefficient cause?)
decapitating things:
decapitated   beheaded
objects
without headings (rebels without a cause)
they capitulate

they return to their un-case
to their (insistent) un-being:
they regress to their stubborn condition of things

Translated by Odile Cisneros

Links for a Renga

the semaphore's red
eye – polyphemic light –
scrutinizes the jet-black light

urine-
yellow sun-
spot
in the chamber-
pot

azure
out of
garbage

crows in the deep-
dark
learning verses
by heart

Translated by Haroldo de Campos

The Left-Winged Angel of History

the landless men at last
are now settled down on land
landing
full-landed landwards:
from landless they change to
landlords: look at them
landlocked
in their shallow graves
exiled from their life-breath
terrorized
from earth
unearthed
dust that to dust returns
plenipossessors
glebe-patroons
of a commonshared
potter (butcher's meat) field:

downwards finally
embedded
into the latiwomb
of the latifundium
(which far from im-
productive re-
veals itself as most fe-
cund: it generates a pin-
guid rubiginous
crop of
bloody clots—
plowmen
without plowland—
look at them
finally converted into larvae
into mortuary
spoils
coffins carved on the
thin timber of

themselves: the killer's bullet
ambushed them
deathscared
dreadseated
decumbentdriven pre-
destinatarian of agrar-
ian re(hungry)
(dis)formation: look
at them – gre-
garious community
of nothingness' pards

a-
shamed
shamefaced –
abashabasedagonizing from
inmostabrasive re-
morse –
fatherland
(how to be proud of?)
fatherlessland
mourns their de-possessed pariah
–parricide fatherland

that perhaps only when
the flaming sword
of the gauche-archangel of
history counterwind flashing
and inflaming
the agromortician associates
of the funereal sodality
where commander-in-chief death
gives orders to a dark
gendarmerie of janizary-jagunzos:
perhaps only the angel
(arch) of counter-
hair brushed history
with his
vortex-whirling sword

would one day
(one dazzling day) per-
haps summon from
the misty mesh of
days to come
the one
(finally super-
venient) day of the
just
adjustment
of accounts

Translated by Haroldo de Campos

Gongorine Tribute to Sá de Miranda

deafening song of nightingales
the sun   so large   it blinds   góngora's sun
("salamandra del sol")   and the chessboard
of stars receding glitters
from facing the sun   yellow-
sulfur jet   crucible   saffron   light radiates

stars await their turn—
to day dim
rotation gives way:
that's when I write   recollection
of solar light   nostalgic   I spell
with diamond nib on tarnished
card   syllables—star-syllables—
I pour sun
sap on the dark
page

Translated by Odile Cisneros

The Poet Ezra Pound Descends to Hell

not to the limbo
of those never alive
not even
to the purgatory of those who await
but to the hell
of those who persevere in error
despite any belated contrition
and the mute old age
—straight with integrity
the old ez
already a ghost of himself

and in such damnation
such splendor of paradise

Translated by Micaela Kramer

II : **Essays**

Reinventing Tradition

Anthropophagous Reason: Dialogue and Difference in Brazilian Culture

> Echte Polemik nimmt ein Buch sich so liebevoll vor, wie ein Kannibale sich einen Säugling zurüstet.
>
> Genuine polemics approach a book as lovingly as a cannibal spices a baby.
>
> —Walter Benjamin*

Avant-Garde and/or Underdevelopment

The question of the national and the universal (notably, of the European) in Latin American culture, a question involving other more specific ones, such as that of the relationship between a universal cultural heritage and local specificities or, even more precisely, the possibility of an avant-garde, experimental literature in an underdeveloped country, is one I addressed in an article from 1962.[1] In that paper, I relied on Engels's reflections on the problem of the division of labor in philosophy contained in a famous letter to Conrad Schmidt (27 October 1890): "But in every

This article was originally published as "Da razão antropofágica: A Europa sob o signo da devoração," *Colóquio/Letras* 62 (July 1981): 10–26. This is a new translation of this seminal essay; a different English version appeared as "The Rule of Anthropophagy: Europe under the Sign of Devoration," trans. Maria Tai Wolff, *Latin American Literary Review* 14, no. 27 (January–June 1986): 42–60. —TRANSLATOR

* Walter Benjamin, "Die Technik des Kritikers in dreizehn Thesen," in *Gesammelte Werke*, vol. 4, part 1, ed. Tillman Rexroth (Frankfurt: Suhrkamp, 1972), 108. In English: "The Technique of the Critic in Thirteen Theses," in *One-Way Street and Other Writings*, trans. Edmund Jephcott and Kingsley Shorter (New York:Verso, 1997), 67. —TRANSLATOR

epoch philosophy, as a definite sphere of the division of labor, presupposes a definite fund of ideas inherited from its predecessors and from which it takes its departure. And that is why economically backward countries can nevertheless play first fiddle where philosophy is concerned. . . ."* For Engels the supremacy of economics is not registered directly but in the "terms laid down by each individual field" (62), that is, indirectly, mediated by the intellectual material transmitted. Engels criticized those who were incapable of taking into account the complexity of this movement, culturally speaking: "What all these gentlemen lack is dialectics" (63). Engels also coined the image of the "infinite group of parallelograms of forces"† leading to the historical event and which, despite the postulated economic supremacy, ultimately cannot be the object of a simplistic, mechanical study, as if it were the case of solving a "simple equation of the first degree" (letter to Joseph Bloch, 21 September 1890, 35).

It always seemed to me that, in terms of literary labor, this complex law of the transmission of a cultural legacy also holds; a law from which poetic production cannot escape and one that could allow us to identify the emergence of the new, even within the conditions of an underdeveloped economy.[2] This is particularly true today, as we witness the real confirmation of what Marx and Engels foresaw: "In place of the old local and national seclusion and self-sufficiency, we have intercourse in every direction, universal interdependence of nations. And as in material, so also in intellectual production. National one-sidedness and narrow-mindedness become more and more untenable, and from the numerous national and local literatures there arises a world literature."[3] Goethe's idea of a *Weltliteratur,* in the context of that passage, can be reread as intersemiotic praxis: it is the realm of communications, the dialogic pressure of generalized intersubjective communication, which orders and configures the universal literary sign as an "ideological sign" (in Voloshinov's—and/or Bakhtin's—sense, as he tried to formulate his Marxist-based "sociological semiotics" in the 1920s);[4] a meeting point of discourses, a necessary dialogue and not a monologic xenophobia, a parallelogram of forces in dialectical tension and not the equivalent of a mimetic-Pavlovian unknown. Thus, any mechanistic reduction, any self-punishing fatalism—according to which, to an economically underdeveloped country must correspond an underdeveloped literature, as

* In Karl Marx and Frederick Engels, *Engels: 1890–92,* vol. 49 of *Collected Works* (New York: International Publishers, 2001), 62. All references to Engels's letters in this essay are quoted from this source. —TRANSLATOR

†In the source quoted, the passage reads "unending multitude of fortuities" (35). I've preserved the author's original geometric allusion. —TRANSLATOR

if by conditioned reflex—always seemed to me the fallacy of a naive soci-
ologism.

Later, I found in Octavio Paz's "Invention, Underdevelopment, Modernity" (*Alternating Current,* 1967) enlightening observations which, by an
intellectual coming from another Latin American country, confirmed my
own reflections on the problem of the Brazilian poet's situation vis-à-vis
the universal:

> A number of Mexican critics use the word "underdevelopment" to
> describe the present situation in Hispano-American arts and letters: our
> culture is "underdeveloped," the work of X or Y represents a breaking
> away from the "underdevelopment of the novel in our country," and so
> on and so forth. As I see it, the word refers to certain currents that are
> not to these critics' liking (or to mine): chauvinistic nationalism, acad-
> emicism, traditionalism, and the like. But the word "underdevelop-
> ment" is a United Nations euphemism for backward nations. The
> notion of "underdevelopment" is an offshoot of the idea of social and
> economic progress. Aside from the fact that I am very much averse to
> reducing the plurality of cultures and the very destiny of man to a sin-
> gle model, industrial society, I have serious doubts as to whether the
> relationship between economic prosperity and artistic experience is one
> of cause and effect. Cavafy, Borges, Unamuno, and Reyes cannot be
> labeled "underdeveloped" writers, despite the marginal economic status
> of Greece, Spain, and Latin America. Moreover, the rush to "develop"
> reminds me of nothing so much as a frantic race to arrive at the gates of
> Hell ahead of everyone else.*

I believe that in Brazil, with Oswald de Andrade's "Anthropophagy" in
the 1920s (revisited in the 1950s as a philosophical-existential cosmic vision
in his thesis *A crise da filosofia messiânica* [*The Crisis of Messianic Philosophy*]), we experienced the strong urge to rethink the national in a dialogic
and dialectical relationship with the universal. Oswald's "Anthropophagy"—as I have written elsewhere[5]—is a theory proposing the critical
devouring of universal cultural heritage, formulated not from the submis-
sive and reconciled perspective of the "noble savage" (idealized following
the model of European virtues in the "nativist" vein of Brazilian romanticism by authors such as Gonçalves Dias and José de Alencar, for example),
but from the disabused point of view of the "bad savage," devourer of

*Octavio Paz, *Alternating Current,* trans. Helen R. Lane (New York: Viking Press, 1973), 19. —TRANSLATOR

whites, the cannibal. This last view does not involve submission (conversion) but, rather, transculturation, or, even better, "transvalorization": a critical view of history as a negative function (in Nietzsche's sense), capable of appropriation and of expropriation, of dehierarchization, of deconstruction. Any past which is an "other" for us deserves to be negated. We could even say, it deserves to be eaten, devoured, with the following clarifying proviso: The cannibal was a "polemicist" (from the Greek *polemos*, meaning "struggle, combat"), but he was also an "anthologist"—he devoured only the enemies he considered courageous, taking their marrow and protein to fortify and renew his own natural energies. For instance, Oswald de Andrade was inspired, to a certain extent, by Blaise Cendrars's nomadic poetic cubism (whom he also, in turn, influenced, during the so-called heroic phase of "Poesia pau-brasil" ["Brazilwood poetry"] in 1923–24). Yet, in lieu of the traveling "pirate of Lac Léman's" *Kodak,* busy recording the picturesque and exotic elements it came across during Cendrars's wanderings in Brazilian lands, we find the *camera-eye* of Oswald's minute-poem shooting a critical element, capturing a satiric note in Brazil's fossilized national life. He detonates a grenade of irreverent humor not found in Cendrars's touristy Brazilian poems collected in *Feuilles de route.* With Oswald, in the 1920s, we are already closer, by anticipation, to the anti-illusionism of Brecht's laconic poetry of the late 1930s (the poems written in "basic German" and sharpened with critical barbs) than to Cendrars's unengagé color slides. The Swiss poet thought he had rediscovered Brazil and poached his Brazilian friend in a cosmopolitan fondue pot.* Oswald borrowed his camera and returned the favor by eating him. Here are the subtleties of the great Indian chief Cunhambebe: "Here comes our dinner, hopping along," as the Tupinamba said at the sight of the European Hans Staden.† The case to some extent parallels that of Huidobro and Reverdy. Bracketing out the idle polemics

---

* The author refers to the trip that Blaise Cendrars took to Brazil with Oswald de Andrade and Tarsila do Amaral. For a full account, see *A aventura brasileira de Blaise Cendrars: ensaio, cronologia, filme, depoimentos, antologia,* ed. Alexandre Eulalio; rev. Carlos Calil (São Paulo: EDUSP/FAPESP/Imprensa Oficial 2001). —TRANSLATOR

† Reference to a sixteenth-century German traveler in Brazil who lived for some time among the Tupinamba Indians, practitioners of cannibalist rites. His 1557 autobiographical account of captivity is entitled *Warhaftige Historia und Beschreibung eyner Landtschafft der wilden, nacketen, grimmigen Menschfresser Leuthen in der Newenwelt America gelegen;* available in English as *Hans Staden, the True History of His Captivity, 1557,* trans. and ed. by Malcolm Letts (London: G. Routledge & Sons, 1928). —TRANSLATOR

over who came first, which of Reverdy's poems could match the force and originality of *Altazor*'s aeroepic synthesis?

Modal Nationalism vs. Ontological Nationalism

I believe that an ontological nationalism, modeled after the organic/biological pattern of a plant's development (a model that secretly inspires any form of literary historiography seeking to identify a "national classicism," a moment of perfection of gradual blossoming, nourished by the "objectivist claim" or by the "immanent teleology" of nineteenth-century historicism),[6] can be contrasted (or, at least, for the sake of "ventilation" of this domain, counterpoised, in the musical sense of the word "counterpoint") with a modal, differential nationalism. In the former case, one seeks the origin and the parousia-like itinerary of a specific national Logos. This is an episode of the Western metaphysics of presence, transferred to our tropical latitudes, one that doesn't quite realize the final meaning of this transfer; a chapter to be added to the Platonizing logocentrism which Derrida, in *Of Grammatology*, subjected to a lucid and revealing analysis, not accidentally at the instigation of two "ex-centrics," Fenollosa, the anti-Sinologist, and Nietzsche, the shatterer of certainties. This first ontological case seeks to locate the moment of incarnation of the national spirit (of the Logos), obscuring difference (the disruptions and infractions, the margins, the "monstrous") to better define a certain privileged course: the straight path of that *logophany* across history. Its apex (comparable to the organic thrust of the tree) coincides with the parousia of this Logos, in full bloom in the domestic backyard. Yet, when it comes to describing this entified substance—the national "character"—one falls into a watered-down and conventional "half-portrait," where nothing is characteristic and the conciliatory patriocentrism must resort to hypostases to sustain itself. Machado de Assis, for example. The great and unclassifiable Machado, swallower of Sterne and of countless others. (He coined the metaphor of the head as a "ruminator's stomach," where, as Augusto Meyer recalls in a subtle study of sources, "all suggestions, after being chopped up and mixed, are prepared for a new remastication, a complicated chemistry where one can no longer tell the assimilating organism from the assimilated matter.")* So Machado—our nineteenth-century Borges—whose works mark the

---

* Quoted from Augusto Meyer, *Machado de Assis*, 3d ed. (Rio de Janeiro: Presença, 1975), 110. —TRANSLATOR

zenith of that parousia in the summa of these logophanic readings, is national because he is not national. Like Fernando Pessoa's mythological Ulysses, who "foi por não ser existindo" [was by way of not being] and "nos creou" [made us].*

Hence the necessity of thinking the *difference*, nationalism as a dialogic movement of difference (and not as the Platonic anointing of origin and a conveniently homogenizing strickle). The need to think the uncharacter, instead of the character; the rupture instead of the linear course; historiography as the seismic graph of subversive fragmentation rather than the tautological homologation of the homogeneous. A rejection of the substantialist metaphor of natural, gradual, and harmonious evolution. A new idea of tradition (antitradition) funtioning as a counterevolution, as a countercurrent opposed to the glorious, prestigious canon. A thesis of Adorno's, recalled by Jauss: "There we find the actual theme of the meaning of tradition: that which is relegated to the side of the road, scorned and suppressed; that which is collected under the name of old junk: it is there, and not in the set of works which supposedly challenge time, where what is truly alive in tradition takes its refuge."[7]

Mário de Andrade, creating Macunaíma, the national antihero "without a character,"[†] denounced, perhaps subliminally (or, we could say here, Oswaldianly), the logocentric fallacy which lurks in any ontological nationalism. The Macunaimic search, seen from this radical perspective, differs from/defers (in the Derridean double meaning of divergence and delay) the talismanic moment of monologic plenitude. It suspends the dogmatic investiture of a single, unique character to be ultimately found. (From this stems the danger of reevangelizing the savage-cannibalesque nature of the Macunaimic project, crowning it with the religious halo of the grail: the danger of putting the "son-of-Mary," candle-bearing Indian, the knightly Guarani ridiculed in Oswald's "Cannibalist manifesto," in the place of the Brazilian anthropophagous trickster. A mistake—or an attempt at exorcism—made by the European missionaries who translated the name of Macunaíma [the "Great Evil" of the Roraima Indians]—as the holy name of the Christian God . . .) After this incessantly deferred and frustrated (deamplified) search remains the difference, the disconcerting, "carnivalized," never thoroughly resolved dialogic movement of the same and

* English translation of the poem "Ulysses" in Fernando Pessoa, *Message,* trans. Jonathan Griffin (London: Menard Press/King's College London, 1992), 17. —TRANSLATOR

†Reference to Mário de Andrade's 1928 novel *Macunaíma;* in English, trans. E. A. Goodland (New York: Random House, 1984). —EDITORS

alterity, of the aboriginal and the alien (the European). A paradoxical critical space, as opposed to the *doxa:* the ever-renewed, instigating interrogation, in lieu of the soothing precepts of the *Boy Scout Manual.*

In this logophanic substantialism, there is little distinction between the two main models for reading tradition put forth by contemporary Brazilian literary historiography: the dysphoric and the euphoric: Antonio Candido's (*Formação da literatura brasileira* [*The Formation of Brazilian Literature*], 1959) and Afrânio Coutinho's (*Introdução à literatura no Brasil* [*An Introduction to Literature in Brazil*], 1959;* *Conceito de literatura brasileira* [*The Concept of Brazilian Literature*], 1960; *A tradição afortunada* [*The Fortunate Tradition*] 1968). Candido economically omits the baroque on the basis of a sociological argument (the absence of printed works and of a reading public) and locates the inaugural "formative moment" in preromantic Arcadianism. Assembling his theory with the elegance and internal coherence of a mathematical construct based on the scheme of transmission of referential (thematic-nativist) messages, Candido privileges, in the process, the communicative and emotional functions of language (expressing its "profound inconstancies") and, by extension, those of literature. On the other hand, he also fuels a certain ironic skepticism with regard to the arbitrariness involved in the critical gesture of objective interpretation and vis-à-vis the aesthetic profitability of the model thus constructed (in this sense, a *dysphoric* model). Coutinho is capable of recuperating the Brazilian baroque without major restrictions or questionable methodological inhibitions through the stylistic-journalistic criteria which mold the work, *latu sensu.* (This important recovery constitutes its principal merit.) He turns to the reconstruction of a supposedly "fortunate" tradition: an ascending evolutionary ladder (not without traces of *ufanismo* [boastfulness])† in which the baroque is naturally integrated as an early blossoming. This approach is less concerned with the rigorous definition of its semiological reading model, which seems to depend on the *fortune* itself—axiomatically declared as such—of such a *tradition.* (Thus, I call it a *euphoric* model.)

---

*Available in English as *An Introduction to Literature in Brazil,* trans. Gregory Rabassa (New York: Columbia University Press, 1969). —TRANSLATOR

† The term *ufanista* (from *ufanar-se,* "to boast"), came to describe a category of Brazilian literature produced in the second half of the sixteenth century and which tended to glorify the land and its riches. Closer to our times, *Por que me ufano do meu país* (1901) by Count Afonso Celso (1860–1938), fostered similar naive and sentimental thought by praising the potential of Brazil, its natural beauty, wealth, and youth. —TRANSLATOR

Both models, however, are bound in the same parousia-like struggle (even if with different, and even antagonistic, ideological overtones): the constitution of the national spirit (or conscience), positing Machado de Assis as the terminus ad quem of this ontological course, as the culmination. In both cases, too, a more rigorous analysis reveals the historiographical culmination of the fundamental project of Brazilian romanticism (with the expected theoretical refinements and the attempt to "normalize" the disturbing interference of Machado de Assis). This project is understood by Antonio Candido as a "process of genealogical construction," a "linear process of Brazilianization," whose naive phase—with Machado, romanticism would become adult and critical—is picturesquely illustrated thus by this critic: "The result would be a kind of spectrogram in which the same color would go from the faintest shades to the most densely tinted, ending in the triumphant nationalism of the romantic Indianist school."*

The Baroque: The Noninfancy

Any logocentric question of origins in Brazilian literature (and this could apply to other Latin American literatures, excluding the problem of the great pre-Columbian cultures, which should be studied as a special case) runs up against a historiographical hurdle: the baroque.[8] The baroque for us is the nonorigin, because it is a noninfancy. Our literatures, emerging with the baroque, had no infancy (*infans:* one who does not speak). They were never aphasic. They were adults at birth (like certain mythological heroes), speaking an extremely elaborate universal code: the baroque rhetorical code (with late medieval and Renaissance traces, already distilled, in the case of Brazil, by Camonian mannerism—which, in turn, stylistically influenced Góngora). To articulate oneself as difference in relation to this panoply of *universalia,* this is our "birth" as a literature: a sort of parthenogenesis without the ontological egg (we could say—difference as origin or the egg of Columbus . . .).

Mário Faustino, a memorable colleague of my generation, wrote, at the end of the 1950s:

---

* "Indianismo," or Indianism, was a literary movement founded during the romantic period and financially supported by the emperor D. Pedro II. Its program centered on the image of the native Brazilian as a way to "valorize our national origins." Its main authors were Gonçalves de Magalhães, José de Alencar, Joaquim Manuel de Macedo, and Gonçalves Dias. —EDITORS.

The Italian or Spanish baroque of the *seicento* is, truly, the first great organized drive in Western poetry toward an "organic poetry," that is, one which grows from the lines of force of the very materials from which it is made; a poetry where the poem reflects a detailed vision of the world as it composes another world, microscopic and reified. The true poetry of the seventeenth-century baroque is evidently, above all, an *erudite* poetry. [And, with regard especially to the Brazilian case:] We emphasize, yet again, that the sophisticated technical level at which poetry began in all its forms in Brazil is surprising. In Brazil, poetry began as an art, as something that could be taught by the skilled and learned and practiced by those possessing a basic level of talent for the goals at hand. In Portugal as in Brazil, in the seventeenth century, one learned to produce verse from manuals like the celebrated *El arte de trobar* [*The Art of Verse-Making*]. Older poets taught the less experienced, and the academies began to flourish. It is, therefore, not at all surprising (considering that they either came from Europe already skilled in the art or would go there to study it) that one finds in our first poets, major and minor, a high degree of technical skill. . . .[9]

To speak the baroque code, in the literature of colonial Brazil, meant to try to extract the difference from the morphing of the same. To the extent that the allegorical style of the baroque was an alternate speech, a style in which, at the limit, anything could symbolize anything else (as Walter Benjamin explained in his study on the German *Trauerspiel*), the "alternating current" of the Brazilian baroque was a double speech of the other as difference: to speak a code of alterities and to speak it in an altered state. Gregório de Matos, a Brazilian educated at Coimbra, a white man among mulattoes and mestizos, antagonized by the nobles of the land and by those born in the kingdom of Portugal. In turn, an unredeemable spiritual hybrid, unable to be either one thing or the other, neither a judge in the kingdom nor a lawyer in the overseas colony, torn, like Brazil, in a situation of dependency, he bursts out cursing as the "Voice of Hell." The same permutation mechanism of the baroque courtly rhetoric lends itself to the disabused virulence of the critic; the ingenious style of praise and courteous worship is the same one that fuels the aggressive mental play of satire and the unrestrained physical play of eroticism. Gregório is already our first cannibal, as Augusto de Campos noted ("the first experimental cannibal in our poetry") in an instigating poem-study from 1974.[10] Our first transculturator, Gregório translated, with a highly personal, differential feature revealed in his ironic handling of the combination of literary topoi, two sonnets by Góngora ("Mientras por competir con tu cabello" ["While to Compete with Your Hair"] and "Ilustre y hermosísima María" ["Illustrious and Most Lovely Maria"] to produce a third ("Discreta e formosíssima Maria" ["Refined and Most Lovely Maria"]), which took apart and made explicit the secrets of the baroque sonnet-making machine. In addition, this sonnet, being Góngora's twice, was also Garcilaso de la Vega's, Camões's, and, more remotely, Ausonius's. (All these poets, in turn, provided Góngora with his paradigmatic sonnets, which Gregório, the Bahian, resonnetized in a *tertius* so mystifying and congenial in its unexpected dialectical synthesis, that even today academic commentators are unable to approach that *monstrous* product without sanctimoniously mumbling the protective charm of the word "plagiarism.". . .) Sor Juana, in Mexico, is another example. About her differential baroque, I will only say—following Octavio Paz's *Las peras del olmo* ([*Pears from an Elm*], 1957)—that at her best, in the "Primero sueño," she does not respond to Góngora but, rather, in a single gesture anticipates German romanticism and the surrealist dreamworld.* She did so from the confinement of her convent, which served her, for the flights of her creative imagination, as a free territory within the colonial space, a space seen as repressive in that it was an exile from the greater cultural centers, and a masculine framework of isolation for a woman poet and scholar.

Speaking the difference in the gaps of a universal code, the Latin American writers of the baroque carried out among themselves a dialogue that only now is being taken up again. A dialogue that could be at times explicit: Sor Juana discusses the theological constructions of Father Vieira, the great prose writer of the Brazilian baroque, in her 1690 polemical piece, "Crisis sobre un sermón" ["Crisis over a Sermon"]† (written while Vieira was still alive). And she discussed them in order to devour them and their author; to impose her feminine wit on Vieira's sacred eloquence and cleverness; to seek revenge for his arrogant and masculine grandiloquence by the artful path of this castrating strategy (in Ludwig Pfandl's spicy psychoanalytic interpretation).[11] Today, we are surprised to find in Borges a reference to Euclides da Cunha's *Os sertões* [*Rebellion in the Backlands*], nothing

---

* Cf. "Sor Juana Inés de la Cruz," *Las peras del olmo* (México: Seix Barral, 1974), 45–46. —TRANSLATOR

† This text is also known as "Carta atenagórica." Cf. Sor Juana Inés de la Cruz, *Obras completas,* 2d ed. (México: Editorial Porrúa, 1972), 811–27. —TRANSLATOR

more than the distant memory of a reading. It so happens that we have become more removed, in terms of spiritual geography, than Sor Juana and Vieira, who operated differentially within a common code. And there was, in addition, an implicit dialogue: Gregório, the Bahian, Sor Juana, the Mexican, Caviedes, the Peruvian—all participated in a discourse tropologically interwoven, even if they were not exact contemporaries nor made direct allusions to one another. This discourse extended itself also as a symposium that went back in time: in attendance were Góngora, Quevedo, Lope de Vega, Garcilaso, Camões, Sá de Miranda, Petrarch. . . . Literature, in the colonies as in the metropolis, was fashioned from other literature. Except that, being eccentric in the colonies, literature could articulate itself as a double difference: a difference of the different. Sor Juana dreaming her pyramidal, presurrealist dream. Gregório de Matos strumming his Goliardic viola, precursor of the electric guitar of the "tropicalist" Bahian Caetano Veloso (as James Amado, the most recent editor of Gregório's poetic manuscripts, sees it). Caviedes biting into the composure of the erudite style, in the disabused Rabelaisian satires of his *Diente del Parnaso*. . . .*

The Baroque and Anthropophagous Reason

Already in the baroque a possible "anthropophagous reason" develops, deconstructing the logocentrism we inherited from the West. Differential within the universal—there began the twists and turns of a discourse which could disentangle us from the same. It is an antitradition, which passes through the gaps of traditional historiography, which filters through its cracks, which goes astray through its fissures. It's not merely an antitradition based on direct derivation—for that would be the substitution of one linearity for another—but rather on the acknowledgment of certain marginal paths or patterns alongside the preferential script of normative historiography. In prose, at a certain point in this meandering process, within a specific configuration, it would produce the vein of the *romance malandro* [novel of the rogue], baptized thus by Antonio Candido in "Dialética da malandragem" ["The Dialectics of Roguery," 1970]. This essay, in my view, represents in a certain way the critic's deliberate "unreading" of the privileged road topographed in his *Formação da literatura brasileira* [*Formation of Brazilian Literature*]. It is a second mode of thought, skillfully projected

---

* Juan del Valle y Caviedes (1652–1695?), Spanish-born Peruvian poet. His *Diente del Parnaso* is a long satirical poem. —TRANSLATOR

over his first straight, chronographic trace, unaligning it, in order to mean-
ingfully carve out the same space, now reorganized as a different constellation. Here, history becomes the product of a construction, of a reconfiguring, a
"monadologic" appropriation in Benjamin's sense. Distinguishing the "novel
of the rogue" from the European picaresque, Candido acknowledges in the
former, archetypal elements from a folk source and the live ferment of popular realism. Remote and ultramodern, the genre is first represented in
Brazil by Manuel António de Almeida's *Memórias de um sargento de milí-
cias* [*Memoirs of a Militia Sergeant*] (1852–53),* a text out of place, almost a
relic, in the preferential series of novels of our canonical romanticism
(which runs from Joaquim Manuel de Macedo to José de Alencar). It is not
by accident that this new possibility of reading the tradition coincided with
the reassessment of Oswald de Andrade's novels-inventions, especially *Serafim Ponte Grande* [*Seraphim Grosse Pointe*] (1933; an experiment in the
semiological transgression of order, in the questioning of the established
legality and legibility, via perennial disorder and anarchic versatility).[12]

To the extent that the "rogue tradition" would be another name for "carnivalization," it acts retroactively on the baroque, on the baroque viewed
by Severo Sarduy as the Bakhtinian phenomenon par excellence: the ludic
space of polyphony and of language in convulsion.[13] Let us not forget that
Quevedo, the Quevedo of the conceptist sonnets, is also the author of *The
Swindler* (1626). Our first *roguish* "hero" (antihero) is the cannibal Gregório
de Matos (as Antonio Candido himself admits, from this new perspective,
in a near postscript to his *Formação,* a work where Gregório, barred by the
lock of sociological argument, has no chance or way of entry). The "Cre-
ole Muse," the "Cursing Muse." The first cannibal-rogue. I'm not speaking
about his biography; I'm speaking of biographical material preserved in the
oral tradition and dispersed in apocryphal manuscripts. Of a persona
behind which a text resonates. A text of texts. Universal and differential.
Parodic. Parallelographic. The "parallel song" of a translator-devourer:
decentered, eccentric.

Concrete Poetry: Another Constellation

In contemporary Brazilian poetry, *concrete poetry* can also claim this
"antinormative" tradition due to another specific redistribution of the

---

* Manuel António de Almeida, *Memoirs of a Militia Sergeant: A Novel,* trans. from the Portuguese by
Ronald W. Sousa, with a foreword by Thomas H. Holloway and an afterword by Flora Süssekind (New
York: Oxford University Press, 1999).

available configuring elements. This redistribution must be equally reconstituted through castings and recastings. From Gregório to Sousândrade, from the "Voice of Hell" of baroque Bahia to the romantic *maudit* of Maranhão, singer of "O Inferno de Wall Street" ["The Wall Street Inferno"] (1870). From Gregório to Sousândrade and from the latter to Oswald, from the mocker of "armadillo-blood" nobility to the high priest of the "Tatuturema" (the black mass of the Amazon Indians), to the *Brazil-wood* reteller of the discovery chronicles.[14] From Oswald to Drummond and Murilo. From all of them to João Cabral de Melo Neto, engineer of "Mondrianesque" structures. A different pattern. Another constellation. An antidiscourse geometrizing baroque proliferation. Father Vieira and Mallarmé, both chess players of language, both *syntaxiers*. The sonorist Tupi poetry and the praise of conciseness (the vocation of Japanese haiku) in Oswald's manifestos:

> Catiti Catiti
> Imara Notiá
> Notiá Imara
> Ipeju . . .
>
> New Moon, oh New Moon!
> whisper in his ear
> memories of
> me . . .*

or:

> Somos concretistas
>
> We are concretists[15]

Concrete poetry represents Brazilian literature's moment of absolute synchrony. Not only can it speak the difference in a universal code (like Gregório de Matos and Father Vieira in the baroque; like Sousândrade recombining the Greek and Latin heritage, Dante, Camões, Milton, Goethe, and Byron in his *Guesa Errante* [*Wandering Guesa*]; like Oswald de

---

*Based on an approximate Portuguese translation by Conto Magalhães in *O selvagem,* 3d ed. (São Paulo, 1935). —TRANSLATOR

Andrade "Brazilwood-izing" Italian futurism and French cubism). Metalinguistically, concrete poetry rethought its own code, the poetic function itself (or the workings of this code). With concrete poetry, the difference (the national) became the place of operation of this universal code's new synthesis. More than a legacy of poets, it became a question of assuming, critiquing, and "chewing up" a poetics. In a way, Max Bense is right when, speaking of Brazilian concrete poetry, he distinguishes first between a traditional (classic) and a progressive (nonclassic) concept of literature. According to Bense, to the former would correspond a work like Curtius's *European Literature and the Latin Middle Ages,* in which past and present converge into a "unity of meaning." To the second corresponds the *Noigandres* group's "Plano piloto para poesia concreta" ["Pilot Plan for Concrete Poetry"] (1958), which announces the end of the "historic cycle of verse."[16] In reality, what was taking place there was a radical change in the dialogic register. Instead of the old question of influences, in terms of authors and works, a new process opened up. Authors belonging to a supposedly peripheral literature suddenly appropriated the entire code, reclaimed it as their patrimony, like an empty shoe waiting for a new historical subject to rethink its function in terms of a generalized and radical poetics. The Brazilian case of this poetics became the differentiating optics and the condition of possibility. The difference could now be thought of as foundational. Below the linearity of conventional history, this gesture, constellationally—by means of an almost subliminal solidarity—"quoted" another gesture: that of the German romantics of Jena, with their dialectical conception of a "universal progressive poetry," which led up to Mallarmé and produced, in the West, the spiritual limit of "Un coup de dés" ["A Throw of the Dice"] (where the East already begins to break through with its synthetic-analogical model of ideogrammatic writing, to disturb the logical-Aristotelic monologism of Western discursive verse).

It was a matter of recannibalizing a poetics. The moment (the decade of the 1950s) was, furthermore, intersemiotic. In Europe, new post-Webernian music was being composed (Boulez, Stockhausen). In the United States, there was Cage and the beginnings of chance indeterminacy on the prepared piano. In Brazil, in popular music, the conditions leading up to the bossa nova of João Gilberto—our pointillist "one note samba" Webern—were blossoming. In architecture, Niemeyer, and in urbanism, Lucio Costa responded to Le Corbusier and to the Bauhaus for our domestic use. In painting: the *Bienal* Exhibitions of São Paulo. And our generation rediscovered and rejuvenated Volpi, our "fourteenth-century Mondrian" (Décio

Pignatari), with his little flags, his striped masts, and his serialized facades with his structural "color-light," who seemed to us more of a painter than the Swiss Max Bill.

Concrete poetry, Brazilianly, thought up a new poetics, national and universal. A planetarium of "signs in rotation," whose point-events were called (like topographic indexes) Mallarmé, Joyce, Apollinaire, Pound, and Cummings, or Oswald de Andrade, João Cabral de Melo Neto, and, further back, retrospectively, Sousândrade—the rediscovered and reassessed Sousândrade of the dizzying ideogrammatic New York Stock Exchange "Inferno" . . . (a Pound avant la lettre, with his financial Hades ruled by a sinister Mammon).

Significantly, this new poetics was accompanied soon afterwards by new reflections on the baroque. My 1955 article (several years before Umberto Eco's book) was entitled "A obra de arte aberta" ["The Open Work of Art"]* and defended a neobaroque rather than the finished, "diamondlike" work.[17]

In 1955, in Ulm, by chance, Décio Pignatari met Eugen Gomringer, at the time Max Bill's secretary in the Hochschule für Gestaltung. From this chance encounter came a mutual discovery. There were many points in common in the poetic program of the Brazilian *Noigandres* group and that of the Swiss poet, author of the *Konstellationen* [*Constellations*]. At that moment, an international movement was outlined, after Gomringer accepted, in 1956, the general title proposed by the Brazilians, "concrete poetry," and which from then on began to circulate widely. (In 1956, São Paulo's Museum of Modern Art hosted the first world exhibition of concrete poetry, an event in which only Brazilian artists—poets and painters—participated. Countless international shows followed this pioneering event.)

Another fact to be noted: Despite its dispossession and voluntary limitation of means (the poem as a collective, anonymous project, Mallarmé's "disparition élocutoire du je," Oswald's and Webern's basic structures), Brazilian concrete poetry, for its critics and observers (and also, clearly, for its opponents) seemed irrevocably baroque, pluralist, multifaceted, in comparison with the austere orthogonality of Gomringer's *Konstellationen*, pure and clear, like a composition by Max Bill.* Our "difference" produced a varying result in the chemistry of the poem, even if the global content of the new poetic program had common points. Aside from the poems open

* This essay is included in the section "The Concrete Moment" in this volume. —EDITORS

to multiple readings (the poems in colors-voices of *Poetamenos* [*Minuspoet*] by Augusto de Campos: Boulez saw them in São Paulo, 1954, at a gathering in the home of the painter Valdemar Cordeiro, where we all enthusiastically discussed Webern and Mallarmé; in his *Troisième Sonate* [*Third Sonata*] from 1957, Boulez uses different colors to distinguish certain alternative routes in the score . . .). Aside from the peculiarities of a more ludic syntax, the semantic dimension: the contextual, even political satire present since the beginning ("coca-cola" by Décio Pignatari, written as early as 1957). Eroticism in the bodily path of our ancestral baroque. Nothing could be more distant from the neutrality or the asepsis of the Zurich school (which is not to deny the merit of the latter, in its own setting—or could it be the case, with new players, of a new "round" of confrontation between the Brazilian Oswald and the Swiss Cendrars?). Contact with the new music was essential, as well as with the young São Paulo composers (Cozzella, Duprat, Medaglia; later Willy Corrêa de Oliveira and Gilberto Mendes). I remember, toward the middle of 1959, in Cologne, Stockhausen's surprise and interest upon seeing copies of the magazine *Noigandres*. At that time, despite his encouragement of Hans G. Helms's experiments, he preferred to compose himself, in the style of montage, the texts he needed. (See, for example, *Gesang der Jünglinge* [*Song of Youth*], with lines taken from the book of Daniel.) In Brazil, some poets were working on texts that intersemiotically incorporated into the syntax of the poem parameters drawn from the theory and practice of the budding new music. (Shortly afterward, speaking on "Musik und Graphik" at the Ferienkurse für Neue Musik in Darmstadt, Stockhausen would leave a written record of that contact: cf. *Darmstädter Beiträge zur neuen Musik* [*Darmstadt's Contributions to the New Music*], Schott, 1960.)

Later, this path of avant-garde (serious) poetry/music would produce a situation unique to Brazil: Augusto de Campos would become the main theorist and supporter of Caetano Veloso's and Gilberto Gil's new popular music. (In instrumental arrangements, at crucial moments, the experimental inventiveness of Rogério Duprat and Júlio Medaglia would converge.) "Prodsumption" (*prodossumo*), as Décio Pignatari put it: the poetry of invention in mass consumption, surpassing Adornian skepticism . . . Let us imagine, by way of comparison and proof this ideal convergence: the Beatles composing in the presence of John Cage on texts by e. e. cummings . . . (It is true that there was Yoko—oh! Yoko!—the Orient . . .) Once again, however, the difference within the universal. Listen to *Araçá azul* [*Blue Guava*] by Caetano . . .

The Alexandrian Barbarians: Planetary Redevouring

> Desarraigada y cosmopolita, la literatura hispanoamericana es
> regreso y búsqueda de una tradición. Al buscarla, la inventa.
>
> Uprooted and cosmopolitan, Spanish American literature is a return and
> the search for a tradition. In this quest, literature invents its tradition.
>
> —Octavio Paz (1961, *Puertas al campo* [*Doors to the Countryside*])*

> Es ist ein Versuch, sich gleichsam *a posteriori* eine Vergangenheit zu geben,
> aus der man stammen möchte im Gegensatz zu der, aus der man stammt.
>
> It is an attempt to give oneself, as it were *a posteriori,* a past in which one
> would like to originate in opposition to that in which one did originate.
>
> —Nietzsche†

I believe that Oswald de Andrade's "Coup de Dents" ["A Throw of the
Bite"] in its Marxillary (Marxist + maxillary) dialectic,[18] in the way it con-
fronts the legacy of European civilization—the first date of his anthropophagous revolution in the history of Brazil would be the year of the
devouring of Bishop Sardinha, a Portuguese missionary official, in 1556—
points to a new fact in the relationship between Europe and Latin America. Already from this point on, Europeans must learn to live together with
the new barbarians who, for some time, in an alternative and different context, have been devouring them and making them flesh of their flesh and
bone of their bone. They have long been resynthesizing them chemically,
through an impulsive and uncontrollable metabolism of difference. (And
they have not only devoured Europeans: Eastern, Hindu, Chinese, and
Japanese ingredients have entered into the "sympoetic" cauldron of these
neoalchemists: in Tablada and Octavio Paz; in the "forking paths" of
Borges and in the rites of passage of Elizondo's *Farabeuf*; in Lezama and
Severo Sarduy; in Oswald and in Brazilian concrete poetry, for instance.)

These are Alexandrian barbarians, equipped with chaotic libraries and
labyrinthine card catalogs. The library of Babel could be called the Bib-

---

* "Literatura de fundación," *Puertas al campo* (México: Seix Barral, 1972), 21. —TRANSLATOR

†"Von Nutzen und Nachteil der Historie für das Leben," *Unzeitgemässe Betrachtungen, Werke in Drei
Banden,* vol. 1, ed. Karl Schlechta (Munich: Carl Hanser Verlag, 1966), 230. In English: "On the Uses
and Disadvantages of History for Life," *Untimely Meditations,* trans. R. J. Hollingdale (Cambridge:
Cambridge University Press, 1983), 76. —TRANSLATOR

lioteca Municipal Miguel Cané and be temporarily located on a modest block of Buenos Aires ("a sad and dingy place, to the southeast of the city"), where Borges worked as an obscure bureaucrat and in whose basement he would escape from the pettiness of the everyday, abandoning himself furtively to infinite readings. . . . Or this library could be lodged, fully, in Alfonso Reyes's vaulted *capilla* in Mexico City, a library-house where he cloistered himself away for nearly twenty years, surrounded by copious bookshelves, a well-traveled, insatiable reader. . . . Or perhaps in São Paulo, on the Rua Lopes Chaves, in the neighborhood of Barra Funda, where Mário de Andrade would fill up note cards and crowd annotations into the margins of the books he perused, between scores of Schoenberg and Stravinsky, catalogs of German expressionists and Italian futurists, volumes of Freud and folklore treatises. Or, finally, the library could proliferate in a house in Old Havana, where Lezama Lima, the "Etruscan," after a ritual immersion into the attics of the Cuban used-book dealers, would spin his immense ringed sphere of readings—decentered, changing, fabulous like a hieroglyphic globe hatched by the mythic "Roc" bird.

For some time, the devouring jaws of these new barbarians have been chewing up and "ruining" a cultural heritage that is ever more planetary. In relationship to this heritage, the barbarians' eccentrifying and deconstructing attack acts with the marginal impetus of the carnivalesque desacralizing, profaning antitradition evoked by Bakhtin in counterpoint to the main road of Lukácsian epic positivism, to monologic literature, to the closed, univocal work. In contrast, the combinatory and ludic polyculturalism, the parodic transmutation of meanings and values, the open, multilingual hybridization are the devices responsible for the constant feeding and refeeding of this "baroquizing" almagest: the carnivalized transencyclopedia of the new barbarians, where everything can coexist with everything. They are the machinery that crushes the material of tradition, like the teeth of a tropical sugarmill, transforming stalks and husks into bagasse and juicy syrup.

Lezama "creolizes" Proust and interconnects Mallarmé with Góngora: his quotations are truncated and approximate, like the leftovers of a diluvial digestion. Leopoldo Marechal's *Adán Buenosayres* (with its "Viaje a la oscura ciudad de Cacodelphia" ["Voyage to the Dark City of Cacodelphia"]) and Julio Cortázar's *Hopscotch* enter into dialogue, at different times and levels, with Joyce's *Ulysses* without losing the distinctive mark of the Argentine condition (even if, in Cortázar's case, we find it has transmigrated with traces of *porteño* nostalgia to Paris's Rive Gauche). Bustrófedon in Cabrera Infante's *Three Trapped Tigers* passes through Lewis Carroll's mirror to shake hands with the "semanticist" Humpty Dumpty and with Shem, the Penman. Dionélio Machado, in *Os ratos* (*The Rats*), re-creates Leopold Bloom's day in the scant, debt-ridden day of an urban Brazilian John Doe of the 1930s (Naziazeno, a no-luck Nazarene struggling for "our daily milk". . .). Guimarães Rosa riddles the backlands of Minas Gerais with metaphysical paths: his *jagunço** is a Mephistaphilologic Faust, trapped in the weft of language like a *caboclo*† Heidegger. Of Carpentier, Carlos Fuentes, and Vargas Llosa, we could say just as much: other concoctions, other amalgams, various and remarkable agglutinations.

The "nightmare of history," for the major writers of Latin America, with all its implications in terms of participation and struggle for the most militant spirits, has been a baroque and obsessive nightmare of writing (a nightmare taken to oxymoronic paroxysm, aware as it is, of being forced into painful cohabitation with the letterless world of the large illiterate segments of the population). "The masses will still eat the ritzy biscuits I bake," prophesied Oswald de Andrade, in a pun‡ inspired by the "Prinzip Hoffnung" like one who prepares the nutritious marrow, the amniotic meal for the cannibalist banquet of an unalienated and communal utopian society of the future.

Octavio Paz, going back to the first decades of this [the twentieth] century, glimpsed an unsuspected and fascinating coincidence: While Pound and Eliot "discovered" Laforgue's French and fed on it, on his ironic "logopoeia," to renew poetry in English, Lugones, in Buenos Aires, and López Velarde, in Zacatecas, Mexico, through different paths which cross ideally in space-time, also turned to the same marginal symbolist. All of them rewrote, differently—independently—the same unfinished universal poem. . . . In Brazil, Pedro Kilkerry, an obscure Bahian daydreamer with an Irish last name, a poor, polyglot mulatto, dead at thirty-two in 1917 from a tracheotomy, contributed to, albeit unacknowledged, the spinning orbit of

---

Jagunços were, historically, the group of fanatical revolutionaries that launched the Canudos rebellion described in Euclides da Cunha, *Os sertões* [*Rebellion in the Backlands*]. More generally, the term describes lawless men of Northeast Brazil, or gangsters, bullies, or hired killers. —TRANSLATOR

†*Caboclo*, literally, "copper-colored," is a term that refers in general to racially mixed people in Brazil, particularly Indian and white or Indian and black. It is also used to describe frontierspeople or people from the backlands. —TRANSLATOR

‡This difficult-to-translate pun hinges on the double meaning of the word *massa* in Portuguese, both "dough" and "crowd, mass." —TRANSLATOR

these ecumenical signs. He translated and metabolized Tristan Corbière (a follower of Laforgue's "coloquial-ironic" line), developing with it a most distinct diction which approximates him as a forgotten pioneer in his beautiful poem "É o silêncio" ["It is the silence"] to the subtle elocution of a Fernando Pessoa.[19]

In sum: All these digestive rumbles, all this hodgepodge, ancestral rumination, already lost in the mysteries of time, could not remain indefinitely ignored in Europe. The "boom," a recent and skin-deep phenomenon, as far as the media is concerned, came as a somewhat unexpected and belated cry of warning to Europeans. (And also to Americans, whose omnivorous pragmatism, when it comes to cultural mastication, was probably best exemplified in the twentieth century by Ezra Pound's *vis paideumica* and in the past by Whitman's universality.) It was a frantic alert to reckless navigators, of the festering and explosive turbulence of a new dialogic relationship, developing undercover, obscured by the monolingual self-sufficiency of the users of "imperial" languages (such as French, decreasingly, and English, increasingly), a relationship that was undermining and eating away at the foundations of the literary koine, predefined in terms of "older" and "greater" literatures, of "trunks," "main branches," and "secondary twigs."

At a certain point, at least with Borges, Europeans discovered they could no longer write their world prose without the increasingly overwhelming contribution made by the voracious Alexandrian barbarians. The books they read could never be the same after being chewed up and digested by the blind Homerian of Buenos Aires, who even dared to rewrite *Don Quixote* under the pseudonym of Pierre Menard. . . . What would be new, without Borges, in Robbe-Grillet's *nouveau roman*? Who could read Proust now without acknowledging Lezama Lima? Could one read Mallarmé, today disregarding the intertextual hypotheses of Vallejo's *Trilce* and Paz's *Blanco*? Or contribute to the "universal continuous poem" without redigesting the Brazilian concrete poetry of the *Noigandres* group? At a meeting in the mid-1960s (in which I remember that Ungaretti, the old Ungaretti full of Brazilian memories also participated during a visit to São Paulo), Nathalie Sarraute told me in conversation that French writing did not include a Joycean experiment. I asked her, in turn (alive in my memory, parallel and equal—joined by common Latin origins—the examples of Mário de Andrade's *Macunaíma* and Guimarães Rosa's *The Devil to Pay in the Backlands*), whether she did not consider Rabelais a French writer.

Since 1963, I had begun to write and publish *Galáxias* [*Galaxies*], a "barraucous ibericane mortalepic," intoned in counterpoint to the "eldolorous galldorado latinamacrid." Since the late 1960s ("Sur Góngora," 1966), Severo Sarduy had begun to "baroquize," through his presence, the Cartesian-Valéry-an space of *Tel Quel.* Fragments of *Galáxias* appeared in German (*Versuchbuch/Galaxien, rot* 25 [1966], edited by Max Bense and E. Walther). Also in 1966: *Compact* by Maurice Roche, a writer-musician who never had any doubts about the renewed viability of the Rabelaisian heritage in his language. Fragments of *Galáxias,* translated into French, appeared in *Change* in September 1970 ("La poétique de la mémoire" ["The Poetics of Memory"]). A remark by Octavio Paz: "I would like to choose the end of the last fragment as a motto: 'el vocablo es mi fábula' ('le vocable est ma fable') ['speech is my story']." One might now look at Philippe Sollers's Joycean and galactic *Paradis.* I have told this story and traced this itinerary in more detail in "Sanscreed Latinized: The *Wake* in Brazil and Hispanic America," (*Triquarterly* 38, *In the Wake of the 'Wake'*), 1977.

To write, today, in both Europe and Latin America will mean, more and more, to rewrite, to rechew. *Oi barbaroi.* The Vandals, long ago, crossed the borders and are crowding the senate and the agora, as in Cavafy's poem. Logocentric writers who imagined themselves the privileged beneficiaries of a proud one-way koine may now prepare themselves for the increasingly urgent task of acknowledging and redevouring the differential marrow of the new barbarians of the polytopic and polyphonic planetary civilization. After all, we might as well recall old Goethe's very timely warning: "Eine jede Literatur ennuyiert sich zuletzt in sich selbst, wenn sie nicht durch fremde Teilnahme wieder aufgefrischt wird" ["Left to itself, every literature will exhaust its vitality if it is not refreshed by the interest and contribution of a foreign one"].* Alterity is, above all, a necessary exercise in self-criticism.

Translated by Odile Cisneros

* Quoted by René Wellek in *The Later Eighteenth Century,* vol. 1 of *A History of Modern Criticism: 1750–1950* (New Haven, CT: Yale University Press, 1955), 221. Original in Johann Wolfgang von Goethe, *Stuttgart 1902–1907,* vol. 38 of *Sämtliche Werke. Jubilaeumsausgabe,* ed. Eduard von der Hellen, 137.
—TRANSLATOR

Disappearance of the Baroque in Brazilian Literature: The Case of Gregório de Matos

Alle Achtung vor euren Meinungen! Aber kleine abweichende Handlungen sind mehr wert!

Well done in your opinions! But deviating a little in your actions is worth more!

—Nietzsche

The "question of origins" has been a persistent problem in the historiography of Brazilian literature. In this context we could say that Brazilian culture is faced—as I have noted in "Anthropophagous Reason"—with "an

The work of Gregório de Matos e Guerra (1636–1695) constitutes a puzzling chapter in Brazilian literature. Born in Bahia and educated in Portugal, de Matos became an important magistrate in Lisbon and later in colonial Salvador, was prosecuted by the Inquisition, and toward the end of his life was deported to Angola due to political problems. His satirical verses, which he never formally acknowledged, were anonymously pasted on the walls of public buildings and were collected by copyists only in the eighteenth century. Haroldo de Campos's essay is an important study on the "segregation" of de Matos's work from the canon of Brazilian literature and a key text to understanding his commitment to the baroque. It took him ten years to fully develop his argument, which began in 1978 as notes for a class that he taught at Yale and was published as a book in 1989: Haroldo de Campos, O seqüestro do barroco na formação da literatura brasileira: O caso Gregório de Matos (Salvador: Fundação Casa de Jorge Amado, 1989). In the context of the present book it was necessary to shorten de Campos's essay for concision as well as to make it more accessible to the English-speaking reader. The missing sections concern basic considerations on reception theory that, although important to the Brazilian audience at the time it was published, do not particularly illuminate de Campos's overall argument. For reason of space, I have also opted, with regret, to exclude a number of lengthy and informative footnotes. —TRANSLATOR

episode of the Western metaphysics of presence, transferred to our tropical latitudes, one that doesn't quite realize the final meaning of this transfer; a chapter to be added to the Platonizing logocentrism which Derrida, in *Of Grammatology*, subjected to a lucid and revealing analysis, not accidentally at the instigation of two 'ex-centrics,' Fenollosa, the anti-Sinologist, and Nietzsche, the shatterer of certainties."

In the Brazilian case, this metaphysical plot is complicated by a peculiar element of "suspense": the name of the father (*le nom du père*) is made present (or absent) through erasure and for reasons of "historical perspective." Wilson Martins wrote in *Gregório, o pituresco* [*Gregório, the Picturesque*] (1970):

> Did a great Brazilian poet named Gregório de Matos really exist in the eighteenth century? Surely not, at least not in terms of literary history. As Antonio Candido writes in *Formação da literatura brasileira*, 2 vols. [*The Formation of Brazilian Literature*] (São Paulo: Editora Martins, 1959) (although his reputation survived in the context of Bahia's local tradition, he did not exist literally in historical perspective until romanticism when he was rediscovered, thanks to Varnhagen;* and only after the 1882 Vale Cabral edition could his work be properly considered. Before that, he did not influence nor contribute to the formation of our literary system, and his manuscripts became so obscure that Barbosa Machado, the rigorous scholar of *Biblioteca Lusitana* (1741–1758),† ignored him completely, although he recorded the achievements of João de Brito e Lima)‡ (1:18). Much later, in the nineteenth century, after the declaration of independence, Ferdinand Denis does not mention him either in his *Resumo da história literária de Portugal e do Brasil* [*Concise History of Literature in Portugal and Brazil*]; his inclusion in seventeenth-century literary chronology is thus one of the most abstruse examples of involuntary historical mystification we can provide.

* Francisco Adolpho Varnhagen (1816–1878), diplomat, engineer, and author of *Historia geral do Brasil* [*General History of Brazil*] (1854), considered the first attempt at Brazilian historiography. De Campos is referring here to another of Varnhagen's books, *Florilégio da poesia brasileira* [*Anthology of Brazilian Poetry*] (1850), where de Matos's work is mentioned for the first time. —TRANSLATOR

† *Bibliotheca Lusitana* was complied by the Abade de Sever Diogo Barbosa Machado and published in Lisbon in four volumes between 1741 and 1759. It is the first catalog of authors and works published in Portuguese. —TRANSLATOR

‡ João de Brito Lima (1671–1747). Also born in Bahia, de Brito Lima received his education from private tutors and entered a monastery early in life. He became known as one of the best poets writing in Portuguese at the time. —TRANSLATOR

Oswald de Andrade, in "A sátira na literatura brasileira" ["Satire in Brazilian Literature"] (1945), voices a diametrically opposite opinion: "Gregório de Matos was undoubtedly one of the greatest figures in Brazilian literature. Technique, verbal richness, imagination and independence, curiosity and strength in all genres, that is what characterizes his work and has since set the path of our national literature."[1]

Borges's Paradox and Pessoa's

We are faced, thus, with a truly Borgesian paradox, since we must add to the "question of origins" that of the identity or pseudoidentity of a "patronymic" author. One of the greatest Brazilian poets of the premodern era, one whose existence is fundamental in order for us to coexist with and feel connected to a living tradition, seems not to have existed literally "in historical perspective." Like Ulysses, the mythical founder of Lisbon, who—in a poem by Fernando Pessoa—"foi por não ser existindo" [was by way of not being]. Grégorio de Matos, too, this "ulterior immemorial demon" (Mallarmé), seems to have founded Brazilian literature precisely by virtue of his nonexistence or by having survived aesthetically at the price of historical death. "O mito é o nada que é tudo" [Myth—nothing, everything], adds Fernando Pessoa in the same poem.*

In this apparent contradiction between poetic presence and historical absence, which makes Grégorio de Matos a kind of retrospective demiurge—abolished in the past for the sake of activating the future—is at stake not only the question of "existence" (in terms of influence on the factual development of Brazilian literature) but, above all, the very notion of "history" according to which existence is denied or given as nonexistence (while retaining "developmental" value in literary terms).

Historical Perspective and Substantialist Ideology

In fact, this "historical perspective" stems from the perspective of a substantialist view of literary evolution grounded in a metaphysical ideal of national identity. If we perform a deconstructive reading of some of the basic assumptions in Antonio Candido's *Formação da literatura brasileira* [*Formation of Brazilian Literature*], the most lucid and elegant attempt at a historical reconstruction of Brazilian literary evolution, we will see that the

---

* These lines are from "Ulysses," in *Mensagem,* trans. Jonathan Griffin (London: Menard Press / King's College London, 1992), 17. —TRANSLATOR

substantialist theme pervades the entire text. Candido's goal, stated in the preface to the first edition, is to follow "the adventures of the spirit," through a "discerning" reading that would cause literary works "to come alive again in our experience," to follow "the adventures of the spirit": "In this case, the spirit of Western tradition, searching for a new home in this part of the world" (1:10). Through the spirit (Logos, Being)'s adventurous path exploration in search of a new dwelling in America, two metaphorical series are introduced, one "animist," the other "organicist." The first is decisively ontological, while the latter is connected to the evolutionist-biological assumption inherent in traditional historiography that sees reproduced in literature a process of gradual blossoming, of organic growth, informed either by a "naturalist teleology" or by the "driving idea" of "individuality" or "national spirit" that regulates, always with teleological dynamism, a closed sequence of events. (This process necessarily culminates in a "national classicism" that corresponds, in political terms, to another "moment of plenitude," the conquest of the "national unity.")

Both metaphoric series converge in the substantialism that colors them. Accordingly one reads in the *Formation:* "Ours is a secondary branch of Portuguese literature, which in itself is but a second-rate shrub in the Muses' garden." The reading of this "poor and weak literature" must be handled with "care and judgment" (maintaining one's "discerning" faculty which is so dear to the "critical spirit"), since "In the absence of love, it will not reveal its message." To read "discerningly," that is, amorously, is what "animates" the literary works. It's worth saying: such type of reading endows them with an anima, a soul, makes them express the voice of Logos, that migrated from the West and transplanted itself in the not so paradisiacal American garden, where its "acclimatization" will be "painful" and will require, to be well understood, that we listen with care (amorous reading): "No one, apart from us, can give life to these works, often fragile, sometimes strong, and always poignant, in which men from the past, from the depths of an uncultivated land, amid the painful acclimatization of European culture, tried to stylize for us, their descendants, the feelings they experienced, the observations they gathered—from which our literature has been formed." This double series of metaphors sounds rather antinationalistic, dysphoric: the transplanted sapling is "secondary" and the shrubbery that it comes from is "second-rate"; on the other hand, transplanting the emigrated Logos and cultivating it in the new setting will be far from paradisiacal (a word that etymologically means "garden"): the land is "uncultivated" and the "acclimatization" (acculturation) will be "painful."

The Literary Incarnation of the National Spirit

The impasse can be overcome through the adoption of a "historical perspective." Since the spirit of Western literature became incarnate in the new lands of Portuguese America, it is up to the critic-historian to retrace the route of parousia of this Logos that, like a shrub, had to be replanted, germinate, and blossom, so that one day, perhaps, it could branch out as a vigorous, fully formed tree: the national literature. The metaphysical concept of history, according Derrida, involves the idea of linearity and continuity: a linear schema of the unveiling of presence, subservient to the "epic" model. It is clear, thus, why it is necessary for this "historical perspective" to determine "when and how the continuity of works and authors was defined, being conscious, as often as possible, of integrating the process of literary formation" (1:25). It is because this "historical perspective" aims at singling out "a continuous tradition" of "styles, themes, forms or concerns." In short, because it requires a "beginning": "Since a beginning is necessary, I took as point of departure the Academia dos Seletos and the Academia dos Renascidos* and the first works of Cláudio Manuel da Costa, and, for simplicity's sake, I rounded the date to 1750, which, in reality, is a mere convention" (1:25).

The "historical perspective" is, thus, an ideological perspective. This becomes apparent when the ruling criteria are made explicit: "The reader will notice that I have deliberately adopted the view of our first romantics and of the foreign critics preceding them. These two groups located the beginnings of Brazil's true literature in the Arcadian phase, by virtue of the themes, notably Indianism,† that would dominate the production of the 1800s." To review "in the present perspective" the opinion of those critics who understood "Brazilian literature as the expression of a local reality and, at the same time, a positive element in the construction of a national identity"—such is the task that the *Formation* sets out to accomplish. This double "effort" (or articulation) of "construction" and "expression" is seen as a "disposition of the *spirit*, historically proven," that "expresses certain literary incarnations of the national *spirit*." On the other hand, Candido

---

* The Academia dos Seletos and the Academia dos Renascidos were two of several institutions opened in Bahia and Rio de Janeiro in the eighteenth century to promote higher education. —TRANSLATOR

† Indianism was a literary program elaborated during the romantic period and financially supported by the emperor D. Pedro II. Its program was centered on the image of the native Brazilian as a way to "valorize our national origins." Its main authors were Gonçalves de Magalhães, José de Alencar, Joaquim Manuel de Macedo, and Gonçalves Dias. —TRANSLATOR

stresses that this very profitable attitude can often be at the expense of the authors' "aesthetic loss and disorientation" which would ultimately lead to the exclusion of some of their production from the "specific field of the belles lettres."

[...]

The Semiological Effect

The exclusion—the "disappearance"—of the baroque in the *Formation of Brazilian Literature* is not merely the result of the adoption of a "historical orientation" that aims to separate literature, as "system," from "literary manifestations" deemed weak and unsystematic. The "perspective" that opts for the nonexistence of Gregório de Matos as necessary to the formation of Brazil's "literary system" (1:24) is also not "historical," in an unequivocal and objective sense. From the point of view of deconstruction, this exclusion, this literary nonexistence, presented to us as "historical," is the latent effect of the very "semiological model" articulated by Candido. This model invests literature as such with the ontological-nationalist characteristics proper to romanticism's literary program. It also emphasizes the "communicative" and "integrative" aspects of literary activity, as they manifest themselves in the peculiar Brazilian synthesis of classicism and romanticism (the "mixture of the neoclassical artisan with the romantic bard," 1:28). From this model emerged "a literature invested" with "a sense of mission," one that repressed, in many instances, the "exercise of the imagination" but that was also capable of conveying a "historical sense and the exceptional power of communication" and thus of becoming the "general language of a society in search of self-knowledge." The baroque evidently does not fit this model, because its aesthetic emphasizes the poetic and the metalinguistic functions, the text's self-reflexivity and the inter- and intratextual self-thematization of the code (metasonnets that dismantle and expose the sonnet's structure, for instance; citation, paraphrase, and translation as plagiotropic tools and so forth). The baroque does not fit in. The aesthetic of "superabundance and waste," as Severo Sarduy has defined it: "Contrary to the language of communication, economical, austere, reduced to functionality—a vehicle of information— the baroque language thrives in supplement, excess, and in the partial loss of its goal." The baroque, the poetic of the "vertigo of the ludic," of the "absolute playfulness of its forms," as Affonso Ávila has noted. The baroque that—according to Octavio Paz, who wrote in regard to Sor Juana Inés de la Cruz, a contemporary of Gregório de Matos—produced, in the American context, "Primero sueño" ["First Dream"] (ca. 1685), a critical, reflexive and metalinguistic poem, a "poem of the adventure of knowledge," that anticipates Mallarmé's *Un coup de dés* [*A Throw of the Dice*], the limit-poem of modernity.

It follows that in *Presença da literatura brasileira²* [*Presence of Brazilian Literature*] (1964), the semiological effect implicit in the model's structure is converted explicitly into value judgment (doubt, restriction). In this work, published almost half a century after the rehabilitation of the baroque by Benjamin, Lorca, Eliot, and Anchesi, among others, both the "authenticity" and "permanence of communication" are called into question, given baroque's "excesses." Here "authenticity" and "permanence" are quoted for their "auratic," noncritical, ahistorical values, in the sense that these values are conferred by an axiological absolute canon, raised to the condition of timeless truth: that of romanticism, with its aspirations to classicism, where a realist vein already pulsates. A romanticism that is purged of its lack of discipline and of its local fixations (on the "picturesque" and on the "raw material of experience") thanks to the "rigor" and the "emotional restraint" of the neoclassic Arcadianism* that served as its native vestibule. In this same anthology, in the part reserved to Gregório de Matos, his contribution is judged severely: "As we know it now, his work is irregular, worth but for only a few lines."

The Linear Model and the Continuous Tradition

The *Formation of Brazilian Literature* favors a certain kind of *history:* the evolutionary-linear-integrative kind, keen on demarcating, in a coherent and progressive way, the route of the "incarnation of the national literary spirit." It also favors a certain kind of *tradition:* that which, "born in the domains of natural evolution," was "transposed to that of the spirit," organizing its productions in a harmonious, "substantial continuity," excluding any disturbances that do not fit in this progression. It favors, in the end, a *vehicular* concept of literature: the "emotive-communicational" kind

---

* Arcadianism was introduced in Brazil around 1768. The poets in this group—Tomás Antonio Gonzaga, Alvarenga Peixoto, Silva Alvarenga, and Cláudio Manoel da Costa—are also well known for their tragic participation in the "Inconfidência Mineira" (Minas Gerais uprising), a pro-independence movement. The main leaders of this group were arrested by the Portuguese authorities and executed in public. Manoel da Costa was arrested and found dead in his cell. Tomás Antonio Gonzaga was also arrested and was deported to Mozambique. —TRANSLATOR

that presides at the onset of Brazilian romanticism. Based on these presuppositions, this evolutionary-linear-integrative kind of history elaborates its descriptive and explicative model. This model is necessarily reductive: What does not fit is set aside, labeled "literary manifestations" as opposed to "literature" itself or literature as "system." In order to establish the model's efficacy, its internal logic is reinforced through a "quantitative" argument. Since we cannot ignore the systematic character of these works and their triadic interaction, it becomes necessary to demonstrate, from a quantitative angle, how relative its public is. Only then can the ontological metaphor of the simplicity of the "origin," conventionally dated (1750), and the genealogical metaphor of a coherent sequence of events, ruled by the tropism of a telos or common zenith, hold and pass for a "historical perspective."

An Integrated Literature

The problem of the audience ("reception," "effect") in the *Formation* ends up being tackled by using a harmonizing principle that emphasizes the integrative aspect of the reception process.

[. . .]

In the *Formation,* audience is a "group of receptors" organically connected to a "group of producers" by a "mechanism" that ensures the "transmission" of a "system of works" interconnected by "common denominators." The audience is seen as the component of a homogeneous system, reconciled and defined in relation to a literature described from the perspective of a closed series and that aspires to become pure classicism. The progressive constitution of a preferential canon of works and authors corresponds to this audience of "aggregation." Such constitution entails a historiography that aims to "represent, through the history of literary products, the essence of a national entity in search of itself."

Within a more flexible perspective, not confined to this "metaphysical cluster," the Gregório de Matos case could be seen in a different light. De Matos is a poet who had an audience in effect (it does not matter, given the circumstances of the time, how limited this audience was) and whose effect is sufficiently documented. And, more importantly, his production is emblematic of the baroque, a style that in turn transcends it and survives in its effects, far beyond in the literary realm, even after the author and his work have undergone a process of occultation, which transformed them from ostensive to recessive in the horizon of reception.

An "objective-reductionist" approach, on the other hand, would have difficulty in dealing with the problem of the reception of ancient literature, when one has to consider "works by unknown authors, obscure authorial intents, relations with sources and models only indirectly discernible." When the virtual readers are inscribed in the very text, in the form of the "context of works that the author deemed, explicitly or implicitly, known to his contemporary public." In the case of Gregório de Matos and Brazil's colonial baroque, these questions are less complex, for although there is no true critical edition of our great poet from Bahia, the oral tradition and the apocryphal writings remain. There is also the testimony of the audience and its reaction to the vicious tongue of the "Boca do Inferno"* [Inferno's Mouth]. There is, above all, the baroque itself that, as a great universal code of the literature of the time, rules over Brazil's literary scene since Camões. The baroque that projected itself in the poetry of the Arcadian poets, in the "monstrosities written in macaronic Portuguese" by Odorico Mendes,† and in the subversive implosion of Sousândrade, who ruined the harmonious construction of our official romanticism. A solution to such questions at the level of reception cannot consist merely of declaring that where there is no "systemic" audience, there is no literature worth recording. That history in formative terms will not be available but rather only "literary manifestations," a "thin" and "sparse" scene, a silent limbo ("without resonance") where the *voice of Being* has still not gained bodily form, a shapeless prehistory which is nonexistent from a "historical perspective." What would happen, for instance, if we had to evaluate through similar "systemic" criteria the literary life of works as remote in time as Provençal poetry?

But in the case of Gregório de Matos, there is yet another paradoxical circumstance to be taken into account: how can an author who is the source of this literary history not "exist" in terms of "historical perspective"? It is through these authors that we can faithfully reconstruct a picture of Brazilian society in the seventeenth century, affirms S. Spina in writing about de Matos and Vieira. "Perhaps the best source of contemporary

---

* Gregório de Matos was often referred to as the "Boca do Inferno" due to the profane nature of his verses against the clergy. —TRANSLATOR

† Known primarily for his translations of Homer and Virgil, Manuel Odorico Mendes (1799–1864) is a highly controversial name in Brazilian literature. For some critics, Antonio Candido among them, his name is synonymous with bad taste and excess. For Haroldo de Campos, however, Mendes is a pioneer of great technical skill and artistic competence and one whose translations will profoundly affect him. —TRANSLATOR

opinion of the *desembargadores* [magistrates] and the Relação* is found not in traditional historical material but in the poetry of the Bahian satirist Gregório de Matos e Guerra," adds Stuart B. Schwartz.[3] How could this historical void be declared without calling into question the very notion of history that gives shape to this exclusive perspective?

Candido necessarily had to tend toward *integration,* disregarding *differentiation,* so that he could configure his work in a preestablished design and execute his program with harmony: "to describe the process through which the Brazilian people became aware of their spiritual and social existence through literature, combining in different ways the universal values with the local reality and, this way, earning the right to express their dream, their pain, their joy, their modest vision of things and their fellow citizen."

Questionable Baroque

This task, as anyone can imagine, was facilitated by the reservations that Candido manifests toward the self-reflexive and ludic aspect of the literary work. He reminds us, as often as possible, of the noncommunicative effect that art, as "mere experimentation of the technical resources," has toward the audience. He also alerts us against "formalism's excessive pretensions," which would end up, "in extreme cases, reducing the literary work to linguistic problems, be it in the broader sense of symbolic communication or in the restricted sense of the language."

This attitude of suspicion will later inspire, in *Presence of Brazilian Literature* by Candido and J. Aderaldo Castello, the reluctance, the judicious hesitation in approaching the Brazilian baroque. At first, the production of that period will be implicitly devalued as hardly original as far as "literary creation" is concerned. Later on, the authors of *Presence* feel compelled to highlight the "nativist sentiment" or the "slow definition of a critical awareness," in other words, romantic-nationalistic characteristics that Brazilian baroque already anticipated. This kind of value judgment, marked by caution and diffidence, in which an argument for "plagiarism" is vaguely insinuated, gains momentum when addressing a poet of considerably less importance than de Matos, but of undeniable gifts: Botelho de Oliveira.†

---

* The Relação da Bahia was the Brazilian equivalent, in the seventeenth century, of the High Court of Appeals. —TRANSLATOR

† Botelho de Oliveira is the author of *Música do Parnaso,* the first book published by a Brazilian author. —TRANSLATOR

Rejection is then clearly expressed: "We are faced with a baroque that is empty and acrobatic, against which the Arcadian poets will rebel, and that went down in history as a pejorative index of that era." A rejection that does not hesitate to comfortably accept, without criticism, a questionable cliché: Gongorism, synonym of bad taste, ornate and hollow style.

Can we recognize, in these passages, the critic that made the defense of "willfulness"? The "willfulness that gives wings to works of art" and which Brazilian authors lack, overburdened instead by a "fidelity to documenting or to sentimentalizing that is connected to raw experience." And he adds, "the courage or spontaneity of willfulness is proof of maturity in the author and civilization as well; to young cultures and authors it comes across as betrayal and weakness."

But it is this same author who, in a gesture contrary to this defense of "willfulness" as creative factor, denies the existence in Brazilian literature, "until modernism," of a "writer truly difficult, except for the pseudodifficulty of verbal ornamentation." What does this formula mean exactly? Is Vieira, with his "ingenious discourse," a facile writer? Are Sousândrade and Euclides da Cunha facile writers? Are they "pseudosophisticates" as were, mutatis mutandis, for hostile critics of their time, Góngora, the "angel of darkness," the "monstrous" Hölderlin of the Sophocles translations, Mallarmé, the "obscure"? Does the communicative success of da Cunha's difficult text make him a "pseudosophisticate" in the pejorative sense of empty verbalism? Wouldn't this argument be enough to elucidate Candido's suspicion of the ornate style of baroque, which coincides with its Hispanic and Ibero-American rehabilitation?

[. . .]

It might not have been a simple decision for Candido to erase the baroque's difference in his model for the development of Brazilian literature. Even more so if we consider that the baroque was, in its own way, an art of ludic communication, of persuasive rapport, as well as of erotic affect and satiric disaffect. Not for nothing did Gregório de Matos provoke the anger of many and get "dispatched" to Angola. The quantitative notion of a rarefied audience, at the time of the production of the work, does not seem to carry sufficient weight, especially when, beyond the colonial period, the relation between writer and audience in Brazil ends up being defined also in terms of absence. We then ask: What has essentially changed in Brazil's "literary system," since the "shallow and sparse manifestations without resonance" of our unsystematic preliterature? The fact that Gregório de Matos was not discovered until the romantic period is not an indisputable argument for those who do not entertain a linear and end-oriented concept of literary history; for those who do not see it from a perspective of a finished cycle but rather as an ever-shifting movement of difference; for those who are more interested in the moments of rupture and transformation than in the "decisive moments" that are linked together in a progression toward an instant of apogee or conclusive moment. From the perspective of this nonrestrictive temporality, the case of Gregório de Matos is not fundamentally different from the case of Góngora in Spain, the case of the Portuguese baroque, or the cases of Caviedes and Hernando Domínguez Camargo in Spanish America.

[. . .]

Góngora was excluded from literary history for more than two centuries. Between Grégorio de Matos's death (1695) and the publication of the second volume of Januário da Cunha Barbosa's *Parnaso brasileiro* [*Brazilian Parnassus*] (1831), in which a few of his poems appear, 136 years passed; 155 years between his death and Varnhagen's *Anthology* (1850); and 187 years until Vale Cabral's edition of *Obras poéticas* [*Poetic Works*] (1882). In this interlude, aside from his fame in Bahia's oral tradition, the "manuscript collection" of his poems was compiled from apocrypha. "Thus, the manuscript tradition could survive throughout the eighteenth century, when Gregório de Matos was no longer alive. . . . The apocrypha writers wanted to preserve Gregório de Matos, apocrypha that, sporadically read, guaranteed the survival of his work."[4]

It is indeed a matter of survival, or *Fortleben,* as Benjamin says when speaking of the survival of literary works beyond the era that fostered them.

History as Constellation

Literary history, renewed by the theory of reception, must, according to Hans Robert Jauss, contain a productive function of the understanding of progress. It must examine both the process of inclusion (the constitution of "tradition") as well as that of exclusion (the critique of "forgetfulness").

Literary history cannot simply accept the feeling of the past as "commonplace," as Candido seems to indicate in the *Formation.* "When we approach a text," Candido writes, "we feel like our immediate forerunners, who formed us, and our contemporaries that the cultural community connects us with; we end up arriving at similar conclusions, the individual character differentiated only by a little timbre in the way of presenting them." Nietzsche has already alerted us to the resigned acceptance of tradition as if it were second nature. In *Daybreak,* we read that "behind feelings there stand judgments and evaluations which we inherit in the form of feelings (inclinations, aversions). The inspiration born of a feeling is the grandchild of judgment—and often of a false judgment!—and in any event not a child of our own! To trust one's feelings—means to give more obedience to one's grandfather and grandmother and their grandparents than to the gods, which are in us: our own reason and our experience."* In this order of things, according to Jauss (and Jean Starobinski), it is necessary for critical interpretation not to annul the "differential function" of the work, its "transgressive function." Criticism should not exclude the exception and assimilate the pariah in order to constitute an immutable canon of works, making it acceptable and turning it into common heritage. Rather, it should "keep or maintain the difference of the works as difference," stressing thus the "discontinuity of literature in relation to the history of society."

"It is well known that tradition—understood as living past—never presents itself as a given: it is a creation," wrote Octavio Paz in "Homenaje a Sor Juana Inés de la Cruz en su tercer centenario" ["Homage to Sor Juana Inés de la Cruz in Her Third Centennial"] (1951).

In fact, if we think, like Walter Benjamin,† that "history is the subject of a structure whose site is not homogenous, empty time, but time filled by the presence of the now [*Jetztzeit*]"; if we understand that "every image of the past that is not recognized by the present as one of its own concerns threatens to disappear irretrievably"; if we ponder that "to articulate the past historically does not mean to recognize it 'the way it really was' (Ranke)," we will have conjured, both the "objectivist" and the "positivist" illusions of the causal chain of facts as the proof of its historicity.

We then understand that the objectively quantifiable determination of the work's first audience is different from the history of its reception. We understand that it involves phases of opacity and prestige, of occultation and renaissance. That it does not feed on a substantialist sense of plenitude depicted as the culmination of a "simple" origin, given once and for all as a precise "date." We can thus imagine, as an alternative, a kind of literary history less as "formation" than as "transformation." Less as a conclusive process than as an open process. A history that stresses its moments of rupture and transgression and that does not understand tradition from an

---

* Friedrich Nietzsche, *Daybreak: Thoughts on the Prejudices of Morality,* trans. R. J. Hollingdale (Cambridge: Cambridge University Press, 1997). —TRANSLATOR

† De Campos quotes from theses XIV, V, and VI of Benjamin's "Theses on the Concept of History," in *Illuminations,* trans. Harry Zohn (New York: Schocken Books, 1988), 255–61. —TRANSLATOR

"essentialist" perspective but rather as a "dialectics of question and answer," a constant and renewed questioning of diachrony by synchrony.

The Vertiginous Origin

Brazilian literature did not have an infancy (*in-fans*, who does not speak). It did not have a "simple" origin. It was never formless. It was born already mature, fully formed, in the plan of aesthetic values, speaking the most elaborate code of the time. In this literature, in the movement of its "rotating signs," the baroque was inscribed since the beginning as "difference." The "movement of difference," according to Derrida, is constantly producing itself; it does not depend on the "incarnation" of a dawning Logos to decide the question of origin like the sun in a heliocentric system. Likewise, the formal (and critical) maturity of de Matos's contribution to Brazilian literature is not dependent on the seasonal cycle proposed by Candido. Preceding and following this cycle, de Matos's work questions the very idea of gradation that informs Candido's sense of history. Brazil's literary "origin" was not *punctual* or "simple" (in the organic, genetic, embryonic sense). It was "vertiginous," like Benjamin's use of the word *Ursprung* in the etymological sense of "leap," of "transformation."

Góngora and Quevedo, and before them Camões, do not abolish the differential contribution—the "differences" called Grégorio de Matos, Caviedes, Domínguez Camargo, Sor Juana Inés de la Cruz. In this sense, there are no "minor literatures," turned passive by a radiant canon, by the "transcendental meaning" of "major" literatures. Since canons are not "eternal" and beauty is historically relative, there is no need to speak of one-way influences that are not reprocessed and differentiated by their new environment. In this differential conception, the American baroque is an art of "counterconquest," as Lezama Lima defined it. We call this process, since the days of Oswald de Andrade, "cannibalist gluttony."

From the perspective of a nonlinear historiography, relevant to the present of creation, that takes into account the "shifting horizons" of reception and the "plagiotropic" machinery of oblique paths and discontinuous derivations; the plurality of *tempi*; the transtemporal constellations. From this other "historic perspective," Gregório de Matos existed and exists, even more so than, for instance, a writer such as Casimiro de Abreu, whose work is now considered kitsch. It is with the work of Gregório de Matos that a poet such as João Cabral de Melo Neto is in dialogue and in sync. It is de Matos's legacy that writers such as Oswald de Andrade and Mário Faustino claim back.

[. . .]

Even though Gregório de Matos was temporarily confined to local memory and to the "manuscript tradition," and his work was rescued in book form only some 150 years after his death; even though the accusation of "plagiarism" weighed over his reputation, his absence was merely virtual, or a masquerade. Gregório de Matos has always been present, as a watermark inscription, at the center of the very baroque code in which he so exceptionally operated. A "collective" or "architectonic style" (Gerardo Diego) that persisted in clear traces even in the work of those who opposed it.

This insidious, rambling style, which migrates to the center of romanticism and later becomes a transepochal repertoire of expressive resources, would explain the apparently dislocated in time, regressive, and progressive insurrection of Sousândrade's *O Guesa errante* [*Wandering Guesa*], an insurrection against the dominant "communicative" code of the period.

[. . .]

The Open Paradigm

> . . . l'impossible "tâche du traducteur" (Benjamin), voilà ce que veut dire aussi "déconstruction."
>
> . . . the impossible "task of the translator" (Benjamin). This too is meant by "deconstruction."
>
> —J. Derrida*

It is necessary to stress, however, that it is precisely Candido who will open the possibility of rethinking his former "historical perspective." In "Dialética da malandragem" ["Dialectics of the Rogue"], his notable essay from 1970, Candido retraces in a different pattern the linear evolution that his 1959 book had established. He deconstructs and reconstructs this evolution in a fractured and transtemporal way and recovers a new perspective through its marginal paths rather than the main road. In this new mosaiclike design, not lines but constellations, the former nonexistent "Boca do Inferno" is given a voice. He is now one of the precursors of the "roguish" comedic spirit in Brazilian literature, valued not as lyrical poetry,

---

Derrida and Difference, ed. David Wood and Robert Bernasconi (Warwick, RI: Parousia Press, 1985), 1–5.
—TRANSLATOR

but for his freewheeling satire. In this autodeconstruction of the *Formation*'s semiological model of reading, through which de Matos's "cursing muse" is finally rescued from its former sociological segregation, the "epic" scheme in search of the logocentric moment is no longer valid. Mário de Andrade was never more right when, in searching for the ontological "character" of the Brazilian man, he arrived not at a conclusive, total identity, but at its difference: the unresolved and questioning "noncharacter" of his antihero Macunaíma.

In "Dialética," Candido is no longer interested in stressing literature's *integrative function,* which would correspond to the "incorporation" of a continuous tradition, until the moment in which the national Logos (the "spirit") would become flesh, mature, and transubstantiate into a conclusive social identity. His aim now is to stress the *anticipatory function,* to devise a subversive, fragmented antitradition, capable of proposing nonmonologic models of behavior, not subject to the laws of identity and homogeneity. And it is precisely in the openness of this nondefined character that we glimpse the antinormative contradictions that, as Candido writes in "Dialectics of the Rogue," "will facilitate our insertion in an open world." "For the character of the comic figure is not the scarecrow of the determinist; it is the beacon in whose beams the freedom of his action becomes visible," writes Benjamin in an essay[5] in which the impossibility of elaborating a noncontradictory concept with character as the center is also stressed. Bakhtin, in considering the crisis of the "epic integrity," also speaks of the joyous excess, the nonrenewable residue of humanity's nonrealized expenditure, which corresponds to a dynamics of discord and that would come across in the *carnivalized* world of laughter.

Translated by A. S. Bessa

The Trans-American Pilgrimage of Sousândrade's *Guesa*

Brazil in the early 1960s witnessed the most tumultuous revision of its literary past, one involving a poet from the state of Maranhão, Joaquim de Sousa Andrade (1832–1902), better known by his nom de guerre Sousândrade. By merging his two last names, the poet sought to achieve a Greek sonority and the same number of letters as in Shakespeare's name, an author he much admired.

Sousândrade, who belonged to the second generation of Brazilian romanticism—*Harpas Selvagens* [*Wild Harps*], his first book, is dated 1857—was marginal during his time, and he remained so until my brother, Augusto de Campos, and I published the anthology *Re/Visão de Sousândrade* (*Re/Vision of Sousândrade*) in 1964. Sílvio Romero (1851–1914), the nineteenth-century patriarch of our literary historiography, saw him as a poet who dared, and whose boldness projected him "far beyond what was ordinary in his time," albeit irregular and hardly understandable (*História da literatura brasileira* [*The History of Brazilian Literature*], 1888). Antonio Candido, Romero's current successor, places the bard from Maranhão among the "minor romantic poets." Although stressing his "originality," he sees the form of his poetry as improper and affected by "a certain degree of preciosity, as a whole to the worst effect, bound to the use of unusual

This essay was first published in Portuguese as "A peregrinação transamericana do *Guesa* de Sousândrade," *Revista USP* 50 (June–August 2001), 221–31. —EDITORS

terms, nearly bordering on bad taste" (*Formação da literatura brasileira* [*The Formation of Brazilian Literature*], vol. 2 [São Paulo: Martins, 1959], 204). Such accusation of preciosity undoubtedly corresponds to Candido's own hesitant attitude toward the baroque phenomenon. On the one hand, Candido places the development of romanticism (preceded by Arcadianism* and by Brazil's political autonomy) as the royal road to evaluating the evolutionary line of our letters; on the other hand, he selects the "common issues" of canonical romantic style: sensitivity and referential transparency as a homogeneous and integrative "general language" capable of working as a manifestation of the "national spirit."

Whether the language of a poet of exceptional originality such as Sousândrade could be impregnated with baroque tints, albeit concurrently exhibiting romantic traits, is something Candido's descriptive scheme does not take into account. After the publication of *Re/Visão,* subsequent historiography began to recognize this landmark poet, and attitudes changed. Alfredo Bosi records the "highly original spirit" of the "astounding intuition of modern times," the "novelty" in regard to "nineteenth-century Brazilian poetry as a whole" of Sousândradian "processes of composition" (*História concisa da literatura brasileira* [*A Brief History of Brazilian Literature*], [São Paulo: Cultrix, 1970]). Massaud Moisés, in turn, states:

> It would not be at all far-fetched to say that we are facing the most powerful voice in romantic poetry, as well as one of the highest and most vibrant in Brazilian literature: A literary history marked by lyricism, not too rarely by overwhelming sentimentality, finds now the epic world outlook that it was missing, thus acquiring a longed-for universalist dimension (*História da literatura brasileira* [*The History of Brazilian Literature*], vol. 2, Romantismo, Realismo [São Paulo: Cultrix, 1984], 258).

A trans-American poem, unified by the topic of the journey (the "mobility in space," as noted by Antonio Candido, being one of its positive aspects), *O Guesa errante* (1868–1888?) brings together, in an epic-narrative setting, dramatic elements (the "Tatuturema" and "Wall Street Inferno"

---

* Arcadianism was introduced in Brazil around 1768. The poets of this group—Tomás Antonio Gonzaga, Alvarenga Peixoto, Silva Alvarenga, and Cláudio Manoel da Costa—are also well known for their tragic participation in the "Inconfidência Mineira" (Minas Gerais uprising), a pro-independence movement. The main leaders of this group were arrested by the Portuguese authorities and executed in public. Manoel da Costa was arrested and found dead in his cell. Tomás Antonio Gonzaga was also arrested and was deported to Mozambique. —EDITORS

episodes inspired by Goethe's *Faust*'s "Walpurgis Nights"), nature's land-scape paintings, and frequent biographical and lyric digressions. Sousân-drade found inspiration for the pilgrim–hero figure (Guesa, the homeless, the exiled) in Alexander von Humboldt's *Vues des cordillères et monuments des peuples indigènes de l'Amérique*, 2 volumes, 1810–1813, and volumes 15 and 16 of Humboldt's *Voyage* (1799–1804) to the equinoctial regions of the New World accompanied by French botanist Aimé Bonpland. The Brazil-ian poet transcribes as an epigraph on the cover of the final version of his poem a long quotation from Humboldt, where the Berlin naturalist com-ments on the mythology of the Muisca Indians from Nueva Granada, Colombia. In the religious rites of those Indians, who worshipped a sun divinity called Bochica, the Guesa was a boy who had been taken away from his parents' home and raised until the age of ten in the sun temple in Sogomozo. At age fifteen, after a pilgrimage to all sites visited by Bochica, the young man was taken to his final destination: the *suna*. There, he was tied to a column and sacrificed by the arrows of priests (*xeques* or *zaques*), who then had his heart taken out and his blood collected in sacred vessels.

The homage paid by Sousândrade, a poet from the equinoctial regions, to Humboldt, in his capacity as a "scientific" narrator of those pre-Columbian legends, reminds me of the tribute of admiration Goethe paid to the great naturalist in his *Elective Affinities* (*Die Wahlverwandschaften*, 1809, part 2, chapter 7). In this work, one of the characters, Ottilie, writes: "We admire only the naturalist who knows how to describe and depict for us the strangest and [most] unusual objects in their proper locality and environment. How I should like to hear only once Humboldt talk."*

Humboldt is named in different ways at different moments of the *Guesa*. In canto 2 (line 62), he is called "father Humboldt," and the poet recalls the naturalist's and Bonpland's experiments with curare. In canto 10 ("Wall Street Inferno," stanza 77), Humboldt enjoys the eminent company of Goethe, Dante, Byron, and others, among the *amautas* (sages or coun-selors in the Inca Empire). Against this Andean backdrop—and that is the most beautiful evocation of the naturalist-traveler in the whole poem—Sousândrade imagines the projection of the brilliant man of science and compares Humboldt's gray hair to the Andean snow:

---

* English translation from Johann Wolfgang von Goethe, *Elective Affinities*, trans. Elizabeth Mayer and Louise Bogan (Chicago: Henry Regnery Co., 1963), 213. —EDITORS

Let us climb farther up, much farther:
up to the horizon the immortal spirit attains,
when sunset is made by roses richer
with so much ice, infinite mountains!
. . . .

Lonesome is glory on the stern attitude,
Humboldt's gray hair: beautiful ethereal light!
His soul in the air, magnificent solitude,
as if in a crystal ball, and quite bright,
feelings were echoed. And oh!
on the snows of Andean solitude contempt
as in man's heights: how could you there go?
it is either death, or divine light attempt.
. . . .

May the man who has climbed up
join calm nature at the top
they are one, and are magnificent.

That dioramic vision of an aged Humboldt, invoked as an Andean guardian spirit, becomes even more relevant when we consider that the Brazilian poet, who had a rigorous training in the Greek classics, does not open his magnificent poem with the traditional (Homeric) exhortation to the Muse but rather with the retrospective view of the grandiose Andean "spectacle," the true source of his "divine inspiration":

Come, divine imagination!
Bare-topped, the volcanic Andes rise,
surrounded by ice, mute, tacit,
clouds floating - what grand spectacle!

—(*O Guesa*, canto 1, 1858)

Those verses flash upon me as a sort of recollection of a unique homage by Goethe to Humboldt: the copper engraving of an "ideal landscape" (1813) that depicts the naturalist-traveler in the Chimborazo heights sending New World greetings to Horace-Bénedict de Saussure, the famous mountain researcher who had climbed Mont Blanc in Switzerland, some 4,900 feet lower than the Andean summit.[1]

Humboldt's influence on the romantics is well known: Chateaubriand attests to it in the prologue to his *Voyage en Amérique* [*Travels in America*] (1828). Ferdinand Denis (1798–1890), a literary scholar who lived in Brazil from 1816 to 1820, is another witness. In his *Scènes de la nature sous les tropiques et leur influence sur la poésie* [*Scenes of Nature in the Tropics and Their Influence on Poetry*] (1824), Denis adopts Humboldt's thesis regarding the influence of the natural environment on progress and on the artistic style. These ideas inspired the young Brazilians who founded the journal *Niteroy* in Paris (1836) under the mentorship of poet Domingos José Gonçalves de Magalhães (1811–1882), whose mediocre *Suspiros poéticos e saudades* [*Poetical Sighs and Nostalgia*, Paris, 1836] is seen as the starting point of Brazilian romanticism, and whose "Ensaio sobre a história da literatura no Brasil" ["Essay on Brazilian Literary History," *Niteroy* 1, 1836] is the expression of the nativist school ideology.*

Inversely to our apologetic and artificial "Indianism," based on the concept of the noble and heroic *bon sauvage,* following the medieval knighthood paradigm, the Indian theme carries a demystifying imprint when addressed by Sousândrade. In his case, the form of the long poem is not affected by obsolescence as is *Confederação dos tamoios* (*Confederation of the Tamoio Indians,* 1856) or *Os timbiras* (*The Timbira Saga,* 1857), the epic attempts by Gonçalves de Magalhães and Gonçalves Dias, respectively. It is, rather, an innovative mixture of genres held together by the journey leitmotif (through the Amazon region, the Gulf of Mexico, and the Antilles all the way up to New York—where the poet lived from 1871 through 1885; along the Pacific Ocean, with stops in Colombia, Ecuador, Peru, Chile, and Argentina—as far down as Patagonia). Except for the southernmost regions, Humboldt had visited many of those places before, during his travels through the Americas (1799–1804).

Only in the twentieth century the Chilean poet Pablo Neruda carried out a project for a trans-American epos of similar reach in his *Canto general* (written between 1937 and 1950). Driven by the travel theme, Sousândrade, probably under the influence of his readings of Humboldt—who could see the clear relationship between the civilizing heroes Bochica

*Nativism is a tendency without clear boundaries, but generally it involves a sentiment of pride in the native soil, particularly the beauties and marvels of Brazil, with varying emphases as evidenced in "ufanismo," "Arcadianism," and "Indianism." *Ufanismo* (from *ufanar-se,* "to boast") refers to a category of Brazilian literature produced in the mid- to late 1500s and which tended to glorify the land and its riches. Arcadianism, described in an earlier footnote, dates to the late 1700s. Indianism, a literary program of the romantic period, valued Brazil's national origins by using the image of the native. —EDITORS

(Muisca), Quetzalcóatl (Aztec), and Manco-Cápac (Inca)—includes, in his *Guesa,* elements of the chronicles of the Inca Empire, of its splendor, its conquests. As Neruda did later, Sousândrade chastises the cruelty of the conquerors and celebrates the revolutionary leaders of the Americas (Bolívar, O'Higgins, Páez, Lincoln, etc.). In addition, the "Inca-Greek" model is idealized as a sort of socialist-utopian republic with Platonic or primitive Christian traits (despite Humboldt's opposition to such a concept when talking about the Inca Empire as "a great monastic entity," a less oppressive "theocracy" that still resembled the Aztec kings' rule). Both Sousândrade in the mid-nineteenth century and Neruda by the mid-twentieth century converge and concur in the epicedial celebration of Incan tragedy. The Brazilian's republican socialist-Christian view as well as the Chilean's Marxist-nationalistic utopia with libertarian ends bring to the fore the social rescue of the conquered peoples. One could compare, for instance, the description of Atahualpa's death, inflicted by Pizarro's perverse maneuvers and incited by Valverde, a fanatical priest (*Canto general,* canto 14):

> In Cajamarca the agony began.
> . . . .
>
> Pizarro, the swine from Extremadura,
> has the Inca's delicate arms
> bound. Night falls
> over Peru like a black ember.*

with canto 11 of *Guesa:* "Atahualpa fasted, in silence." The scene to which the magnificent decasyllable "O sol, ao pôr-do-sol, (triste soslaio!)" ["The sun at sunset (sadly slanting)!"] belongs concludes:

> Obfuscated, the Sun disappeared.
> Atahualpa, by the skies unprotected
> finding himself in a crater, shattered:
> as in astonishment he petrified![2]

Sousândrade indeed had a utopian-idealizing view of the Inca Empire. Regarding the Brazilian indigenous people, his attitude was one of fervent criticism against the corruptive effect of the whites and of catechizers. (The

---

* English translation from Pablo Neruda, *Canto General,* trans. Jack Schmitt (Berkeley and Los Angeles: University of California Press, 1991), 55. —EDITORS

"Inferno" in canto 2, the Amazonian "Tatuturema," a word from the merging of the Portuguese and Tupi languages, is an orgiastic pandemonium under the sign of Jurupari, the indigenous devil according to missionaries.) The republican-representative model inspired by the "avant-garde young people" (the United States and its founders), a form of government admired by Sousândrade and by Humboldt (a democrat, heir to the French Revolution, Jefferson's friend and correspondent), is also not safe from corruption:

> Oh! How sad; in the Republic ultimate
> moral lies fraud, in its bosom!
> In its pure bosom—as it were—
> Christ's body in decomposition![3]

Sousândrade, in his multilingual "Wall Street Inferno" (canto 10), captures and harshly satirizes speculation through the figure of the New York Stock Exchange god Mammon (the Greek *Mammonas*), the *usura* deity, during the so-called Gilded Age (1870–1884) of American capitalism.

Another aspect that stands out in *O Guesa* is the descriptions of nature, full of graphic beauty and visual images. Sousândrade's pictorial power is akin to (here, I do not mean influenced by) Humboldt's style in his "nature paintings" (*Ansichten der Natur*), which the erudite traveler intermingles with his scientific reports, developing, as it were, his "poetic prose" (*dichterische Prosa*). The description of the Tequendama Falls is a good example, since both Humboldt (*Vues des cordillères*) and Neruda (*Canto general*, section "Los ríos acuden" ["The Rivers Come Forth"]) were impressed by the magnificent view of the Colombian falls. Atop the Andes, nature is sublimated in the eyes of Guesa, the wandering poet. He ends up catching a glance of the "Eternal Spirit," the "One-Infinite" in the "Andes that rise up high, enlarged / into the skies like transparent clouds." He glimpses in a "white light / diamond," in "tellurian crystal," the "natural moral process, / colorless principles, existence / absolute in its beauty—here and beyond." A visionary of light, Sousândrade envisages the "One-God" in the glittering telluric mineral: "Oh! the Diamond, so pure / a burning flame / and also Eternal! Should I contemplate / it, How can I tell the gleam from what glows?"[4]

Would this, again, rather than influence, be somewhere close (by sensitive kinship) to the "holistic" concept of the cosmos—that *Synthese von physischer und moralischer Natur* [synthesis of physical and moral nature] which so deeply fascinated the great naturalist-philosopher from Berlin?

Translated by Diana Gibson, edited by Odile Cisneros

An Oswald de Andrade Triptych

A Poetics of the Radical (Selection)

Being Radical

If we wanted to characterize in a meaningful way the poetry of Oswald de Andrade in the panorama of Brazilian modernism, we could say that his poetry articulates a poetics of the radical. It's a radical poetry. What does "being radical" mean? In a famous text, Marx wrote: "To be radical is to grasp things by the root. But for man the root is man himself."* How can we understand, in that sense, the radical quality of Andrade's poetry? Once again, Marx provides us with a clue: "Language is as old as consciousness, language *is* practical consciousness that exists also for other men, and for that reason alone it really exists for me personally as well; language, like consciousness, only arises from the need, the necessity, of intercourse with other men. Where there exists a relationship, it exists for me: the animal

This section comprises excerpts from three essays originally published as introductions to works by Oswald de Andrade: "Uma poética da radicalidade," in *Poesias reunidas,* vol. 7, *Obras completas* (1966; reprint, Rio de Janeiro: Civilização Brasileira, 1972), republished in *Pau Brasil* (São Paulo: Editora Globo, 2000), 7–53; "*Miramar* na mira," in *Memórias sentimentais de João Miramar* (1964; reprint, Rio de Janeiro: Civilização Brasileira, 1972), xiii–xlv, and (São Paulo: Editora Globo, 1997), 5–33; "*Serafim:* Um grande não livro," in *Memórias sentimentais de João Miramar/Serafim Ponte Grande,* vol. 4, *Obras completas,* 4th ed. (Rio de Janeiro: Civilização Brasileira, 1972), 101–27, republished in *Serafim Ponte Grande* (São Paulo: Editora Globo, 1996), 5–34. —EDITORS

*Karl Marx, "Critique of Hegel's *Philosophy of Right,*" trans. T. B. Bottomore, in *The Marx-Engels Reader,* ed. Robert C. Tucker (New York: W. W. Norton, 1972), 19. —TRANSLATOR

does not enter into '*relations*' with anything, it does not enter into any relation at all. . . . Consciousness is, therefore, from the very beginning a social
product, and it remains so as long as men exist at all."[*] The radical nature
of Andrade's poetry can be gauged, thus, insofar as this poetry affects, at the
root, that practical, real consciousness which is language. Since language,
like consciousness, is a social product, a product of man as a being in a relationship, it is worthwhile to locate Andrade's project in its historical framework. What was the state of literary language at the time when the
Oswaldian poetic revolution was fermenting and broke out?

Intellectually, the Brazil of the first decades of this [the twentieth] century, around the Modern Art Week of 1922, was still a Brazil under the spell
of the "myths of the *mot juste*" (Mário da Silva Brito[†]), where an "ornamental patriotism" reigned (Antonio Candido[‡]), full of tribune rhetoric, the
counterpart of a oligarcho-patriarchal regime that lasted until well into the
republic.[§] Rui Barbosa, the Eagle of the Hague, Coelho Neto, the Last of
the Greeks, and Olavo Bilac, the Prince of Poets,[**] were the uncontested
gods of an official Olympus, in which the Parnassian Pegasus dragged its
heavy metrifying armor, and word wealth (understood merely in a cumulative sense) was a sort of thermometer for an "enlightened" consciousness.
Evidently, literary language in that context functioned as a jargon of castes,
a diploma of intellectual "nobiliarchy."

Between the language full of pointillist correction written by the atten-
dees of the literary banquets and the language carelessly spoken by the people (mostly of São Paulo, where the migratory currents led, accompanied
by their peculiar oral deformations) an apparently unbridgeable gap
opened. Oswald de Andrade's *Poesia Pau-brasil* [*Brazilwood Poetry*] represented, as we can easily imagine, a 180-degree shift in that status quo,

[*] Karl Marx, "The German Ideology," in *The Marx-Engels Reader*, 122. —TRANSLATOR

[†] Critic (b. 1916), author of the important *História do modernismo brasileiro* [*History of Brazilian Modernism*] (Saraiva: São Paulo, 1958). —TRANSLATOR

[‡] Critic and university professor (b. 1918), author of *Formação da literatura brasileira* [*Formation of
Brazilian Literature*] (1959). —TRANSLATOR

[§] The Brazilian Republic was proclaimed on November 15, 1889, by Marshall Deodoro da Fonseca.
—TRANSLATOR

[**] Barbosa, a writer and liberal politician and thinker (1849–1923), was considered a Parnassian stylist
of the language in his writings and oratory. Neto, a novelist and short-story writer (1864–1934), was the
prolific author of more than 120 works. Bilac, a Parnassian poet (1865–1918), attained extreme popular-
ity in his day; his *Poesias* was an uncontested best seller for years. Because of extreme attention to perfection in style, Bilac came under attack by the modernists of 1922. Mário de Andrade called him "the
most brilliant juggler of the Portuguese verse." —TRANSLATOR/EDITORS

where—to use Oswald's* own expression—"the stable values of the most backward literature of the world prevented any kind of renovation." He called everything into question in terms of poetry. Being radical language-wise, he found, while drilling into the fossilized strata of convention, the restlessness of the new Brazilian man. This modern subject was being forged speaking a language stirred by the "wealthy contribution of all the mistakes," in a country that had begun—precisely in São Paulo—a process of industrialization with deep structural repercussions. "If we look for the explanation of why the modernist phenomenon emerged in São Paulo and not elsewhere in Brazil, we'll see that it was the result of our industrial con-sciousness. São Paulo had long been swept by all the cultural winds. Not only did the coffee trade produce the resources, but also industry, with its zeal for the new, its stimulation of progress, made competition enter all fields of activity." That was Oswald's hindsight in 1954.[1]

The Evils of Eloquence

When Paulo Prado,† in May of 1924, writing the preface to Oswald's first book of poems (1925), defined "Brazilwood poetry" as "the egg of Colum-bus" and hailed it as the "first systematic attempt to liberate Brazilian poetry," he touched on the nerve of the problem. Not only because Prado saw in this poetry the "rehabilitation of our everyday speech, sermo ple-beius, which pedantic grammarians wanted to eliminate from written lan-guage." But, beyond this, because he foresaw in it something more fundamentally far-reaching:

> Let us hope that "Brazilwood" poetry may also eliminate once and for all one of the greatest evils of our race—the evil of eloquence, fluffy and rustling. In this era hastened by fast activity, everything tends to the simple and naked expression of sensation and feeling, in complete and synthetic sincerity. "Le poète japonais / Essuie son couteau: / Cette fois l'éloquence est morte," says the Japanese haiku in its stony conciseness. That will be a glorious day for Brazilian poetry. To obtain, in capsules, minutes of poetry.

* Brazilian literary history is rich in writers bearing the last name "Andrade." For this reason, and partic-ularly when referring to the two contemporaneous main players of Brazilian modernism, Oswald de Andrade and Mário de Andrade (who were not related by blood), authors often refer to them by their first name. For reasons of clarity, this peculiarity has been preserved as it occurs in the original. —TRANSLATOR

† Prominent member of the São Paulo bourgeoisie (1869–1943). He was a lover and patron of the arts who actively supported the 1922 Modern Art Week. Published *Retrato do Brasil* (1928), an essay that attempts to define the Brazilian national ethos. —TRANSLATOR

It is true that before *Brazilwood,* Mário de Andrade,* another great name of Brazilian modernism, had already published two books of poetry: *Há uma gota de sangue en cada poema* [*There's a Drop of Blood in Each Poem*] (1917) and *Pauli céia desvairada* [*Hallucinated City*]† (1922), books of undoubtedly great historical import and which would go on to powerfully instigate Oswald. (On May 27, 1921, in an article that provoked scandal and controversy even with Mário himself, Oswald introduced the author of the then unpublished *Pauli céia* as "My Futurist Poet.")² In none of those books, however, do we find the radical attitude vis-à-vis language which emerges from Oswald's first collection and which is already present in the novel-invention *Memórias Sentimentais de João Miramar* [*Sentimental Memoirs of John Seaborne*],‡ begun between 1914 and 1916, written and rewritten successively until 1923, and published in 1924. Many of its sections are literally made up of poems that could have been included in *Brazilwood:*

Mont-Cenis

The alpinist
from alpenstock
descended
upon
the Alps

In reality, the language of Mário's first book (published under the pseudonym Mário Sobral and later gathered in a volume of *Obra imatura* [*Juvenilia*] of his *Complete Works*) is still quite traditional, exclamatory, and dotted with rhetorical sentimentality. In it, there are only a few scattered moments of nonconformity, such as "Somente o vento / continua com seu oou . . ." [Only the wind / goes on with its oou . . .], which Oswald enthusiastically admired when the two Andrades first met.³ On the other hand, *Hallucinated City* is already an aesthetically representative book, comprising poems such as "Ode to the Bourgeois Gentleman" and the profane oratorio "The Moral Fibrature of the Ipiranga," examples of the best Marioandradian diction. In spite of this, there is nothing in it that points to the strip-

* Poet, critic, novelist, short-story writer, and musicologist (1893–1935). He was one of the pivotal figures of the Brazilian modernist movement. —TRANSLATOR

† In English: *Hallucinated City,* trans. Jack E. Tomlins (Kingsport, TN: Vanderbilt University Press, 1968). —TRANSLATOR

‡ In English: *Sentimental Memoirs of John Seaborne,* trans. Albert G. Bork and Ralph W. Niebuhr, *Texas Quarterly* 15, no. 4 (Winter 1972): 112–60. —TRANSLATOR

ping, the reduction, the synthesis that distinguishes Oswald's "Brazilwood" poetry. That is because Mário did not question the foundations of rhetoric; he tried instead to lead it into a new bed, to disturb it with the introduction of unusual semantic conglomerates, but he allowed the verse to flow liberally, only here and there interrupted by the broken "harmonic verse" ("Raptures . . . Struggles . . . Arrows . . . Chants . . . Populate!" in the body of a poem such as "Tietê"). Also, the thematics and rhyme schemes (frequently their force, their unexpectedness, and dissonance) were affected by an unconquerable symbolist component of the urban kind à la Verhaeren. [. . .] So thus, *Hallucinated City*, for all its novelty, still was not the revolution; it was a reform, carrying its sandbags of conciliation and wordiness. The revolution—the Copernican revolution—came with "Brazilwood" poetry. From there emerged an entire line of substantive poetics, of contained poetry, condensed to its essential process of signs, which passes through Drummond in the 1930s, informs the poetic engineering of João Cabral de Melo Neto, and projects itself into today's concrete poetry.[4] An industrial-grade poetry, we could say, as opposed to the old discursive craft, institutionalized in rhetorical models by Parnassianism, or already thawed, revitalized in new lyric-interjective streams by the poet of *Pauliceia*. [. . .]

Like Paulo Prado, João Ribeiro* understood with perspicacity the pioneering and radical meaning of Oswald's poetics. His subsequently much-quoted verdict—"Mr. Oswald de Andrade with *Brazilwood* marked a definitive era of national poetry"—is formulated in an article from 1927, dedicated to the author's second poetry collection.[5] In that article, written looking back two years to Oswald's poetic début, João Ribeiro managed to evaluate with accuracy the impact of that landmark work:

> He attacked with decisive energy, the lines, arabesques, planes, perspective, colors, and light. He had the childlike intuition of wrecking toys to see what was inside. And he saw nothing. He began to devise, without help from the Muses, a new art, an unconscious one capable of the maximum of triviality vis-à-vis the rigid style and grandiloquence of the masters. He geometrized reality, achieving that primeval, Assyrian or Egyptian quality of African sculpture; he created frightful fetishes; and opposed to the Greek vase the rhomboid beauty of earthen pots [. . .] That's how a national poetry was born, one that lifting the import tariffs, created a Brazilian industry. [. . .] For me, he was the best critic of national emphasis, the one who reduced the complexity of rhetorical

---

* Symbolist critic (1860–1934). —TRANSLATOR

garb to the simple and proverbial fig leaf, which was already uncomfortable enough. He arrived at the childlike and decimal conception that one must have of man: an 8 perched on two legs equals 10.

In another article from 1928,[6] João Ribeiro speaks again of "Brazilwood" poetry: "He [Oswald] was, like all of us, sick of the usual imitations, and he proceeded a bit like Descartes, eliminating one by one all preconceptions, until he arrived at Brazil, still pre-historic, revealed by the *conquistadores*. With that reduction, poetry earned a new and original meaning. And here the simultaneous influx of his colleague Mário de Andrade must not be forgotten."

Miramar on the Mark (Selections)

The First Crucible

In 1922—the year that in Brazil would be marked by the blast of the "Modern Art Week"—Shakespeare and Co. (the now legendary publishing house owned by Sylvia Beach) published in Paris the first edition of a book that was to change the course of modern fiction: James Joyce's *Ulysses*. In 1923 the Irish novelist began to write *Finnegans Wake,*[7] which from then on would be published in installments under the title *Work in Progress* in the international avant-garde magazine *Transition,* edited by the poet Eugène Jolas.

In 1923, Mário de Andrade wrote to Manuel Bandeira:* "Osvaldo[*sic*] and Sérgio† are arriving in December. Sérgio is bringing his newly published *Oeil de bœuf* [*Eye of the Ox*]. Osvaldo is bringing a novel, *Memórias de João Miramar,* which, from what I hear, is unbelievably interesting, unbelievably modern, exaggeratedly unruly. I'm dying to see it."[8] *Memórias Sentimentais de João Miramar* [*Sentimental Memoirs of John Seaborne*]—carrying the inscription "Sestri Levante/Hotel Miramare, 1923"—was published in 1924, dedicated to Paulo Prado and Tarsila do Amaral,‡ with a cover by Amaral (Livraria Editora Independência, São Paulo). This is the novel that Oswald de Andrade, with due justice, called "the first crucible of

---

* Poet and critic, (1886–1968), important and influential in the Brazilian modernist movement. A selection of his works is published in English in the volume *This Earth, That Sky,* trans. and with notes and introduction by Candace Slater (Berkeley and Los Angeles: University of California Press, 1989). —TRANSLATOR

† Sérgio Milliet, poet and critic (1898–1966), also affiliated with the modernist movement. —TRANSLATOR

‡ Tarsila do Amaral (1886–1973), an artist influenced by cubism, studied painting in Paris with Albert Gleizes and Ferdinand Léger. She was an important figure in the Brazilian modernist movement and was married to Oswald from 1926 to 1930. —TRANSLATOR

our new prose" in an article from 1943 ("Antes do *Marco Zero*" ["Before the *Ground Zero*"]) republished in his collection *Ponta de lança* [*Spearhead*].⁹ This fundamental book, now a rare item and practically unknown to the new generations, is—finally!—being republished and put again into circulation, forty years after its launch and ten years after the author's death. In reality, people haven't always remembered to cite this watershed work when it comes to tracing the evolution of modern Brazilian prose. There was even, for a long time—and with echoes until today—a systematic campaign of silence against Oswald, which resulted in the minimization, if not deliberate obliteration, of his important literary contributions. The creator of *Seaborne,* in his usual combativeness, had already denounced this campaign in another essay from *Spearhead* ("Fraternidade de Jorge Amado" ["Brotherhood of Jorge Amado"]):

> Then arose the fable that I only produced jokes, and a wall of silence tried to obscure the pioneer work that created *Pau-Brasil* [*Brazilwood*], from where, as Vinícius de Moraes has recently noted, all the elements of modern Brazilian poetry emerged. The renewal in prose of 1922 was deliberately forgotten, an experiment to which I contributed with *Memórias sentimentais de João Miramar.*

[. . .]

Ulysses and Miramar

Parody constitutes a fundamental device in Joyce's *Ulysses.* It would even be unnecessary to resort to episode 14 of the book, "The Oxen of the Sun," the parodic chapter par excellence. There, the embryonic development up until the moment of birth is presented through an elaborate paraphrase of the evolution of the English language and literature: from the primitive, monosyllabic, and alliterative Anglo-Saxon to the cockney or slang of the streets, passing through an imitation of all the main stylists of the language. Even the parody of the Homeric epic in the one-day flânerie of an obscure Dubliner already involves, in a sort of general program, its technical aspects.¹⁰ In both *Sentimental Memoirs of John Seaborne* and Mário de Andrade's *Macunaíma,** parody is present as a stylistic and structural device, a technique crucial to the understanding of some of modern literature's

---

* Novel by Mário de Andrade, one of the fundamental texts of Brazilian modernism, discussed in an earlier part of the essay not included in this selection. Available in English: *Macunaíma,* trans. E. A. Goodland (New York: Random House, 1984). —TRANSLATOR

greatest works, as well as to the understanding of certain literary works of the past not easily pigeonholed: Folengo, Rabelais, and Cervantes. As we noted, both de Andrades—Oswald and Mário—perfectly incorporated parody into the Brazilian context, endowing it with an active satiric function. But, focusing on Oswald, it is not just from this angle that one can compare *Seaborne* to *Ulysses,* although the parallel must be approached with caution and the appropriate reservations. In reality, *Sentimental Memoirs* is far from possessing the intricate and complex structure, the monumental nature of Joyce's *Ulysses,* a veritable encyclopedia of modern novelistic techniques. It would be sufficient to consider the meticulous guide to the labyrinth (prepared by the author himself and first made available by Stuart Gilbert)[11] in order to have an idea of the distance separating the Joycean macromicrocosm—carefully planned to the minutest details—from the Oswaldian novel, composed in a streak of brilliant improvisation, a small masterpiece of 163 fragments-episodes condensed in little more than one hundred pages.

Seaborne, as a whole, could more readily be compared with an isolated chapter from *Ulysses* (chapter 7: Eolus), set in a newspaper's editorial room, where the techniques of the headline, the captions, and the topics of the daily press are employed. *Seaborne,* with its telegraphic style, is more a mix of sentimental diary and a *faits divers* newspaper of a provincial and idle society whose barometer was the ups and downs of the coffee trade.[12] Antonio Candido provides this eloquent synthesis of the book:

> *Sentimental Memoirs of John Seaborne,* apart from being one of the greatest books in Brazilian literature, is a most serious endeavor in style and narrative as well as a first sketch of social satire. The moneyed bourgeoisie exposes, the world over, its emptiness and conventionality in a show of terrifying sterility. Seaborne is a *pince-sans-rire* [deadpan-faced] humorist who attempts to nonchalantly "Kodak" life using a synthetic and dazzling language, full of bold weldings and lapidary conciseness.[13]

Evidently, in *Ulysses'* "Aeolus," preordained or superimposed intentions are imbricated through constant reworkings (the exploitation of journalistic techniques joins a sampler of rhetorical devices with its wealth of figures), all of which are alien to the associative immediacy of the collage of fragments in *Seaborne.* But they are similar in the topical and condensed character of the takes. *Seaborne* also does not lack the idea of the voyage. And this is already in the title, which onomastically infuses the character with a perpetual sea-bound vocation, and, in Joyce's *Ulysses,* is transposed to the terrestrial and pedestrian journey in the urban enclave of Dublin. It is that

"Odyssean quality that the novel consciously acquired with Joyce" and to which Oswald alludes with utter conviction.[14] But the journey in *Seaborne* apparently has no consequences: it is a journey for the sake of the bohemian consumption of freedom, at the end of which the hero rejoins his bourgeois context (marriage - lover - separation - poetasterings - financial vicissitudes). A bit out of phase, it is also true that *Seaborne* is also his post-travel journal and the negation of that context through mockery. Seaborne, the protagonist, is a naive Ulysses without the slyness of Homer's *rusé personnage* [cunning character], but for whom the journey represents an initial possibility, even if vague and undefined, of an opening to the world and of a "critical" stance. "And he would return, innocent as he had gone, down the slope of an endless sea. He had only a new dimension in his soul—he had encountered freedom" (Oswald, *Um homem sem profissão* [*A Man with No Profession*], 79).* But the Odyssean destiny of the character journeys to the novel that was sparked by *Seaborne* and which surpasses it ideologically and formally: *Serafim Ponte Grande* [*Seraphim Grosse Pointe*] (1929/1933).† There, "the veneer of a bourgeois and conformist upbringing is washed away by the utopia of a permanent and redemptive journey in search of plenitude via mobility."[15] The myth of the "permanent voyage" is also the anarchic counterpart of the permanent revolution that becomes a positive will to political engagement in the important retrospective and prospective preface to *Seraphim*. That new Odysseus, Seaborne/Seraphim, will only find again, vivid and long-suffered, his spiritual Ithaca in the *Cântico dos cânticos para flauta e violão* [*Song of Songs for Flute and Guitar*] (1942), song of peace in the aftermath of war where the beloved woman is celebrated thus: "Port of my life / seven times departed / Port of my life broken / In the prisons / Sweated in the streets / Wrought / In the vague dawn of hospitals."[16]

Serafim: A Great Un-Book (Selections)

"The most surprising symptom of modern literature is perhaps to witness the appearance under our noses of a form of writing so new, unitary, and global that the radical abandonment of the distinction of genres gives way to what could be called 'books.' But books for which, it should be

* Oswald de Andrade, *Um homem sem profissão: sob os ordens de mamãe. Memórias e confissões: Vol. 1, 1890–1919* (Rio de Janeiro: Civilização Brasileira, 1974). —TRANSLATOR

† In English: *Seraphim Grosse Pointe,* trans. K. D. Jackson and Albert Bork (Austin: New Latin Quarter Editions, 1979). —TRANSLATOR

noted, no reading method has yet been practically devised."[17] The author of this reflection is a young French writer, Philippe Sollers, from the generation of the so-called *nouveau roman* and gathered, since the early 1960s, around the experimental forum of the journal *Tel Quel.*

The invention/novel[18] *Seraphim Grosse Pointe* by Oswald de Andrade, "written from 1929 backwards" (or "finished in 1928," as the preface reads) and published in 1933, is one of those works that calls into question the traditional idea of genre and literary work, proposing a new concept of the book and of reading. In *Sentimental Memoirs of John Seaborne* (concluded in 1923, published in 1924), Oswald had already experimented with boundaries, abolishing the border between poetry and prose. Now, he radicalized the experiment in another dimension, making use of his previous stylistic conquests, but going deeper—if it is possible to say this—into the disassembly of the traditional novelistic form.

The challenge to the idea of the book as a well-defined object in a codified literary past including its cultural rituals begins here, of course, as an attack on the materiality, the physicality of the object itself. In the place usually reserved for the "Works by the Same Author," the list is headed by the expression "Rejected Works," and the very book that one is about to read, *Seraphim Grosse Pointe,* is included among the discarded titles. The copyright—which sanctions the rights of the author and of literary property—is paraphrased in a mocking tone ("No rights reserved. May be translated, reproduced, and deformed into all languages"). There is a "Printer's Error" slip dislocated from its habitual place, functioning autonomously, as an independent chapter. Finally, what corresponds to a colophon (indicating the date and place of printing of the book) is also subject to an unusual treatment: the chronology is listed backward, as if seen through the distancing lenses of a pair of binoculars placed in reverse: "This book was written from 1929 (the era of Wall Street and Christ) backwards." Not to mention the parody included in the classical dating conventions (B.C., A.D., year of the Lord, anno Domini, etc.).

Such *indexical* signs (in Peirce's classification system)[19] point like arrows toward the reality of an object that we know through these localizing and characteristic markers—just as traffic signs show us the way or alert us to the presence of a school or hospital. However, these signs simultaneously "estrange" the object, or "defamiliarize" it to our perception, through the very act of pointing to it or emblematizing it.

Ostranenie—That's how the Russian formalist critics in the first decades of the twentieth century tried to define this technique used to demolish "automatization," the inertia that we are subjected to by routine. What is familiar appears to us as new, unknown, if we alter the normal relations that the familiar is presented under through an "alienation effect." Viktor Shklovsky, who made use of this concept in his 1917 study "Iskusstvo kak priem" ("Art as Technique"),* considered a true manifesto of Russian formalism,[20] also developed the idea of "exposing the technique" (or "procedure"—*obnazhenie priema*) as a measure of the work of art's specificity. For him, Laurence Sterne's *Tristram Shandy* was the most typical novel of world literature (instead of the exceptional or extravagant case, as was previously held) precisely because it exposed the very structure of the novel by disturbing it, "deautomatizing" it for the reader's reception. "Formalistically, Sterne was an extreme revolutionary," says Shklovsky; "it was characteristic of him to 'lay bare' his technique."[21] *Tristram Shandy,* this apparently bizarre and idiosyncratic work written in the second half of the eighteenth century (1759–67), is in reality a pioneer milestone of the revolution of the book as object. This revolution projects itself in an overwhelming and irreversible way into our [the twentieth] century, having now as allies (or at least, as instigators) the new technologies for reproduction and transmission of information, the mass communication of new media and intermedia.

Oswald de Andrade's *Seraphim,* like Sterne's *Tristram,* is a book that, from the start, questions its own structure. Already in *Sentimental Memoirs of John Seaborne* Oswald had developed the project of a fractured, fragmentary book made up of elements that had to be articulated by the reader's inner spirit, a book that looked like an anthology of itself.[22] But in *Seaborne,* even if the shattering of chapters might produce the effect of disintegrating the norm of linear reading, there is still a rarefied chronological thread, traced from a residual form of the bildungsroman, that presents us with—in parodic terms, to be sure—the stages of childhood, adolescence, the educational travels, marital and extramarital loves, the separation, the widowhood, and the meditative disenchantment of a hero, the "memorialist"/litterateur who gives the book its title.

Now, in *Seraphim,* Oswald's concern with the framework of the book leads him to a sort of *continuum* of invention, the protean, labile structure of a surprise box. If in *Seaborne* the great novelty was in the realm of syntax, at the microaesthetic level of the stylistic linking of text units (words and phrases), in *Seraphim* it is the *great syntagmas* of narrative that merit the

---

* *In Russian Formalist Criticism: Four Essays,* trans. and with an introduction by Lee T. Lemon and Marion J. Reis (Lincoln: University of Nebraska Press, 1965). —TRANSLATOR

author's special attention. In *Seaborne,* we can recognize a cubist style, or at least a metonymic one, in the manner in which Oswald recombined the phrasal elements at his disposal, arranging them in new and unusual neighboring relationships, altering them through a tie of contiguity. It is as if he were a cubist painter disjoining and conjoining through a new optics the fragmented objects on his canvas. Now, in *Seraphim,* that cubist technique, that metonymic treatment, seems to operate at the level of the general architecture of the work itself, hence, at the macrolevel.[23] *Seraphim* is a composite, hybrid book made up of pieces or "samples" of various possible books, and all of them propose and challenge a certain mode of the narrative genre or of the so-called art of prose (or, for that matter, of writing *tout court*). Each one of these excerpts or "trailers" of virtual books works—at the macrosyntagmatic level, at the level of the framework of the text—as a metonymic allusion to a certain cataloged type of prose, be it conventional or pragmatic, that never manages to impose itself completely on the Oswaldian book, giving it a unified directive. Instead, the excerpts point—allusively and elusively—to a literary mode *that could be but isn't.* The metonymic operation—or, more precisely, the synecdoche, in the *pars pro toto* form of traditional rhetoric (the pieces of books which, taken for the whole, indicate a certain genre or a certain species in the stock of literary holdings)—acquires then a *metalinguistic* function. It is through this operation that the book effects the critique of the book (of the novel in particular and, by extension, of prose and of "artistic" and "nonartistic" writing). In this manifestly parodic exercise, a review of the very history of the novelistic genre, of its diachrony, is not lacking; in a chaotic way, admittedly, but not because of this less significantly. Wellek and Warren, in their exposé of André Jolles's theory of how complex literary forms represent the development of simpler units (*Legende, Sage, Mythe, Rätsel, Spruch, Kasus, Memorabile, Märchen, Witz*), note that the maturity of the novel also fed on the *einfache Formen* [simple forms], such as the letter, the diary, the travel book, the memoir, the essay, and so on.[24]

Even in metonymy's projection on the *great syntagmas* of narrative, as they occur in *Seraphim,* it is possible to identify a technique that is typical of cubism: collage, the critical juxtaposition of diverse materials, which in cinematic terms may be equated with montage. Collage and even montage—to the extent that they work with a set of tools and materials, making an inventory of them and manipulating their primitive functions—may be characterized as the type of activity that Lévi-Strauss defines as "bricolage" (composition of structured sets, not directly but through the use of residues and fragments), which, while typical of the *pensée sauvage* [savage mind], also has much in common with the concrete, combinatory logic of poetic thought.[25]

Oswald, *bricoleur,* made a book out of residues of books, from pieces metonymically significant which are telescoped and imbricated in it in an apparently disconnected fashion. But he does so while exhibiting, through that very critical hybridity which could be called a structural "technique of quotation," the most profound calling of the Oswaldian project: to produce an "un-book," an antibook, from the parodic accumulation of the habitual ways of making books or, by extension, of writing prose (or even, and also, of written language). Antonio Candido, in a seminal study of Oswald's prose, referred to *Seraphim* as the "fragment of a great book."[26] This assessment, which reveals Candido's appreciation of the Oswaldian experiment—"there is much in it of a great book," he insists in another passage—simultaneously evidences some reservations vis-à-vis a certain "aesthetic self-indulgence" in the technique employed, which would not allow for an elaboration of compositional problems. Today [in the 1970s], with insights gained in the last twenty years, the question could be reformulated: it is precisely through the syncopated technique and the resulting unfinished quality that the construction becomes apparent, that the woodwork of the traditional novel, as *priem,* as procedure, was exposed. Elaborating on Antonio Candido's definition, we would like to reformulate it thus: *Seraphim* is a great un-book made up of book fragments.[27]

Translated by Odile Cisneros

The Concrete Moment

Pilot Plan for Concrete Poetry

Augusto de Campos, Haroldo de Campos, and Décio Pignatari

Concrete poetry: product of a critical evolution of forms. Assuming that the historical cycle of verse (as formal-rhythmical unit) is closed, concrete poetry begins by being aware of graphic space as structural agent. Qualified space: space-time structure instead of mere linear-temporal development. Hence the importance of the ideogram concept, either in its general sense of spatial or visual syntax or in its specific sense (Fenollosa/Pound) as a method of composition based on direct—analogical, not logical-discursive— juxtaposition of elements. "Il faut que notre intelligence s'habitue à comprendre synthético-idéographiquement au lieu de analytico-discursivement" ["Our brain must get used to thinking synthetico-ideographically instead of analytico-discursively"] (Apollinaire). Eisenstein: ideogram and montage.

Forerunners: Mallarmé ("Un coup de dés" ["A Throw of the Dice"], 1897): the first qualitative jump—"subdivisions prismatiques de l'idée"; space ("blancs") and typographical devices as substantive elements of composition. Pound (*The Cantos*): ideogramic method. Joyce (*Ulysses* and *Finnegans Wake*): word-ideogram; organic interpenetration of time and

Originally published by the authors in *Noigandres* 4, São Paulo, 1958; reproduced in Augusto de Campos, Décio Pignatari, and Haroldo de Campos, *Teoria da poesia concreta* (*Textos críticos e manifestos, 1950–60*) (São Paulo: Edições Invenção, 1965; republished São Paulo: Duas Cidades, 1975; and São Paulo: Brasiliense, 1987). English translation by Jon Tolman published in *The Avant-Garde Tradition in Literature,* ed. and with an introduction by Richard Kostelanetz (Buffalo, NY: Prometheus Books, 1982) and *Manifesto: A Century of Isms,* ed. Mary Ann Caws (Lincoln: University of Nebraska Press, 2000). —EDITORS

space. Cummings: atomization of words, physiognomic typography; expressionistic emphasis on space. Apollinaire (*Calligrammes*): the vision, rather than the praxis. Futurism, Dadaism: contributions to the life of the problem. In Brazil: Oswald de Andrade (1890–1954): "in compressed minutes of poetry." João Cabral de Melo Neto (1920–99—*the engineer,* and his "Psicologia da composição" ["Psychology of Composition"] and "Anti-ode"): direct speech, economy and functional architecture of verse.

Concrete poetry: tension of word-things in space-time. Dynamic structure: multiplicity of concomitant movements. Thus in music—by definition, an art of timing—space intervenes (Webern and his followers: Boulez and Stockhausen; concrete and electronic music); in visual arts—spatial, by definition—time intervenes (Mondrian and his *Boogie-Woogie* series; Max Bill; Albers and perceptive ambivalence; concrete art in general).

Ideogram: appeal to nonverbal communication. The concrete poem communicates its own structure: structure-content. The concrete poem is an object in and of itself, not the interpreter of exterior objects and/or more or less subjective feelings. Its material: word (sound, visual form, semantic charge). Its problem: a problem of functions-relations of this material. Factors of proximity and similitude, Gestalt psychology. Rhythm: relational force. The concrete poem, using phonetics (digits) and analogical syntax, creates a specific linguistic area—*verbivocovisual*—which shares the advantages of nonverbal communication without giving up the word's virtuality. The phenomenon of metacommunication occurs with the concrete poem: coincidence and simultaneity of verbal and nonverbal communication; but—it must be noted—it deals with the communication of forms, of structure-content, not with the usual message communication.

Concrete poetry aims at the lowest common denominator of language. Hence its tendency toward nominalization and verbification. "The concrete wherewithal of speech" (Sapir). Hence its affinities with the so-called isolating languages (Chinese): "the less outward grammar the Chinese language possesses, the more inner grammar inheres in it" (Humboldt via Cassirer). Chinese offers an example of pure relational syntax, based exclusively on word order (see Fenollosa, Sapir, and Cassirer).

We call isomorphism the form-subject conflict looking for identification. Parallel to form-subject isomorphism, there is space-time isomorphism, which creates movement. In the first stage of concrete poetry practice, isomorphism tends toward physiognomy, that is, movement imitating natural appearance (*motion*) where organic form and phenomenology of composition prevail. In a more advanced stage, isomorphism tends to resolve itself into pure structural movement (*movement* proper); in this phase, geometric form and mathematics of composition (rationalism of sensibility) prevail.

Renouncing the struggle for the "absolute," concrete poetry remains in the magnetic field of perennial relativity. Chrono-micrometric measuring of chance. Control. Cybernetics. The poem as a self-regulatory mechanism: feedback. Faster communication (problems of functionality and structure implied) endows the poem with a positive value and guides its own making.

Concrete poetry: total responsibility before language. Total realism. Against a subjective and hedonistic poetry of expression. To create precise problems and to solve them in terms of sensible language. A general art of the word. The poem-product: useful object.

Postscript

1961: "There's no revolutionary art without revolutionary form" (Mayakovsky).

Translated by Jon Tolman, edited by A. S. Bessa

The Open Work of Art

In order to bring to focus a willfully "drastic selection" in the pragmatic-utilitarian terms of Poundian theory, one could name the works of Mallarmé ("Un coup de dés" ["A Throw of the Dice"]), Joyce, Pound, and Cummings as the radial axes that generate the vectorial field of contemporary poetry. From the convergence of these axes and depending on the development of the productive process, certain results, some predictable, some not, will emerge.

It is not necessary here to enter deeply into the multiple problems which the mere mention of these names together provokes on the threshold of contemporary experiments in poetry. Instead it will be sufficient to merely give some hints of the morphocultural catalysis caused by their works.

The Mallarméan constellation-poem has as its base a concept of multi-divisions or capillary structure. This concept liquidates the notion of linear development divided into beginning-middle-end. It substitutes in its place a circular organization of poetic material that abolishes any rhythmic clockwork based on the "rule of thumb" of metrification. Silence emerges from that truly verbal rosette, "Un coup de dés," as the primordial element of rhythmic organization. As Sartre has said: "Silence itself is defined by its

Published originally in *Diário de São Paulo*, March 7, 1955. Republished in Rio de Janeiro in the following year in *Correio da manhã*. The present revised version was published in *Teoria da poesia concreta* (São Paulo: Editora Perspectiva, 1965). The English translation by Jon Tolman appeared in *Dispositio* 6, no. 17-18 (Summer–Fall 1981): 5–7, and is reproduced by kind permission of *Dispositio: Revista Americana de Estudios Comparados y Culturales/American Journal of Comparative and Cultural Studies,* published by the University of Michigan, Department of Romance Languages and Literatures. —EDITORS

relationship with words, just as the pause in music receives its meaning from the group of notes which surround it. This silence is a moment of language."[1] This permits us to apply to poetry what Pierre Boulez affirmed of music: "It is one of those truths so difficult to demonstrate that music is not only 'the art of sounds' but that it is better defined as a counterpoint of sound and silence."[2]

The Joycean universe also evolved from a linear development of time toward space-time or the infusion of the whole in the part ("allspace in a notshall"), adopting as the organogram of *Finnegans Wake* the Vico-vicious circle. Joyce's technique evolved pari passu with his own work[3] and under the influence of Bergson's concept of "durée."

Mallarmé developed a visual notion of graphic space, served by the prismatic notation of poetic imagination in ebbs and flows which are dislocated like the elements of a mobile, utilizing silence in the way that Calder used air. Joyce, on the other hand, holds to the materialization of a "polydimensional limitless flow"—the "durée réelle," the "riverrun" of "élan vital"—which obliges him to undertake a true atomization of language, where each "verbi-voco-visual" unit is at the same time the continent-content of the whole work and instantly "myriad-minded."

Mallarmé practices the phenomenological reduction of the poetic object. The eidos—"Un coup de dés jamais n'abolira le hasard" ['A throw of the dice will never abolish chance"]—is attained by means of the ellipsis of peripheral themes to the "thing in itself" of the poem. In the structure of the work, however, what Husserl notes with relation to his method also occurs: "Said with an image: that which is placed between parentheses is not erased from the phenomenological table, but simply placed between parentheses and affected by an index. But with this index it enters again into the major theme of investigation."[4]

Joyce is led to the microscopic world by the macroscopic, emphasizing detail—*panorama/panaroma*—to the point where a whole metaphoric cosmos is contained in a single word. This is why it can be said of *Finnegans Wake* that it retains the properties of a circle—the equal distance of all its points in relation to its center. The work is porous to the reader, accessible from any of the places one chooses to approach it.

For Cummings, the word is fissile. His poems have as their fundamental element the "letter." The syllable is, for his needs, already a complex material. The "tactical modesty" of that poetic attitude is similar to that of Webern: interested in the word on the phonemic level, he orients himself toward an open poetic form, in spite of the danger of exhausting himself in the one-minute poem, as he faces the hindrances of a still experimental syntax. As Fano has said with respect to Webern's early works, they are "Short organizations materializing a 'possibility' and concluding on the eventuality of new transformations. A catalytic procedure in which certain base elements determine the disintegration and clustering of a substance which is transformed, without themselves being affected."[5]

Ezra Pound's *The Cantos,* in particular "The Pisan Cantos," also offer the reader an open structure. They are organized by the ideogrammatic method, permitting a perpetual interaction of blocks of ideas which affect each other reciprocally, producing a poetic sum whose principle of composition is gestaltian, as James Blish has observed in "Rituals on Ezra Pound."[6]

The contemporary poet—having at his disposal a lexicon which encompasses acquisitions from the symbolists to the surrealists, and in a reciprocal way, Pound's "precise definition" (the poetic word comprehended in the fight of an art of "gist and piths"), and also having before him a structural syntax, whose revolutionary perspectives have been only faintly glimpsed—cannot allow himself to be enveloped by the Byzantine nostalgia for a fallen Constantinople, nor can he, polyplike, stagnate at the margins of the morphocultural process which beckons him toward creative adventure.

Pierre Boulez, in a conversation with Décio Pignatari, manifested his lack of interest in the "perfect" or "classic," the "diamond-like," work of art, in the sense of the diamond, and stated his concept of the *open work of art* as a kind of modern baroque.

Perhaps the idea of a neobaroque, which might correspond intrinsically to the morphological necessities of contemporary artistic language, terrifies by its mere evocation those slack spirits who love the stability of conventional formulas.

But this is not a cultural reason for failing to enlist in the crew of Argos. It is, on the contrary, a prompting to do so.[7]

Translated by Jon Tolman, edited by A. S. Bessa

The Informational Temperature of the Text

Concrete poetry has been accused of impoverishing language. This rebuke has often been made in almost apocalyptic terms, with some accusers speaking of "willful castration" and others going so far as to threaten the concrete poets with a "season in Dante's Hell."

Any artistic discipline implies a voluntary restraint. In poetry, this can be seen in the terza rima of Dante or, even more pronouncedly, in the rigorous melopoetic texture of Arnaut Daniel's sestinas. In both examples, the form chosen drastically limits the poets' linguistic options. But without delving further into such generic considerations, we will attempt to develop our discussion in the objective field of modern aesthetic analysis. Information theory provides us with precise tools, free of visceral emotional appeals. In this way we can attempt to identify straightforwardly the linguistic and aesthetic characteristics which gave rise to the aforementioned censure and proceed to locate them and the poetic object which they distinguish in a wider process of formal evolution, as well as in the cultural context from which they derive their necessity and their justification.

Max Bense, in laying out his *theory of text,*[1] introduced, for aesthetic and literary purposes, B. Mandelbrot's theorem on *the informational temperature of a text.*[2] If we take 1 as the highest limit of a text's informational temperature, that temperature, in a given text, will be higher the nearer it is to

Originally published in *Revista do livro* 18, no. 5 (June 1960). The English translation by Jon Tolman appeared in *Poetics Today* (Tel Aviv, Israel) 3, no. 3 (Summer 1982): 177–87 and is reproduced here by kind permission of Duke University Press. —EDITORS

1. In such cases, for Mandelbrot, "the available words are 'well employed,' even rare words being utilized with appreciable frequencies. Low temperature, on the other hand, means that words are 'badly employed,' rare words being *extremely* rare" (30). Of the first case, Mandelbrot, basing himself on Zipf,[3] gives James Joyce, whose vocabulary is "quite varied," as the example; of the second, *the language of children*.

It is necessary, however, in order to transpose these concepts into aesthetic terms, to remember Bense's admonition: Mandelbrot "limited himself to linguistic investigations," that is, his theorem is linked to "documentary or semantic information," to "factual information," and not, therefore, to "aesthetic information" (which is "inseparable from its actual accomplishment"). However, the "statistical-linguistic dimension" he reveals can furnish us an aesthetic indicator, precisely because of what "it says with respect to the text's productive process."

First conclusion: aesthetically, the concept of informational temperature is not necessarily linked to a criterion for evaluating *good* and *bad* use of words in a text, as it appears in Mandelbrot's linguistic formulation. Rather, Mandelbrot's theorem agrees with an idea of "richness of vocabulary," since he defines the "macroscopic description of the statistics of a text" as "a measure of the potential richness of its vocabulary" (28). However, richness of vocabulary and its stylistic opposite, "simplicity of vocabulary," are not, by themselves, sure indicators of the aesthetic value of a text (see appendix at the end of this essay, section 1).

Mandelbrot himself makes this felt, permitting us to suggest a fundamental aesthetic corollary at this point, when he criticizes Zipf for having considered the Joycean example as "the best model at his disposal, because of the length and variety of his works," and for having accepted the informational temperature of Joyce's texts as being the "best estimate" of the "maximum potential number of different words" for all authors, "when, in reality, that value is due to the exceptionally great potential variety of Joyce's text" (30).

Concerning "aesthetic information," it is doubtlessly true that the degree of "informational temperature" is an element in its accomplishment, an integrating factor in the artistic process that leads to it. The relative intensity or weakness of temperature, separate from any aprioristic norm of merit or demerit, can be correctly approached only when it is considered as a function of the specific creative process to which it contributes. Therefore, it will be factors of an aesthetic order, and not necessarily those of an exclusively linguistic-statistical order, which will involve the need for a higher or lower proportion, a maximum or minimum, in the informational temperature of a given artistic text, such as a poem or a piece of prose. There is, distinct from the linguistic sense, a self-sustaining concept of the "informational temperature of an aesthetic text," decidedly linked to the evolution of forms on the creative plane.

And thus we are ready to proceed to the second phase of our study. As an element of contact between both orders of ideas, we will use some remarks of G. A. Miller,[4] another linguist, who in passing touches on problems which can be applied to aesthetics. Miller focuses on Basic English,[5] comparing it with the language of James Joyce. Ogden's Basic English, according to Miller, is "an attempt to take advantage of the statistical aspects of language," reducing English to "850 lexical units . . . carefully chosen so that, through combinations, they could be made the equivalent of a much larger vocabulary. . . . By reducing the number of word types to 850 lexical units the potential size of the audience is greatly increased." This, of course, makes possible rapid, easily assimilated communication. Ogden himself defines the process: "A reduction may be effected in the number of words that need to be used; i.e., how a given field of reference may be covered with the greatest economy. . . . What is really required is, in fact, a scientifically selected vocabulary minimum; and it is this selection that Basic claims to provide." As Miller points out, however, "there has been an artistic and scientific swing to the opposite direction. The desire for verbal diversification in literature is typified by James Joyce." These two aspects of language usage are synthesized by Miller in the following terms: "An increase in the size of the vocabulary is balanced by decrease in the size of the audience. A decrease in vocabulary is balanced by an increased audience. There seems to be no simple way to have a large vocabulary and a large audience at the same time."[6] Evidently, considered in relation to the vocabulary potential of English, Basic English will exhibit, as compared to the texts of Joyce, an extremely low "informational temperature" in Mandelbrot's sense (see appendix, section 2).

Moving on to "aesthetic information" and to the "artistic process" which makes it possible, it can be said that the notion of a "high informational temperature of the text" is linked to something like a craftsman's manipulation of poetry and prose. In such a procedure, the creative artist exhausts the possibilities of diversification and nuance in his or her linguistic arsenal, holding redundancy to a minimum and elevating to the maximum the number of syntactic-semantic options. Joyce in English literature and Guimarães Rosa in Brazilian literature exemplify that artistic process, which seems in itself, in each work—or more exactly in the unified work *in progress*—to tend toward the closing of a whole cycle in the craft of verbal invention, putting it at the same time into crisis. The linguistic artifacts of both authors (Joyce's more than Rosa's) acquire a unique quality of highly personal workmanship through the elaborate handling of words and perfectionist refinement of linguistic textures. This is merely a stylistic observation and is in no way an attempt to play down the exceptional importance of these authors in the redimensioning of their respective literatures. Both were instrumental in staking out the limits of a stage of craftsmanship, well captured by Harry Levin: "The novel to end all novels."[7] This statement, which critically summarizes the position of Joyce's work, can also well characterize the correlative if less extreme position that Guimarães Rosa has come to assume in Brazilian literature.

Concrete poetry is included in a different historical and cultural dimension. Its point of departure is the "crisis of verse" generated at the end of the last [nineteenth] century by Mallarmé's "Un coup de dés" ["A Throw of the Dice"]. It responds to a notion of literature not as *craftsmanship* but, so to speak, as an *industrial* process. Its product is a prototype, not the typical handiwork of individual artistry. It tends toward a minimal, simplified language, increasingly objectified and, for that reason, easily and quickly communicated. This presumes that the semantic reactions of the audience have been correctly conditioned toward structure instead of "swarms of inarticulate feelings." Its program is "the least common denominator" of language, or (paraphrasing Ogden) of an "artistically selected vocabulary minimum" (see appendix, section 3). In this way it coincides with the sense of a progressively technical civilization within which it is postulated.[8] That is why it rejects the airs and graces of craftsmanship—in spite of the seriousness with which it considers the artisan's contribution to the stockpile of extant forms—from the *art of verse* to the elaborate diversification of vocabulary in prose.[9] It has recourse in its turn to factors of proximity and likeness on the graphic-gestaltic plane, to elements of recurrence and redundancy on the semantic and rhythmic plane, to a visual-ideogrammatic syntax (when not merely "combinatory") for controlling the flux of signs and rationalizing the sensible materials of a composition. This is how it limits *entropy* (the tendency to dispersion, to disorder, to the maximum informational potential of a system), fixing the informational temperature at the minimum necessary to obtain the aesthetic achievement of each poem undertaken (see appendix, section 4).

A counterpart of the same problem is the fact that in detail, in their minuteness, both Joyce and Guimarães Rosa, whose extensively crafted macrocosms involve microcosms which are intensively wrought and reduced to essences or chains of essences, are much closer to concrete poetry than the whole literature of dreamy, hedonistic alienation, the paradigm of which is surrealism. It is impossible to discern in surrealism any constructivist organization, any semantic system after the manner of the interconnected "complexes of meaning" which Adelheid Obradovic[10] recognizes in Joyce's art, for example, when comparing it with the destructive avant-gardes of this [the twentieth] century's beginnings.

It is not by chance that Joyce's portmanteau word "silvamoonlake" can be considered a concrete unit of composition, given that it is possible at all times to individualize series of concretions, perfectly defined as such, in his verbal cosmology:

> With Kiss. Kiss Criss. Cross Criss. Kiss Cross.
> Undo lives' end. (*Finnegans Wake*)

The same can be said of Guimarães Rosa: "Os urubus—os, os, os" ["The vultures—the, the, the"].*

At this point the apparent "impoverishment of language"—in reality, reduction and simplification of vocabulary within a syntax, not of the logical-discursive kind but of the analogical-visual type—which some thought to see in *concrete poetry,* comes to be correctly redefined. This so-called impoverishment, emptied of the naive pejorative connotations attributed to it only in the heat of argument or in the levity of a less-than-rigorous observation, comes to assume, analytically and aesthetically, the character of a true "stylistic principle." As such, it is verifiable as a device and worthy—in a successfully achieved concrete poem—to be considered an integrating factor in its generative process. The question thereby is placed in a historical and cultural context, which, notwithstanding the schematic way it has been outlined here, we can leave at this point as an all instigating subject for the

---

* From the short story "Cara de bronze" ["Bronze Face"] in *Corpo de baile* [*Corps de Ballet*]. This literal translation ignores the vowel play in the Portuguese original, which renders it like Joyce's verbal games. In phonetic transcription: uz urubuz uz uz uz. —TRANSLATOR

creative mind (especially for the young generation of poets which still has not been contaminated by petrifying routines). Commitment to past artistic experience proves fruitful only when it leads to the disclosure of the vectorial field of a new sensibility, contemporaneously valid and active.

Appendix: Parallel Themes

1—Verbal opulence alone cannot be equated with true artistic achievement. This is the case of Coelho Neto, whose vocabulary is calculated at around 20,000 words.* Even if one wanted to see in him a forerunner in the formal handling of texts, the truth is that his notion of stylistic richness was almost always quantitative and not qualitative (re-evaluative). His erudite use of lexical rarities, archaisms, Lusitanisms, Orientalisms, Latinisms, and so on for their own sake was purely ornamental, like a decorative and cumulative tapestry reminiscent of the worst Flaubert. (The Flaubert we have in mind here is not the defender of *le mot juste*, to whom Pound traces the whole "colloquial-ironic" line of French symbolism—Laforgue, etc.— but the exoticist of *Salammbô*.) That is why he was debunked by the Brazilian modernists (1922) and, symptomatically, in Oswald de Andrade's preface to *Seraphim Grosse Pointe* (1933), a book which represents a landmark of verbal invention, of qualitative lexical and syntactic manipulation in Portuguese. On the other hand, it is to the verbal *magrezza* of Machado de Assis, whose "informational temperature" would be comparatively low (from Mandelbrot's linguistic point of view), that we owe, in Brazilian literature, the finest examples of textual structuring prior to modernism. We cite the extreme examples of chapters 55 and 139 in *Epitaph of a Small Winner* where punctuation marks alone substitute for words in the best Sternian tradition, conveying a psychological situation perfectly handled from an aesthetic point of view.

2—Claude Shannon observes that "two extremes of redundancy in English prose are represented by Basic English and by James Joyce's *Finnegans Wake*. The Basic English vocabulary is limited to 850 words and the redundancy is very high. [. . .] Joyce on the other hand enlarges the vocabulary and is alleged to achieve compression of semantic content."[11] In Joyce, therefore, redundancy would be minimal. A curious sample of these two directions of English can be studied by means of the parallel between a frag-

---

* Coelho Neto, a writer from the northern Brazilian state of Maranhão, famous for his luxuriant style, was quite popular in the premodernist era. —TRANSLATOR

ment of "Anna Livia Plurabelle" and its version in Basic English by Ogden.[12] One should keep in mind, however, in order not to distort the terms of this comparison between the "simplest and most complex English, Mr. Ogden's language of strict denotation and Joyce's language of extreme connotation,"[13] that while the Joycean text strives for "aesthetic information" and toward "aesthetic achievement," Ogden's Basic English was conceived as an instrument for conversation and practical communication.

3—The aesthetic possibilities of a method of reducing vocabulary essentials, as developed by Ogden for communicative purposes, are hinted at by Ezra Pound, preoccupied as always with his slogan program *dichten: condensare,* in his preface to Fenollosa's *Chinese Written Character.*[14] There, Pound attempts to offer a valid contribution to "basic English" by means of the ideogram. The principle of verbification peculiar to written Chinese is emphasized:

> Many of the nouns in the Ogden list of 850 words could very well serve as verbs, thereby giving considerably greater force to that brief vocabulary. [. . .] I suggest also that the limited gamut of actions included by Ogden in this essential vocabulary might be considered almost a declension of a yet briefer set of main root possibilities.[15]

Evidently, a "basic poetry" has its lexical potential not as a function of a reduction in language to facilitate semantic communication but as a function of the communication of a poetic product for the accomplishment of which this basic concision is a structural principle. Its lexicon, therefore, will be potentially greater, since it is not limited exclusively by a standard of linguistic (denotative) utility, but by a principle of aesthetic functionality, varying from poem to poem, according to the problem to be solved. Pound's *Cantos,* apart from the ideogrammatic method of composition, are included in the craftsman's cycle of creativity and thus offer a high "informational temperature" or, more exactly, a high "referential temperature." (Its richness is less due to lexical diversification than to referential complexes—to facts, events, characters, cultural contexts, implying a corresponding continuous variation and incorporation in style, from the Dantesque mode to colloquial American, from Provençal cantabile to the archaic English of *The Seafarer,* etc.) Pound, however, does come to speak of a "basic canto": "I propose starting a nice lively heresy, to effek, that gimme 50 more words, and I can make Basic into a real licherary and muledrivin' language, capable of blown Freud to hell and getting' a team from Soap Gulch over the Hogback. You watch ole EZ do a basic Canto."[16]

This "basic Canto" is implicit in the very ideogrammatic macrostructure of *The Cantos,* where discursive language (from which Pound has not completely dissociated himself) is criticized. As the work progresses, however, along with a stylistic plurality, which aspires to monumental craftsmanship, there occurs a parallel fragmentation of discourse. The device of ideogrammatic montage invades the microstructure of the composition and—beginning with the Pisan Cantos—it can be said that the tension for the "basic Cantos" constantly shows up in details:

2 on 2

what's the name of that bastard? D'Arezzo, Gui d'Arezzo 黃
notation

       3 on 3

     chiacchierona   the yellow bird   鳥

  to rest   3 months in bottle
by the two breasts of Tellus   止

                (auctor)

Or:

      Hot   hole   hep   cat

Or:

      8th day of September
        f   f
    d
     g
    write the birds in their treble scale
    Terreus! Terreus.

Or even (from *Rock - Drill):*

They who are skilled in fire

    shall read   旦   tan the dawn.

Or:

And from far
  il tremolar della marina
   chh   chh
the pebbles turn with the wave
     chh   ch'u

    The Cantos, as a San Francisco practitioner of oral poetry once observed (by way of censure), "end as a complete palimpsest of ideographs."[17]

    4—It is necessary to clarify (Bense mentions it only once) that Mandelbrot used Shannon and Weaver's concepts of *information* and *entropy* in developing his theorem of "the informational temperature" of the text: "Let us clarify, therefore, that when we speak of *information* it will always be in Shannon's sense of the word, which is precise because extremely limited" (12). In Shannon's theory of information, which is "normative, prescribing how to encode a message, given certain desires and constraints typical of a telegraphic situation," information is "a measure of one's freedom of choice when one selects a message" (9). In that theory, always related to an *information source, entropy* is a "measure of information": "The quantity which uniquely meets the natural requirements that one sets up for 'information' turns out to be exactly that which is known in thermodynamics as entropy" (12). That is to say, the expression *entropy* is related to "the amount of freedom of choice we have in constructing messages" (13), just as "in the physical sciences, the entropy associated with a situation is a measure of the degree of randomness, or of 'shuffledness' if you will, in the situation" (12). Entropy always grows, physical systems tend to become increasingly disorganized. Thus, Weaver adds that for a communication source one can say, just as he would also say it of a thermodynamic ensemble: "This situation is highly organized, it is not characterized by a large degree of randomness or of choice—that is to say, the information (or the entropy) is low" (13). It is in that sense, of *maximum de l'information,* that Mandelbrot uses the term "entropy." We can therefore conclude that a "high informational temperature" means a high degree of chance, and of *entropy.* On the other hand, Wiener[18] sees the informative content of a system as a measure of its degree of organization, and *entropy* as a measure of disorganization, one being the opposite of the other. Thus *informative content* is "essentially a *negative entropy,*" while processes leading to a loss of information are strictly analogous to those in which entropy is increased. In his "Informational

Aesthetics,"[19] Bense uses "information" and "entropy" to some extent in Wiener's sense of the terms. The first is defined as a measure of the "degree of order," characterizing "aesthetic cosmo-processes," where there is an "exceptional, selected distribution of elements," and the second measures the "degree of disorder," characteristic of "physical cosmo-processes." With relation to that aesthetic application, based on cybernetic nomenclature, it seems valid to say that if the limitation of the "informational maximum" in the production of a text (concrete poem) lowers the "informational temperature" in Shannon's sense (freedom of choice, chance, in relation to the lexical potential of language), it also diminishes *entropy* and consequently, in Wiener's sense of the term, increases the *organization,* the *negative entropy,* the *informative content* of the system. It is true that Bense in other essays resorts to Shannon's concept of *information,* which, as has been seen, is formulated from a different point of view from that of cybernetics. As, for example, when he studies the principle of *repetition* in the work of Gertrude Stein. There, Bense defines repetition with the term "redundancy" as "reduction in the total of aesthetic information in the process of its achievement," by means of which "the primitive originality also wanes," making it "thus possible to develop this aesthetic information as a principle of style."[20] The following text will serve as a sample of the process:

> Money is what words are.
> Words are what money is.
> Is money what words are.
> Are words what money is.

In this case, it is evident that rather than speaking of "a reduction in aesthetic information," it would be better to speak of a reduction in "informational temperature," à la Mandelbrot via Shannon, linked to the linguistic (semantic) idea of "richness of vocabulary." As Bense himself indicated in another text: "We cannot refrain from observing that concrete painting offers, in reality, little semantic information, but nevertheless relatively high values of aesthetic information."[21] This passage seems to support our proposition that there is a concept of "aesthetic informational temperature" (high or low) different from "linguistic or semantic informational temperature" (high or low). This concept can be readily applied to Stein's "exhibit," one of her best texts, and one which is quite close in its structural articulation to the "combinatory technique" of Eugen Gomringer's "constellations."[22]

worte sind schatten
schatten werden worte
worte sind spiele
spiele werden worte
sind schatten worte
werden worte spiele
sind spiele worte
werden worte schatten
sind worte schatten
werden spiele worte
sind worte spiele
werden schatten worte

words are shadows
shadows become words
words are games
games become words
are shadows words
do words become games
are games words
do words become shadows
are words shadows
do games become words
are words games
do shadows become words

The same concept may also be applied as a general rule to *concrete poetry*. If aesthetic information is "information about structure," "informative content" being the structure itself, the richer the former, the richer will the latter be in the sense of innovation, of inventiveness. Therefore, concrete art by reducing the work "to the aesthetically essential, to the thematics of signs," manifests in a particularly clear way the distinctive feature of aesthetic information. The selection of a structure, the choice among "x number of" structural possibilities of that one which best renders the particular problem of the poem, will be in the concrete work the Mallarméan moment of creation. This moment organizes and defines, in the sense of an irreversible decision, the raw materials of sensibility, that "torsion du concerté sur l'instant" [twisting of the concerted upon the instantaneous], in the words of the French composer Michel Fano. The dialectical poles of this decisive moment are reason and chance, intelligence and intuition, rigor and liberty. It implies not an "abolition" but a *control,* an integration of chance in the compositional process. "The most lucid intellectual work for the clearest intuition."[23] It is there that the problem of originality is posited. It will no longer be described in terms of a thematics of content but as a *thematics of structure.* (Something altogether different, it must be once again emphasized, is that concrete poets in no way renounce the content of words. The semantic charges of the words selected are as important a working material as their sound or their graphic shape and converge with them toward the articulation of the desired structure.) It will no longer be pertinent, therefore, to speak of a "richness of vocabulary" but of a *richness of structure* which will coincide, in *concrete poetry,* without programmatic contradiction, with the most rigorous simplification and lexical transparency. In that sense, one last observation of Max Bense's seems to us to be meaningful, and we transfer it *mutatis mutandis* to concrete poetry: "In presenting instruments of perception, eternal objects of that perception[24] such as colors themselves, the measure of information and the measure of redundancy converge into a singular conjunction: Both contribute to perception, to presentification. In concrete painting *information* and *redundancy* manifest themselves as mutually integrative, complementary evidence of a single aesthetic fact."[25]

Translated by Jon Tolman, edited by A. S. Bessa

Concrete Poetry–Language–Communication

The Aristotelian principle of identity, according to Alfred Korzybski, "tends to obscure the difference between words and things." When we say, for instance, "this is a pencil," we tend to identify the object with its verbal expression; but Korzybski affirms that "as words are not the objects that they represent, the structure, and only the structure, becomes the exclusive link connecting our verbal processes to empirical facts."[1] Hence the transformations that have occurred in the traditional practice of thinking; the cosmic vision that is now offered to us by the current state of science demands an analogous revolution in the structure of language, one that would enable language to adapt itself to the description of the world of objects. In place of the metaphysical, prescientific, animistic dualism that the traditional linguistic structure insists on fomenting, and which obscures and erases functional relations—for instance, the concepts of space and time separated in an autarchic way—a linguistic structure closer to reality would give way to the Joycean notion of "spacetime."[2] In order to renew language, Korzybski proposes a "mathematical method": "systems of propositional functions, deliberately emptied out of any content, that would then be receptive to any content."[3]

These formulations present a fascinating perspective when put in the context of the problematics of concrete poetry. The concrete poem puts in

Originally published in the *Suplemento dominical do "Jornal do Brasil"* (Rio de Janeiro), 28 April 1957 and 5 May 1957. Republished in various forms, most recently in Augusto de Campos, Décio Pignatari, and Haroldo de Campos, *Teoria da poesia concreta* (*Textos críticos e manifestos, 1950–60*) (São Paulo: Brasiliense, 1987). —EDITORS

check the logical structure of traditional discursive language, since it finds in it a barrier to accessing the world of objects. The poet's position is nevertheless fundamentally different from that of the semanticist. The former envisions a communication of forms; the latter aims to communicate content. Yet they both want to communicate in the most direct and efficient manner, and hence they reject structures that are unable to achieve this level of efficiency.

The *kulturmorphologie* produced in the last sixty years, leaning toward a synthetic-ideogrammatic compositional technique, has provided the poet with a linguistic instrument closer to the real structure of things and has placed him face-to-face with the modern creations of scientific thought. The concrete poem, which establishes an entire field of optical, acoustic, and signifying relations through its spatiotemporal structure, is an entity that carries an isomorphic link with the "total world of objective actuality," which, according to Trigant Burrow, is denied to modern man from his early education, "enveloped within a field of vicarious symbols."[4]

By searching for an instrument capable of bringing language closer to things—a language superior to that of verbal-discursive poetry, enough to encompass a spatial (visual) as well as temporal structure—concrete poetry does not aim at a faithful description of objects.[5] Its scope is not to develop a system of signs structurally apt to transmit, without deformations, a vision of the world rectified by modern scientific knowledge. Its aim is to put this rich and flexible instrument of intellectual work—ductile, close to the real form of things—at the service of an unexpected goal: the creation of its own object. For the first time, it no longer matters if a word is not a given object, since, in reality, it will always be, in the special domain of the poem, the object given. Hence, a language that is able to communicate the world of things in a quick, clear, and efficient way, exchanging it for structurally isomorphic systems of signs, opens an arsenal of possibilities to a new venture: to create, out of its own material, a new form, or rather, an entire parallel world of things—the poem. This flux of linguistic possibilities back to themselves—now powerfully renewed—mirrors and explains the special verbal process that is unleashed in the poetic field. If, for a moment, the paths of the language scientist and of the artist become entangled, this reflux also makes evident how they soon disentangle. A description of these processes is made necessary, succinct as it will be in this essay, for a basic clarification of how they operate in one's mind.

Commenting on Korzybski's call for the development of, "by the wider application of physical-mathematical methods, new languages of physic-mathematical kind which would correspond in structure with the structure of human behavior, individual and social," Hayakawa notes that "there are two fields in which this program began to be realized: mathematical biology and cybernetics."[6] Olivier Bloodstein, addressing the same problem, adds that, like mathematics, modern art is a "non-Aristotelian system."[7]

If we apply these concepts to concrete poetry, we will notice that it partakes of the same form of linguistic evaluation in a very radical way. The concrete poem, to use Gomringer's notion of "constellation," "is a reality in itself, and not a poem about something or other." Since it is not linked to the communication of contents and uses the word (sound, visual form, fixed concepts) as compositional material rather than a vehicle of interpretation of the objective world, its structure is its true content. Only in the historical and cultural fields we find a relationship between the poem-object (concrete) and a content exterior to it, even though this relationship will be once again structural. Hence, the physiognomy of our era is to be found rather in structures prone to content which are related to the content-structure of the concrete poem. Not in this or that object, nor in one or another subjective feeling rescued from the poet's inner world or the world outside, despite the fact that semantic reactions that often occur through the manipulation of words, will leave traces in the poem, which the reader will hang on to as a lifesaver. Certainly, these traces of content do exist in an art such as poetry, whose instrument—the word—unlike color or sound, cannot be treated as an entirely neutral element but rather carries an immediate cluster of meanings.

Concrete poetry's function is not, as one would imagine, to empty the word of its charge of content but rather to utilize this charge as working material in equal conditions with all other material that is available to it. The word-element is used in its entirety and not mutilated through the unilateral reduction to descriptive music (*Léttrisme*) or to decorative pictography (*Calligrammes*). The simple act of tossing on paper the word *terra* (earth, hearth) could denote an entire georgic. What the reader of a concrete poem needs to know is that a given connotation is valid (and even unavoidable) in an exclusively material plane, as long as it reinforces and corroborates the other elements that are being manipulated; as long as it participates with its particular effects in the content-structure which constitutes the poem. Any other cathartic *démarrage,* or subjectivist detour, is foreign to the poem and happens because of the tendency toward nomenclature—that is, the exchange of objects by vague nominative labels—so well identified by Hayakawa in this anecdote:

A trivial but revealing instance of this adjustment to names occurred in my own home recently, where I have hanging on the wall an abstract painting by the late László Moholy-Nagy. A woman who was visiting us couldn't keep her mind on the conversation; she kept turning to stare at the painting. Apparently it was disturbing her a great deal. Finally, she walked up to it, found a tiny typewritten label on the frame saying, "Space Modulator, 1941." "Space modulator, is it?" she said. "Isn't that nice!" She sat down, much relieved. She never even glanced at it again after that.[8]

If we go back to the word "terra," it will provide an excellent test for the understanding of the special kind of language operation that occurs in the concrete poem and how the question of content is expressed therein. Dadaism, according to Gide, strove to dissociate verb from thought by displaying words side by side without any connection whatsoever, each word an island of pure tone that would eventually resonate with other tones. This is the opposite of the concrete poet's procedure, for whom the poem is a question of relations. In "terra," Décio Pignatari has taken on the challenge of constructing a poem composed basically of a single word, an experiment that echoes Pierre Boulez's "Étude sur un son" ["Study on a Sound"], a work mentioned by Pierre Schaeffer in *À la recherche d'une musique concrète* [*In Search of a Concrete Music*], p. 197. The word *terra* would be the generator of the relational complex that embodies the poem:

```
ra terra ter
rat erra ter
rate rra ter
rater ra ter
raterr a ter
raterra terr
araterra ter
raraterra te
rraraterra t
erraraterra
terraraterra
```

"terra—erra—ara terra—rara terra—erra ara terra—terra ara terra" (earth/hearth—err—tend the earth—rare earth—err tend the earth—earth tends earth): these are the thematic elements that originate from this nucleus, besides the expression "terra a terra" (down to earth), that follow throughout like a virtual phonetic chorus.

From cybernetics, Pignatari borrowed the process of "feedback" as a structural device for the poem. W. Sluckin writes in *Minds and Machines:*

The machines which perhaps impress us most are not those which are merely capable of performing complex calculations, but rather the ones that work in a manner reminiscent in some striking way of animal or human behavior. All such machines incorporate some form of automatic regulation, or as it tends to be nowadays called automatic control. This is achieved by a mechanism, which in most cases is referred to as a servomechanism. It operates in such a way that it regulates the performance of the machine at every moment according to the result produced by the machine's performance immediately before. In other words, the output of the machine is made to control its operation with a view to not allowing the output at any time to exceed or to be less than a certain value. . . . Any arrangement employing negative feedback, whether known as servomechanism or not, may be regarded as "error-actuated" and "self-correcting" (or "error-compensating"). This is because it operates when the output deviates from a required level, or is *in error* with respect to it; the operation of the negative feedback compensates the error, correcting the output.[9]

In the seventh member-line of the poem "terra"—which up to this point had been composed solely of this word, articulating and interrupting itself, as in the running of a teletype band or in the running words on an LED—there is the sudden introduction of a new element generated by its very initial nucleus: the syllable *ra* which forms *ara* when it connects with the discarded *a* of the word *terr* in the preceding member-line; this new element (which stands as an *error* in relation to the expectation of the reader, who would simply expect the continuous formation of the word *terra* and not the duplication of its final syllable) is *memorized* by the poem and begins to control its subsequent role, improving it and unleashing another element, apparently unexpected, but nevertheless required by the process itself—*rara* (rare)—until it reaches the climax—*terraterra*—which balances the poem's field of action as a necessary and deliberately pursued goal. This structure regulated by feedback is corroborated by the thematic elements in the most efficient manner: the word *erra* (to err), already produced in the poem's second line, and which is constantly insinuating itself in the poem's body, makes explicit the structure-content: at once the operation of the poem, the poet's "olhar de errata" (errata eye),[10] who rights (writes) through wrongs or who transforms his errors into profit in the semantic "field" produced by him; and—at once, we said—the very structure isomorphically produced, ideoform. The error, as we have seen earlier, at the verbal and process level, expresses the autocorrection to which the poem subjects itself, coerced by the will for structure with which the poet forged his working method. Another correlated topic of cybernetics that should here be addressed: the method of solving problems through "trial and error," which is also of interest to Gestalt psychologists. The "trial and error" behavior, according to Sluckin, can be described in terms of "negative feedback."

> The solution of the problem may be regarded as the creature's immediate goal or equilibrium level. Information as to the distance from the goal is fed back to the center of control. It is—it may be said—this stream of information which controls the creature's steady movement towards the goal.[11]

This is the system that explains the deciphering mechanisms of labyrinths built in the last few years [mid-1950s] by Shannon, I. P. Howard, and J. A. Deutsch. The poem *terra* also deciphers itself, concretely.

But not only that. The other thematic elements are also vectors that compose the content-structure: the poem that generates itself, the active error—*errar arar* (to err, to plow)—as an earth (hearth) that cultivates itself (*terra ara terra*), a rare earth (*rara terra*) and yet an operation so *down to earth* (*terra a terra*), so elemental, so characteristic of the human condition as the act of man plowing the land. A concrete painting holds a certain *chromatic number* that controls, quantitatively and qualitatively, the array of colors required for the solution of the particular problem it sets to resolve; the concrete poem also holds its *thematic number:* the charges of content of the words, taken from the point of view of material, allow only a certain number of meaningful implications, exactly those that act as the poem's structural vectors and that participate definitively in its gestalt. No ornaments nor any effect of subjective pyrotechnics.

At this point, it is necessary to fundamentally distinguish concrete poetry from surrealism. The latter, facing the barrier of traditional logic, did not try to develop a language that would go beyond it; on the contrary, it established its "headquarters" on the *maudit* side of logical-discursive language where are produced admirable propositions such as "A ring-tailed baboon is not a constitutional assembly."[12] Bréton's "white haired revolver" rules over an absurd reign that is unleashed amid the language ordained by the Aristotelian system, when the latter is taken, as a process, to its last consequences. It's the reign of paradox, nonsense, whose laws are the "confusion of levels of abstractions." Surrealism, although voicing against logic, is its bastard son. Hayakawa (on Korzybski):

> Traditional Aristotelian language structure and accompanying semantic reactions tend to ignore a fundamental fact of the functioning of the human nervous system, namely, that we abstract at an indefinite number of levels—by abstracting from abstractions, by abstracting from abstractions of abstractions, etc. In mathematics, the procedure of symbol manipulation is such that, should a confusion of orders of abstraction occur, the system will at once make the confusion evident by exhibiting a contradiction. The efficiency of mathematics in this respect is shown by the way in which many traditional logical paradoxes, in which shifts of orders of abstraction are concealed by everyday language, are simply solved by mathematical methods.[13]

Concrete poetry—which, like mathematics, is a non-Aristotelian system of language—also has, in its *thematic number,* a control instrument that sorts and eliminates elements that would clash with its rigorous structure. Hence, in "terra," words such as the noun *era* or the interjection *arre* (gosh!), for instance, would have been rejected as strange bodies by the regulation device of the poem's content-structure, although they could apparently be part of its phonetic structure. The concrete poem rejects traditional logic and its crippled brother, "psychic automatism": logic, as Fenollosa pointed out, "has abused the language which they left to her mercy. Poetry agrees with science and not with logic."[14]

The poem "terra" is intrinsically connected to its structure both graphically as well as visually. The generation of the poem—beginning with the syllable *ra,* which immediately forms *terra* and goes on to take out of this nucleus the word *erra* (err)—creates in the spatial field a movement all its own, supported by elements of proximity and similarity: (1) the section which decreases from *terra* until *a* (upper center in triangle-rectangle) connects to another rectangle-triangle through one of the vertices, which decreases from *terr* until *t;* (2) on the upper left section of the poem, an orthogonal column formed by the reiteration of the element *ter;* (3) finally, a larger triangle-rectangle, including in its area the other elements already described, with the smaller base in *terra ter* and one of the vertices in *t.*

Another great triangular section with inverse orientation—with the smaller base in *terraterra* and one of the vertices in *ra* (truncated)—is visible, in opposition to the other by the square angle; inside, delimited by a gap that runs between the lines of *aa* and *tt,* interact, confronted, a truncated triangle (*ra* to *terrara*), a rectangle (the orthogonal column formed by the element *ra* repeated six times) and a trapeze (the sides delimited by the line of *tt,* by *terra* in the eleventh line and by a straight line that goes from *t* to *a* forming the larger base of the trapeze); by its turn, the trapeze generates visually a small triangle rectangle (apex in *t,* smaller base in *terr*) and a parallelogram (element *terra* repeated six times). The whiteness of the paper acts on the thin gap already mentioned as well as on the larger gaps (one, separating the two larger triangles in opposition to each other; another, the upper center triangular sector—*terra* until *a*—from the column of elements *ter*). A large rectangle frames the poem's general area and levels the game. The conflicting directions of the main triangular elements; the perceptual production of shapes onto other forms; the two parallel gaps in space, and the other perpendicular two, whose intersection creates a kind of visual flexion toward reading; the sections that dwindle from word to letter; all that imposes a graphic-spatial-temporal structure to the poem, whose verbal flux has suddenly been altered, rectified, and conducted to its profit/climax through feedback, through autocorrective error. A passage from the physiognomic (white gaps = furrows in the cultivated land) to the isomorphic (visual structure = verbal structure). It should be added that the analytical minutia here employed to didactically describe a process do not imply a greater difficulty in the field of perception, where the eye's geometry simply and naturally rules over the senses.

A similar phenomenon happens at the acoustic level. The poem's interior dialectics, the cuts and coagulation of phonetic elements—from the word-source *terra,* producing *erra, rara, ara*—become one with the desired content-structure and demand elocution (the interplay of timbre, pauses, etc.), a human voice that would emphasize, reflect, through a creative vocalization, its proper movement. Only those who are not used to the activating techniques for voice in modern music (Schönberg's use of the *Sprechgesang* in "Pierrot Lunaire" and "Ode to Napoleon," for instance) could question the aural effect of a concrete poem. Even a plain silent reading will be richer the closer it gets to the effects of such vocalization.

We should also briefly consider the opinion of a critic from São Paulo,[15] for whom the poetry of E. E. Cummings, fundamental to the concretist movement, is "impossible to be heard" for being predominantly visual. It is an opinion contrary to Susanne Langer's, who, in studying the role of sound in poetry, wrote: "There is poetry that profits by, or even demands, actual speech (E. E. Cummings, for instance, gains tremendously by being read aloud)."[16]

Since "terra" is not a georgic, and it narrates nothing that could appease an imagination prone to discourses on nature or pastoral eclogues, its content, such as a concrete painting, is also its structure. This structure will find a structural connection, at the historical and cultural level, to a problem that is exterior to itself—cybernetics' idea of feedback—integrated to the cosmic vision of modern man. The local contents of words and sequences of words required by the *thematic number* of "terra" are connected and adapted to the poem's structure to such a degree that they will not satisfy the demand for catharsis that would eventually overcome certain readers. Learning how to see and hear structures will thus be the key to the understanding of concrete poetry.

But for a scholar of general semantics like Bloodstein, modern art is a non-Aristotelian system precisely because it considers structure, relations, and order the very content of art. This implies, obviously, in a revision of the reader's habitual semantic reactions, which are accustomed to looking in the poem for objects other than its object, to making the artwork a pretext for meta-artistic divagations. Korzybski (quoted by Oliver Bloodstein): "Any fundamentally new system involves new semantic reactions; and this is the main difficulty which besets us when we try to master a new system. We must re-educate, or change, our older semantic reactions."[17] If this is a valid claim for any new language system, it will impose itself more forcefully in regard to concrete poetry, where the concern with structure is not transitive (i.e., designed to convey another structure—that of reality—such as in other non-Aristotelian systems) but self-sufficient, depleting itself in its own realization. It is here where the problem of communication lies.

It has been wrongly suggested that the concrete poets of São Paulo believe that "the speed with which a work of art acts on a spectator decides its validity and efficacy as a work of art."[18] What we have affirmed, and is self-evident, is that the concrete poem has the virtue of putting into effect an immediate form of communication. A communication of forms, of structures, not of verbal contents. As a matter of fact, supported by verbivocovisual elements that integrate in structural consonance, the concrete poem attacks, on all sides and at once, the perceptive field of the reader who is seeking in it what it has to offer: a structure-content.

Thus, the concrete poem, by regarding the word as an object, accomplishes the feat of bringing to the domain of poetic communication the virtual possibilities of nonverbal communication without losing any of the peculiarities of the word. In other words, since a concrete poem communicates its structure, the content charges of the words being manipulated are controlled by the thematic number for the sake of the structure, and for that reason, they appeal to the reader's sense of nonverbal understanding.[19] Jurgen Ruesch and Weldo Kees establish the following distinction between verbal and nonverbal communication: The former is based on a codification of information of the digital kind, whose main examples are the phonetic alphabet and the numeric system ("information transmitted through such a system is obviously coded through various combinations of letters or digits"); the latter uses analogical codification ("various kinds of actions, pictures, or material objects represent analogic types of denotation"). And they add:

> In terms of codification, "digital" contrasts with "analogical"; in language terms, "discursive" contrasts with "non-discursive." Discursive language depends upon logic, made up of a set of artificial rules that have been agreed upon, expressed in verbal terms about a circumscribed kind of work. Logic dispenses with analogical codification altogether, in spite of the fact that most of our thinking and communication is dependent upon the nonverbal as well as the verbal.[20]

By rejecting the logical discursive order and opening itself to the possibilities of the ideogramic method of composition, concrete poetry sets out to create with digits, with the phonetic system, a nondiscursive linguistic area that shares the advantages of nonverbal communication (greater proximity to the object, preservation of the continuity of action and perception), without mutilating its instrument—the word—whose special power to express abstractions, to communicate interpolations and extrapolations, and to frame wide-ranging aspects of diverse events and ideas in comprehensive terms are not rejected but rather used toward the creation of a total communication. The notion of metacommunication explains the relations between verbal and nonverbal codification; any message can be considered as having two aspects: the proposition itself and the explanations pertinent to its interpretation. The nature of interpersonal communication requires that both parts coincide in time, and that can only be attained through another means. Thus, when a proposition is verbally phrased, one tends to give nonverbal instructions. The effect is similar to the arrangement of a musical composition for two instruments, where the voices move independently in different directions, modifying and supplementing each other, and yet integrated in one functional and organic unity. A phenomenon akin to metacommunication occurs within a concrete poem: the main difference resides in the fact that the concrete poem does not communicate an outer message and content, but rather it uses these resources to communicate forms, to create and corroborate, verbivocovisually, a content-structure.

Corollary observations to the problems discussed earlier: the concrete poet's task will be the creation of forms, the production of artistic content-structures whose material is the word. Value of this task: to place the poem in correspondence with a series of speculations taking place in the science and philosophy of our times. Consequence of this task: the immediate stimulation that a concrete poem can bring to the clarification of mental habits, to the creation of new semantic reactions that stir the reader's perception of the real structure of everyday communication and prepare him for non-Aristotelian systems of communication;[21] the appeal to the non-verbal level of communication makes the mind extremely sensitive to the relationship between words and things, warning us against the "distortions of meaning" generated by the manipulation of verbal symbols toward abstraction, teaching us to use words in a scrupulous way and with a sense of integrity. At this juncture, Mallarmé's and Pound's mottoes complement each other: "Donner un sens plus pur aux mots de la tribu" / "Artists are the antennae of the race."

The production of content-structures poses questions that are not exhausted in the poem itself. New tendencies in the visual arts instigated a new world of forms in the field of industrial production (Bauhaus). The concrete poem instigates a new kind of typography and propaganda and even a new kind of journalism, besides other possible applications (TV, cinema, etc). Here is a cogitation to be renewed: Mayakovsky's plight for a propaganda that would also be poetry of the highest quality. Another constant source will be Mallarmé's theory of the book and his interest in journalistic techniques: a reversal of interests, from journalism toward the techniques of concrete poetry, wouldn't be so disconcerting.

Translated by A. S. Bessa

A Laboratory of Texts

Brazilian and German Avant-Garde Poetry

Introduction

The influence of French culture on Brazilian letters is well known. In poetry, for example, during the romantic, Parnassian, and symbolist periods, the French influence is crucial. The case of Parnassianism is typical: Perhaps only literature in France and in Brazil (the latter as a tributary of the former) may have had a movement so distinct. Its aesthetic contribution in both countries, was—despite the major sway it held in Brazil—fairly modest, it could be said in passing. The Brazilian modernist movement of 1922 was more universally aware. Nonetheless, the presence of the French literary or artistic avant-garde—through the poetry of someone like Paul Dermée, or Apollinaire, or Cocteau, or the Swiss French Blaise Cendrars, or Max Jacob, etc., and of cubism, as seen in the first group shows of the Salon d'Automne [Autumn Exhibition]—made itself felt. This, as always, in counterbalance to the contribution of Italian futurism and its supranational "inseminatory" activities. (Marinetti, as a matter of fact, promoted his manifestos in Paris and wrote a great deal of his work in French.) Mário de Andrade, a spirit drawn to new trends, in his essay on modernist aesthetics "A escrava que não é Isaura" ["The Slave Who Is Not Isaura"] (1924), surveys a number of major and minor authors from various countries (among them, significantly, the German poet August Stramm).

Originally published in *A arte no horizonte do provável e outros ensaios* (São Paulo: Perspectiva, 1969).
—EDITORS

But the main accent in the landscape of Brazilian letters was still the French influence. In the 1940s, mainly thanks to a renewal of the methods of literary criticism, there was a great interest among Brazilians in Anglo-American culture: the new critical approaches of I. A. Richards, Eliot, and the contribution of American New Criticism; this in parallel to poetry in English, particularly Eliot's neoclassicism. Also, during the 1940s, Rainer Maria Rilke began to acquire prestige in Brazil. But mainly the Rilke of the *Elegies* and the *Sonnets to Orpheus;* not the Rilke of the *Neue Gedichte* [*New Poems*] or of the *Ding-Gedichte* [*Thing Poems*] (considered by critic Otto Maria Carpeaux the poet's "major work" and, in my view, probably the most currently relevant).[1]

In the 1950s, with the advent of concrete poetry, launched by the poets gathered around the São Paulo magazine *Noigandres,* an avant-garde movement of national and international traffic was historically created for the first time—one which did not follow analogous European movements. This movement, while taking into account, in its theoretical configuration, the contribution of French authors such as Mallarmé and Apollinaire, on the one hand, and of English-language ones, such as Pound, Joyce, and Cummings on the other, exhibited an unusual trait in Brazil: it was born in contact with the work of a German-language poet, the Swiss-Bolivian Eugen Gomringer, and chronologically coincided with it. Concrete poetry spread simultaneously to the two main Brazilian cities (São Paulo and Rio) and to Switzerland, Austria, and Germany as well. We can now [in 1969] say that it has an active presence in Brazilian and German letters, having transnationally migrated to other countries—from Japan to Czechoslovakia, from Italy to England—mainly thanks to the militant work of the Brazilian group.

The Connection with Eugen Gomringer

It's worthwhile here to stop to consider the figure of Eugen Gomringer. Born in 1925 in Cachuela, Esperanza, Bolivia, to a Swiss father and a Bolivian mother of Indian descent, he was educated in Europe. From 1954 to 1957, he was Max Bill's secretary at the Hochschule für Gestaltung in Ulm, Germany, the industrial design school that succeeded the Bauhaus. Between 1957 and 1958, Gomringer was director of the press division of the school, from which he later withdrew when Max Bill left. In 1953, he published a book of poems in German, English, French, and Spanish under the title *Konstellationen* [*Constellations*]. Together with the painter and visual artist Marcel Wyss, he then founded the international art review *Spirale* [*Spiral*] (Bern). In 1955, in that magazine, he launched his manifesto "From Verse to Constellation: Function and Form of a New Poetry."[2]

In turn, after various experiments with fracture and montage of words, including experiments privileging words spatially in poems such as "O jogral e a prostituta negra" ["The Minstrel and the Black Prostitute"] (1949) by Décio Pignatari and my "Ciropédia ou a educação do príncipe" ["Cyropedia or the Prince's Education"] (1952), Brazilian concrete poetry reached its first systematic achievement in Augusto de Campos's series *Poetamenos* [*Minuspoet*] (January–July 1953). These are poems in colors that respond, on the one hand, to Mallarmé's concept of the "prismatic subdivisions of the Idea" and Pound's technique of ideogrammatic montage. On the other hand, musically they echo the *Klangfarbenmelodie* [melody of timbres] by Anton Webern, the most radical of Vienna's twelve-tone trinity, music with a power of synthesis comparable to that of Japanese haiku, according to critic Antoine Goléa. Just as when in Webern a continuous melody migrates from one instrument to the next continuously changing color (timbre), in these poems every color indicates a different theme, which is to be articulated by a different vocal timbre, producing, as a whole, a lyric ideogram. (Almost all the poems had lyrical and love themes within a new concept of lyricism, not a sentimental-discursive one but rather an existential-pointillist one, so to speak.)

Given the high costs of color printing, *Poetamenos* was only printed using different typefaces in February 1955, in the second issue of the book-magazine *Noigandres*. However, in January 1954, Pignatari, in collaboration with the composers Damiano Cozzella and L. C. Vinholes, organized the first public performance of the poems in that series, on the occasion of the Fifth International "Pro Arte" Summer Course (in Teresópolis, directed by H. J. Koellreuter). At that time also, as professor of the poetry and literature division, Pignatari lectured on the theoretical tenets of the new poetry and on the basic list of authors that such poetry required.[3] In the first half of 1955, Augusto de Campos's article-manifestos "Poesia estrutura" ["Poetry, Structure"] and "Poema, ideograma" ["Poem, Ideogram"] and my "Poesia e paraíso perdido" ["Poetry and Paradise Lost"] and "A obra de arte aberta" ["The Open Work of Art"] were published. All texts dealt with the aforementioned issues.[4]

In October 1955, the label "concrete poetry," launched as the title of an article by Augusto de Campos (in *Forum* [publication of the Centro Acadêmico in São Paulo], no. 3, August 22), began to circulate in the local press, announcing a concert-recital commemorating the first anniversary of the movement Ars Nova, conducted by maestro Diogo Pacheco. (At this concert, which took place in November of that year at the Teatro de Arena, there was a performance of pieces by the young Brazilian composers Ernst Mahle and Cozzella, as well as readings and visual presentations of three poems from *Poetamenos*.) In November 1955, Pignatari visited the Ulm Hochschule. By chance and without any previous contact or knowledge, he then met Gomringer. After living in Europe for two years, especially in Paris, Gomringer was the first poet that Pignatari met who was carrying out experiments similar to those of the Brazilian group *Noigandres*. In Paris, Pignatari was mainly in contact with musicians (the composer Pierre Boulez, the Domaine Musical concert group; it would be only years later that the new poetry would manifest itself noticeably in France).

The poet from Ulm acknowledged a list of basic authors almost identical to that of the Brazilians: instead of Pound, he quoted William Carlos Williams (a disciple and friend of Ezra Pound); and he added, for the German context, the *Phantasus* by Arno Holz. Gomringer practiced an extremely concise poetry, with a rigorous and orthogonal construction, thematically limited to notes from nature or an urban landscape, or instead abstract motifs of dynamical structures. He called his poems "constellations," following Mallarmé's example. "A constellation," Gomringer explained, "is the simplest way of structuring a poem founded on the word. As a group of stars, a group of words forms a constellation. Two, three, or more words—there don't have to be a lot of them—vertically or horizontally laid out: an 'idea-thing' relationship is established. And that's all!" Brazilian concrete poetry—as it appears in *Poetamenos* and in some other unpublished poems—was more complex. It employed, instead of a two-dimensional (orthogonal) construction, a multidimensional, less concentrated one. This structure partakes of a visual baroqueness that is perhaps one of the formal constants in the Brazilian spirit as is evidenced, for instance, in our modern architecture. Contact between the Brazilians and Gomringer was mutually beneficial, resulting in an exchange of encouragement and influences respecting each other's paths.[5] In December 1956, concrete poetry was officially launched, with a large exhibit at the Museum of Modern Art in São Paulo (later shown at the exhibition space of the Ministry of Education in Rio de Janeiro). In a letter to Pignatari dated August 30, 1956, Gomringer had already accepted the name "concrete poetry," suggested by the Brazilians, as a general label for the movement, while still keeping the term "constellations"[6] to characterize his own experiments.

Later on, the Brazilian group popularized Gomringer's theoretical writings and poetry in Brazil, while he promoted the work of the *Noigandres* team in Switzerland, Austria, and Germany. In 1960, in issue 8 of *Spirale,* Gomringer published a *Kleiner Anthologie konkreter Poesie* [*Little Anthology of Concrete Poetry*], presenting sixteen poets from various countries: seven Brazilians, three Austrians, two Germans, two Swiss, one Japanese, and one Italian. That same year Gomringer began publishing a series entitled *Konkrete Poesie/Poesia Concreta* [*Concrete Poetry*] with the epigraph: "Concrete poetry is the aesthetic chapter of universal linguistic form of our time." (Individual volumes of selected poems by Brazilian poets are planned, and an anthology in collaboration with the *Noigandres* group, *Ideogramme/Ideogramas* [*Ideograms*] has already been published.)

Making the balance of contemporary German poetry, Anatol Rosenfeld argued in 1964: "It must be noted that Brazilian concretism has been exerting a certain influence on German concrete poetry, and even recently Gomringer has specifically made reference to Brazilian concretism (in the afterword to *33 Konstellationen*, 1960)."[7] Let's turn now to a typical example of a Gomrigerian "constellation" (that the reader may compare with poems from the series *Poetamenos,* republished in *Antologia Noigandres,* São Paulo, 1962, since it is impossible to reproduce them in color here):

Eugen Gomringer:

Constellation

words are shadows
shadows become words
words are games
games become words
are shadows words
do words become games
are games words
do words become shadows
are words shadows
do games become words
are words games
do shadows become words*

*All poems translated from the original languages by essay translator, unless otherwise noted. —TRANSLATOR

Arno Holz, Schwitters/Sousândrade, Oswald

A characteristic common trait of the international concrete poetry movement originating from those two main matrices (Brazil and the German domain) was precisely the attempt to demarginalize the avant-garde, integrating it to a living tradition. This required a revision of the literary past, in order to substitute the morose and conventional view of literary historians by another one, the *inventive* one of the creative artist. In the German case, the works of Arno Holz (1863–1929) and Kurt Schwitters (1887–1948) were reconsidered in light of the new poetic experiments. Gomringer, as was said, included the poems of *Phantasus* (first edition: 1889–99, two issues) on the basic list of his article-manifesto (1955): "New poetry is grounded in historical evolution. Its origins must be sought in the experiments of Arno Holz (*Phantasusgedichte*) as well as in those of the last Mallarmé and of Apollinaire's *Calligrammes*. In these poets, a new layout of the poem announces itself. Arno Holz gathers, in a single line, words rhythmically interrelated, hence the well-known contour of short and long lines in *Phantasus*."[8] Holz, until fairly recently, had been the "disinherited of the disinherited" of German literature, a name that was negated or omitted, according to a statement by the novelist Alfred Döblin in a volume dedicated to the poet, part of a series eloquently titled *Disappeared and Forgotten* (Mainz: Akademie der Wissenschaften und der Literatur, 1951). Today he reappears, full of life and instigation, not only for concrete poetry but also for the experiments of new prose writers such as Ferdinand Kriwet and Hans G. Helms.

In 1962, I had the opportunity to study at length Holz's *Phantasus* in two articles, "A revolução da lírica" ["The Revolution of Lyric"] and "Elefantíase do projeto" ["Elephantiasis of the Project"].[9] I argued there that that "masterly baroque book," as Döblin called it, could be placed next to Joyce's *Finnegans Wake* thanks to its sense of elaborate and grandiose farce, where language—inflated in a series of word-montages that take the natural proclivities of the German language to their last consequences—was the protagonist of a Cyclopean struggle, a veritable clash of Titans against the basaltic strata of tradition. Between 1961 and 1962, the *Phantasus* was published by Luchterhand in its definitive three-volume version, unpublished until then, and under the care of the poet's widow, Anita Holz (an Argentine by birth), and Wilhelm Emrich. In 1964, Max Bense devoted a magnificent essay to Holz ("Textalgebra Arno Holzes"), reassessing his value in light of his own new aesthetics based on statistics and semiotics.[10]

The visual aspect of Holz's poetry must be stressed: the poems are laid out on the page, governed by the "middle axis" (hence the term *Mittelachsenpoesie*)—a typographic/virtual backbone—that the poet used in an effort to respond optically to the oral nature of his poetry, preserving the single *tone* of words, the breath and pauses of spoken poetry. The subject matter of *Phantasus,* in Otto Maria Carpeaux's synthetic formulation (*A literatura alemã* [*German Literature*] [São Paulo: Cultrix, 1964]), is the "impressionistic impressions of everyday life." I would add that the poem also contains mythological allegories, travel scenes, polyglot and burlesque dialogues, an encyclopedic gallery of heroes and illustrious men; it is also lyric poetry about nature and the big city, childhood memories, and even philosophic meditations, especially on destiny and the poet's role ("Ecce Poeta," last part of the third volume).[11] In the monumental edition of 1916, the poem had 355 pages, in a 32-by-44 centimeter format [12.6 by 17.3 inches]. In 1926, three years before the poet's death, a new, revised edition appeared. Masses of adjectives and adjectivized participles form, for instance, a gigantic, 743-line sentence, which goes on for fifteen pages and whose organic laws of growth gradually impose themselves on the author, until he ends up becoming (as he himself admits) "a creature of his own work, which self-creates itself." A kind of polypary of predicates anchored to a verb or a final noun, that is how one could define the usual syntactic figure of the *Phantasus,* a poem that the scholar René Lasne compared to a kind of "poetic encyclopedia" (giving the expression a negative ring . . .). I quote below a fragment of the initial *Barocke Marine* [*Baroque Seascape*] episode, from part 3—Götter und Götzen [Gods and Idols] —in the first volume of the poem:

Arno Holz:

Baroque Seascape

Sea
Sea, sunniest, sea
as far as
you . . . see!
Over the rolling water here,
rage-

roarromping,
unruly, rejoicehowling, rapturexulting, lustlaughing, swarming
gruntmoaning, waltzhurling,
backslinging,
warming
hollowhandcalling, hollowhandcrying,
hollowhandsbawling
greenseaweedhairy, shimmerscalebellied, sturgeontailfloating
swimdiveblinkering, swimpuffnimbling
swimpuffpanting
like
raging mad trumpetsnailhorn blowing
thousand . . . tritons!

So Brazilian concrete poetry, aside from having contributed to the process of rehabilitation of Arno Holz, also promoted a parallel revision on the Brazilian front. It is the case of the poet from Maranhão, Joaquim de Sousa Andrade (Sousândrade, 1833–1902), belonging to the second generation of romantics and author of the long epic-dramatic-narrative poem *O Guesa errante* [*The Wandering Guesa*]. Sousândrade was unfairly criticized by his contemporaries because his innovations exceeded the aesthetics of his age. Only recently, with the book *Re/Visão de Sousândrade* [*Re/Vision of Sousândrade*], a critical essay, anthology, and glossary,[12] has Sousândrade been put back into circulation. Only now can we appreciate Sousândrade's vertiginous semantical innovations (as in the creation of new compound words, doing violence to the genius of the Portuguese language: *fòssilpetrifique* ["fossilpetrify"] *sôbre-rum-nadam* ["over-rum-swimming"], *florchameja* ["flowerflickering"], *lágrima-pantera* ["tear-panther"]); as well as in the realm of syntax: a montage of news items from newspapers of his time and of events and characters from the past and present in a chaotic, polyglot whirl set in the New York Stock Exchange in the 1870s, the time when Sousândrade lived in the United States.

In the article "De Holz a Sousândrade" ["From Holz to Sousândrade"],[13] Augusto de Campos and I drew parallels between both poets. We showed that while Holz had to his advantage the nature of the German language in creating his lexical montages, something that allowed him to go farther and systematize his process, Sousândrade must be credited with having had the unusual nerve to fight against the genius of his language, twisting it for his creative purposes. It's important to note that for the episode of the Stock Exchange (entitled *The Wall Street Inferno*) as well as for another similar episode (*Tatuturema,* which focuses on the Jurupari rituals performed by Amazon forest dwellers corrupted by the white man), Sousândrade followed the model of Goethe's *Faust* (the *Nights of Walpurgis*). He also followed Heine's *Atta Troll* (*A Midsummer Night's Dream,* 1847), a satire against the philistine bourgeois personified in Atta Troll, the bear, who tries to give wise moral and theological lessons to his offspring, warning them against the treachery of the young "barbarians."[14] Goethe's paradigm is specifically mentioned by Sousândrade in the lines that precede the Inferno of the New York Stock Exchange:

> Romantics I saw you, dance
> at night from Brocken in Amazona.
> Behold classic Pharsalia, on glacial days
> By the Hudson. Guesa stops to gaze.

The witches' Sabbath on Mount Brocken (*Faust,* part 1) is reproduced in the pandemoniac dance of the Indians on the banks of the Amazon; Sousândrade's second *Walpurgisnacht,* parallel to the classic *Pharsalia* of the *Second Faust,* takes place next to the Hudson River, in New York. Note the last stanza of the second Inferno episode in Sousândrade:

> (A magnetic handle-organ; ring of bears sentencing the architect of the
> PHARSALIA to death; an Odyssean ghost in the flames of
> Albion's fires:)

> – Bear . . . Bear is beriberi, Bear . . . Bear . . .
> = Mahmmuhmmah, mahmmuhmmah, Mammon!
> – Bear . . . Bear . . . ber' . . . Pegasus
> Parnassus
> = Mahmmuhmmah, mahmmuhmmah, Mammon!

The poet, in the persona of the Guesa (an adolescent who must be sacrificed to the Sun God by a ring of priests), is about to be ritually killed by a ring of bears (one of the circles of Tammany, the North American secret society; by extension, in this episode, the bear also designates the Yankee, placed under the sign of the northern constellations of Ursa Major and Minor; "bear," in stock exchange jargon, was a speculator who caused an artificial drop in market prices). The poet was also the architect of the

Pharsalia of Wall Street in the same way that Lucan was of the epic *Pharsalia* and Goethe of the Faustian one. An infernal chorus, speaking with the nasal twang of a barrel organ, praises the god of the Stock Exchange ("Mammon" or "Mammonas"), and their refrain is an amalgam of the words *Mamma* (German for "mama") and *Mumma* (the Bear-Mother, wife of Atta Troll in Heine's poem). Speculation ("Bear") generates disease ("beriberi"). In this financial Inferno, the "Pegasus" of the poetic "Parnassus" is grotesquely transformed into a bear. An Odyssean ghost is witness to this, since Ulysses also descended to hell ("Nekuia," book II of the *Odyssey*). The flames are realistic, drawn from a true incident (the famous fire that destroyed the city of London in 1666), substituting the symbolic infernal blaze. "Albion" is the ancient name given to England by the Greeks. Because of his fragmentary style, of his fusion across time of events and characters, Sousândrade can be seen as one of the precursors of modern poetry internationally and, without a doubt, the forefather of Brazilian avant-garde poetry.[15]

Another first-rate poet rehabilitated by the German-language avant-garde is Kurt Schwitters. Schwitters was a notable innovator in the visual arts, combining Dadaist trends with the contributions of Russian constructivism in his painting and sculpture, which he named *merz* (a syllable from the word *Kommerz:* the process of clipping a term found in urban signs embodies an entire creative agenda). Schwitters's production—painting and sculpture as well as literature—is characterized by the constant use of collage. It profits from the humor that arises from unforeseen associations of everyday detritus, whether it be tram tickets and letter envelopes placed in sudden assemblage or bits of ordinary conversation, slang and newspaper lingo, the stock of clichés, and so on. Now [1969] the neo-Dada trend is taking over all fields: avant-garde music, with its aesthetic of the unfinished and chance; poetry, with its techniques of syntagmatic montage (one of the main techniques of concrete poetry, for instance); painting, with pop art, happenings, and neorealism.

It is thus evident that "Dadá não está gagá" ["Dada is not senile"], as Anatol Rosenfeld put it when he wrote about the large Schwitters show included in the Fourth São Paulo Biennial (1961).[16] With this colorful formulation, not unworthy of the linguistic findings of the *merz* poet, Rosenfeld tried to emphasize the currency of Schwittersian issues. Brazilian concrete poetry, since 1956 (five years before the Fourth Biennial and seven years before the large Schwitters retrospective at the Wallraf-Richartz

Museum in Cologne) had been issuing a cry of warning, stressing the importance of his poetry. This was also two years before the acknowledgment of his importance in England (where the poet, fleeing Nazi persecution, spent the last years of his life), a recognition that came with the book by Stefan Themerson, *Kurt Schwitters in England* (London: Gaberbocchus, 1958). In "Kurt Schwitters ou o júbilo do objeto" ["Kurt Schwitters or the Joy of the Object"],[17] I tried to show the contribution of the creator of *merz* art to new poetry in terms of his correlation with the latest musical experimentation, which culminates in the piece "Gesang der Jünglinge" ["Song of Youth"] by Karlheinz Stockhausen, written between 1955 and 1956. Between 1921 and 1923, Schwitters composed a "Primordial Sonata" or "Pre-Syllabic Sonata" ("Ursonate"), the most radical and consistent of all experiments carried out to our day in the field of phonetic (sound) poetry and which renders pale all that was attempted by the French *léttristes* under Isidore Isou. Schwitters was also a virtuoso of diction, having left behind recordings of his compositions using the sound material of language. Stockhausen, for his part, in his "Gesang der Jünglinge," did nothing but fragment and reassemble eighteen lines from a biblical psalm from the book of Daniel, so that the words, set in the context of an electronic composition, may wander from a state of asemantic noise (devoid of meaning) to one of intelligibility (where some words or syntagmas are gradually allowed to agglutinate semantically: *Sonne, Mond, Winde, Himmels, Jubelt dem Herrn,* and are perceived as momentary islands in a sea of phonetic residue). Commenting on this, Stockhausen writes: "Language can approach music and music, language, until the boundaries between sound and meaning are abolished," explaining that in his work he created "a series of degrees of intelligibility" with a structural function.[18]

Alongside its interest in Schwitters—as an associate and even a forerunner of today's German avant-garde—Brazilian concrete poetry, from its earliest manifestos, fought for the reexamination of the oeuvre of Oswald de Andrade (1890–1954), who, in many respects, occupies a place similar to Schwitters's in the Brazilian context. Oswald was the most dynamic figure of the 1922 modernist movement: the creator of our new poetry (*Brazilwood* poetry) and our new prose (the novels-inventions *Memórias sentimentais de João Miramar* [*Sentimental Memoirs of John Seaborne*] and *Serafim Ponte Grande* [*Seraphim Grosse Pointe*]),* and of our

---

*See the selections from "*Miramar* on the Mark" and "Seraphim: A Great Un-Book" in the essay "An Oswald de Andrade Triptych" in this volume. —EDITORS

new theater (*O rei da vela* [*The Candle King*], *O homem e o cavalo* [*The Man and the Horse*], *A morta* [*The Dead Woman*], a Brechtian-style theater written between 1933 and 1937, i.e., before Brecht's most notable phase). Speaking only of the poetry, it could be said that Oswald was the forerunner of concrete poetry, thanks to his "poemas-minuto" (minute-poems) which can be reduced to a mere two words—title: *amor* (love); poem: *humor*. Also thanks to his direct juxtaposition of phrases and situations gathered from the quotidian; thanks to his sensibility (taste) which Décio Pignatari accurately termed Dadaist and "pop"[19] avant la lettre; thanks to his simplicity that countered the national vice of rhetoric. Compare this "ready-made" poem by Oswald with *Anna Blume* [*Anna Flower*] by Schwitters.

Oswald de Andrade:

Berlitz School

All pupils have an eager face
But the teacher-suffragette
Mistreats the poor pretty typists
And hates
  The spring
      Der Frühling
          La primavera scapigliata
There's a bunch of books to be bought
We're left sort of waiting
The bells alert us
The doors close

Is the peacock beautiful?
What color is Senhor Seixas?
Senhor Lázaro, bring me some ink
What's the first letter of the alphabet?
Ah!

Kurt Schwitters:

Anna Blossom Has Wheels

O Thou, beloved of my twenty-seven senses,
I love thine
Thou thee thee thine, I thine, thou mine.—we?
That belongs (by the side) not here!
Who art Thou, uncounted woman?
Thou art—art Thou?—
People say, Thou werst,—
Let them say, they don't know, how the churchtower stands.
You wearest your head on your feet and wanderst on your hands,
On thy hands wanderst Thou.
Hallo thy red dress, clashed in white folds,
Red I love Anna Blossom, red I love Thine!
Thou Thee Thee Thine, I Thine, Thou mine,—we?
That belongs (by the side) in the cold glow.
Red Blossom, red Anna Blossom, how say the people?
    Price question
      1. Anna Blossom has wheels.
      2. Anna Blossom is red.
      3. What color are the wheels?
Blue is the color of thy yellow hair.
Red is the whirl of thy green wheels.
Thou simple maiden in everyday-dress,
Thou dear green animal,
I love thine!
Thou Thee Thee Thine, I Thine, Thou mine,—we?
That belongs (by the side) in the glow box.
Anna Blossom,
Anna,
A—N—N—A
I trickle your name.
Thy name drops like soft tallow.
Does thou know it, Anna,
Does thou allready know it?
One can also read thee from behind,
And thou, thou most glorious of all,

Thou art from the back, as from the front:
A—N—N—A
Tallow trickles to strike over my back.
Anna Blossom,
Thou drippes animal,
I
Love
Thine!*

A poem that makes one think about Wittgenstein's dictum: "Philosophy exists because languages are absurd."

Morgenstern, Stramm, Kandinsky, Klee

In this effort to create its own tradition—or its *antitradition*—and to withdraw the living literary past from the timorous custody of literary historians in order to reestablish the obscured paths of an evolution of forms, directed by creation, Brazilian concrete poetry—its concerns in sync with the new guard of German poetry—chose also to promote in Brazil the work of authors such as Christian Morgenstern, August Stramm, Kandinsky, and Klee.

In 1958, I devoted an essay to the linguistic fabulation of Christian Morgenstern (1871–1914).[20] I tried to show there how, in the *Galgenlieder* [*Gallows Songs*], there are contributions to the sonorist trend of the new poetry ("Das Grosse Lalula" ["The Big La-lu-la"]), to the visual trend ("Fisches Nachtgesang" ["Fishes' Nightsong"], a poem without words where the opening and closing of the mouth of a fish in an aquarium—its "nocturnal song"—is indicated by symbols of long and short syllables), the trend of lexical and vocabulary humor (the transfiguration of animals and objects into fable characters through mere linguistic manipulation). The following examples belong to this last trend in which the visual element is also important.

Christian Morgenstern:

---

*English version by Kurt Schwitters in *Das literarische Werk*, vol. 1, ed. Friedhelm Lach (Cologne: DuMont Buchverlag, 1974), 150, reprinted by kind permission of DuMont Literatur und Kunst Verlag, Cologne, Germany. —TRANSLATOR

The Aesthetic Otter

An otter
sets his daughter
on gravel near swift water
Do you know,
though, why?

The mooncalf, whispered low,
And told me, on the sly:

That sublime
-ly keen beast does
because
he can't resist the rhyme.*

The Lonely Rocking Chair on the Deserted Terrace

"I am a lonely rocking chair
And I rock in the wind,
                in the wind

That moves so cool on the terrace where
I rock in the wind,
                in the wind

And I rockle and knockle the livelong day
While knockles and crockles the linden.
Who knows what more might rock and sway
In the wind,
            in the wind,
                    in the wind,
                        in . . ."†

---

* English translation from Christian Morgenstern, *Gallows Songs,* trans. W. D. Snodgrass and Lore Segal (Ann Arbor: University of Michigan Press, 1967), 72. Reprinted by kind permission of the translators. —TRANSLATOR

† English translation from Christian Morgenstern, *Gallows Songs,* trans. W. D. Snodgrass and Lore Segal (Ann Arbor: University of Michigan Press, 1967), 65. Reprinted by kind permission of the translators. —TRANSLATOR

August Stramm (1874–1915) is a true precursor of the creations of Schwitters, a poet in whom expressionism meets futurism. His poetry, through visual verticalization, reveals at times the influence of the "median axis" of Arno Holz; through the composition of words, it also shows the lesson of *Phantasus,* although in a more radical way through the lexical crumbling he practices. To this effect, consider the poem:

Brothel

Lights wench out of windows
contagion
straddles at the door
and offers moaning whores for sale!
Women's souls shame shrill laughter!
Mothers' wombs yawn child-death!
Unborn things
spook
mustily
through the rooms!
Aghast
in a corner
through the rooms!
shame-mortified
cowers
sex!*

A word such as *Schamzerpört* fuses *Scham* [shame], *Empörung* [disgust], and *zerdrückt* [crushed] to mean "crushed and disgusted by shame." In "Os estenogramas líricos de August Stramm" ["The Lyrical Shorthand of August Stramm"],[21] I tried to study the telegraphic style (*Telegrammstil*) of the poet (who, by the way, was a postal worker . . .). This style, by virtue of its synthesis, imagetic surprise, and speed, also has something in common with Oswald de Andrade's writing style (defined in those same terms in the jocular-serious preface to *João Miramar* [*John Seaborne*]: "telegraphic style" and "piercing metaphor"). There is also something else worthy of

---

*English version quoted from August Stramm, *Twenty Two Poems,* trans. Patrick Bridgwater (Wymondham, Eng.: Brewhouse Press, 1969), reprinted by kind permission of the translator. —TRANSLATOR

note: the book of war poems written between 1914 and 1915 and titled *Tropfblut* [*Dripblood*], where what was ardent and exclamatory in Stramm's lyrical-love shorthand gives way to a dry and sorrowful pointillism. Now, the first book by Mário de Andrade (who knew the entire work of his German confrere) is precisely called *Há uma gôta de sangue em cada poema* [*There's a Drop of Blood in Every Poem*] (1917) and is made up of texts equally inspired by the war of 1914. It is true that *Tropfblut* was only published in 1919, but many of Stramm's poems appeared before in the magazine *Der Sturm* [*The Storm*], founded in 1910. Compared to Stramm's, the poems of Mário de Andrade's first poetry book seem pale and conventional.

Mário de Andrade:

Howitzer Refrain (fragment)

. . . .
But in the supreme glory of ascending,
to feel
that strength will fail:
and to come back to Earth;
and to serve as an instrument of war;
and to explode,
and to kill! . . .

August Stramm:

Signal

The drum plods on
The horn rises
And
Death props
Its head on a fluttering death
Bristles
Going Going
Bristle

Goes
And goes and goes
And goes and goes
And goes and goes and goes and goes
Goes
Plods
Goes

Concrete poetry also became interested in poet-painters, such as Kandinsky and Paul Klee, who transmuted into verbal language the new syntactic inventions and the new visual art of their pictorial worlds, managing to shake the literary convictions that professional poets frequently seemed incapable of fracturing. Consider the following examples:

Kandinsky:

White Horn

A circle is always something.

Sometimes very much.

Sometimes—seldom—too much.

Like a rhinoceros is sometimes too much.

In com-pact violet it sits at times—the circle.
The circle of white
And necessarily gets smaller. And smaller.

The rhinoceros lowers its head, its horn. It threatens.

The com-pact violet looks angry.
The white circle has gotten smaller—a small dot, an ant's eye.
And it flickers.

But not for long. It swells up again—the little dot (ant's eye).
It swells in swelling.

Swelling twitches the little dot (ant's eye)
Until it becomes the white circle.
It twitches once—only once.

All white.

Where is the com-pact violet?

And the ant?

And the rhinoceros?
(Paris, May 1937)

Paul Klee:

                              Last

        In the heart's middle
        As sole request
        Fading steps
        A cat's act:

        her ear spoons a sound
        her leg runs off
        her look
        burns thin and thick
        she faces no return
        pretty as a flower
        yet full of weapons
        and has, on the whole, nothing to do with us.

The *Anthologie der Abseitigen* [*Anthology of the Marginal*] (Bern, 1946), compiled by the distinguished Swiss essayist and art critic Carola Giedion-Welcker, played a decisive role in the recovery of that lost tradition. All the poets cited participate in that anthology, as well as Paul Scheerbart (author of an 1897 sonorist poem *Kikakoku! Ekoralaps!*) and the Dadaistas Hugo Ball and Hans Arp, poet-painter-sculptor.

Current Situation of the German Avant-Garde

German-language poetry is the one that, nowadays in Europe, reveals the most experimental line of action, which is particularly interesting for Brazilian poets who locate writing in the category of invention.

To begin with, I'd like to mention the name of Helmut Heissenbüttel (b. 1921), who lives in Stuttgart, and is cultural editor of the Süddeutscher Rundfunk [South German Radio]. He is the author of *Kombinationen* [*Combinations*] (1954), *Topographien* [*Topographies*] (1956), and a *Textbuch* [*Textbook*] in five fascicles (1960-65). In his first books he reveals expressionist and surrealist influences, especially in the use of images. However, he gradually strips and rarefies his language through his contact with the experiments of Gertrude Stein, to whom he dedicated an essay in 1955.[22] In this way, he manages to obtain a poetry that essentially operates with the "formal apparatus of logistics" with the "elementary functional schemes of language," a poetry that, in many aspects, can be considered concrete. (Max Bense has classified it thus.) Heissenblüttel's texts gradually reveal a "thematics-of-being" irradiating a Kafkaesque aura imbued with Wittgenstein's philosophy of language, which plays with the ambiguities and the absurdities of the discursive structures of Western languages. More wide-ranging semantically than Gomringer's work, this poetry encompasses problems that could be defined as ideological; in this way, it comes close to Brazilian concrete poetry. Consider for instance these examples:

Helmut Heissenbüttel:

the remaining standing
the remaining standing   of the one who remained standing
the fall   of the one who remained standing
the fall   of the one who fell
the remaining standing   of the one who fell
of the one who fell

Political Grammar

Persecutors persecute the persecuted. But the persecuted become the persecutors. And because the persecuted become persecutors this made the persecuted persecuting persecuted and the persecutors persecuted persecutors. But persecuted persecutors become in turn persecutors [persecuting persecuted persecutors]. And the persecuting persecuted become in turn persecuted [persecuted persecuting persecuted]. The persecutors produce persecuted. The persecuting persecuted produce persecuted persecutors. The persecuting persecuted persecutors produce persecuted persecuting persecuted. And so on ad infinitum.

Heissenbüttel's poetry represents the radicalization of a premonitory line already present in the poetry of Bertolt Brecht (1898–1956). This can be verified either through the dialectical manipulation of the phrase structure, or via the elliptical rarefaction of the poems of Brecht's last phase, where the poems seem to follow a path that goes from the "epigram to the pictogram," under the influence of Chinese poetry, especially of Japanese haiku.[23] Two examples:

Bertolt Brecht:

Pleasures (The First Look Out the Window)

The first look out the window in the morning
The old book, found again
Inspired faces
Snow, the change of seasons
The newspaper
The dog
Dialectics
Showering, swimming
Old music
Comfortable shoes
Understanding
New music
Writing, planting
Traveling
Singing
Being friendly

It's evening. Two inflatable
boats glide by. On them,
Two naked youths. Rowing side by side
They talk. Talking
They row side by side.

Another important name is Hans G. Helms, a young author working
with the team of experimental musicians of the Cologne Radio Studio. His
poem-novel *Fa:m' Ahniesgwow* (1960), a satire of Nazism and its survival in
postwar Germany, is a polyglot experiment modeled after Joyce's late prose,
with an emphasis on the phonetic values of words and syntagmas. (The
book comes with a "synchronization plan" and a record.) The title of the
work is already programmatic and can be interpreted as: FAME
(from/*vom*): AMIGAU and/or ANISGAU, i.e., SAGA (from Latin, *fama*
= legend) OF THE (from, *vom*) DISTRICT (*Gau* = district, in the Nazi
administrative organization, where *Gauleiter* = chief of district) OF THE
FRIEND (*Ami* = colloquial expression used to designate Americans during
the time of the German occupation) and/or OF ANIS (aromatic liqueur).
In this amalgam, there are other reverberations: the idea of prediction or
premonition (*ahnen*); the onomatopoeia of a dog's barking (*gwow*); an
exclamation of relief ("wow" in American slang).[24]

The launch of this book allowed T. W. Adorno to make the defense and
illustration of experimental literature through an instigating essay, where,
at a certain point, he affirms that "the maligned word 'experiment' must be
used in a positive sense; only as experimentation, not as something kept
away from danger, can art, in the end, have a chance."[25] *Golem, Polemic for
9 Solo Voices* (1962) is Helms's second composition. It is an operetta of
phrases in freedom taken from books by Heidegger (*Sein und Zeit,
Holzwege, Einführung in die Metaphysik*). In it, Helms, in the guise of a
bouffe assemblage of fragments that succeed themselves and cross over,
criticizes the philo-Nazi inclinations he detects in the writing of the exis-
tentialist philosopher. (The opening of this satire caused great uproar in
Germany.) Currently, Helms is working on a text of political analysis (the
problem of statistic obedience in a society of advanced economic and technological development, the "Anonymous Society" as he calls it).[26]

Ferdinand Kriwet, based in Düsseldorf, also wrote a poem-novel, *Rotor*
(1961), inserting in an oneiric mixture isolated images, clichés, reminis-

cences of family-circle idle-talkers and of the urban hubbub. In this way, for critic Philippe Jaccottet, he manages to go beyond, say, a Beckett or a Nathalie Sarraute.[27] Today, invoking as slogan a phrase by Walter Benjamin ("The typewriter will alienate the hand of the man of letters from the pen only when the precision of typographic forms has directly entered the conception of his books"),* Kriwet develops a literature of optical perception, the *Sehtexte,* panels of words in space, collected and commented on by the author in *Sehtextkommentare* (1965) with the suggestive subtitle "Leserattenfänge."[28] Franz Mon, who in 1959 published an anthology of concrete poetry (*Artikulationen*), has also done research on typograms, fusing poem/graphic image. Following this line in Brazil, there are examples of various trends, in the new visual work by Wlademir Dias Pino, in the semiotic poems (code-poems) created by Décio Pignatari and Luiz Ângelo Pinto, in the "popcrete" poems by Augusto de Campos, in the tactilograms by Edgard Braga, and in the labyrinths by Pedro Xisto.

It's also important to mention the Swiss Diter Rot, who lived in Iceland and currently works in the United States, a creator of books without words, which are purely typographical (he was connected to Gomringer and Marcel Wys of *Spirale* magazine); Claus Bremer, professor at the School of Ulm, author of poems composed according to tables of semantic variation; the Austrian concrete group: Gerhard Rühm, Friedrich Achleitner, Oswald Wiener, and Ernst Jandl (this last one in an interesting line of oral poetry, a "cabaret" poet, a concrete *Minnesänger*);[29] Reinhard Döhl, assistant professor of German literature at the Technical University in Stuttgart, whose *Fingerübungen* [*Finger Exercises*] date back to 1962; and Ludwig Hrig, from Saar, author of a permutational prose piece (the short story "Das Fussballspiel" ["The Soccer Game"], 1962); in East Germany, Carlfriedrich Clause, whose pictographic poems were published in 1964 by Typos Verlag in Frankfurt (*Notizen zwischen der experimentellen Arbeit* [*Notes between Experimental Work*]). Markus Kutter, Swiss, is a name that cannot be forgotten: in 1957 he published an experiment-novel *Schiff nach Europa* [*Ship to Europe*], optically organized by Karl Gerstner, a graphic designer and painter from Basel. Influenced mainly by Joyce's *Ulysses,* Kutter seeks a "synthetic novel," a "hypothetical theater" in which reality is "produced" rather than "reported"; in a word, "writing as an exact process, not a romantic one," an "intoxication of things, not of feelings."[30] Two antholo-

---

* Walter Benjamin, "Teaching Aid," *Reflections: Essays, Aphorisms, Autobiographical Writings,* trans. Edmund Jephcott (New York: Schocken Books, 1986), 79. —TRANSLATOR

gies followed in 1959 and 1961, containing texts, concrete poems, and typograms (*Leser gesucht* [*Reader Sought*] and *Inventar mit 35* [*Inventory with 35*]). Other names could be mentioned, if it were not too long to list them. It's enough to say that the weight of the avant-garde is felt even in the case of a poet of a less extreme experimental bent, such as Hans Magnus Enzensberger (b. 1929), perhaps the best-known poet of the young German literature, for some, the equivalent of the Beat poets, the "angry young men," or of the Russian Yevtushenkos and Voznesenskys. While criticizing the radical avant-garde, Enzensberger—a poet in the conversational-ironic line of Pound and Brecht—allows himself to become influenced and fascinated by it. It's instructive to know that he was in contact with Max Bense and was a visiting professor at the Hochschule of Ulm. When Enzensberger presents the poem as an "object for use," he is echoing, albeit in a personal way, Max Bill's aesthetic of the "objects for use by the spirit." ("These poems are objects for use, not gift items in a strict sense.") This aesthetic has had repercussions on Gomringer's theory of concrete poetry and on the *Noigandres* group. The Brazilian case's definition is very close to what would interest Enzensberger because it is linked to Mayakovsky's technological conception of the poem as an industrially produced form.[31] It's important to see how, in a traditional poetry scheme, Enzensberger makes use of combinatory techniques and sound effects reaped from the most radical avant-garde.[32]

Hans Magnus Enzensberger:

Bait Song

My wisdom is a rush
Cut your finger with it
and paint a red ideogram
on my shoulder
Ki wit Ki wit

My shoulder is a fast ship
Lie down on its sunny deck
and rock your way to an island
made of glass of smoke

Ki wit
My voice is a gentle dungeon
Don't get caught
My rush is a silk dagger
Don't listen
Ki wit Ki wit Ki wit

The fact that I have dealt with works nominally in prose, while speaking of experimental poetry, should not be surprising. For an avant-garde literature under the sign of invention, the traditional genres of *poetry* and *prose* prevail only for the purposes of didactic reference, but they are abolished, they lose their character of waterproof compartments, under a new concept, a more encompassing and illuminating one as far as the goals of experimentation are concerned, the category of *text.* Thus, it should not be surprising that we would attribute to a prose writer, Arno Schmidt (born in 1914, now living in Bargfeld bei Celle), a prominent role in anticipating the currents of contemporary avant-garde literature in German. An apparently marginal and isolated figure possessing a very personal style termed "a dead end"[33] by critic Otto Maria Carpeaux in his excellent *A literatura alemã [German Literature]*, Arno Schmidt is, however, inevitably present in experiments such as those of Helms, Kriwet, or Kutter. In his short-story trilogy *Leviathan* (1949), two stories are written from the perspective of antiquity and the third, main one is set in occupied Nazi Germany on the eve of capitulation. It forms a skillfully linked triptych in which the values of freedom and of the individual fight against totalitarianism and oppression (Nazism being the modern incarnation of the monster) and reveal a suggestive fusion of an expressionist heritage and Joycean techniques. (Schmidt, who performed a devastating critique of the German translation of *Ulysses*,[34] has devoted himself to translating into German fragments of *Finnegans Wake*.) A "staccato" style, a succession of images, slang, words derived from Latin and Greek, legends, oneiric flights, erudite digressions where notions of astronomy, mathematics, and philosophy intervene, all of this constitutes Schmidt's verbal environment in *Leviathan,* which, being his first book, is prototypical in relation to the later ones. His theoretical notes on the new formal modalities required by prose ("Berechnungen" ["Calculations"], parts 1 and 2, in *Rosen and Porree,* 1959) are also of major importance. Although the author thought of them in relation to the development of his own work, they undoubtedly offer stimulus to younger writers. Some examples of note are the following procedure: when Schmidt invokes a combination of units of image and commentary ("photo album" or "photo-text") in order to capture "complex living" data; when he studies the phenomenon of the "porous present" of "existence in a mosaic"; when he proposes substituting the uninterrupted "epic flux" for the interrupted "epic waterfall"; when he discusses "mind games" of the "passive" dream to the waking "chosen," "active" dream.

I deliberately reserved the conclusion of this essay for the case of the personality of Max Bense. Born in 1910 in Strasbourg, Bense is professor of philosophy and theory of knowledge at the Technical University of Stuttgart. His new aesthetics in four volumes, the first of which was published in 1954, is based on semiotics, on information and communication theory, and on a statistical analysis of style.[35] Bense is also a critic (*Rationalismus und Sensibilität* [*Rationalism and Sensibility*], 1956) and the creator of experimental texts (*Bestandteile des Vorüber* [*Components of the Past*], 1961; *Entwurf einer Rheinlandschaft*, 1962; *Die präzisen Vergnügen* [*The Precise Pleasure*], 1964, etc.). Bense's critical and aesthetic work has been popularized in Brazil by the concrete-poetry group. From his creative work, I translated the essay-poem about Brasilia "Esboço de uma Paisagem Renana" ("Entwurf einer Rheinlandschaft" ["Draft of a Rhineland Landscape"]).[36] In turn, Bense and his assistant, Elisabeth Walther (also essayist and translator, specializing in semiotics),[37] have intensely promoted Brazilian concrete poetry in Germany since 1959 through exhibits, lectures, and studies.[38] Thus, he is today the main mediator between the *Noigandres* group, the *Invenção* magazine team, and German-language avant-garde literature. In Stuttgart, in 1964, and at the invitation of Max Bense, I had the opportunity to deliver a series of lectures in which I dealt with, aside from concrete poetry, the most creative work of contemporary Brazilian literature: Oswald de Andrade, Guimarães Rosa, and João Cabral de Melo Neto.[39] Having visited Brazil already four times, in contact with its literature and visual arts, Max Bense published in 1965 a book entirely devoted to the new artistic manifestations of our country. Regarding literature, he specifically dwells on Guimarães Rosa (*The Devil to Pay in the Backlands* and "My Uncle, the Iauaretê") and on concrete poetry. In the introduction to his *Brasilianische Intelligenz* [*Brazilian Intelligence*] (Wiesbaden: Limes Verlag, 1965), he writes:

> Also, this small book, dedicated to my Brazilian friends and which owes its birth to four stays in that country, should call attention to the fact

that a progressive civilization does not conquer general interest through power relations but through its relations of intelligence; that mercantile relations are not the decisive ones but rather the spiritual ones; that the global organizer is not the businessman but rather the intellectual.

There is a Brazilian progressive intelligence that maintains internal and external relations with Europe, America, and Asia, that develops, in an original and creative way, themes, styles, knowledge, points of view, and experiments which are worthy of the highest esteem and which do not discourage the tension of spiritual life and show themselves to be free from metaphysical decadence and barbarism.

It also seems that the idea and practice of humanity in the tropical centers of civilization possess dimensions that are not found elsewhere; that this idea and practice constituted themselves less historically than in a continuous present; that creativity, rather than contemplation, is the main point; and that existential relations are dictated less by the idea of (theoretical) separation than by that of (practical) absorption.

These formulations recall Oswald de Andrade's new "cannibalist" humanism,* placed under the double sign of antimessianism and critical devouring (the creative, rather than contemplative, "absorption" of the legacy of tradition, carried out in a synchronic, a "continuous present" perspective, rather than a diachronic one).

Translated by Odile Cisneros

*See "Anthropophagous Reason: Dialogue and Difference in Brazilian Culture" in this volume.
—EDITORS

The Ghost in the Text (Saussure and the Anagrams)

The *aesthetic function* of language hardly lends itself to analysis, being as tightly woven as it is with the communicative and expressive functions. This, at least, according to A. Martinet, in his *Elements of General Linguistics.*[1]

It is especially appropriate that a linguist, Roman Jakobson, be the one to challenge this difficulty and lift this interdiction. In his essay "Closing Statement on Linguistics and Poetics," originally presented at an interdisciplinary conference on problems of style hosted by Indiana University, we can read, by way of a conclusion:

> The present conference has clearly shown that the time when both linguists and literary historians eluded questions of poetic structure is now safely behind us. . . . If there are some critics who still doubt the competence of linguistics to embrace the field of poetics, I privately believe that the poetic incompetence of some bigoted linguists has been mistaken for an inadequacy of the linguistic science itself. All of us here, however, definitively realize that a linguist deaf to the poetic function of language and a literary scholar indifferent to linguistic problems and unconversant with linguistic methods are equally flagrant anachronisms.[2]

This essay originally appeared in *A operação do texto* (São Paulo: Perspectiva, 1976), 103–17. —EDITORS

I have standardized and expanded the bibliographic citations in the original essay, keeping all of the original notes but providing full citations and including references to English-language translations where appropriate. —TRANSLATOR

In his analysis of a poem by Bertolt Brecht, Jakobson insists on the same point:

> Among the literary studies of various countries, languages, tendencies, and generations, there are always some that regard the structural analysis of poetry as the trespass of linguistics into a prohibited zone; on the other hand, there are linguists of various schools who, from the start, exclude poetic language from the circle of topics of interest to their science. It is a problem of troglodytes remaining troglodytes.[3]

One would say that Jakobson is not exactly a linguist. Or rather, he is more than simply a linguist: he is a genius. Even if the argument does justice to Jakobson, it doesn't do justice to the science of language, which in this way is reduced to the condition in which it exists in certain American universities—the same ones that Jakobson himself spoke of and which demonstrated a pettiness that was unable to embrace the genius of a man like Charles Sanders Peirce.[4] In his excellent *Survey of Structural Linguistics,* Giulio C. Peschy reports, in agreement with this, that a curious critique has been made of Jakobson: his "excess of intelligence." Because of this "excessive intelligence," the Russian-American maestro would be seen to cast his shadow over certain still nascent problems, anticipating and sometimes predetermining their normal development, thanks to the intuitive foresight of conclusions which, lacking adequate data and thorough and systematic research, would not be able to be satisfactory to everyone . . .[5]

The relatively recent publication of Ferdinand de Saussure's notebooks has demonstrated that, quite contrary to what one would expect, Jakobson, with his heuristic talents and a phonological imagination quick to uncover the arcana of poetic structure, was not alone in this endeavor, nor was he an extravagant case in the field of linguistics. Rather, the professor from Geneva, the recognized father of structural linguistics, proves to be a premonitory and illustrious companion.

Those who have read Jacques Lacan's celebrated study "The Insistence of the Letter in the Unconscious" know that Lacan, the man responsible for expanding the scope of structuralist psychoanalysis, critiques the principle of linearity of Saussurian linguistics in terms that presuppose Saussure's ignorance or a lack of interest with regard to poetry. Lacan writes:

> The linearity that F. de Saussure holds to be constitutive of the chain of discourse, in conformity with its emission by a single voice and with its horizontal position in our writing—if this linearity is necessary in fact, it is not sufficient. . . . But one has only to listen to poetry, something Saussure was perhaps not in the habit of doing, to hear a true polyphony

emerge, to know in fact that all discourse aligns itself along the several staves of a score. There is in effect no signifying chain which does not have attached to the punctuation of each of its units a whole articulation of relevant contexts suspended "vertically" from that point.[6]

In 1957, when Lacan published his study, Saussure's unpublished work on the problem of the "anagrams" had not yet been disclosed; it would come to light only in 1964, in the *Mercure de France,* thanks to Jean Starobinski.[7]

In an interview conducted by Jean Pierre Faye, Jakobson considers the congruence of linguistics and poetics. Taking these and other unpublished Saussurian texts into account, he was already able, in 1966, to respond:

> One such unity can already be drawn from Saussure's lessons. Consider his "Anagrams." I have just seen the Geneva manuscripts, thanks to Starobinski. It is his most inspired work, which managed to frighten even his disciples. And so they tried to keep this part of the Saussurian oeuvre a secret for as long as possible. Saussure, however, wrote to Meillet that it was his masterwork.[8]

But, after all, what are the "Anagrams," where Saussure, surely, would have displayed an excess of intelligence and imagination to such a degree, that zealous disciples, bereft of equal creativity, would have prudently decided, for the sake of the master's reputation, to delay their publication?

Starobinski, whose commentaries accompany the fragments of Saussure's text, explains:

> In the years in which he was presenting a course to his students at the University of Geneva—the notes to which would form the posthumous publication of the General Linguistics—Ferdinand de Saussure turned his attention to some quite different problems. To judge from the ninety-nine notebooks left unpublished, the most important of these preoccupations concerned a particular type of *anagram,* which Saussure termed, successively: anaphone, hypogram, and paragram.[9]

Properly speaking, the anagram, as we know, deals with letters: the graphic signs, or digits, of a phonetic alphabet. As defined by Mattoso Câmara Jr., it is a question of an "artifice which, based on the written form, consists of disguising a word by exchanging the position of the letters and, thus, of the corresponding phonemes."[10] In this way, "Eva" is the anagram of "ave," "Roma" of "amor," and vice versa.[11]

Saussure, however, was interested in the anagram exclusively at the phonemic level, in the anagram as an "acoustic image," as Jakobson would say: the anagram as constituted by the repetition of certain sounds whose combination *imitated* a given word. Hence Saussure's consideration of the name "anaphone," which he subsequently reserved for a phonically imperfect anagram, in which the repetition of the phonemes of a theme-word were not complete. A simple vocal correspondence (alliteration, rhyme, assonance), which Saussure called "phonic harmonies," should not be confused with the anagram, nor with the anaphone, because they do not include the imitative aspect of a given word. Saussure recognized this theme-word (an onomastic, the name of a god or hero) quite freely and without regard to the successive, linear sequence of phonemes—as if some "privileged" elements (as it would be appropriate to say in the technical sense of Gestalt theory) would have stood out against a phonetic frame of less relevant elements.

Saussure's observations emerged from his examination of Latin Saturnian poetry, which is characterized by its alliteration. By the end of his studies, that alliterative practice in Saturnian verse appeared to be only a particular and minor manifestation of fixed phonetic laws, whose fulcrum would lie exactly in the anagram and anaphone. Thus, in the example *Taurasia Cisauna Samnio cepit,* Saussure recognized the name of *Scipio,* ghosting up and phonetically reconstructed by the syllables *Ci* (of "Cisauna"), *pi* (of "cepit"), and *io* (of "Samnio"). He then caught a glimpse of another almost perfect repetition, of the same theme-name, in the phonemes of *Samnio cepit* (the initial syllable and the final vowels of the first word, plus the four first phonemes of the second). In another example, *Mors perfecit tua ut essent,* Saussure discerned the ordered repetition of a vocalic series: *o - e - i - u,* modeled after the vowels in the name "Cornelius," with a single imperfection: the first short *e* of *perfecit,* which did not exactly correspond to the long *e* of the theme-name, although it still maintained the vocal quality of the *e.*

Saussure also thought of giving his discovery the name "hypogram," a word whose denotations—"to allude to"; "to reproduce in writing, like a notary, a secretary"; "to emphasize with cosmetics the features of a face"— all adapted themselves completely to the definition of the phenomenon in question: "emphasizing a name, a word, making a point of repeating its syllables, and in this way giving it a second, contrived being, added, as it were, to the original of the word."[12]

Ultimately, however, he came back to the term "paragram," always insisting that the use of the root "gram" should not imply that figure being studied would be of a graphic or written nature. "Anagram" would be reserved, in this last terminological specification, for cases in which a theme-word was contained within a delimited phonic space (one or two words), almost as in the traditional definition of the device. In this way, the anagram would represent only a restricted and less important aspect of a broader phenomenon of the phonic mimetism of the paragram.

This paragram (or hypogram), notes Starobinski, "inserts a simple name into the complex array of syllables in a poetic line; its function will be to recognize and reassemble its leading syllables, as Isis reassembled the dismembered body of Osiris."[13] The metaphor is all the more appropriate, to add my own twist to this trope, when one also notes that the name of Osiris, in its turn, contains the redistributed, *anagrammatized* phonemes of Isis . . .

But Saussure didn't leave it at that. Besides the paragram, in its various modalities, or concomitant with it, he also deciphered phonic harmonies resulting from the repetition of elements in equal number (which he called "coupling"). Thus, in the line *Subigit omne Loucanam opsidesque abdoucit*, he discerned the following phonic elements, each repeated twice: *ouc, d, it, i, o, n, m.*

From the evaluation of his research, Saussure concluded that, taking all the syllables into consideration to contribute to a phonic symmetry, there exists in the *carmen* a second combinatory principle, independent of the metrical scheme of the verse, but that allies itself with that metrical pattern to constitute a poetic form. In order to satisfy this second principle, *poets had to devote themselves to the phonic analysis of words.* Saussure stressed that a science of the vocal form of words is what, since the most ancient Indo-European times, would have accounted for the superiority and extraordinary quality of the Hindu *kavys* and the Latin *vates.**

In fact, Saussure encountered the same phenomena in his analysis of Vedic poetry. In the hymns dedicated to Agni Angiras, for example, he detected a series of calembours such as *girah* (songs), *anga* (union), and so on, which aimed at replicating the syllables of the sacred name. In the first hymn of the Rig-Veda, he discovered a poetic-grammatical analysis instilled in the phonopoetic analysis of the base. (This hymn, according to Saussure, declined the divine name *Agni.*) In this way, Saussure also recognized paired vocal symmetries in Hindu poetic art.

Extending his investigations to medieval German alliterative poetry, Saussure made a curious etymological digression. It was the poets' duty, by

---

* Cf. Starobinski, *Words upon Words* (New Haven, CT: Yale University Press, 1979), 22. Saussure uses the term *kavis* (*kavys*), which actually refers to a type of poetry. Because in this passage he is referring to the abilities of the poet, not the texts, he most likely meant *kev* the Hindi term for poet. —EDITORS

the timeless precepts of their art, to analyze the phonic substance of words (whether by the organization of purely acoustic series governed by proportional rule or by the constitution of imitative-allusive series—paragrams—around a theme-name). So it follows that one should investigate how a poet would compute the analyzed phonic elements. This thought allowed Saussure to interpret the German word *Stab,* in its triple sense of "rod," "alliterative poetic phoneme," and "letter." While composing a song, the poet, who would have to combine sounds in determined number, would use pebbles of different colors or small rods of various sizes to mark those sounds already used. The connection between "rod" and "phoneme" would thus make historical sense, since the poet counted phonemes by means of rods. Antedating writing, this *Stab* (computing instrument of phonemes, or simply phoneme by metonymy) would later have been agglutinated with *Buch* (from *buoch,* the beech bark on which characters would be traced) in order to form the modern composite *Buchstabe* (letter).

The nodal point of Saussure's reflections on the anagrammatic phonemes is exactly the point at which they touch on the question of the linearity of language. It is a matter, as Starobinski says, of the question of *time* in language, which, by virtue of the anagram, appears in a new light, as the phonemes of the theme-word are dislocated from their proper initial order and are motivated to undergo a fugal treatment.

As we know, one of the fundamental postulates of Saussurian linguistics is the linearity of the signifying aspect of the linguistic sign ("[A]coustic significations only have at their disposal a temporal line; elements present themselves one after the other; they form a chain"; this "linear character of language excludes the possibility of two elements being pronounced at the same time" [Saussure, *Course*]). Jakobson contested the validity of this assertion, invoking, in order to weaken it, the nonlinear but simultaneous character of the distinctive traces which constitute the phoneme. The author of "For a Phonemic Structure" writes: "Yes, it is clear that two sounds cannot be articulated at the same time in speech, but when there are two or more phonic properties, it is clearly possible!" This is exemplified by showing that the conjunction of two distinctive qualities—clear tonality and muffled acoustic effect—in the same phoneme is a relation of two simultaneous elements *in praesentia.*[14]

From the point of view of structural psychoanalysis, we see the refutation that Lacan also made to the linearity principle, using as argument precisely the *polyphonic* character of poetry and, by extension, the scored arrangement that all discourse implicitly bears.

So it is of the utmost importance to know that Saussure himself went on to admit a weakening of his axiom, at least in the field of poetic language, in the study of the paragram, which does not obey the principle of temporal consecutivity. The master muses:

> Can one give TAE by *ta* + *te*, i. e., by inviting the reader to what is no longer a juxtaposition in consecutivity, but to a mean of acoustic impressions beyond time, beyond the order in time these elements have and the linear order which is observed if I give TAE by TA—AE or TA—E, but is not if I give it as *ta* + *te*, to be amalgamated outside time, as could be done with two simultaneous colors?[15]

Here, in the phonic plane, is a Mallarméan precept, of the more general "prismatic subdivisions of the Idea," which inspired an explicitly scored configuration (horizontal/vertical) in *Un coup de dés* [*A Throw of the Dice*] (1897) and which subsequently led to the *simultaneity* of futurism and Dada. Jakobson, in 1914, would write to Velimir Khlebnikov about the problem of "simultaneous semiotic units" of "simultaneity" (*odnovremennost*) in poetry, and of the analogies with music notes, without knowing that some years before, a great many identical preoccupations had been obsessing Saussure, who would die in 1913.[16]

In Brazilian concrete poetry, we have an emphatic example of an even programmatic denial of the dogma of linearity (from the very first manifestos, culminating in the "Pilot Plan" of 1958: "space-time structure instead of mere linear-temporal development," like the creative manipulation of the effects of simultaneity for the production of texts destined for a nonlinear but plural reading).[17] In the poem "Lygia fingers," from Augusto de Campos's series *Poetamenos* (1953), inspired by the *Klangfarbenmelodie* (timbral melody) technique of composer Anton Webern, there is, for example, a true, gradual anagrammatization of the theme-name, running through the entire piece, with all of its complete or partial phonemes redistributed through other words (*digital, linx, felyna, figlia,* etc.), which themselves function as metonymic or metaphoric emblems of femininity and its attributes. Like the ancient Germanic poets, who used colored stones to mark the phonemes of their composition, the concrete poet made use of his own notation, in which different colors distinguish different reading "parts" (in the musical sense). Each phonothematic collection must be executed by a different vocal timbre (five voices in all in the poem under consideration).[18]

But let's go back to the Saussurian notebooks. In them, Starobinski reports, strictly expositive texts are rare, standing out in counterpoint to the exercises of paragrammatically deciphering Homer, Virgil, Lucretius, Seneca, Horace, Ovid, Plautus, and so on.

Spurred by the results of his analysis, and considering undeniable the general worth of the observed phenomena, the master questioned himself about the origins of the anagrammatic process. Was it a matter of an "occult" or "secret" tradition? Saussure found no evidence to confirm this in the ancient writings. However, he concluded hypothetically:

> 1. One can never know precisely how to measure the strength of this kind of tradition. There are many nineteenth-century French poets who would not have written in the style foreseen by Malherbe if they had felt free to do otherwise. But, additionally, if the practice of anagram had already been established, a poet like Virgil must have easily seen the extended anagrams in Homer . . . [and] would have wished to remain within the rules and not be inferior to Homer on a point which the latter had valued.

> 2. Poetic difficulty could serve as the instigator of composition (as in the case of rhyme). Recognizing that the fundamental and habitual method of poetry would consist in the presupposed decomposition, the theme-word, then the difficulty of the anagram would also serve the poet, who would be inspired by the syllables of the word for expressing ideas to choosing expressions.[19]*

But the problem continued to preoccupy him. Could the paragrams not be mere products of chance? For the observer predisposed to discern significant structures through the conjunction of dispersed phonemes, would language, by its internal dynamics, not engender them almost automatically? Starobinski mentions Saussure's following observation as representative of the dilemma that confronted the thinking of the master in his final stage: "Can the materiality of the fact be a matter of chance? Are not the laws of the 'hypogram' sufficiently spacious that inevitably, and without surprise, one finds within them every proper name?"†

Just as Mallarmé, pursued by *Le Hasard* and trying to abolish it through ("perhaps") a "constellation" (*compte total en formation*), Saussure (*Le*

---

* De Campos paraphrases Saussure in this passage. Cf. Starobinski, *Words upon Words*, 96. —EDITORS

† De Campos paraphrases Saussure in this passage. Cf. Starobinski, *Words upon Words*, 97. —EDITORS

Maître / hors d'anciens calculs) fought with chance, seeking to capture it in the motile figure (*dispersion volatile*) of his paragrams, harnessing it in the combinatorial web of his "phonic harmonies." In both examples, chance if not eliminated is irrevocably incorporated into the reflections of its antagonists ("si c'était le Nombre / ce serait le Hasard" ["if it was the number / it would be chance"], warns Mallarmé). Just as the genius poet of "Un coup de dés" queried Valéry, upon showing him his poem—"Does it not seem to you an act of madness?"—Saussure also wrote to Meillet, on doubting that he was falling victim to a subjective illusion. Meillet, in his reply— Starobinski reproduces the letter—invokes the example of Bach, in order to justify that which, to the eyes of outsiders, could seem a foolish and groundless idiosyncrasy:

> I don't know whether you've seen a general thesis by André Pirro, *L'esthétique de Bach.* In it, one can see very well how preoccupations apparently as puerile as that of the anagram obsessed Sebastian Bach and in no way prevented him from writing highly expressive music but rather guided him in the labor of expressive form.[20]

Starobinski concludes his first presentation of the Saussurian notebooks with a suspension of judgment. For Saussure, classical poetry would be a combinatorial art; but all language is combination. The field is thus open for the decoders, whether they be cabalists or phoneticists. And will there not be ciphers to decipher (a "latent depth," a "secret language within the language")? There will always remain—concludes Starobinksi—the "attraction of the secret," an "anticipated discovery" of "steps astray in the labyrinth of exegesis. . . ."[21]

The fact remains, however, that although focused on the art of classical poetics, Saussure's inspired theory of the paragrams—his final "throw of the dice"—appears as an invaluable instrument for evaluating the essence of poetry. The paragram (which is, as Lepschy says, a type of "spatialized paraphrase" of the theme-word) achieves, in the final analysis (and here it is not necessary to know a timeless poetic ritual is in operation behind the figure), a fusion of sound and sense characteristic of the "poetic function" of language, which Jakobson independently investigated in his first works.[22] In the simultaneity of paragrammatic reading is mirrored that projection of the paradigm over the syntagma that, according to Jakobson, distinguishes poetry. In fact, the paragram takes the form of a phonic paradigm, in which the theme-word functions as the center of an associative constellation, and the combinatorial variants of the phonemes of that word-nucleus play the role of the coordinated terms that converge on that nucleus. (Paradigm, in the traditional definition, denotes a schema, a table of inflections of a word given as the model of a series, of a declension.) Paronomasia (wordplay, pun), the queen figure of poetry in Jakobson's estimation, is merely another, broader way of seeing the phenomenon of the Saussurian paragram.[23] By virtue of this, phonological similarity is felt as a semantic relationship, as is the case of anaphony (paragram), whereby the theme-name repeatedly takes shape against the signifying horizon of the poem. When Poe, in the famous Jakobsonian analysis, has his crow ("raven," ra'v n) pronounce its own name backward ("never")—R.V.N. / N.V.R.—he has anagrammatized a theme-word, just as Virgil, in the Saussurian decoding, makes the phonemes of Priamides appear in those lines of the *Aeneid* that describe the apparition in a dream, to Aeneas, of Hector, son of Priam (canto 2, verse 268 and following): "Tempus erat quo prima quies mortalibus aegris / Incipit, et dono divum gratissima serpit" ["It was the hour when gentle sleep first comes, / welcome, by God's grace, welcome to weary men"],* etc.

In this way, Saussure's reflections on the paragram, extrapolating from a pure phonological investigation, touch on the very essence of poetry. More importantly, although thriving on classical poetry, they fully project themselves into the present, as if demonstrating the continuity of poetic invention, the synchronic coexistence of cultural past and creative present. Starobinski, though emphasizing that the Saussurian analyses do not consider modern poetry, notes that they nonetheless suggest the potential of the method. He notes, for instance, that the compositional method of Raymond Roussel (a pioneer of contemporary French *écriture*) could be approached using paragrammatic criteria, mentioning, in connection to this, Michel Foucault's 1963 book on the author of *Impressions of Africa*. And it is not surprising that Julia Kristeva, a member of the group associated with the journal *Tel Quel*, has again taken up Saussure's final speculations as directives for an important and ambitious semiotic research of textual production: "Pour une sémiologie des paragrammes."[24] There are, as Kristeva establishes, starting from Saussure, a set of principles which could lead to a revision of the general concept of the literary text:

a) Poetic language "adds a second mode of being, an artificial, supplementary mode of being, so to speak, to the original mode of the word."

* Virgil, *The Aeneid*, 2d ed., trans. Frank O. Copley (Indianapolis: Bobbs-Merrill, 1981), 32. —EDITORS

b) There is a correspondence between elements, through pairing and through rhyme.

c) These *binary* poetic laws go so far as to transgress the laws of grammar.[25]

d) The elements of a *theme-word* (even a letter thereof) can "extend over the entire text or be concentrated in a tiny space, such as one or two words."[26]

Thus, in a corollary mode, Kristeva's three theses:

1. Poetic language is the only infinity of code.

2. The literary text is a double: writing-reading.

3. The literary text is a network of connections.[27]

In this last thesis there is a challenge to "linearity," by way of a "tabular model," a system of multiple connections, a polyvalent web, a "dynamic and spacial graphism designating the over-determination of meaning."

Saussure is thus transformed, by his extreme and most daring "throw of the dice," into a theoretician of the avant-garde. His work, like that of Mallarmé, whose exact heuristic profile only the future would be able to define, ends also at a cliff.[28]

Translated by Craig D. Dworkin

Poetic Function and Ideogram/
The Sinological Argument

Poetic Function and Ideogram

As a practitioner of poetry, Ernest Fenollosa was not able to go beyond the conventional horizon of the belles lettres of his time. Yet as a theoretician—as a poeticist—it must be recognized that he intuitively captured the fundamental structures of his art and was able to provide the instruments with which to meet future needs. Something analogous might be said of Saussure, who was out of tune with contemporary poetic practice—Mallarmé, above all—and entirely concerned with the poetry of antiquity (Vedic, classical Greek and Latin, or Germanic and considered his contemporary Giovanni Pascoli worthy of attention only as a scholarly cultivator of the Latin versifying art).[1] At the same time, his work on anagrams put forward a conception of how poetry is engendered, which was to meet with its most definitive counterpart not in the sealed mysteries of the past but

---

This section comprises two parts of a longer essay in eleven parts entitled "Ideograma, anagrama, diagrama: Uma leitura de Fenollosa," published as introduction to *Ideograma: Lógica, poesia, linguagem,* 2d ed., ed. Haroldo de Campos (São Paulo: Cultrix, 1986; reprint, São Paulo: EDUSP, 2003), 9–113 [page numbers refer to the 1986 edition]. This English translation by Kevin Mundy and Marc Benson with an introductory note by Lúcia Santaella Braga (here omitted) was originally published in *Dispositio* 6, no. 17–18 (Summer–Fall 1981): 9–39. The translation is reprinted, with minor editorial alterations, by kind permission of *Dispositio: Revista Americana de Estudios Comparados y Culturales/American Journal of Comparative and Cultural Studies,* published by the University of Michigan Department of Romance Languages and Literatures. —EDITORS

in the breakthroughs of the future, inaugurated precisely by Mallarmé's exemplary radicalism. (Indeed, after the manner of an amateur linguist, Mallarmé provided him in advance with his own alphabetic-alliterative theory in unwitting circumstantial counterpoint, while at the same time dreaming of how science would one day write the "history of the letters of the alphabet," as he wrote in 1877 in his *Les mots anglais* [*English Words*], also entitled *Petite philologie à l'usage des classes et du monde* [*Short Philology in the Usage of the Classes and of the World*]. . . .)[2]

At this point, it might be useful to stress that one of the primary aims of Fenollosa's essay is the *translation of poetry*, understood as a re-creative operation. It is here that his dispute with the Sinologues begins:

> It was perhaps too much to expect that aged scholars who had spent their youth in gladiatorial combats with the refractory Chinese characters should succeed also as poets. Even Greek verse might have fared equally ill had its purveyors been perforce content with provincial standards of English rhyming. Sinologues should remember that the purpose of poetical translation is the poetry, not the verbal definitions in dictionaries.[*]

In this sense, it can be said that as a translator-inventor of Chinese poetry, Ezra Pound was not only Fenollosa's cultural heir but also the most faithful and providential executor of his testament.

Fenollosa was opposed to those who considered Chinese and Japanese poetry to be a trivial and childish amusement, and he distrusted translations whose lack of skill created this futile image of "milk-and-water poetry." He set out to make an intrinsic analysis of Chinese ideographic characters and thereby to discover the sources of the aesthetic pleasure Chinese and Japanese poetry gave him. In order to do so, and precisely because the object of study—written Chinese—was evidently so extremely distant from Western forms (indeed, in this sense there was the widest possible gulf, at least apparently, between it and phonetic-alphabetic languages), Fenollosa resolved to investigate those "universal elements of form" which constituted a "poetics" (as did Jakobson, later on, in his "poetry of grammar") and the way that such elements worked in this peculiar and alien body of poetry. It must be pointed out that for Fenollosa the study of

---

* All references to this essay quoted from Ernest Fenollosa, *The Chinese Written Character as a Medium for Poetry*, ed. Ezra Pound (1936; reprint, San Francisco: City Lights Books, 1968). Quotation on p. 5. Hereafter, page references to this work will be given in parentheses directly after the passage quoted in the text. —EDITORS

poetry was rooted in the study of language, and the criterion for distinguishing between language as a means to transmit a "prosaic meaning" (its *referential function,* as we would now put it) and language which can be recognized as poetry (its *poetic function*) was a difference *in form.* The "plastic" character of this language, as evidenced by a "regular and flexible sequence," was the poetic itself. Although Fenollosa's formulations are a far cry in technical and linguistic precision from those of Jakobson, it is relevant here to recall certain passages from the latter's "Linguistics and Poetics." There he points out, following an "empirical criterion," that the "poetic function" is designed to "promote the palpability of signs":

> The repetitiveness effected by imparting the equivalence principle to the sequence makes reiterable not only the constituent sequences of the poetic message but the whole message as well. This capacity for reiteration whether immediate or delayed, this reification of a poetic message and its constituents, this conversion of a message into an enduring thing, indeed all this represents an inherent and effective property of poetry.*

In his scrutiny of poetry written in phonetic languages, Jakobson sought out the interchanging recurrence of "figures of sound and sense" (as Saussure before him, in his vertiginous deciphering of anagrams, had yielded to the "frenzy of the phonic interplay," the "Chinese puzzle" [*sic*] of words resounding beneath other words).[3] In Chinese written poetry, on the other hand, and thus at the level of graphemes, Fenollosa was able to recognize the "overtones" which vibrated before the eyes, "coloring" all the semantic planes like a "dominant."

This is indeed Fenollosa's main contribution to the understanding of how poetry works *in any language*—for the "Chinese model" to him was simply a touchstone for the approach to the problem of English-language poetry (and, by extension, of all poetry in the phonetic languages of the Western world). Despite his insistence on the directly "pictorial" aspect of the ideogram in relation to external nature (and we shall soon see the precise meaning of this problem of *relation*), Fenollosa is lucid enough to tone down his hyper-philological hypothesis by the end of his essay. There he stresses its qualities as a model, above all, and its effectiveness as a functional framework: "Such a pictorial method, *whether the Chinese exempli-*

---

* Roman Jakobson, "Closing Statement: Linguistics and Poetics," in *Style in Language,* ed. Thomas A. Sebeok (New York: Technology Press of MIT, 1960), 371. —EDITORS

fied it or not, would be the ideal language of the world"(31, emphasis added). Ideal in what sense? Most directly, in the sense that Fenollosa (like Vico before him and the transcendentalist Emerson) defended the mythopoeic thesis of an original language, the language of Eden or Adam, where words reverberated the halo of things in a paradisiacal communion, radiating out through the tropological force of metaphors. Vico even made the distinction between a "holy language" invented by Adam, endowed by God with the gift of *onomathesia* (the faculty of granting original names to things in accordance with the nature of each one), and the "primitive speech" of "theologian poets," the "Atlantic language," which reclaimed part of this divine faculty through "poetic logic," whose corollaries were the "tropes," and among them the most "luminous" and "necessary": metaphor. Thus, the argument continued, the ideas of things were conceived "through fantastic characters of animated substances," figurative personifications always related to the "nature of things" with their "natural properties." (Joyce, a self-confessed disciple of Vico, expresses through his "persona," the young artist Stephen Dedalus, the intention of reading in nature "the signature of things," *signatura rerum,* as he writes in *Ulysses.*)

In his famous 1844 essay, Emerson writes: "The poet is the Namer or Language-maker, naming things sometimes after their appearance, sometimes after their essence, and giving to every one its own name and not another's, thereby rejoicing the intellect, which delights in detachment or boundary. The poets made all the words, and therefore language is the archives of history, and, if we must say it, a sort of tomb of the muses." And he continues: "For, though the origin of most of our words is forgotten, each word was at first a stroke of genius, and obtained currency, because for the moment it symbolized the world to the first speaker and to the hearer. The etymologist finds the deadest word to have been once a brilliant picture. Language is fossil poetry."[4]

Fenollosa believed he had found a living instance of Emerson's hypothesis, miraculously preserved, in the "Chinese model." He is echoing the poet he so admired during his Harvard years when he declares:

> Metaphor, the revealer of nature, is the very substance of poetry. . . .
> Poetry only does consciously what the primitive races did unconsciously.
> The chief work of literary men in dealing with language, and of poets
> especially, lies in feeling back along the ancient lines of advance. . . .
> [P]oetry was the earliest of the world arts; poetry, language and the care of
> myth grew up together. . . . Our ancestors built the accumulations of

metaphor into structures of language and into systems of thought. Languages today are thin and cold. . . . Nature would seem to have become less like a paradise and more and more like a factory. . . . Only scholars and poets feel painfully back along the thread of our etymologies and piece together our diction, as best they may, from forgotten fragments. (24)

Hence, for Fenollosa, the exemplary and revivifying nature of the Chinese paradigm:

In this Chinese shows its advantage. Its etymology is constantly visible. It retains the creative impulse and process, visible and at work. . . . Their ideographs are like bloodstained battle-flags to an old campaigner. With us, the poet is the only one for whom the accumulated treasures of the race-words are real and active. Poetic language is always vibrant with fold on fold of overtones and with natural affinities, but in Chinese the visibility of the metaphor tends to raise this quality to its intensest power. (25)

Jacques Derrida highlights the fact that at the end of the seventeenth century and during the eighteenth the "Chinese model" functioned (at least apparently) as an interrupter of Western logocentrism and acted as "a kind of European hallucination." It matched contemporary concerns to find a "universal language," a goal formulated by Descartes and later by Leibnitz. The latter saw ideographic writing as a philosophic language par excellence, although he had an idealized conception of its nature. This "model" of a supposedly artificial, ahistorical language gave Leibnitz the basis for his projected "universal characteristics," a set of combinations or a "calculus" which was to culminate in the invention of a script with all the advantages of Chinese characters, "because everyone would understand it in their own language," but at the same time none of the obstacles to rapid learning so intrinsic to Chinese. The second moment of this Sinological fascination was to be seen in America with Fenollosa and Pound. (Though it should be remembered, as Hugh Kenner argues, that Emerson's organicism and, more broadly, New England transcendentalism had also had their "Chinese affinities" before Fenollosa through readings of the same neo-Confucian works of Jesuit missionaries in China which had stimulated Leibnitz to write his *Specimen calculi universalis*. . . .) There was a difference, however. The first moment saw the constitution of the "Chinese model" as a means to fertilize a renewal of Western logic in terms of an algebraic combination (the "calculus" developed by Leibnitz—wrote R. H. Robins, in *A Short History of Linguistics* [Bloomington: Indiana University

Press, 1967]—"anticipates certain features of modern symbolic logic, though it is based on the Aristotelian syllogism"[113]). The second, on the other hand, highlighted the poetic and rose up against Aristotelian logic: instead, it proposed something in the order of a "poetic logic" (to use Vico's expression), a logic of analogy or imagination, which in its turn embraced another aspect of Aristotle, now brought back into the limelight not as the father of the syllogism but as the theoretician of metaphor, the distinguishing mark of poetic genius. . . .

Both moments, for their seminal purposes, idealized the Chinese paradigm, endowing it with virtues which could even be seen as opposites. For Leibnitz, the important element in Chinese was what he presumed to be its purely institutional and purely arbitrary character, free of historicity. (Chinese was invented, according to this view, as an artificial means of communication between the different peoples who inhabited the great Chinese Empire.) Whereas to Leibnitz Egyptian hieroglyphs represented a "sensory" and "allegorical" script, Chinese characters seemed "more philosophical," as they were "founded upon more intellectual considerations" and made up of "disconnected strokes which are not aimed at resembling any kind of body in any manner." (In his *Cours,* Saussure echoes this conception, seeing in Chinese the "ultralexicological" type par excellence, among languages where lack of motivation reaches its apogee and arbitrariness is thus subject to minimal restrictions: this is derived from the assumption that the "grammatical instrument" is irrelevant in Chinese.) Fenollosa, on the other hand, saw Chinese as the mirror of nature because of its "pictoriality," which brought it close to the active world of things: for him, the absence of explicit grammatical canons was an obvious proof of this language's fidelity to the dynamics of the natural processes of energy relations and transfer, something in the way of a structural, morphological, organic-evolutionary mimesis. According to Fenollosa's reading, ideograms are rooted deep down in history or rather in a quasi-paradisiacal arche-history. They are, as it were, the mnemonic records of mankind, where diachrony is exhibited in a dioramic display: "The prehistoric poets who created language discovered the whole harmonious framework of nature, they sang out her processes in their hymns" (32). This radiant, Emerson-like vision of the poet as a "translator of nature" in fact coincides with the legendary Chinese tradition of the origins of writing as a transcription (an "emblematics," as Marcel Granet would say) of natural signs. It is said that during the reign of the semimythical Emperor Huang Ti (twenty-sixth century B.C.), a minister invented writing "after studying the celestial bodies and their formations as well as the natural objects around him, especially the footprints of birds and animals" (M. Granet, *La pensée chinoise* [*Chinese Thought*]; V. Alleton, *L'écriture chinoise* [*Chinese Writing*]).* In strictly semiotic terms, this "myth of origin" can be interpreted as the translation of indices (vestiges) into icons with progressively accentuated conventionalization through stylizations of a symboloid tendency . . ."5

The Sinological Argument

How would a scholar be received if he were to lean down from the narrow chair of his specialty in order to pore over the *Scienza nuova,* only to condemn its pseudoetymological whims and lucubrations, its fanciful overdoses of mythopoeia, all in the name of philological rigor and without any grasp of the fundamentals of the philosophy of language at the heart of Vico's revolution?

This is the procedure followed by the Sinologists (with a few honorable exceptions) with regard to Fenollosa's legacy. "Fenollosa's essay is a small mass of confusion," declared George Kennedy in 1958. Kennedy is the most acrimonious of such censors; at the same time, he hails Pound as a poet but never as a translator, for Pound has the practice but lacks the necessary knowledge ("Fenollosa, Pound and the Chinese Character").†

The most shocking aspect of Fenollosa's view to the specialists is the argumentative stress he places on the "pictorial appeal" of Chinese. Its refutation is—without G. Kennedy's acrimony—properly summarized in a study by Yu-Kuang Chu.‡ Of the four principles on which the construction of Chinese characters was based, only the first centers on pictorial representation (the second, according to the same view, is a kind of diagram of the idea, such as a dot over a stroke to indicate "over"; the third is a means to evoke something through suggestion, by combining two characters in order to release a third ideative element; the fourth—from which most Chinese words are derived—is a combination of one of the 214 "radical"

*Michel Granet, *La pensée chinoise* (1934; reprint, New York: Arno Press, 1975), 48; Viviane Alleton, *L'écriture chinoise,* 2d ed. (Paris: Presses Universitaires de France, 1976), 71. —EDITORS

† In *Selected Works of George A. Kennedy,* ed. Tien-yi Li (Li Tianyi) (New Haven, CT: Far Eastern Publications, 1964). —EDITORS

‡ The essay that de Campos refers to is "Interplay Between Language and Thought in Chinese," *Etc: A Review of General Semantics* 22 (1965): 307–29, a translation of which was published in *Ideograma: Lógica, poesia, linguagem,* the same volume containing the original version of the present essay. The quotation at the end of the paragraph appears on pp. 312–13. —EDITORS

elements, or rather "semantic classifiers," with a "phonogram" or indicator of the pronunciation of the composite whole: a necessity in order to avoid the high incidence of homophony in a basically monosyllabic language— at least as regards classical Chinese). Moreover, the author proceeds, the growing stylization of the pictograms and the changes introduced over the ages by, among others, the learned lexicologists, with their transcription errors and/or imaginative idiosyncrasies, have made the original pictography largely unrecognizable. Finally, in ordinary use, Chinese readers treat ideograms in the same way as users of alphabetical languages treat script, as conventionalized symbols, without any longer seeing in them the visual metaphor—the visible etymology—which so impressed Fenollosa and which he is alleged to have overestimated. It is curious that, having conveniently "discredited" Fenollosa's reading, Yu-Kuang Chu feels compelled to make a reservation: "However, it remains true that the Chinese treat the written character as an artistic design. It is perhaps no coincidence that Chinese art excels in the visual field."

If we consider the practice of the *poetic function,* in the sphere of phonetic languages themselves, we can see how the main stress shifts when dealing with a similar problem. Whereas for the referential use of language it makes no difference whether the word *astre* ("star") can be found within the adjective *désastreux* ("disastrous") or the noun *désastre* ("disaster"), or whether there are affinities between *espectro* ("specter") and *espectador* ("spectator"),

> Calme bloc ici-bas chu d'un désastre obscur
> —Mallarmé
>
> Stern block here fallen from a mysterious disaster*
>
> Spectros espectadores que surgiam
> Vindo ao espetac' lo horrendo horríveis de palor
> —Sousândrade†
>
> Specters spectators that emerged
> coming to the horrendous spectacle horribly pale

for the poet this kind of "discovery" is of prime relevance. In poetry, warns

---

* From the English version of the poem Mallarmé himself made in 1877 for Sarah Helen Whitman in Stephane Mallarmé, *Oeuvres complètes,* ed. Bertrand Marchal (Paris: Gallimard [Pléiade], 1998), 1193. Translation suggested by Richard Sieburth. —EDITORS

† From *Poesia e prosa reunidas de Sousândrade,* ed. Frederick G. Williams and Jomar Moraes (São Luís de Maranhão, Brazil: Edições AML, 2003). —EDITORS

Jakobson, any phonological coincidence is felt to mean semantic kinship (not only those coincidences which can be etymologically justified, as in *parekesis,* but more extensively, as in the case of paronomasia in the broad sense, any phonic similarities which can be semantically confronted in an overall fecundating process of pseudoetymology or poetic etymology; thus, in the foregoing quotation from Sousândrade, the last word in the sequence, *palOR* ("pallor"), shares the same phonic figure as in *hORrendo* ("horrendous") and *hORríveis* ("horrible"), thus being, as it were, prepared for by the emphatic repetition which precedes it).

What the Chinese example enhanced for Fenollosa was the homological and homologizing virtue of the *poetic function.* Because it was written in characters, Chinese poetry gave Fenollosa the chance to explore (inspect) these "homologies" within a visual framework from the point of view of the grapheme.[6] Now, leaving aside the comparative degree of stylization or conventionalization (the "symboloid features," to use the terminology coined by Peirce, that remarkable fellow countryman and contemporary of Fenollosa's), the fact is that if the question is not examined from the philological but rather from the semiotic standpoint, the "iconicity" factor always seems to be present in varying degrees in Chinese writing ("iconicity," like "artistic realism" in Jakobson's demonstration, is a matter of degree and depends on variable codes of perception, immersed in tradition and history). This factor is at work, with varying levels of "mimetic" intensity, in each of the four principles behind the formation of characters listed by Yu-Kuang Chu. It can at once be seen that the "pictogram" is undeniably an "icon": it is a painting whose characteristics give it some kind of relationship, by similarity, with reality, although this "representative quality" may well be derived not from servile imitation but from a differentiated pattern of relationships, in accordance with a selective and creative criterion. (At this point it must be recalled that Fenollosa refused to admit "copybook" naturalism in painting; on the contrary, he encouraged a reorganization of natural relations in a new creative synthesis, taking nature not as a mold for transfer-like imitation, but as a dynamic model.) If imagined inside its potential frame at the stage of evolution it had reached when Fenollosa examined it, the "pictogram" already forms a small cubist painting, an aggressively metonymized metaphor. (Eisenstein, whose 1929 essay on the cinematographic principle and the ideogram* coincides with so many points of Fenollosa's, was well aware of this aspect

---

*Sergei Eisenstein, "The Cinematographic Principle and the Ideogram," in *Film Form [and] The Film Sense,* ed. and trans. Jay Leyda (New York: Meridian Books, 1957), 28–44. —EDITORS

when, with his filmmaker's eye focusing on the process, he stressed the antinaturalism of the psychological "disproportions" in Japanese art. Indeed, he considered this "method of expressive representation," in its turn, "organically natural," spontaneous in children, and traceable to sources as far back as prehistory. The "natural scale" always gives way to an intrinsic "pictorial scale," while "absolute realism" is by no means "the correct form of perception," but simply a function of given social structures which are also absolutist. . . .)

The sign that results from the application of the second formative principle (called "diagram" by Yu-Kuang Chu himself) can be described in Peirce's terminology as a "hypo-icon" with indexical features, a small map or topological graph. The third principle is that of "suggestive" association. (Eisenstein calls it "copulative" or "combinatory," emphasizing that its result is not a mere sum total but a "product," a value of a different degree.) Two "pictograms" are joined to suggest a new relation that was not present in the individual elements in isolation. Or in the words of V. Ivanov ("Eisenstein et la linguistique structurale moderne," 1970):* "The association of two representations (two "pictographic" hieroglyphs or cinematographic images) leads to the designation of the abstract concept which representation in itself is unable to evoke." (Ivanov points out that a study of this phenomenon is especially relevant to present-day semiology as it entails transforming syntax into a means for a study of semantics.) Now, this is exactly the "ideographic method of composition" described by Fenollosa and which he places on a par with "metaphor": the use of "material images" to suggest "immaterial relations," or, as Eisenstein puts it, the passage from "thought through images" to "conceptual thought." But in Peirce's triadic classification, metaphor is also a "hypo-icon," although it is a tertiary "hypo-icon," close to the pole of conventionality of the symbol. (However, whereas in metaphor properly speaking, as Jakobson explains it, there is an equation at the level of meanings between a "primary" and another "secondary" meaning, in the ideogramic complex the visual or grapheme notation corroborates the metaphorical equation at the level of the *signans* as a kind of paragraphia, which can be assimilated to Jakobson's paronomasia.)[7]

Finally, in the fourth formative principle iconicity is fully manifest in the form of the "semantic classifier" (also known as "radical"). This belongs to the family of "pictograms," analyzed above: each one of these 214 "radi-

* Viacheslav Ivanov, "Eisenstein et la linguistique structurale moderne," *Cahiers du cinéma: Russie années vingt* 220–21 (May–June 1970): 46–50. —EDITORS

cals" points to, or rather "displays," the "general category of things" to which the compound ideogram into which it fits refers. The "phonogram" element, however, apparently plays an arbitrary role in the compound, as a mere orthoepic reminder (that is, a record of the pronunciation of the resulting word). And yet even here what is arbitrary a priori may often become (in Lévi-Strauss's words) interrelated a posteriori, at least for the poet engaged in the practice of his craft (or for the imaginative etymologist and lexicologist). Thus, in the very example given by Yu-Kuang Chu, the ideogram for ocean,

洋

we have, on the one hand, the "semantic classifier" indicating the presence of something "liquid" (the pictogram for "water"—radical no. 85— metonymized visually by a few laconic strokes resembling trickles of water from a spring); on the other, there is the phonogram which indicates the pronunciation yang (i.e., yang uttered in the second of the four tones of classical Chinese); this is also individually the pictogram for "ewe" or "sheep" (a zoomorphic head, detached from the animal's body by a stroke of synecdoche and stylized so as to represent the muzzle and horns with six brushstrokes). According to Yu-Kuang Chu, the second element has nothing more to do with "sheep" but is now a mere phonetic graph. However, the mind of a poet can hardly resist this Vicoesque "miniature fable," which seems to throb in the juxtaposition of the "radical" and the "phonogram" as if already pushing its product toward the third category, that of "associative" or "suggestive" ideograms. The Portuguese verb *encarneirar* (referring to the curling of small choppy waves in the sea *as if* it were a flock of sheep) and the French verb *moutonner* help to make explicit the metaphorical process thus intuitively sensed (or constructed?) a posteriori. In their book *Pictorial Chinese-Japanese Characters* (1950), Oreste and Enko Vaccari, who as analysts are aware of the fascination of the visual, provide some confirmation of this "discovery" by the poetic imagination.* According to these authors, the idea of representing the ocean by means of this combination of characters originated precisely in the immemorial perceptive fact that "a flock of sheep in motion reminds one of the rolling of white-capped waves on the open sea."[8]

To Fenollosa, "relations" between things were more important than

---

* Oreste Vaccari and Enko Elisa Vaccari, *Pictorial Chinese-Japanese Characters: A New and Fascinating Method to Learn Ideographs,* 6th ed. (Tokyo: Vaccari's Language Institute, 1968). —EDITORS

things themselves. This genuine structuralist credo *ante litteram* is expressed in the same passage of his essay as the section where he discusses the question of "homologies" or "sympathies" between poetry and nature. This excludes, on the grounds of oversimplification, any reading which claims (in ignorance of Fenollosa's ideas on painting) to reduce his view on the mechanics of the ideogram (grounded in a supposed "identity of structure") to the mere "imitation" of reality, to figuration understood as a servile "copy" of an external object. Fenollosa was interested in deepening this "structural analogy," discerning the lines of force in nature and capturing them within a new harmonious synthesis.

> Relations are more real and more important than the things which they relate. . . . Similar lines of resistance, half-curbing the out-pressing vitalities, govern the branching of rivers and of nations. Thus a nerve, a wire, a roadway, and a clearing-house are only varying channels which communication forces for itself. This is more than an analogy, it is identity of structure. Nature furnishes her own clues. Had the world not been full of homologies, sympathies, and identities, thought would have been starved and language chained to the obvious. (22)

(This puts the whole of McLuhan in a nutshell, including his "new media" as "extensions of man.") Nature is a web of multiple dynamic tensions. For Fenollosa, the ideograph—and, as an expansion of it, poetry—is the written homologue of these tensions in the abbreviated world of the text. (An " 'imagist' transformation of the dialectical principle," concluded Eisenstein, attempting through the notion of "conflict"—"montage is conflict"—to replace a description of the "progressive-evolutionary" type with a synthesis of the "dialectical substance of events.")*

In his essay, Fenollosa makes his way through a suggestive endeavor to "naturalize" grammatical processes—all of which are traced back to their energy source in the transitive verb through, as Kenner points out, a kind of pre-generative-transformational grammar. I would add, however, that Fenollosa's is diachronic and evolutionary, or "genetic," rather than synchronic and formal, as Chomsky's. He then proceeds to condemn the tyranny of medieval logic and the syllogistic pyramid (an aspect to be considered below with all due emphasis). It is only toward the end of his essay that Fenollosa finally touches on what seems to me the essence of his problem:

* Eisenstein, "Cinematographic Principle," 38. —EDITORS

It is true that the pictorial clue of many Chinese ideographs cannot now be traced, and even Chinese lexicographers admit that combinations frequently contribute only a phonetic value. But I find it incredible that any such minute subdivision of the idea could ever have existed alone as abstract sound without the concrete character. (30)

(The reference to a "minute subdivision of the idea" reminds one of those "subdivisions prismatiques de l'Idée" which, like a Hegelian spoor, permeate Mallarmé's preface to "Un coup de dés" ["A Throw of the Dice"]. . . .) Fenollosa then proceeds in terms which might be read as an anticipation of Derrida's hypothesis on "arche-writing":

Therefore we must believe that the phonetic theory is in large part unsound?[9] The metaphor once existed in many cases where we cannot now trace it. Many of our own etymologies have been lost. . . .The poet can never see too much or feel too much. His metaphors are only ways of getting rid of the dead white plaster of the copula. He resolves its indifference into a thousand tints of verb. His figures flood things with jets of various light, like the sudden up-blaze of fountains. . . . Thus in all poetry a word is like a sun, with its corona and chromosphere; words crowd upon words, and enwrap each other in their luminous envelopes until sentences become clear, continuous light-bands. (30-32)

Here we have a description of the recurring structure (or "isotopic" structure, as Greimas puts it, elaborating on Jakobson) of the poetic message. "Poeticalness," recalls the Russian linguist, echoing Mayakovsky's remark before the members of the Moscow Linguistic Circle in 1919, "is not a supplementation of discourse with rhetorical adornment but a total re-evaluation of discourse and of all its components whatsoever."[*]

Fenollosa now moves on, still using quasi-Jakobsonian terms, to define the modus operandi of the poetic function: "Poetry surpasses prose especially in that the poet *selects* for *juxtaposition* those words whose overtones blend into a delicate and lucid harmony"(32). I have underlined "selects" and "juxtaposition" because these terms correspond exactly to the operations "selection" (in the paradigm) and "combination" (in the syntagma), "the two basic means of arrangement utilized in verbal behavior" to which Jakobson is obliged to resort in order to answer a question as to what the essence of poetry is.

* Jakobson, "Closing Statement," 377. —EDITORS

What is the empirical linguistic criterion of the poetic function? In particular, what is the indispensable feature inherent in any piece of poetry? To answer this question, we must recall the two basic modes of arrangement used in verbal behavior, *selection* and *combination*. . . . The selection is produced on the base of equivalence, similarity and dissimilarity, synonymy and antonymy, while the combination, or the build up of the sequence, is based on contiguity. *The poetic function projects the principle of equivalence from the axis of selection into the axis of combination.* Equivalence is promoted to the constitutive device of the sequence.*

Fenollosa aims to designate something similar to this "projection" of the "equivalence principle" during the unfolding of the "sequence" when he refers to music and the theory of harmony in music, which "tints" or "colors" the horizontal development of the melodic line with vertical effects: "All arts follow the same law; refined harmony lies in the delicate balance of overtones. In music the whole possibility and theory of harmony are based on the overtones. In this sense poetry seems a more difficult art" (32). (It was in "music heard at a concert" that Mallarmé sought out the inspiration for his arrangement of "Un coup de dés" as a music score, whereby he borrowed back from music something that he considered always to have belonged to literature as well. . . .)[10]

"How shall we determine the metaphorical overtones of neighboring words?" (32) This is Fenollosa's next question, of capital importance, for here he put his finger on the nerve ending of the problem. It is the example of Shakespeare that at once springs to his mind, yet Chinese offers a better vantage point from which to make this objective identification of the "empirical criterion" required to apprehend the mechanism behind this "concord" or "harmonizing" (Fenollosa's way of understanding the "equivalence principle projected into the sequence"). To him, it seemed less easy to single out this aspect "tangibly" in poetry written in phonetic languages. He goes on: "Here also Chinese ideography has its advantage, in even a simple line; for example, 'The sun rises in the east'" (32). He then shows how, in the Chinese sequence,

日 昇 東

sun   rises   east,

*Jakobson, "Closing Statement," 358. —EDITORS

the pictogram for "sun" is redistributed through all the signs which make up the line, passing through the sign for "rise" and that for "east," as if one single overtone in grapheme form were governing the whole filmlike chain of the phrase with its changing figures.

This, then, is the "Chinese model" (*vero* or *ben trovato*) as established at the ideal level of poetic fruitfulness; but its validity (if not veracity) can only be measured properly by the exercise of the relevant function, that is, the *poetic function* of language, ultimate aim of Fenollosa's analysis. In poetry, "sentences must be like the mingling of the fringes of feathered banners, or as the colors of many flowers blended into the single sheen of a meadow" (31).

The Sinologists share a common tendency to reject as completely fanciful this possibility of an etymo-poetico-graphemic reading. A further example of this disapproving attitude can be seen in J.Y. Liu's book devoted precisely to the art of poetry (*The Art of Chinese Poetry*), wherein he reduces to a mere "suggestive" excrescence the importance of the visual parameter in Chinese poetry but frequently fails to notice how far the examples he himself quotes contradict him.[11]

Hugh Kenner has commented humorously on one of them, the compound sign, translated as "loyalty":

心 ₊ 中 ₌ 忠
heart middle loyalty

"Heart" + "middle": J.Y. Liu gives this second part as a mere phonogram, although a few pages farther on, he is forced to admit: "It would not be out of the question to think of *loyalty as having someone's heart in the center*, although etymologically this is incorrect."[12] This quotation gives a very clear idea of the philological opposition between "etymological truth" and "pseudoetymology" as an ad hoc product of the poetic imagination. Another elucidative example: in his analysis of a reputedly "obscure" poem by Li Shang-yin, the "Chinese Mallarmé," J.Y. Liu associates the word "ashes" (*huei*) with the compound ideogram "despair" (*huei-hsin*), represented graphically by "ashes beside the heart." He does this without showing any sign of noticing that this association in absentia might have been caused by the presence of the pictogram "heart" in the sign which corresponds positionally to *huei* in the line below, that is, *ch'ou₂* (melancholic, sad), and which can be interpreted "à la Verlaine" as "autumn over the heart":

灰   灰心   愁   火

ashes   ashes+heart=despair   autumn over heart=feel sad, melancholic   fire

Significantly, the pictogram of "fire" is present, as an "overtone" in grapheme form, both in "ashes" and in "autumn," that is, in both ideograms placed parallel in the text. It is moreover well known that perception of this kind of parallelistic affinity is a feature of the "translinear" reading proper to Chinese verse (cf. Viviane Alleton).[13] My own alertness to the visual nature of the ideogram (following the lesson of Fenollosa/Pound) led me to translate the line as follows,

> *A lâmpada se extingue em lágrimas: coração e cinzas*

> The lamp goes out in tears: heart and ashes

breaking down the suggestive concreteness of the ideogram for "despair" and capturing the intertextual allusion between *huei* and *huei-hsin* noted by J.Y. Liu. The English translation he himself gives is feeble and conventional:

> The candle will drip with tears until it turns to ashes grey.[14]

It is of course true that some exceptions must be registered even among academic Sinologues. H. G. Porteus, for example, took pains to highlight the following when speaking of Pound's translations stimulated by Fenollosa's ideas: "His pseudo-Sinology releases his evident clairvoyance, just as the pseudo-sciences of the ancients often gave them above normal vision" ("Ezra Pound and His Chinese Character: A Radical Examination").[*] A further noteworthy aspect of Porteus is that, when evaluating the heuristic balance of Pound's poetic re-creations inspired by the Fenollosian method of "intelligent reading," he remains undisturbed by the fact that Pound, in his hesitant and as yet amateur "deciphering" of the plates of ideograms which illustrate Fenollosa's essay, did perpetrate certain "preliminary" reading errors. For example, he confused "radical" no. 64

---

* In *Ezra Pound: A Collection of Essays to be Presented to Ezra Pound on His 65th Birthday,* ed. Peter Russell (London-New York: P. Neville, 1950), 203–17. —EDITORS

("hand") with no. 93 ("bull"), and both of them with a third, no. 68 ("measure"). Porteus remarks:

> What is remarkable about Pound's Chinese translations is that so often they do contrive to capture the spirit of their originals, even when, as quite often happens, they funk or fumble the letter. Pound's knowledge of Chinese, at least up to the time of his second version of the *Ta Hsüeh,* was so inadequate that he had been incompetent even to use a Chinese dictionary properly. This has however, by no means impaired the value of his achievements. In his edition of Fenollosa's essay, "The Chinese Character As a Medium for Poetry," Pound provides an illuminating commentary on his own practice, in the form of "some notes by a Very Ignorant Man." And one might go so far as to argue that it is rather because of that frankly acknowledged ignorance than in spite of it that his Chinese "inventions" (to follow up Eliot's hint) are so valuable.[15]

Later on, in the same work, Porteus stresses: "Plainly Pound, handicapped as he necessarily is, sees something—or at any rate looks for something—that Sinologues in general are blind to."[16]

A decisive contribution to this kind of analysis has recently been made by François Cheng, head of the Chinese Linguistics Center at the École Pratique des Hautes Études in Paris, in his essay "Le 'langage poétique' chinois" ["The Chinese 'Poetic Language'"] (in the collective work *La traversée des signes* [*The Passage of Signs*]). Cheng seems to have returned in a determined fashion to Fenollosa's hypothesis of a "harmonic reading" (although he does not mention this specifically in this work), and he has elaborated on it and strengthened it in the process, with new, up-to-date arguments. The author writes:

> More than being mere supports for sounds, ideograms bring all the weight of their physical presence to bear. They are sign-presences rather than sign-utensils, and they attract our attention by their emblematic force and the gestual rhythm they contain. Because of their writing, the Chinese have the impression that they learn the universe through the essential strokes whose combinations reveal the dynamic laws of transformation. It is no accident that, in China, calligraphy, which exalts the visual beauty of the characters, has become a major art form.[17]

He goes on to analyze a line by the poet Wang Wei, which is valid as a splendid illustration of Fenollosa's fundamental postulate concerning "overtones" vibrating before our eyes and coloring all the semantic planes of the text:

木 未 芙 蓉 花

"branch"　"tip"　　"hibiscus"　"flowers"

("at the tip of the branch hibiscus flowers")

NB: "radical" for plant = 艸

François Cheng comments that this example "shows how a poet exploits the possibilities offered by ideograms, their evocative visual appeal and their multiple semantic levels."[18] As if replying to Fenollosa's detractors, Cheng goes on:

> Any reader, even if he knows no Chinese, can be sensitive to the visual appeal of these characters, whose succession harmonizes with the meaning of the line. If we contemplate the characters in order, we do indeed have the impression that we are watching a tree in the very process of flowering (first character: a bare tree; second: something buds at the tips of the branches; third: a new shoot appears, represented by the "radical" for plant; fourth: branching out of the new shoot; fifth: a full-fledged flower). Yet being what is shown (visual aspect) and what is denoted (normal meaning), a reader who knows Chinese could not fail to discover, through the ideograms, a subtly concealed idea, that of a man who, in spirit, enters the tree and takes part in its metamorphosis.[19]

(Here we feel tempted to recall that passage of Eisenstein's essay where, having referred to the two complementary aspects—"denotation" via "image"; "figurative representation" via "expressive deformation"—which coexist within the "hieroglyphic principle," the author compares them to the unfolding of the arches of a hyperbola, which, mathematically speaking, should meet only in infinity. This might be imagined to happen through successive instances of dialectical mediation, one of which could be exemplified by Japanese puppet theater and another by Joycean word-montage.)* François Cheng proceeds:

* "Thus we have seen how the principle of the hieroglyph—'denotation by depiction'—split in two: along the line of its purpose (the principle of 'denotation'), into the principles of creating literary imagery; along the line of its method of realizing this purpose (the principle of 'depiction'). . . . And, just as the two outspread wings of a hyperbola meet, as we say, at infinity . . . so the principle of hieroglyphics, infinite splitting into two parts . . . unexpectedly unites again from this dual estrangement, in yet a fourth sphere—in the theater." Eisenstein, "Cinematographic Principle," 35. —EDITORS

The third character in fact contains the element "man," which in its turn encompasses the element "homo" (the tree in the first two characters is henceforth inhabited by a human presence):

"lotus"
(part of the
compound
ideogram
hibiscus)

"man"
(adult)

"homo"
(simplified
form,
representation
by synecdoche:
2 legs)

The fourth character contains the element "face" (the new shoot branches out in the form of a "face"), which in turn encompasses the element "mouth" (something which speaks). Finally, the fifth character includes the sign for "transformation" (sharing in universal transformation):

"hibiscus mutabilis"

"face"
("persona,"
"facies")

"mouth"

"transformation"

Thus, with an astonishing economy of means, and without resorting to external commentary, the poet brings a secret experience alive anew under our very eyes, in all its successive stages.[20]

This detailed demonstration gives us palpable evidence of the nature of the "continuous moving picture" effect (similar to a "cartoon," we might say today) captured by Fenollosa in his reading of poetry in Chinese characters. In a footnote, François Cheng makes the reservation that his analysis "is not based exclusively on etymological data";[21] for example, etymologically speaking, there is no "necessary link" between the ideogram he translates as "homo" and that for "tree." He stresses the fact that his purpose is to "show the graphic relations which exist between the characters."[22] Would it not be true to say that Pound's "eye for errata" (even when he committed those "primary" errors in ideographic deciphering, later counterbalanced by his "empathetic" perception of the whole) was hunting precisely for those "more-than-etymological" affinities, "gestalt" links by irradiation and reciprocal contagion of the forms (graphemes) in themselves? Moreover, would this not be a more extreme consequence of the "hyper-etymological" method put forward by Fenollosa, at least as a possibility of a "plural" reading? If this assumption is developed on the acoustic plane, the following quasi haikai could represent a phonic paraphrase ("paraphone") of the "Zen" line by Wang Wei:

hibisco:	(*hibiscus*
na trama	*in the web*
dos ramos	*of branches*
brilhos	*gleams*
de chama	*of flame*)

(The sparkling floral flame of *chAMA is* already resplendent in *trAMA* and *rAMos,* while the *BrIlhOS*—gleams—are like an echo of *hIBIScOS,* in an overall process of luminous metamorphosis within the text.)

In what follows, I would like to use this criterion of "visual-harmonic" reading to examine the fifth line of the famous poem by Li-Tai-Po, "saying farewell to a friend." Pound translated it thus:

Mind like a floating wide cloud.

Based on Pound, Mário Faustino rendered it as follows in Brazilian Portuguese:

A mente é ampla nuvem flutuante.

My own "hyper-Poundian" translation, returning to the original, is:

nuvens voláteis: o ânimo de quem viaja

volatile clouds: the mood of one who travels

The line by Li-Tai-Po (here laid out in the Western fashion, for ease of horizontal reading) unfolds like this:

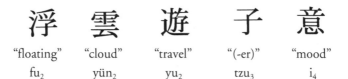

浮	雲	遊	子	意
"floating"	"cloud"	"travel"	"(-er)"	"mood"
fu_2	$yün_2$	yu_2	tzu_3	i_4

I wish to focus on the course of this character:

("boy,"   "child,"   "pup"),

which in isolation represents "radical" no. 39, through the poem. It appears at once, in the first ideogram, to the right of the "radical" for "water"; it consists of the representation of the "feet" of a bird, metonymically set over a "child," as if in the act of protecting it (by "suggestive" extension, this connotes "sympathy," "trust"):

(old form)   (present form);

the whole thus obtained, including the pictographic "radical" for "water" (no. 85):

(old form)   (present)   (abbreviated),

is usually translated as "floating." However, it could be interpreted metaphorically through the following "miniature fable": "floating with the tranquillity and security a child protected by its mother reposes with." The same sign for "child" reappears later, in the third ideogram, whose radical, to the left of the complex character, is a pictographic abbreviation for "foot" or "boot," giving the idea of "walking" ("radical" 162):

辶

On top of the "boot," there are graphic elements which can be interpreted as "hanging branches, lianas, in undulating movement," beside or falling onto "a swimming man." (The man is represented by the pictogram for "child" because when he swims his legs are underwater, like a newborn baby wrapped in a shawl; it should be noted that in a noncontracted form, this complex ideogram would also contain the element "water"):

「hanging branches」 (old form)   idem (middle form)   idem + "child"   "undulating movements of a swimming man" (present form, abbreviated, of preceding complex)   idem (present form, uncontracted)

Thus, the idea of "traveling," through the implicit sign for "water" (in "undulating, swimming movements"), involves that for "floating," so that the third ideogram of Li-Tai-Po's line makes a "chord" with the first. Finally, in the fourth character, which can be counted as a simple "suffix" (like the "-er" in "traveler") but which is also translated as "man" or "nobleman," the pictogram we are tracing as an "overtone" can be seen in full focus. In its three appearances, the character for "boy" shifts its position, its graphic framing and its semantic scope, culminating in a magnified close-up inside the imaginary frame (the "four-sided cage of the shot," as Eisenstein puts it).

These are the "visual rhymes"—the "overtones" vibrating before our eyes—that Fenollosa the philosopher-poet, who lacks the Sinologues' professional cataract, manages simply to teach us to *see*.[23]

The Italian scholar Girolamo Mancuso, in the chapter entitled "Lingua cinese como metodo di poesia" of his book *Pound e la Cina* [*Pound and China*] (1974)* has also given us a sound contribution to a fresh consideration of the problem at the theoretical level. Mancuso writes:

> Since in China there is no clear differentiation between painting, calligraphy, and poetry, a poet is often both calligrapher and painter. At the root of the impersonality and atemporality of Chinese poetry, there is thus the influence of the writing system, but in a very different sense from that understood by Fenollosa and Pound. What matters is not its *ideo*-graphic, but its *graphic* nature; this becomes completely manifest

* Milan: Feltrinelli, 1974. —EDITORS

in the "cursive" forms, which are as distant as possible from icono-graphic reproduction, and where the purely graphic quality of the sign is enhanced. Once again, Fenollosa was after the right thing, although in the wrong direction. His interest in and sensibility toward the figura-tive arts made him attentive to the pictorial qualities of Chinese poetry, which in contrast had escaped the notice of so many Sinologues. The same happened with Pound, who had always been aware of the visual qualities of poetry. Yet both were led astray by prejudice with regard to the ideographic nature of Chinese characters.

Here it is worth considering, once again, that the problem is not so much *graphic* as *iconic*, not in the usual sense of *iconology* as an imitative represen-tation, but rather that of *semiotic iconicity*, which includes degrees of con-ventionality (codes of "stylization") and does not permit realization in a "pure" state, as Peirce stresses, but through "attenuated" ("degraded") medi-ations, or "hypo-icons." Thus, despite the force of its initial impact (with its eminently "cathartic" function of unblocking perception), the important aspect of Fenollosa's essay is not the "pictographic" argument (the ideogram as a painting of ideas via things), but rather the "relational" argument (the ideogram as a relational process, as a structural metaphor). For this to be-come clear, it is enough to recall Fenollosa's remarks on painting:

> I do not like the word *decoration*. It seems to imply too much artificial-ity, a superficial prettiness. The word we ought to use is structural. The lines, the spaces, the proportions lie in the structure of the thing itself. . . . Representation is not art, it is literature. That a picture represents a man does not interest us. . . . It is a question of spacing, of how the pat-tern is worked out, that interests us. . . . Not the representational ele-ment but the structural element . . . not the realistic motive but the desire to find a finer space relation and fine relations.*

This manner of conceiving of painting ("intelligent seeing") undeniably underlies Fenollosa's manner of interpreting the ideogram ("intelligent reading"). In one of his Boston lectures (referred to by L. W. Chisolm), Fenollosa shocked his audience by a statement that, as an "extensional device," could be compared to Moholy-Nagy's anecdote as retold by Hayakawa. "The Japanese," Fenollosa maintained, before his suspicious

*Quoted by Van Wyck Brooks in "Fenollosa and His Circle," *Fenollosa and His Circle and Other Essays* (New York: Dutton, 1962), 49. —EDITORS

audience, "would just as lief at first see a picture upside down; that is, they admire beauty of line and color in art, rather than . . . merely depicting nature. . . ."* (We should perhaps point out that Fenollosa delivered this lecture in 1892. . . .) For him, imagination is distinguished by its "power of construction"; it acts upon reality not in an "imitative" but a "creative" (selective) manner. The "image" is the result of this "quick power of the imagination which seems in a moment to explore a million possible combinations and to seize upon the right one" ("Imagination in Art," an essay written in 1894). To rephrase the point in Jakobson's terms, it is the metonymic aspect which breaks through the metaphoric movement.[24]

This aspect occurs in the "psychological disproportion" and "expressive deformation" of Chinese script (cf. Eisenstein). Yet far from removing its iconic nature, this aspect retains it and tints it with indicial and/or symbol-like features (subordinating the characters to "notation codes" of a graphemic order and giving them, as we have seen, the semiotic nature of "hypo-icons").

In his lectures on art and education, Fenollosa endeavored to show that the historical development of artistic capabilities had led the perfecting of a skill in "creating spatial relations" to predominate over that of making imitative copies of nature. Thus, when Pound refers to the ability of his friend, painter and sculptor Gaudier-Brzeska, to sight-read certain ideograms without any knowledge of Chinese, because he was "accustomed to looking at the real shape of things" (*ABC of Reading*)† and "used to consider all life and nature in terms of planes and of bounding lines,"‡ we should not be surprised (without exaggerating the primarily apologetic aim of the anecdote): Gaudier's Cubist-Vorticist eye was above all a metonymic eye. . . .

Fenollosa was eminently concerned with *relations* ("relations are more real and more important than the things which they relate"[22]; "in this process of compounding, two things added together do not produce a third but suggest some fundamental relation between them"[10]), and as such he was able to glimpse in Chinese poetry the workings of a *relational intracode,* similar to harmony in music: the "chromosphere" of the "overtones" flooding over the visual strip of a poem in characters. This *intracode* translates a "saturation" process on the semiotic level which Fenollosa was able to formulate in a pioneering manner, using his vividly "organicist" vocabulary.

* Lawrence W. Chisolm, *Fenollosa: The Far East and American Culture* (New Haven, CT: Yale University Press, 1963), 94. —EDITORS

† Ezra Pound, *ABC of Reading* (New York: New Directions, 1960), 21. —EDITORS

‡ Ezra Pound, footnote in Fenollosa, *Chinese Character,* 31. —EDITORS

First he describes the "new calculus," which the sensibility of the artist must carry out to make use of the manifold possibilities for colors and lines at his disposal. This would entail the ability "to feel their several tensions vibrating in a microscopic balance; to rush along the criss-cross paths of their subtle affinities and actually see them displaying the secret process of their crystallization. . . ."[25] And he concludes:

> In short, the trained soul of the artist, while not itself the principle of crystallization, is just the peculiar solvent or medium in which the crystallization occurs. The real crystallization is in the units of the art itself; . . . "Art is a saturated solution of all the involved elements in terms of each other." ("The Logic of Art," 1906)[26]

When Décio Pignatari writes, following Peirce's line, "The quasi sign is not a thing, but a relation, a process. It is contained in all basic, foundational semiotic operations—in all operations of code saturation, all translations, all inter- and pansemiotic operations,"[27] he is unwittingly returning, through an involuntary (and all the more illuminating) convergence, to a proposal already outlined by Fenollosa.

Translated by Kevin Mundy and Marc Benson, edited by Odile Cisneros

Translation as Creation and Criticism

In 1958, the essayist Albrecht Fabri, professor at the Hochschule für Gestaltung in Ulm, Germany, wrote an article on the problem of artistic language for the journal *Augenblick*.[1] In this article, which he entitled "Preliminary Notes to a Theory of Literature," Fabri develops the thesis that "the essence of art is revealed by the fact that art is tautological," that works of art "do not *mean* but *are*." In art, he says, "it is impossible to distinguish between what is representation and what is represented." Then, turning to literature, he adds that what is unique to the language of a literary work is the "absolute phrase," the phrase "which has no content other than its own structure" and "which only exists as its own instrument." For this very reason, maintains Fabri, such an "absolute" or "perfect phrase" cannot be translated, because "translation begins with the possibility of separating word and meaning." That is to say, translation is based on the "discrepancy between what is said and what is said." For Fabri, then, translation indicates the less perfect or less absolute (or, it could be said, the less aesthetic) character of the phrase. It is in this sense that Fabri affirms that "all translation is criticism," because translation "is born from the deficiency of the phrase," from its insufficiency to be something by itself. "One does not translate what is language in a text, but what is not-language." And, "both the possibility and the necessity of

This essay was originally written for the Third Brazilian Congress on Criticism and Literary History, held at the University of Paraíba in 1962. It was published soon after in the journal *Tempo brasileiro* (Rio de Janeiro) 4–5 (June–September 1963). It has since been republished a number of times, most recently in *Metalinguagem,* 4th ed. (São Paulo: Editoria Perpectiva, 1992), 31–63. —TRANSLATOR/EDITORS

translation depend on the fact that sign and signified (*signatum*) may be separated and alienated from each other."

In the same issue of *Augenblick,* writing on the same problem but transplanting it into the terms of his New Aesthetic, an aesthetic founded on a semiotic and theoretical-informative base, the philosopher and critic Max Bense establishes a distinction between "documentary information," "semantic-information," and "aesthetic information."[2] It should be remembered that for Bense, *information* is any process of signs that exhibits a degree of order. "Documentary information" reproduces something observable and forms an empirical phrase, a phrase that may be scientifically proven or verified. We may illustrate Bense's theory with this example:

The spider spins her web.

"Semantic information" goes beyond what is purely documentary and transcends the limits of what is observed, and thus, it is information about an element that is not in itself observable, a new element such as the concept of true and false: "The spider spins her web" is a true proposition, an example of "semantic information." And finally, "aesthetic information" transcends "semantic information" inasmuch as it corresponds to the "unpredictability, the surprise, and the improbability of the order of signs." So, when João Cabral de Melo Neto writes,

> A aranha passa a vida
> tecendo cortinados
> com o fio que fia
> de seu cuspe privado

> (The spider spends her life
> weaving webs
> with the thread she spins
> from her private drivel)

> —from "Serial" ["Serial"], "Formas
> do Nu" ["Forms of Nakedness"], in
> *Terceira Feira* [*Third Fair*]

we have an example of "aesthetic information." These distinctions are fundamental and allow Bense to develop the concept of the "fragility" of aesthetic information as their corollary, a concept that refers to all that is inherently fascinating in a work of art. While both documentary and semantic information may have different codification and may be transmitted in many different ways ("The spider makes her web," "The web is woven by the spider," "The web is a secretion of the spider," etc.), aesthetic information *cannot be codified except in the form in which it was transmitted by the artist.* (Here Bense refers to the impossibility of an "aesthetic codification"; it would perhaps be more exact to say that aesthetic information is identical to its original codification.) The *fragility* of aesthetic information is, therefore, colossal. (In fact, any modification in the sequence of verbal signs in João Cabral's poem, no matter how small, no matter how minimal, would profoundly disturb this text's aesthetic realization.) In semantic and documentary information, Bense adds, "redundancy" (the predictable and replaceable elements that may be reconstituted in another form) is high, while, in contrast, in aesthetic information, such redundancy is minimal; "in a successful work of art, the difference between maximum possible aesthetic information and the aesthetic information found in developed form in the work is always minimal." Aesthetic information is inseparable from its realization; "its essence, its function, are tied to its instrument, to its singular realization." Bense comes to the conclusion that "the totality of information in aesthetic information is, in all cases, equal to the totality of its realization" and that this very fact accounts "at least in principle, for its *untranslatability.*" "In another language, the aesthetic information will be different, even though it may be semantically equal to the language of the original text. It follows, then, that aesthetic information cannot be semantically interpreted." Here Bense makes us think of Sartre's distinction between poetry (*mot-chose*) and prose (*mot-signe*), between the use of the word in poetry and prose. In *Situations II,* Sartre says, with regard to Rimbaud's verses "O saisons! O châteaux! / Quelle âme est sans défaut?":

> Nobody is questioned; nobody is questioning; the poet is absent. And the question involves no answer, or rather it is its own answer. Is it therefore a false question? But it would be absurd to believe that Rimbaud "meant" that everybody has his faults. As Breton said of Saint-Pol Roux, "if he had meant it, he would have said it." Nor did he *mean* to say something else. He asked an absolute question. He conferred upon the beautiful word "soul" an interrogative existence. The interrogation has become a thing as the anguish of Tintoretto became a yellow sky. It is no longer a signification, but a substance.[3]

It is true that the problem of the untranslatability of Fabri's "absolute phrase" or Bense's "aesthetic information" becomes particularly acute in the case of poetry. Nevertheless, it may be shown that the Sartrean dichotomy is artificial and inconsistent (at least as an absolute criterion) once we take into account prose works that give great importance to the treatment of the word as an object and thus come to possess certain qualities of poetry. We think, for example, of Joyce's *Ulysses* and *Finnegans Wake* or, to mention a few Brazilian works, of Oswald de Andrade's *Memórias sentimentais de João Miramar* [*Sentimental Memoirs of John Seaborne*] and *Serafim Ponte Grande* [*Seraphim Grosse Pointe*], of Mário de Andrade's *Macunaíma* and of João Guimarães Rosa's *Grande sertão: Veredas* [*The Devil to Pay in the Backlands*]. Such works, like poetry (and to a greater extent than some poetry), postulate the impossibility of translation; in these and other cases, it seems to us more exact to replace the concepts of prose and poetry by that of "text."

Once we admit, in principle, the thesis of the impossibility of translating "creative" texts, it seems that we may also admit, in principle, the corollary of this thesis, the possibility of re-creating the texts. The texts may exist, then, as Bense wishes, in two languages and as two bodies of autonomous aesthetic information, which, we should like to add, will be linked to each other through an isomorphic relation: they will be different in language, but like isomorphic bodies, they will crystallize within the same system.

This very idea was discussed by the Hungarian-Brazilian writer Paulo Rónai, who, in his book *Escola de tradutores* [*School of Translators*],[4] remarked that the demonstration of the theoretical impossibility of literary translation implies the affirmation that translation is art. As Rónai says, "Isn't the objective of all art something impossible? The poet expresses (or tries to express) what is inexpressible, the painter reproduces what is unreproducible, the sculptor molds what cannot be molded. It should not be surprising, then, that the translator seeks to translate what is untranslatable."

We may say, then, that every translation of a creative text will always be a "re-creation," a parallel and autonomous, although reciprocal, translation—"transcreation." The more intricate the text is, the more seducing it is to "re-create" it. Of course in a translation of this type, not only the signified but also the sign itself is translated, that is, the sign's tangible self, its very materiality (sonorous properties, graphical-visual properties, all of that which forms, for Charles Morris, the *iconicity* of the aesthetic sign, when an iconic sign is understood as that which is "in some degree similar to its denotation").[5] The signified, the semantic parameter, becomes just a kind of boundary marker for the "re-creative" enterprise. We are, then, at the opposite end of the "spectrum" from the so-called literal (or servile) translation.

In our time, the prime example of the translator/re-creator is, of course, Ezra Pound. Pound's poetic career was always marked by his adventures as a translator, by means of which he was able to criticize his own linguistic instrument and subject it to the most varied diction and to accumulate material for his poems in progress. In this way, Pound developed a whole theory of translation and an entire vindication of the aesthetic category of translation as re-creation. It is thus that in "Notes on Elizabethan Classicists" he writes: "A great age of literature is perhaps always a great age of translations; or follows it."[6] And in "How to Read": "Curiously enough, the histories of Spanish and Italian literature always take count of translators. Histories of English literature always slide over translation—I suppose it is an inferiority complex—yet some of the best books in English are translations."[7] He adds that after the "Seafarer" and a few other fragments of primitive Anglo-Saxon literature, "English literature lives on translation, it is fed by translation; every new exuberance, every new heave is stimulated by translation, every allegedly great age is an age of translations, beginning with Geoffrey Chaucer, Le Grand Translateur, translator of the *Romaunt of the Rose,* paraphraser of Virgil and Ovid, condenser of old Stories he had found in Latin, French, and Italian."[8] In still another essay, "Date Line," Pound enumerates the functions of criticism and upholds translation as a mode of criticism. "Criticism by translation." This idea becomes perfectly comprehensible once we recall that, for Pound, the two functions of criticism are: (1) The attempt to theoretically anticipate creation, and:

> 2. Excernment. The general ordering and weeding out of what has actually been performed. The elimination of repetitions. . . . The ordering of knowledge so that the next man (or generation) can most readily find the live part of it, and waste the least possible time among obsolete issues.[9]

Thus, Pound, animated by these proposals, embarks on the task of translating Chinese poems and Japanese Noh plays; Provençal troubadours; Guido Cavalcanti; French symbolists; and making use of his experiences in the handling of Laforguean *logopoeia* ("the dance of the intellect among words"), he rewrites Propertius in "vers de société" and translates the *Trachiniae* of Sophocles into a colloquial American speech driven by the beats of slang. His work is both criticism and pedagogy, since while it diversifies the possibilities of his poetic of idiom, it also offers up to new poets and readers of poetry a whole repertory (often unsuspected or obscured by the conventions of academic taste) of basic poetic products, now reconsidered and revivified. "Make it new": give new life to the valid literary past via translation. To understand this better, it suffices to recall T. S. Eliot's observations about the translations that Professor Murray, the eminent Hellenist, did of Euripides:

> We need a digestion which can assimilate both Homer and Flaubert. We need a careful study of Renaissance Humanists and Translators, such as Mr. Pound has begun. We need an eye which can see the past in its place with its definite differences from the present, and yet so lively that utilizing it shall be as present to us as the present. This is the creative eye; and it is because Prof. Murray has no creative instinct that he leaves Euripides quite dead.[10]

Of course it is true that many times (in tribute to the expression *traduttori-traditori*) Pound "betrays" the words of the original text, but even when he does so, not by choice but through a flagrant error,[11] he almost always succeeds—a kind of miraculous intuition or perhaps through a greater solidarity with the final "gestalt" of the work to which he adapted his technical skills—in being faithful to the "spirit," to the particular "climate" of the translated text; and the new effects and variations which he adds to it are like a continuous accumulation of heuristic strata and are, in fact, authorized by the inventive virtuality of the original. Hugh Kenner stresses in his introduction to *The Translations of Ezra Pound:*

> Since he doesn't translate the words, he may deviate from the words, if the words blur or slide, or if his own language fails him. . . . If he doesn't translate the words, the translator remains faithful to the original poet's sequence of images, to his rhythms or to the effect produced by his rhythms, and to his tone. Insofar as he is faithful, he does homage to his predecessor's knowledge of his job.

And he concludes:

> The labor that precedes translation is therefore first critical in the Poundian sense of critical, an intense penetration of the author's sense; then technical in the Poundian sense of technical, an exact projection of one's psychic contents, and so of the things on which one's mind has fed.[12]

Kenner's opinion is that Pound's best translations stand midway between pedagogy and personal expression, participating in both.

When Kenner speaks of Pound's enterprise of translating the tone, or "tonus," of the original, he employs the same words that Pasternak, another great translator and theorist of translation, used:

> Among us, Rilke is virtually unknown. The few attempts that have been made to translate him have not been very fortunate. It is not the translators who should be blamed. It is a habit to translate the meaning, not the tone, of what is said, and with Rilke, everything is a question of tone.[13]

In fact, it was from this perspective, which goes beyond the specific case of Rilke and can be extended to creative texts in general, that Pasternak sought to translate Shakespeare, with an unmistakably personal tone, allowing himself the luxury of great liberty in its re-elaboration.[14] A similar creative freedom may be found in the case of Ungaretti, another great poet-translator, who translated not the plays but the sonnets of Shakespeare.

In Brazil, it does not seem possible to speak of the problems of creative translation without mentioning the one person who was the first to propose and put into practice what could be called a true theory of translation. We call the attention of the reader to the preromantic Brazilian from the northeastern state of Maranhão, Manuel Odorico Mendes. Much ink has been spilled in an effort to disparage Mendes the translator, to criticize his irritating preciosity and the "bad taste" of his compound words. Indeed, it is very easy to take a negative approach to his translations, and from Silvio Romero (who considered them to be "monstrosities" written in a "macaronic" Portuguese)[15] on, that is what almost everyone has done. Still, it should be recognized that Odorico Mendes, an admirable humanist, was able to develop a coherent and consistent system of translation in which his vices (undoubtedly numerous, but to some extent the result of his period) are counterbalanced by his virtues. From the very beginning, his project of translation included the idea of synthesis (for example, according to the comparative chart that accompanies the edition of his translation of the *Odyssey*,[16] he reduced Homer's 12,106 verses to 9,302 verses), be it to prove that Portuguese is capable of as much concision as Greek and Latin, or more, or to accommodate the Homeric hexameters in blank heroic hendecasyllables, or to avoid the repetitions and the monotony that arise when an inflected language, in which one may manipulate the different case endings and give new sonorous values to the same words, is transplanted into a noninflected language. In this respect, Odorico Mendes declared: "If

Homer's repetitions were translated slavishly, the result wouldn't be as pleasing as his: the worst kind of infidelity."

Inspired by the examples of Monti and Pindemonte, the Italian translators of Homer, he attempted to translate the "fixed metaphors," the characteristic Homeric epithets, by creating compound words in Portuguese—at times taking this paradigm to an extreme, because he found Portuguese to be "ever more receptive than Italian to compound words, and even more daring." He strove to be realistic and reproduce exactly the crudities of certain passages in the Homeric cantos. (His sharp criticism of the euphemisms used by the French translator Giguet for the rendering of the scene in which Ulysses appears before Nausicaa is noteworthy.) He insisted upon the "right term," be it for the reproduction of a hue of the sea's water or for the denomination of a piece of armor. His notes to the translated cantos give an idea of the care he took to capture the liveliness and animation of the Homeric text so that he might later, within his chosen aesthetic coordinates, transpose these qualities into Portuguese. (Note the comparison that he makes between Ulysses' raft [*Odyssey*, book 5] and the scows used by the *jangadeiros* [raft-fishermen] in the northeastern state of Ceará, or even better, the passage where he alludes to the use, in Maranhão, of a large iron kettle, similar to the Greek tripod.) He discusses, and many times refutes harshly, the solutions of the translators who preceded him in other languages. He adopts the technique of interpolation, incorporating verses of other poets (Camões, Francisco Manoel de Melo, Antonio Ferreira, Filinto Elíseo) when he suspects that a certain Homeric passage can be translated through these references. Obviously, his practice is not as good as his theory, and many of his solutions, his intricate syntax and especially his compound words, are truly sesquipedalian, bizarre, and unacceptable. The excesses of his period also seemed to have played a role. Thus, "velocípede Aquiles" (velocipedalian Achilles), for "swift-footed," or simply "rapid Achilles" is today patently out of the question, since a "velocipede" has come to mean a kind of tricycle. Nonetheless, considering our present way of evaluating literary texts enriched by Joycean coining of word montages or by Guimarães Rosa's inexhaustible lexical inventions, and *free* from prejudice against mannerism and the baroque, other "cultist" neologisms, such as "Iris alidorada" (goldenwinged Iris), "criniazul Netuno" (bluemaned Neptune), or, for a river, "amplifluente" (amplyflowing) or, better yet, "bracicândida" (albescentarmed/white-armed) for Helen are stylistically successful in Portuguese within the context Odorico Mendes created and the rules of the peculiar game he proposed. In many cases, Mendes is able to reproduce the *melopoeia* that, according to Pound, reaches a peak in the Homeric epic and would have the tone of pure poetry for a modern ear educated in the theories of Bremond:

> Purpúrea morte o imerge em noite escura
> Brilha puníceo e fresco entre a poeira

> Purple death immerses him in obscure night
> He shines Punic and fresh amid the dust

In matters of sonority, which, through its impressive and uninterrupted parade of Greek names and patronymics approaches a kind of "sonorism," it is worth noting the great care taken by Odorico Mendes in transposing into Portuguese the list of names of the captains of the Greek ships and their places of origin in verse 429 and following of book 2 of the *Iliad*,[17] resisting the idea of omitting this part in his text.[18] He also succeeded in the onomatopoeic transcription of the sounds of the sea, a constant occurrence in the Homeric epic:

> Muge horrísona vaga e o mar reboa
> Com sopro hórrido e ríspido encapelam
> o clamoroso pélago

> the horrisonous waves roar and the sea resounds
> with a horrible and harsh blow they swell
> the clamorous sea

One "touchstone" that Ezra Pound chooses as an example of "untranslatable melopoeia" is the verse:

> pará thina polyphóisboio thalasses-

"The impetus of the waves on the beach and their reflux," says Pound,[19] gains (once hyperbaton is admitted) a lovely sonorous quality in Odorico Mendes's version:

> pelas do mar fluctissonantes praias

> along the beaches of the polysonorous sea

Odorico Mendes also has, frequently, good moments of *logopoeia*. Note, for example, in book II of the *Odyssey,* this description of the specter of Hercules about to shoot an arrow:

> Cor da noite, ele ajusta a frecha ao nervo
> Na ação do disparar, tétrico, olhando

> The color of night, he girds the arrow to his nerve
> In the act of shooting, gloomily, gazing

Clearly, it is a laborious task to read Odorico Mendes's translations (a task more difficult than that of reading the original texts, according to the ironic opinion of João Ribeiro,[20] who, nonetheless, did praise him whole-heartedly). But in the general panorama of the creative history of Brazilian poetry—a history still in the process of formation (and in many cases, one that has to be developed by selecting verses, extracts of poems, "corner-stones," rather than entire poems)—it would be an error to deny Odorico Mendes's honorable and pioneering role. And, for those who decide to study his theory of translation, expounded fragmentarily in the commentaries to his versions of Homer and Virgil, there awaits an intriguing adventure: that of accompanying *pari passu,* and within the context of his language of special forms and conventions, the successes and failures of the poet in the plan he sought to follow. The argument that, provided with a "preestablished system," he coldly ("without emotion") gave himself over to his task, which Sílvio Romero uses to criticize him, is actually what makes his efforts all the more interesting.

Chapman's mannerisms, his "excesses of added ornaments," his "parentheses and inversions," which impede the reading at many points, did not prevent Ezra Pound from recognizing him as the best English translator of Homer; the idea that Pope was out of fashion did not prevent Pound from holding his inventive topoi in high esteem—even though he did temper his praise ("full of beautiful passages") with the remark that they "remain almost wholly unsuccessful, or rather, there are glorious passages but no long or whole satisfaction."[21] Paraphrasing Pound, writing in regard to Chapman and Pope, the translations of Odorico Mendes are "of interest to specialists."[22] This does not mean, however, that their importance should be denied. For they do become very important, once one recognizes Mendes's influence on a writer like Sousândrade, the most revolutionary poet of Brazilian romanticism, who called Odorico Mendes our "Rococo father." In *Novo Éden* [*New Eden*], Sousândrade follows Mendes's example and seeks to achieve a Greek sonority:

Alta amarela estrela brilhantíssima
Cadentes sul-meteoros luminosos
Do mais divino pó de luz; véus ópalos
Abrindo ao oriente a homérea rododáctila
Aurora!

High, yellow, most brilliant star
Declining, luminous, south-meteors
Of most divine dust of light; opal-veils
Opening to the Orient the Homerean rhododactilian
Aurora![23]

When the *Noigandres* poets proposed the task of reformulating contemporary Brazilian poetics, they linked their theoretical and productive activities to a systematic work in the field of translation. In so doing, they were conscious of the didactic method that emanates from Pound's theory and practice of translation and from his ideas with respect to criticism's function—via translation—as "nutriment for the creative impulse." With Pound's ideas in mind, they began a team translation of seventeen of his cantos,[24] trying to bring to this modern master of the art of the translation of poetry the same criteria of creative translation that he himself expounded in his writings. Shortly after, Augusto de Campos undertook the translation into Portuguese of ten poems by E. E. Cummings, poems in which even "optical data" had to be translated (through typographical spacing, fragmentation, and interlinear relations), and which, at times, necessitated taking into account the number of letters and physical (plastic, acoustic) coincidences in the verbal material to be employed.[25] After other experiments with "difficult" texts (ranging from German avant-garde poems to Japanese haiku; from Dante's *Rime petrose* and the Provençal troubadours to the English Metaphysic poets), Augusto de Campos and I tried to re-create in Portuguese some fragments of *Finnegans Wake*,[26] many of which had not previously been translated into other languages. These experiments carried out with *intelletto d'amore,* with patience and devotion, did, at the very least, permit the realization of an intensive work in poetic translation, a fact that does allow us to have a definite point of view on the problematics of this field.

Translation of poetry (or of prose with an equal degree of difficulty) is, above all else, an experiment in introspection into the world and technique of the text to be translated. It is as if one took apart and, at the same time, put back together again the machine of creation, that frail and apparently inaccessible beauty that offers us a finished product in a foreign language but which, nevertheless, is able to give itself over to an implacable vivisection, to an operation in which it will be literally disemboweled and then re-formed, reconstituted, in a new and different linguistic body. It is for this very reason that translation is criticism. In *Escola de tradutores*, Paulo Rónai quotes J. Salas Subirat, the Spanish translator of Joyce's *Ulysses:* "Translating is the most attentive way of reading." And Rónai adds, "It is precisely this desire to read with attention, to better understand complex and profound works, that is responsible for many modern versions, including this Castilian one of Joyce."

The main stakes for a translator, when he is a poet or prose writer as well, are in the outlining of a live tradition (from which it may be deduced that the choice of the text to be translated is not an indifferent one but always revealing and worthwhile) and the acquisition of a deep understanding of the text and thus the aptitude for carrying out an operation of living criticism. One of the most important consequences that such stakes, when achieved, would bring about would be the enactment of a pedagogy that is neither dead nor obsolete but, rather, fertile, stimulating, and active. Much is said, for example, about the influence of Joyce on the work of Guimarães Rosa. Nevertheless, no example of such influence would be more clear or eloquent than a simple comparison of the text of *Grande sertão: Veredas* with fragments of *Finnegans Wake* that have been re-created in Portuguese. This is the "ideogrammatic" method recommended by Ezra Pound: the analysis of the materials and their comparison (criticism via translation).

Years ago, I began to study Russian, with hopes of translating Mayakovsky and other Russian avant-garde poets. For the initial experiment, the poem chosen was "To Sergei Esenin," a poem written by Mayakovsky on the occasion of the suicide of his contemporary—and adversary in aesthetic ideals. This poem, "Sierguéiu Iesiéninu," was the basis for a whole theory of poetic composition which Mayakovsky developed in his admirable essay "How Are Verses Made?" [1926]. My translation of this poem, first proposed as an exercise in re-creation—on its sonorous, conceptual, and formal level—of the formal elaboration of the original through the use of equivalent Portuguese structures, was carried out bearing in mind the scope and the demands of Mayakovsky's essay. The result was the remaking, step-by-step, of the stages described by Mayakovsky in his theoretical work and, *mutatis mutandis,* the repetition, in every line of the poem, of the operations of trial and selection among all the different possibilities of choice that came to my imagination. It was then the best reading that I could ever have made of the poem, linking the text to its theoretical matrix and reproducing its praxis, a truly critical reading. One example: There exists in the original a case of alliteration that receives special emphasis in Mayakovsky's commentaries:

> Gdié on
> bronzi zvon
> ili granita gran?

The lines refer to the monument which has not yet been erected to the dead poet and could be literally rendered as "Where the resounding of bronze or the edge of granite?" Fidelity to the effect desired by the poet gave rise to a version that does not depart from the general semantic field of the original but does "translate" more of the alliteration than of the meaning:

> Onde
> o som do bronze
> ou o grave granito?

> Where
> the sound of bronze
> or the grave granite?

The noun "edge" is replaced by the adjective "grave," and thus the sound scheme of the original is maintained.

From experiments such as this comes the conviction that it is impossible to teach literature, particularly poetry (and the prose that is comparable to poetry in its formal quests), without first giving a demonstration of the problems of criticism via translation. Since our literary patrimony is universal, we cannot think of a cloistered teaching of literature. Thus, no theoretical work on the problems of poetry, no aesthetics of poetry, will be valid as an active pedagogy if the materials to which they refer, the creative patterns (texts), are not placed in evidence. If translation is a privileged form of critical reading, it will be by means of translation that one can lead other poets, readers, and students of literature to an understanding of the most profound workings of the artistic text, its most intimate mechanisms and gears. The aesthetics of poetry constitutes a kind of "metalanguage" whose real value can be measured only in relation to its *language-object* (the poem, the text). It is not for nothing that so many poets, since Poe's exemplary essay, "The Philosophy of Composition," have undertaken to trace the genesis of their poems, to show that poetic creation can be the object of rational analysis, of methodical approach (an approach that does not completely exclude but is complemented by sensitive intuition and phenomenological description).

The problem of creative translation can only be resolved in ideal cases, when linguists and poets (who have at least some acquaintance with the language of the original text to be translated) work together as a team. It is necessary to replace the barriers between language professors and verbal artists by productive cooperation. It is, of course, necessary for the artist (poet or prose writer) to understand that it is a highly specialized task that demands both devotion and meticulous care, and, on the other hand, it is necessary for the language professor to possess what Eliot called a "creative eye": he should not be restricted by academic prejudices, and he should find in the re-creation of a verbal work of art that peculiar joy that emanates from a noncontemplative beauty, an active beauty, a beauty in motion. In "Ezra Pound and his Chinese Character: A Radical Examination," Porteus speaks of this dilemma when he compares the versions of the Chinese poems done by the Orientalist Arthur Waley (very competent in their fidelity to the text) and those of Ezra Pound (notable as creations):

> Pound is first and last a poet. Waley is first and last a Sinologue. In Sinological circles, no doubt, Pound's excursions into Chinese raise no more than a wry smirk. . . . On the other hand, those responsive to the subtle niceties of Pound's verse cannot be expected to take seriously the hit-or-miss poetic technique of Mr. Waley.[27]

Such problems must be overcome through the project of a Laboratory of Texts, where the two contributions, that of the linguist and that of the artist, will complement each other and be integrated into a work of translation that is simultaneously competent as such, and valid as art, in a product that only ceases to be faithful to the textual meaning in order to be inventive and that is inventive to the same degree that it deliberately transcends faithfulness to meaning in order to achieve a greater loyalty to the shaping spirit of the translated original, to the very aesthetic sign seen as a total entity, indivisible in its material reality (in its physical base, its *signans,* something particularly important for the translator) and in its conceptual weight, its *signatum.*

In this Laboratory of Texts, with the collaboration of linguists and guest artists, it would be possible to have a series of experimental publications of re-created texts and, at the seminar level, a series of pedagogical experiments in which students would collaborate in collective works of translation that would include such matters as the exposition of the adopted solutions, the proposal and discussion of possible variants, and so on.

Translated by Diana Gibson and Haroldo de Campos, edited by A. S. Bessa

Hölderlin's Red Word

La littérature, c'est la contestation de la philologie.

Literature, the refutation of philology.

—Michel Foucault

Around Easter 1804, Johann Heinrich Voss, who had gained renown with his German translations of the *Odyssey* (1781) and the *Iliad* (1793), wrote to a friend:

> What do you say of Hölderlin's Sophocles? Is the man really crazy or does he only pretend to be. . . . The other night while I was having supper with Schiller and Goethe at Goethe's house, I regaled both poets with the question. Read for instance the fourth chorus from his *Antigone.* You should have seen the way Schiller laughed; or *Antigone,* line 21: "Was ists? Du scheinst ein rotes Wort zu färben." ["What's happening? You seem to color a red word."] I offered this passage to Goethe as a contribution to his Optics.[1]

In July of the same year, the philosopher Schelling wrote to Hegel about these translations and their author, who was a mutual friend: "His translation of Sophocles shows he is a complete degenerate."[2]

This essay was originally intended as an introduction for Haroldo de Campos's excellent translation into Portuguese of act 1, scene 1 of Hölderlin's *Antigone* (1967). The English translation by Albert J. Bork was published in *20th Century Studies* 11 (September 1974): 4–10, and is reproduced by kind permission of the translator and Professor Stephen Bann, former editor of *20th Century Studies.* —EDITORS

One of the most laughable products of pedantry. Had Sophocles spoken to his Athenians in so stiff, so drawling, and so un-Greek a fashion as these translations are un-German, his audience would have left the theater at a run! In every respect, Mr. Hölderlin's translations of Sophocles' two plays must be included among the worst. It's up to the reader to guess whether Mr. Hölderlin has undergone metamorphosis, or whether he wished by a veiled satire to appeal to the public's depraved taste.[3]

In these terms—as a subject of scorn or as evidence of insanity—the Swabian poet's contemporaries denounced his translations of Sophocles. And if Hölderlin was to survive by around thirty years this lack of comprehension by his peers, he was also pushed by it toward a long period of madness; this he was to spend at Tübingen, in a small room with a view on the Neckar, referring to himself as "Mr. Librarian" or "Scardanelli," composing fragmentary poems,[4] fingering a piano whose strings he had cut, and bearing in mind right up to the end, to the very year of his death, those slandered translations of the Greek tragedian. ("I have tried to translate Oedipus, but the bookseller was a . . . !"[5] wrote the poet in the winter of 1842–43; it was the carelessness of his publisher that accounted for the typographic mistakes which added to and perhaps aggravated the contempt with which the work was received.) Three years before the First World War, Norbert von Hellingrath, a member of Stefan George's circle, undertook his own reedition of Hölderlin. Reevaluating the unjustly treated poet's activities as a translator, von Hellingrath categorically affirmed:

> For the first time, the linguistic form of Greek poetry was clearly understood and transposed into living language in a new form suited to it, without suffering, in the transition, adulteration from that which was foreign to it, such as is introduced by other translators when they have recourse to traditional forms, whether of the national poetry or of Latin poetry. The historic place of these translations corresponds to their significance for the present: To those whose knowledge of Greek is not sufficient for a total blossoming of the original, they are the only means of access to the Greek words and images. The next best translations by German translators follow them at a great distance: Humboldt's *Agamemnon* and Voss's *Homer*.[6]

In 1923, in his famous essay "The Task of the Translator" (more than a mere *physics,* a veritable *metaphysics* of translation), Walter Benjamin did not hesitate to say of Hölderlin's versions:

In them the harmony of the languages is so profound that sense is touched by language only the way an aeolian harp is touched by the wind. Hölderlin's translations are prototypes of their kind; they are to even the most perfect renderings of their texts as a prototype is to a model. . . . For this very reason Hölderlin's translations in particular are subject to the enormous danger inherent in all translations: the gates of a language thus expanded and modified may slam shut and enclose the translator with silence. Hölderlin's translations from Sophocles were his last work; in them meaning plunges from abyss to abyss until it threatens to become lost in the bottomless depths of language.[7]

In the winter of 1947–48, upon returning to Europe, Bertolt Brecht took it upon himself to prepare a version of Sophocles' *Antigone*. He used as a source, deliberately, Hölderlin's text, simplifying it and adapting it to the exigencies of the scenic oralization. And he recorded on the margin of his attempt: "The language of Hölderlin's *Antigone* deserves a closer study than I can presently give it. It is admirably radical."[8]

The bibliographic fate of Hölderlin's translations is, as can be seen, exemplary. From the supercilious mockery or stigma of madness with which his contemporaries received them, to the awed recognition and reverence of modern criticism, their path illustrates a fundamental break: with these translations, and unbeknownst to those who were eyewitnesses to the fact, an entire concept of literature was suddenly quashed, and poetic modernity was founded. Schiller's amused laughter, in the illustrious company of Goethe and Voss, was in truth the ironic epitaph (in the sense that it blithely failed to recognize itself as an epitaph) of a certain vision of poetry and artistic decorum. The same translations which the German nineteenth century branded as "monstrous," in the words of its most recognized and representative authors, the twentieth century would revive as ideal landmarks of their genre.

But what was so strange about these works? Wolfgang Schadewaldt, allying his competence as a Hellenist and philologist with the acuity of one who brings sensitivity to bear on the aesthetic aspects of a problem, clarifies this for us. Hölderlin's knowledge of Greek was quite limited, even when one considers the state of research in this field during his time. For that reason, he fell into frequent mistakes in reading and interpreting the original text. Moreover, the poet relied on a little recommended edition of Sophocles's text, and to cap it all, the printing of the translations, as has been mentioned, was tainted by typographical errors. (Hölderlin prepared an erratum for *Oedipus Rex,* and in subsequent editions, various passages had to be reconstructed by means of conjecture.) Notwithstanding all of that, and after having painstakingly enumerated the semantic and syntactic errors of Hölderlin's translations with reference to the Greek text, Schadewaldt refers us to the words with which von Hellingrath describes these translations in the following quotation:

> . . . A strange mixture of familiarity with the Greek language and a keen understanding of its beauty and character, combined with ignorance of its simplest rules and a complete lack of grammatical precision . . . Scarcely could the dead language be more congenial and alive while Greek grammar and all of its philological apparatus remained unfamiliar to one and the same person.[9]

And Schadewaldt adds, after stressing that the sum of Hölderlin's errors signifies neither the first nor the last word about his creations:

> When as a translator he blazed his own trail through completely unexplored territory, he took some false steps and stumbled. Nevertheless, he was thus able to avoid the beaten paths of conventional translation and treat with originality Sophocles' original word. . . . Hölderlin as a translator of Sophocles, metaphorically speaking, can be compared to those excavators of the Greek soil, who, without formal training or method, set to work on their own, their hearts full of enthusiasm, and guided by great instinct: They went about it violently many times and destroyed many things; however, they also managed to get to the depths and in this way indicated the path of discovery to their successors.[10]

Hölderlin's mistakes, given his existential predisposition to his task, his privileged bond with the essence of tragedy, were *creative errors:*

> The larger part of Hölderlin's linguistic errors is made up of creative errors, errors which are due to peculiarities of the text, behind which, notwithstanding, there is a general truth, whatever it may be, be it that the translation error led to a new and peculiar verbal vision or that Hölderlin's mistakes were from the outset guided toward a creative goal.[11]

In addition to *common understanding,* which goes from the particular to the general and surely and by degrees arrives at the *essence,* there exists another, *genial-anticipatory understanding,* which, emerging from "a minimum of facts, penetrates directly to the center and with an objective capacity for premonition grasps the essential."[12] This type of understanding, Schadewaldt concludes, was Hölderlin's.

At this point one is tempted to establish a comparison between Hölderlin and that other prime poet-translator, Ezra Pound. Hölderlin is an "exegetical" translator, performing a kind of liturgical translation, transubstantiating the language of the original into the language of the translation like the hermeneutical officiant of a sacred rite who attempts to conjure the primordial word (and this is why in his *Hyperion,* before Mallarmé, the Swabian poet "reads" the stars like letters, through which "the name of the book of heroes is written in the sky"). Pound, on the other hand, is a pragmatic, "laical" translator, performing his translation in the fashion of a lesson, as a critical-creative reinvention of a tradition. Both Hölderlin and Pound resemble each other with respect to the results which, by their different paths, they finally achieve.[13] For both poets, *translating the form* is a basic criterion. Pound (among whose translations from various languages the most serious scholars never tired of gleaning mistranslations) proposed to draw forth from Chinese ideograms, through a return to the pictographic elements composing them, the original vibrations, which had been smothered by the routine of repetitions; thus compensating almost by some kind of empathy, of revealing intuition, for his deficiencies as a Sinologist and his resultant reading mistakes, he managed to confer on his recreations a strength and beauty which the versions of the most notable Orientalists did not come close to possessing. (As Eliot has pointed out, "Pound is the inventor of Chinese poetry for our time.")*

H. G. Porteus ("Ezra Pound and his Chinese Character: A Radical Examination") explains for us this process of "elective affinity" which occurs between Pound's mind and the Chinese text:

> What is remarkable about Pound's Chinese translations is that so often they do contrive to capture the spirit of their originals, even when, as quite often happens, they funk or fumble the letter. . . .His pseudo-Sinology releases his latent clairvoyance, just as the pseudo-sciences of the ancients sometimes gave them a supernatural insight.[14]

With reference to Hölderlin, a characteristic of his method of translation is his stressed literalness, a literalness as regards the *form* (not merely the content) of the original. It is a matter of "superliteralism," in Schadewaldt's expression. (It is worth remembering that Brazil's own Mário de

---

*This often-quoted line is from Eliot's introduction to *Ezra Pound: Selected Poems* (London: Faber and Gwyer, 1928). —EDITORS

Andrade spoke of "supertranslation," to conceptualize a form of translation in which the "order of dynamogeneity" of the words of the original was captured.) Thus, for example, that *red* word—that *speech which is turbid with red*—which Hölderlin's divinatory instinct wrested from the Greek text to the glee of Goethe's dining companions (Voss, let it be remembered, offered it to the master of Weimar as a contribution to his *Farbenlehre) appears,* in the Les Belles Lettres edition of *Antigone,* simply as "quelque propos te tourmente" [what troubles you]. The Bailly dictionary explains that the verb *kalkháino,* in Greek, means "to have the dark color of purple," and that in the figurative sense (a meaning which the lexicographer notes expressly for the Sophoclean passage in question), it means "to be somber, to be immersed in thought, reflection, to meditate something profoundly, deeply." Schadenwaldt adds: "The Greek expression would sound in a literal imitation: 'you purple a word.' *To purple . . .* stems here from the dark red color that the sea assumes when a tempest is approaching."[15] Hölderlin scandalized his contemporaries (including the poets . . .) because he preferred, to the pallid convention of the translated sense, the concrete force of the original metaphor (in the same way as Pound made emerge from the *lexicalized* ideograms, distinguishing, for example, the abbreviated paintings of *sun* and *moon* together where a linguist would see only the noun "brightness," or the adjective "bright," or the verb "to shine").[16] There is no doubt that the sense (its denotative content) of the original in that fashion refines itself and becomes hermetic; but the poetic compulsion of language, by contrast, increases considerably. Recall, for example, the tactile concreteness of those "parole di colore oscuro" [words of dark color] inscribed on the portico of Dante's *Inferno.*

According to Walter Benjamin, next to Goethe's "Notes" for the *West-östlicher Divan,* the best material in German on the theory of translation is this passage by Rudolf Pannwitz:

> Our translations, even the best ones, stem from a wrong premise. They want to turn Hindi, Greek, English into German instead of turning German into Hindi, Greek, English. Our translators have a far greater reverence for the usage of their own language than for the spirit of the foreign works. . . . The basic error of the translator is that he preserves the state in which his own language happens to be, instead of allowing his language to be powerfully affected by the foreign tongue.[17]

Hölderlin (and Pound, with his versions of the Chinese, for example, where the exploration of the pictographic strata of the ideograms is stressed together with the syntactic propensity of the English language for the isolating kind of sentence) did not commit this fundamental error, whatever the imperfections of "content" of his re-creations of Sophocles may be. In the translation of a poem, the essential is not the reconstitution of the message but the reconstitution of the system of signs in which this message is incorporated, of the *aesthetic information,* not of the mere semantic information. For this reason, Walter Benjamin holds that a bad translation (of a work of verbal art, be it understood) is characterized by being a mere transmission of the message of the original, or in his own words, "the inaccurate transmission of an inessential content."[18]

Goethe, in the "Notes" quoted by Benjamin, understood this problem profoundly, from the theoretical viewpoint. So much so that he admits to the existence of three types of translation and describes the highest and last type or stage as being that in which one would like to make the translation identical to the original, so that the former would not merely approximately replace the original but would in actuality assume its very place. Nor did the effect of "estrangement," so to speak, which occurs in this phase, escape him, when the translator broadens the frontiers of his own language and subverts its dogmas to the influx of the foreign syntax and morphology; in that sense, he writes (Pannwitz, using other terms, touched upon the same point, as can easily be seen): "This method encounters at the outset the most vigorous opposition, for the translator who clings closely to the original is up to a certain point renouncing the originality of his own nation, whence comes a third term to which the taste of the public must begin to adapt itself."[19] Paradoxically, Goethe and Voss (who, for the author of *Faust,* would be the ideal of that type of translator), did not understand Hölderlin's translations, which as a matter of fact took to the most extreme consequences this same methodological assumption.

This lack of comprehension, by its very proportions, is extremely significant and should warn us against the noncritical repetition of the clichés of historiographical evaluation, against the automatic reiteration of judgments without appeal, with which certain authors were, once and for all, labeled and forgotten in the more or less immutable sepulchre of the anthologies and literary histories. Hölderlin's *red word* may be considered as a paradigmatic case for the type of historical poetics based on successive synchronic approaches envisaged by Roman Jakobson.

Translated by Albert G. Bork, edited by A. S. Bessa

Eucalypse: The Beautiful Occultation

In Octavio Paz's last book of poems, *Árbol adentro* [*A Tree Within*] (1987),* there is a composition particularly notable for its structure and its intriguing thematic development, the former exerting a magnetic field over the latter. This poem is "La guerra de la dríade o vuelve a ser eucalipto" ["The Dryad War or Return to Being Eucalyptus"].

First Tempo (1–17)

The poem articulates itself through a play of metamorphic figures that bring about its transformations. Anaphoric structures of repetition conduct what I call the *first tempo:* the adventures of the *enorme perro* (huge dog), three-headed like the mythological and Dantesque Cerberus (5–6), unleashing, in a vortex, successive mutations:[1]

1. *el enorme perro* . . . (the huge dog)
9. *el gato* . . . (the cat)
10. *el perro* . . . (the dog)
11. *el gato* . . . (the cat)
12. *el perro* . . . (the dog)

This essay was presented on July 3, 1990, in a summer course on the work of Octavio Paz at the Universidad Complutense de Madrid, at Escorial. It was first published in Portuguese in the *Revista USP* 8 (December-February 1990–91): 70–80. —TRANSLATOR

* For a complete translation of this poem, see Octavio Paz, "The Dryad War," *A Tree Within,* trans. Eliot Weinberger (New York: New Directions, 1988), 118–25. This essay does not follow that translation. References to the line numbers of the poem are given in parentheses in the text. —TRANSLATOR

13. *el humo* . . . (the smoke)

14. *el cielo* . . . (the sky)

15. *la tempestad* . . . (the storm)

16. *el rayo* (. . .) (the lightning)

17. *las cenizas* (. . .) (the ashes)

19. *el cuarto* (the room)

22. *el trueno* (thunder)

25. *el agua* (water)

As in the "fantastic" tales analyzed by Vladimir Propp in *Morfológia skázki* [*Morphology of the Folktale*] (1928),[2] the developments of the action in Paz's poem are produced through the exploration of the conflicts between archetypal antagonists: in the particular case mentioned earlier, *el enorme perro* [the huge dog] on the one hand and *el gato montés* [the wild cat] on the other (8). From their confrontation emanate two axes of mutation. As the *gato* (upsetting our natural expectation) manages to win over the three-headed *perro,* he is in turn struck by a *rayo* [lightning bolt] that fulminates and reduces him to *cenizas* [ashes] (16–17). This action occurs in the middle of a numbered sequence that is fantastic although not chaotic (in the manner of enumeration systems considered by Spitzer). To this end, the logic of the "absurd" is rigorously used, such as in the logic of "semiology" that presides the engendering of folktales. Hence, an antecedent, seen in regard to its position as a cause, necessarily produces (and motivates) a consequence:

11. *gato* wins over *perro* ("le sacó un ojo" [ripped an eye])

12. *perro* transforms into a *humo* ("ladrido de" [woof of])

13. *humo* ascends to *cielo*

14. *cielo* transforms into *tempestad*

15. *tempestad* produces *rayos* ("bajó armada de" [came down armed])

16. *rayo* fulminates *gato* (reducing him to *cenizas,* 16)

Second Tempo (17–25)

With the combustion of the *gato montés* [wild cat], the poem moves into its second metamorphic tempo: the feline cinders are spread over the entire universe (17–18). After spreading its spatial limits in such an incalculable manner, the poem, like a photographic camera adapting its lens for a close-up, opts to focus in on a precise site: a *cuarto* (room). The demarcation of this strictly domestic setting leads us to imagine a protagonist (the "I" of the enunciation that is also the composition's lyric "I"), subject and agent of this series of transformations: a man (the poet?) who sleeps in the bedroom and dreams of these voracious mutations. The bedroom, thanks to a typical oneiric amplification—since dreams are characterized, in their metaphoric and metonymic workings, by a lack of limits[3]—is converted immediately into the vastness of the Sahara. The descriptive notations are then distributed through two semantic networks. On one side are aligned the elements that have to do with the domestic environment announced by the word *cuarto:*

> a) *cuarto* (19)—*azotea* (rooftops) (22)—*cielo raso* (ceiling) (25)

On the other side is aligned a series that I would define as "universal" (by opposition to the particularization of the spatial marking characteristic of the foregoing series). This series takes off from the fantastic geography of line 18 ("las cuatro esquinas del universo" [the four corners of the universe]), stretching the image of the Sahara evoked in line 19. From there it evolves, by an effect of compulsive contiguity, into that of the *simún* (sirocco) (20: "sopló el simún" [the sirocco blew]). Then comes the "thunder" (*el trueno,* 22) and the torrential "rain" (23–25: "llovió sin parar" [it rained without stopping]), crisscrossed by "lightning" ("cuarenta relámpagos" [forty lightning bolts], 24). Thus we have:

> b) Sahara—*simún*—*trueno*—*lluvia*—*relámpagos* (Sahara—sirocco—thunder—rain—lightning bolts)

The two series will eventually meet and blend into each other but not until the flooding rain has reached the *cielo raso* [ceiling]* (25: "el agua llegó al cielo raso" [the water reached the ceiling]). It is a conventional expression, a lexical metaphor meaning that which the *Diccionario manual de la Real Academia Española* [*Small Dictionary of the Royal Spanish Academy*] defines as "trecho de superficie plana en lo interior de los edificios" (piece of flat ceiling inside a building). And again we find ourselves in the particular space of a "bedroom" by virtue of this sudden translation that takes us from *cielo* (indicated by the word *arriba* in line 23: "se quebraron los cántaros de arriba"[4] [the pitchers of the sky cracked open]) to *cielo raso.* The metaphorical stereotype is revitalized in a context charged with references to atmospheric or meteorologic phenomena that are made from line 20 ("sopló el simún") until line 25.

* The expression *cielo raso* (ceiling) literally means "flat sky." —TRANSLATOR

Third Tempo (26–38)

The second character in the poem's plot is introduced in line 26: the warrior woman. She is the personification, perhaps, of the loved one who does not let herself be conquered. It is the theme of the "amorous fight" that Dante, for instance, developed so dramatically in the *Rime petrose:*[*]

> Così nel mio parlar voglio esser aspro,
> com'é ne li atti questa bella petra . . .
> Ed ella ancide, e non val ch'om si chiuda
> né se dilunghi da 'colpi mortalli
> che, com'avesser ali,
> giungono altrui e spezzan ciascun'arme:
> s'I ch'io non so da lei né posso atarme.

> I want to charge my speech with so much harshness
> as this enchanting Stone . . .
> 'tis she who slays, however one may manage
> to hide or run from all her mortal blows
> which, as endowed with pinions
> reach everybody and all armors break;
> so there is no defense that I may take.

The woman-antagonist comes into the scene through a reference to the *cama* (nuptial thalamus?) that is transformed into a rocking boat, with bed-sheets improvised as sails (26: "en el vértice de la cresta tu cama se bande-aba" [your bed bobbed at the top of a wave]; 27: "con las sábanas armaste un velamen" [with the sheets you rigged a set of sails]; 28: "de pie en la proa de tu esquife inestable" [standing at the prow of your unstable skiff]). At this point begins the description of the "combat." Standing at the prow, the Amazon captains her *cama-esquife* [bed-skiff], which is at once ship and triumphal tram since it is carried "por cuatro caballos de espuma y un águila" [by four sea-foam horses and an eagle] (29). Her hair is compared to a "llama ondeante" [rippling flame] (30: "una llama ondeante tu cabel-lera eléctrica" [your electric hair a rippling flame]). Sailing on (31–32), the warrior woman "attacks" the male protagonist with her "artillery." Not by

---

[*] For the two excerpts from Dante's "I want to charge my speech with so much harshness," I have used Joseph Tusani's translations from *The Age of Dante* (New York: Baroque Press, 1974), 206, 208.
—TRANSLATOR

chance, line 32 is split in two segments, the second part projecting itself on the page, in isolation (33):

> y te hiciste a la mar
> tu artillería
> disparaba desde estribor (32–34)
>
> and you set out to sea,
> your cannons
> fired from starboard

Here design plays the role of a "relational icon," as in diagrams, and aims to evoke, isomorphically, as a syntactic film still, the "cannons" aiming, shooting. . . . The composition resorts to its iterative aspect, no longer through the anaphora as introduced by the determinative article (*el* or *la*, 1–25), but rather through a succession of verbs that function as signs of the bellicose action unchained by the "warrior":

tu artillería (your cannons)	34. *disparaba* (fired)
	35. *desmantelaba* (dismantled)
	36. *hacía* (*añicos*) (shredded)
tus espejos ustorios	38. *incendiaban* (cremated)
(your incendiary mirrors)	

Notice that this series was preceded by still another dynamic sequence:

31. *levaste* (*el ancla*), (raised [anchor])
31. *capeaste* (*el temporal*), (lay [to the storm])
32. *te hiciste* (*a la mar*), (set out [to sea])

Another aspect to be underlined is that the battle happens on the rhetorical level of a metaphor, since the effects of the bellicose attempt are produced on this level. Hence, *premisas* (premises) are dismantled (35); *consiguientes* [consequences] (i.e., "segunda proposición del entimema o del argumento que sólo tiene dos proposiciones" [second proposition of the enthymeme, or of the argument that has only two propositions] in the specific sense given by Dialectics, *Diccionario de la Real Academia*) torn to pieces; *convicciones* (convictions) burned. The male character is assaulted at the level of language, by the formation of syllogisms and of logical thinking. Stemming from this specific semantic area, terms such as *premisas,* *consiguientes,* and *convicciones* produce an effect of contrast with the verbs of which they are the objects. Verbs that rule concrete actions, as in the case of English metaphysical poetry or that of the Mexican poet Sor Juana ("silogismos de colores" [syllogism of colors])—residues of the baroque.

Fourth Tempo (39–51)

The fourth tempo of the poem is focused around the "exit of the male character" and in his decision to "react" against the implacable Amazon, exacting revenge. And again we find in Dante's *Rime petrose* a similar situation:

> S'io avessi le belle trecce prese,
> che fatte son per me scudiscio e ferza,
> pigliandole anzi terza,
> con esse passerei vespero e squille:
> e non sarei pietoso né cortese,
> anzi farei com 'orso quando scherza;
> e se Amor me ne sferza,
> io mi vindicherei di più de mille.

> Oh, if I could but seize those lovely locks
> which have become both whip and lash for me
> from very early matins
> I'd make them ringing bells unto the night:
> and I would not be pitying or kind,
> but like a playful bear with her I'd play;
> and since Love whips me still
> I would avenge myself a thousand-fold.

The I-narrator (the afflicted "lover"?) exits the scene. The serialization of active signs that sublimate the agent's motion occurs once again:

39. *me replegué* (*hacia la cocina*); [I retreated (to the kitchen)]
40. *rompí* (*el cerco en el sótano*); [broke (a grate in the cellar)]
41. *escapé* (*por una alcantarilla*). [escaped (through the gutter)]

During his flight, it occurs to him to organize his resistance and plot revenge against the cruel Amazon who antagonizes him:

(*en el subsuelo*) [underground]   42. *hallé* (*madrigueras*) [I found (burrows)]
(*el insomnio*) [insomnia]   43. *encendió* (*su bujía*) [lit (its candle)]
(*su luz díscola*) [its flickering]   44. *iluminó* (*mi noche*) [filled (my night)]

The deliberation to resist is underlined in line 45 by a sequence of nouns derived from the verbs "to inspire," "to conspire," and "to immolate" (*inspiraciones, conspiraciones, inmolaciones* [inspirations, conspiracies, immolations]). These verbs mark the evolution of the idea of revenge that will be concretized with the premeditated "immolation" of the warrior woman. In that endeavor, the breathless pursuer searches for a weapon (48): "(forjé) un puñal de misericordia" [I forged a dagger of mercy], which has the characteristic of the "magic objects" used by the heroes in Propp's fantastic tales. Hence the dagger to immolate the beloved woman is forged:

46. *con rabia verde* [with green rage] (Chomsky's "green ideas"?)
46. *una llamita iracunda* [a furious little flame]
47. *el soplete de ¡me las pagarás!* [the blast of "you will pay for this!"]

Having now in his possession the magically prepared weapon, the pursuer sets off to punish the Amazon, even undergoing "trials" or "difficult tasks" (whose execution constitutes another paradigmatic element in Propp's analysis).

49. *me bañé* (*en la sangre del dragón*) [I bathed in the dragon's blood]
50. *salté* (*el foso*) [I leaped over the moat]
50. *escalé* (*las murallas*) [I scaled the walls]
51. *aceché* (*en el pasillo*) [I ducked down a corridor]
51. *abrí* (*la puerta*) [I opened the door]

Fifth Tempo (52–63)

A new movement (the fifth tempo) is set forth in the poem by a string of events—"encounter with the antagonist," "escape," and "persecution":

52. *te mirabas* (*en el espejo*) [you were watching yourself in the mirror]

52. *sonreías* [you smiled]

53. *desapareciste* (*en un destello*) [you disappeared in a flash]

This time around it is the warrior woman who runs away from her adversary in an inversion of the functional schema in lines 39 to 41. He chases her or tries to:

54. *corrí* (*tras esa claridad desvanecida*) [I run after this vanishing brilliance]

55. *interrogué* (*a la luna del armario*) [I asked the mirror in the closet]

56. *estrujé* (*las sombras de la cortina*) [I punched shadows in the curtains]

Notice that in "la luna del armario" we have yet another lexical syntagma, of the metaphoric kind, which is revitalized in this context since *luna,* in this case, means "mirror" ("tabla de cristal o de vidrio cristalino, de que se forma el espejo" [slab of crystal or crystalline glass, of which mirrors are made], in the *Diccionario de la Real Academia*). The chase concludes with the realization of the Amazon's "escape" (*ausencia*) and with the lover-hunter finally understanding his inescapable solitude. The images that carry these semes are the following:

57. (*plantado en el centro de*) *la ausencia* [planted in the center of absence]

58. (*fui estatua en una*) *plaza vacía* [I was a statue in an empty square]

59. (*fui palabra*) *encerrada en un paréntesis* [I was a word enclosed in a parenthesis]

60. (*fui aguja de un*) *reloj parado* [I was the hand of a stopped watch]

61. (*me quedé con un*) *puñado de ecos* [I was left with a fistful of echoes]

62. (*baile de*) *sílabas fantasmas* [dance of phantom syllables]

63. (*en la cueva del cráneo*) [in the cave of the skull]

In this passage we find once again the "baroque-metaphysical" artifice of mixing notations related to concrete objects and/or situations with terms from another semantic zone (related to language, to grammar terminology: *palabra, paréntesis, sílabas* [word, parenthesis, syllables]).

Sixth Tempo (64–82)

The sixth tempo corresponds to what I would like to call "revelation" or the Dryad's APOCALYPSE. In fact, the "cruel" beloved reappears in line 64:

64. *reapareciste (en un resplandor súbito)* [you reappeared in sudden splendor]
65. *llevabas (en la mano derecha un sol diminuto)* [you carried in your right hand a small sun]
66. *(en la izquierda un cometa de cauda granate)* [in the left a comet with garnet tail]
67. *(los astros) giraban* [stars whirled]
    cantaban [and sang]
68. *(al volar) dibujaban (figuras)* [drawing figures as they flew by]
69. *se unían* [they gathered]
    se separaban [they departed]
    unían [they gathered]

The anaphoric chain of verbs again propels the movement of phrase-verses. It is important to notice that to the "reapparition" in line 64 corresponds the "disappearance" in line 53 ("al verme desapareciste en un destello" [seeing me you disappeared in a flash]). The luminous and cosmic images of lines 64–66 ("resplandor súbito" [sudden splendor], "sol diminuto" [small sun], "cometa de cauda granate" [comet of garnet tail]) were also anticipated by lines 53–55 ("destello" [in a flash], "claridad desvanecida" [vanished clarity], "luna del armario" [mirror in the closet]). The change of attitude of the "former warrior" toward the male character is already glimpsed in line 52 ("sonreías" [you smiled]): a "smiling" that is later associated with the *seme* of "luminosity" (such as in Dante's Beatrice: "e cominciò, raggiandomi di un riso" [and begun, with a glowing smile]; *Paradiso,* canto 7, 17). The same "smile" is present in line 81, key to the "revelation" (APOCALYPSE) of the dryad ("tú reías en mitad de la pieza" [you laughed in the middle of the room]). The *cuarto* of line 19 is reintroduced in line 81, just as the *espejo* in line 52 has returned in line 79 ("el espejo era un arroyo detenido" [the mirror was a still stream]). There is no "battle" any longer, no more confrontation between the "lover" and his cruel and bellicose "beloved." The poem is now on its way to the finale, under the sign of pacification, of the reconciliation of opposites. The agent of this transformation is apparently the "doble pájaro de lumbre" [double bird of fire] that emerges in line 71 as the avatar of the "sol diminuto" (65) and of the "cometa de cauda granate" (66), cosmic elements that design "figuras" and that unite in line 70. This luminescent bird affects the "lover" immediately:

72. *anidó* (*en mis oídos*) [nestled in my ears]
73. *quemó* (*mis pensamientos*) [burned my thoughts]
73. *disipó* (*mis memorias*) [dissipated my memories]
74. *cantó* (*en la jaula del cerebro*) [sang in the cage of my brain]

The memory of the humiliations suffered by the "lover" is dissipated by the luminous bird's lenitive action. The bird also sings a nuptial hymn in the narrator's mind ("en la jaula del cerebro," which is a reworking of "cueva del cráneo" in line 63). The canticle, through hyperbolic images, is defined as "el solo del faro en la noche oceánica" [the lighthouse solo in the oceanic night] (75), and also as "el himno nupcial de las ballenas" [the whales' nuptial hymn] (76). It is the festive moment of harmony that succeeds the aggressive confrontation. The "beloved" (former warrior) assumes her condition of dryad (a tree nymph, whose life was associated with, and preserved the life of, a particular tree). Although the designation "dryad" appears only in the title, the "revelation" or "unveiling" (*apo-kálypsis*) of the nymph, hidden under the persona of the bellicose and cruel "beloved," happens in the transfigured image of a "columna de luz líquida" [column of liquid light] (82). An eidetic image, nonetheless, since it unveils the character's essence, reuniting the *seme* of "luminosity" and that of the "aquatic" nature proper to dryads. The elevation to the condition of dryad occurs after a new series of transformations: The dagger (from line 48) blossoms ("el puñal floreció" [the dagger flowered], 77); the dog, who was aggressive in the initial lines, is now domesticated, licking the nymph's feet ("el perro de tres cabezas lamía tus pies" [the three-headed dog licked your feet], 78); the mirror of line 52 is morphed into "arroyo" [stream] (79), and the cat from line 8 also rises from ashes as fish, bucolically, "imágenes en el arroyo" [images in the stream] (80).

Seventh Tempo (83–91)

This last section is governed by the phrase "Vuelve a ser eucalipto" [Return to being eucalyptus] (83), uttered by the nymph and through which the "lover" is transformed into a tree. Just as in Ovid's *Metamorphosis,* the nymph Daphne is transformed into a laurel by Phoebus:

Atque conjunx quoniam mea non potes esse,
Arbor eris certe—dixit—mea

Since you cannot be mine
My tree—he said—you shall be

—*Metamorphosis,* book 1, 556–57

Or just as in Pound (whose poetry is a weaving of "magic or metamorphic moments"), when Neptune's son, Cygnus, is killed by Achilles and is transformed into a swan, an episode that Pound takes from book 12 of Ovid's poem:

. . . Victum spoliare parabat:
Arma relicta videt. Corpus deus aequoris albam
Contulit in volucrem, cujus modo nomen habebat

. . . He went to strip the dead:
the vanished body from the arms was fled.
His Sea-God Sire, to immortalize his frame,
had turned into a bird that bears his name

—*Metamorphosis,* book 12, 143–45

In Pound's version, the entire operation is synthesized into a sole phrase or movie still: "The empty armor shakes as the cygnet moves" (canto 4).*

As in both examples, the transformation in Paz's poem is given at once, without major transitions: "el viento mecía mi follaje" [the wind moving my foliage] (84). The following verses complete the description of the vegetal metamorphosis:

Yo callaba y el viento hablaba,
murmullo de palabras que eran hojas,
verdes chisporroteos, lenguas de agua,
tendida al pie del eucalipto
tú eras la fuente que reía (85–89)

I was silent and the wind spoke,

---

*Ezra Pound, *The Cantos of Ezra Pound* (New York: New Directions, 1998), 15. —EDITORS

> whisper of words that were leaves
> crackles of green, tongues of water,
> stretched out by the eucalyptus
> you were the laughing fountain

Also involved in the metamorphic process, the dryad now shows herself in her aquatic condition: "lenguas de agua" (of a stream that flows from under the tree, and also referring to the mirror-streams in lines 79–80); "fuente que reía" (laughing fountain, remission to 52 and 81).

The nymph is now at rest, in peace and not at war, amiable instead of belligerent. She veils over her "eucalyptus" for the "lover," once made hostile but now hidden under the arboreal cover (*eu-kalyptós,* in Greek, means "beautifully occulted").[5] An idyllic distich closes the poem:

> 90. *vaivén de los ramajes sigilosos* [swaying of secret branches]
> 91. *eras tú, era la brisa que volvía* [it was you, it was the moving breeze]

The dryad here returns in a new, complementary shape, as the *brisa* [breeze] that blows through the branches. The branches are now "silent," having become "mute" before the wind's "voice" (85). The "lover" transformed into eucalyptus also becomes "mute": the nymph now "smiles" as a *fuente* [fountain] (89) and "murmurs" (as wind or breeze, 85–86 and 91), moving through the tree's boughs in which her destiny is forever sealed. The words, one by one, yield the idyllic theme. The verb *volver* (*vuelve,* 83; *volvía,* 91; although of slightly distinct shades, are in this context harmonic) seals this magic instant of reconciliation, the closure of the entire metamorphic cycle which unravels through out the poem.

Up to this point, I have attempted to articulate the narrative syntagmas, to reveal the "diegetic" progress of the composition. Now we can backtrack and try to piece together a little of what goes on in the poem when confronted with the literary series to which it is affiliated.

This poem, regardless of its clear Ovidian matrix, belongs nevertheless to the tradition of visionary literature that has its roots in the biblical prophets and in the New Testament's apocalypse, a tradition that has been followed by authors such as Dante and Blake, to name a few.[6] We find a hint of this linkage in lines 28–29, in the description of the *esquife inestable* [unstable skiff], which belongs to the same realm of triumphal chariots and war vessels. The verse mentions that the bizarre vehicle was "tirado por cuatro caballos de espuma y un águila" [pulled by four sea-foam horses and an eagle]. Standing at the prow, the warrior woman, whose electric hair resembles a "llama ondeante" [rippling flame] (30), sets out to attack the male character (the narrator).

The vision of the chariot or war vessel reminds one of Dante's encounter with Beatrice (*Purgatorio,* canto 30, 31: "donna m'apparve sotto verde manto / vestita di color di fiamma viva" [a lady appeared under a green cloak / dressed in the color of live flame]). She appears on a triumphal chariot pulled by a griffin (eagle and lion in one). The image of the chariot was inspired, as Dante himself mentions, by the prophet Ezekiel's visionary theophany (Ezek. 1:15–21), but we might also add by the prophet Elijah's "chariot of fire" (2 Kings 2:11): "un carro, in su due rote, triunfale, / ch'al collo d'un griffon tirato venne" [a chariot, in two wheels, triumphal / harnessed to the neck of a Griffon came] (*Purgatorio,* canto 29, 107–8). Borges, in his *Nueve ensayos dantescos* [*Nine Dantesque Essays*],[7] has thus interpreted this "encuentro en un sueño" [encounter in a dream] between Dante and Beatrice: "Negado para siempre por Beatriz, soñó con Beatriz, pero la soñó severísima, pero la soñó inaccesible, pero la soñó en un carro tirado por un león que era um pájaro y que era todo pájaro o todo león cuando los ojos de Beatriz lo esperaban (*Purgatorio,* canto 31, 121)" [Forever denied Beatrice, he dreamed of Beatrice, but dreamed her as terribly severe, dreamed her as inaccessible, dreamed her in a chariot pulled by a lion that was a bird and that was all bird or all lion while Beatrice's eyes were awaiting him]. A dream that is also a nightmare ("Tales hechos pueden prefigurar una pesadilla" [Such images can prefigure a nightmare]). The woman whom the narrator in *La guerra de la dríada* meets in his dream is not dressed in flames but has flaming hair. Sea-foam horses and an eagle pull her triumphal chariot. But their encounter, even though tumultuous and aggressive at first (in the poem's third tempo), manages to avoid becoming a bad dream to end in apparent appeasement. After escaping her antagonist's revenge, the warrior woman reappears amid a "resplandor súbito" [sudden splendor] (64) and, bathed in this luminosity, takes over the male character, who then enters in a process of amorous combustion (73, "Quemó mis pensamientos, disipó mis memorias" [burned my thoughts, dissipated my memories]). Manifested, in her condition of dryad, as a "columna de luz líquida" [column of liquid light] (82) around which the poem's ferocious animals are pacified (78 and 80), this new and most essential transfiguration of the warrior woman is now celebrated in a "himno nupcial" [nuptial hymn]. As a counterpoint to this revelation—the unveiling of the dryad in her luminous and benign condition—to this APO-CALYPSE, corresponds, symmetrically, the process of EU-CALYPSE ("beautiful occultation") of the male character, metamorphosed into a tree by the nymph's very will (83). "Tree" and "stream/breeze (Dryad)," united in their final destiny, apparently overcoming conflict. The war to which the title refers seems to conclude in the idyllic conciliation of the antagonists. No mismatch (like in Borges's reading of Dante), but true encounter: a reunion of opposites now made complementary through consummated love. The poem's last scene conjures up the Edenlike atmosphere of a paradise regained. But a final shadow still lingers. This reconciliation was only possible in nature, while a natural accord between elements in a landscape: "tree" and "stream/breeze." On the anthropomorphic level, on which the poem is developed up to lines 82–83, an understanding was not possible; there, in fact (from 1–63), the dream is constantly invaded by nightmarish images (war, conflict). The ultimate feeling elicited by the poem is "melancholy." The "vegetal/fluvial" harmony is developed against a backdrop of refusal and absence (the settings of 57–63 evokes a De Chirico painting). It is from this refusal and absence, this evasive void, that the melancholic character,[8] under Saturn, falls in love—as Sor Juana Inés de la Cruz has masterfully expressed in her baroque-conceptual way ("Détente, sombra de mi bien esquivo, / imagen del hechizo que más quiero, / bella ilusión por quien alegre muero, / dulce ficción por quien penosa vivo" [Tarry, shadow of my scornful treasure, / image of my dearest sortilege, / fair illusion for which I gladly die, / sweet unreality for which I painfully live]),* and as have Paz, in his exegesis of Sor Juana's poetry and personality, and Walter Benjamin, in his analysis of allegory and ruin in the German baroque theater.[9]

In Paz's poem, melancholy seems to intervene as a shadow, as the flapping of a dark wing against the quasi-pastoral clarity that takes over at the end. Melancholy insinuates itself in the text, not as intentional effect but as a theme so that the reader's animus, approaching the poem reflexively, dwells in the instant of "naturalized" reconciliation that follows the "war" between the characters. Hence the reader does not lose sight of the fact that for this conciliation to take place, an irremediable erasure of the human

* *Anthology of Mexican Poetry,* ed. Octavio Paz, trans. Samuel Beckett (London: Thames and Hudson, 1958), 83. —TRANSLATOR

aspect was necessary, for the characters are reconciled not as man and woman but rather as "tree" and "stream/breeze." Not exactly as partners of a fulfilled affair but rather as "accidents" (whose union the dryad myth secures and deems fatal) or elements of a landscape.[10] As in Hegel's *Aesthetics*, where "natural beauty" (*Naturschönes*) is but an echo, an imperfect "reflex" of "artistic beauty" (*Kunstschönes*),[11] here too the harmony of nature is a precarious substitute that does not supply our need for harmonic realization on the interpersonal, interhuman level. Hence it is not true plenitude of the magnitude where the human element becomes foreign. It can only serve as a nostalgic, deferred mirage.

Translated by A. S. Bessa

Light: Paradisiacal Writing

White on White

Writing about Guido Cavalcanti's "Donna mi prega" ["A Lady Asks Me"] in an essay that should be read in the manner of a Borgesian visionary fiction rather than as a cautious piece of philological erudition, Ezra Pound defined it as a "metaphor on the generation of light."[1] T. S. Eliot, in turn, tried to characterize the whole of Dante's *Commedia* as a "vast metaphor."[2] The *Paradiso,* the *Commedia*'s third and last installment (*cantica*), could then be seen, in an essential dimension, as the gradual expansion of that metaphor on light, now under the influence of the theology of Aquinas.

In the aforementioned canzone by the "freethinker" Cavalcanti, a heterodox with shades of Averroes, *Amore,* generated as "diafan di lume d'una schuritade" [a mist of light upon a dusk], was the lyric-esoteric sign of the Provençal tradition rather than the "*appetitus rationalis* for wisdom" (Auerbach), hypostatized by Dante in Beatrice, his theological muse. Cavalcanti's canzone is an inspired exercise in natural philosophy (Physics), which seeks support in the sensorial proof against the "tyranny of syllogism" ("non razionale, / ma che sente, dico" [not by reason / but 'tis felt, I say])—as Pound realized it many years before Derrida, in *Of Grammatology,* alerted us to the "logocentric" tendency in Western philosophy.

This 1975 essay appeared in book form in a volume of Dante translations and essays by Haroldo de Campos: *Pedra e luz na poesia de Dante* (Rio de Janeiro: Imago, 1998), 67–83. —EDITORS

For Cavalcanti, *Amore* is not divine but human love. His canzone does not move from "accident" toward "substance" but instead concentrates on examining the modus operandi of the phenomenon of love as such (*accidens in substantia*), annexing it to the "sensitive soul," rigorously separated from the "intellect possible" (Nardi, via Contini). In this sense, by condemning Averroes's doctrine of the non-immortality of soul, Dante (*Purgatorio,* canto 25, 62–66), would be implicitly refuting Cavalcanti's concept of the philosophical canzone.

In the *Paradiso,* invested in conciliating the Thomist system with the mystic-amorous ideology of *cor gentile* (Auerbach), Dante stretches, sustains, and totalizes that radiant speculation on the kind of Love that is Light. He moves from *accident* and towards *substance,* since in God, *simplicissima substantiarum,* Eternal Light, *nihil accidens:* substance, accident and its manifestation unite in the same knot (*Paradiso,* canto 33, 88–91). However, between Dante's text and Cavalcanti's, a subtle dialogic screen is established. The two texts interact through diverse semantic threads, vestigewords that allow Pound, in his translation of "Donna mi prega," to transcribe (in the musical sense) Cavalcanti in terms of Dante, to clarify the lexical and syntactic abstruseness of the "philosophical canzone" with the supplement of the luminous paradisiacal material. This mediation is made possible through the hypothesis that Guido Cavalcanti (ca. 1259–1300), in some way, had knowledge of the philosophy of light through Robert Grosseteste (1168–1253), for whom: "Lux ergo, qual est prima forma in materia creata. . . . Lux enim per se in omnem partem se ipsam diffundit" [this light, which is the first form created in matter, . . . Light of its very nature diffuses itself in every direction]. Or, as Umberto Eco (who glimpsed the possibility of a parallel "between this metaphysics of energy and contemporary concepts of physics such as *electric fields*")[3] explains:

> Grosseteste's cosmos was an enormous explosion of luminous energy solidifying in mathematical relations . . . *lux* is, above all, free diffusion, origin of all movement, and it penetrates the entrails of earth, forming minerals and the germs of life, bringing to them a *virtus stellarum* [starry quality].[4]

Thus, when the *sdegnoso e ardito* [scornful and daring] Cavalcanti, in one of the most controversial points of the *elegantissima e mirabile canzone* [most elegant and wonderful canzone], concludes in regard to *Amore:*

> E non si po conoscer per lo viso
> compriso
> bianco in tale obietto cade,

Pound, in a splendid tour de force, reads *compriso bianco* in the sense of "understood as a whole," clarified by a total light ("all colors united in white"),[5] which remits us to the verb *imbiancare*, used by Dante in *Paradiso* ("vuo' tu che questo ver piu ti s'imbianchi?" canto 8, 112; "per che del lume suo poco s'imbianca," canto 7, 81), and translates (transreads?/translights?) thus:

> Nor is he known from his face
> But taken in the white light that is allness
> Toucheth his aim,

Which I dare to hypertranslate into Portuguese (Cavalcanti via Pound via Dante):

> O rosto não vê de Amor que tal
> Na luz total
> alveja branco no alvo.

"Augustinian *dealbatio*"—Pound would conclude. Transcultural synchronicity. Malevich: white on white.

Stars

Commentators of the *Commedia* often note that the three sections of the poem end with the word *stella* [star], as if to underscore the three stages of the ascent—the excelsior vocation—from the *infima laguna* [bottomless lake] of the *Inferno*.

As he leaves hell, the poet, in a transport, exclaims: "e quindi uscimmo a riveder le stelle" [from there we came out to see once more the stars]; later, at the conclusion of his stay in the *Purgatorio*, already preparing for his last ascent:

> Puro e disposto a salire alle stelle

> Pure and prepared to leap up to the stars

and finally, at the end of line 145 of canto 33 of *Paradiso,* leaving the final stellar point, apex of the journey and restart (or revolution) of everything in the wheel of divine Love, *principium et finis* [beginning and end]:

L'amor che move il sole e l'altre stelle.

The love that moves the sun and the other stars.

Having passed through the first two prestellar stages (although marked, indexed, as star), the whole poem is configured in the last, as a constellation, when the paradisiacal matter is progressively consubstantiated in semantic light—a kind of isomorphism that the *Paradiso* promotes, elaborates, and, in the final canto, sublimates.

The Op Poem

Paradiso, for that matter, will be the least dramatic *cantica* of the *Commedia.* At any rate, less popular and less read than the *Inferno.* T. S. Eliot has observed that "we have (whether we know it or not) a prejudice against beatitude as material for poetry."[6] From this perspective, the *Paradiso* can be seen as a truly *abstract poem* (in the sense that a modern art critic would speak of "abstract constructivism" in order to define certain operative and evolutionary tendencies from Malevich and Kandinsky to op art). A poem in which those "sujets d'imagination pure et complexe ou intellect" [subjects of pure and complex imagination or intellect] that so deeply moved Mallarmé—who strove not to exclude them from poetry—were already anticipated by several centuries. Dante's eye, here, is that of an optical artist, kinetic, apt at devising the light in light, iris in the iris, fire in the flame: luminous specimens, different shades of clarity. (I think of the lucid sculptures of Vantongerloo, who sometimes preferred the photographs of them instead, for only they—he often said—captured a radiant ectoplasm, nimbus, or fluorescence, dissolving the crystal in crystals.) And the mystery, the theological enigma, resolves itself in epiphany, phaneroscopia, paradisiacal writing: *light.*

From Kinetic to Iconic

Like a cosmonaut in luminous transnavigation—just like before he was a speleologist of terrestrial depths in his infernal, chthonic descent—

Dante, at the culmination of the *Sacrato poema* [sacred poem] witnesses the conversion of the kinetic into figural, of the optical into iconic, by witnessing the transfiguration of the reverberating vortex of the Trinity ("tre giri di tre colori" [three circles of three colors]; *Paradiso,* canto 33, 116–17) into the face of Christ: the true effigy (*vero icon* = veronica) stamping itself in the iris of the iris. In the hypostatic union of three in one, light incarnating itself, transubstantiated: Christ. And the face of Christ was also his face. "La nostra effige" [our effigy].

The face of Man. Of any man. Of HCE/Here Comes Everybody ("Hoc est enim corpus meum"), as Joyce, another writer influenced by Aquinas, would write in the ecumenical dream of *Finnegans Wake.*

Lucifer: The Reversed Metaphor

From those apexes where the mind "in-paradises" (*imparadisa*) itself, emerges the possibility for a retrospective reading of the *Inferno* as the symmetrical inversion of the light metaphor. Satan as the antithetical double, "degraded," of the Trinity-God (*Inferno,* canto 34, 38–44). According to Jüri Lotman's cultural typology, the Middle Ages offer a cultural model of dominant paradigm: at the top of the semiotic hierarchy, the "text," charged with the highest coefficient of truth, reducible to a sole significant opposition, is omnipresent. "The entire group of particular semantic oppositions tended to be reduced to fundamental cultural antithesis (heaven-earth, eternal-temporal, salvation-ruin, good-evil, etc.), which in turn would generate semantic series that, on a more abstract level, were reduced to a sole fundamental semantic opposition."[7] Auerbach has already observed that Dite, the *civitas diaboli* [city of the devil] in the *Inferno* (canto 8, 66–68), is the antithesis of the *civitas Dei* [city of God] in the *Paradiso* (cantos 30–33). He also added that Dite "is represented, to be sure, as part of the total divine order which includes evil, and in that sense it is well ordered; but it persists in impotent rebellion against the high power of God. . . ."[8] Numerological semiotics of the degrees of sin and virtue in preestablished correspondence. Whereas the paradisiacal splendor is all flames (the *beatos* of the *milizia santa* [holy army] and the angelic choir burn in divine Love), the deepest recesses in Dante's *Inferno* are made not of "fire," but of its opposite, "ice" (Giudecca, the last circle of the frozen lake formed by Cocito: "quindi Cocito tutto s'aggelava" [this was the cause, Cocytus was all iced]; *Inferno,* canto 34, 52), implying, on a symbolic level, the absolute absence of *Love* (light, fire). Hibernating in the central ice, suspended in the void, reigns Lucifer, the ancient "light-bearer" (Latin: *lucifer*), also Lusbel, the most beautiful of all angels ("la creatura ch'ebbe il bel sembiante" [the creature who was once so beautiful]; *Inferno,* canto 34, 18), but now fallen light, ex-lumen ("colui che fu nobil creato" [him who was created noble] and that has fallen *folgoreggiando* [like a streak of lightning]; *Purgatorio,* canto 12, 25–27).

In his transition from Inferno to Paradise, passing through purgatory, Dante will be first helped by Luzia, the illuminating grace, *gratia illuminans* (*Purgatorio,* canto 9, 55; *Inferno,* canto 2, 97–100). Later on, before stepping into Earthly Paradise (a place of transition, *status viatoris*—pre-Paradise already, or *quasi coelum*), the pilgrim-poet will be subjected, under a guardian Angel, to a purification through "fire" (*Purgatorio,* canto 27, 10-12: "Più non si va, se pria non morde, / anime sante, il foco . . ." [you may go no further, holy souls, / unless the fire sting you]) and will find himself compelled to cross a "measureless fire" ("incendio senza metro," *Purgatorio,* canto 37, 51). Igneous indexes of the oppositional-complementary disjunction/conjunction between the Kingdom of Reverse Light (whose center is the eternal ice of the Cocito) and the Kingdom of Triumphal Light, the Empireo, with its flaming celestial Rose. Dante, in his letter to Cangrande della Scala (a text that serves as an authentic metalinguistic description of the *Commedia*), clarifies: "It is called Empireo, which is the same as the sky inflamed with fire or ardor; not because there is fire or material ardor, but spiritual, which is saintly love or charity." The seme "fire," in the *Commedia,* is pervasive, coloring three distinct, although interconnected, functions: jubilant fire, *Amore,* in *Paradiso* (*Empireo,* from Greek *pyr,* fire); purifying fire, in *Purgatorio;* and punishing fire, in *Inferno* (in the infernal Seventh Circle, those who raged against God are punished under a *rain of fire;* "d'un cader lento, piovean di fuco dilatate falde" [falling slowly, flakes of flame came floating down]; *Inferno,* canto 14, 28–29). Thence the possibility of Norman Brown's unifying reading in *Love's Body:* "Love is all fire; and so heaven and hell are the same place. As in Augustine, the torments of the damned are part of the felicity of the redeemed. Two cities; which are one city. Eden is a fiery city: just like Inferno."[9] This hypothesis shows that, at the extremity of the paradigm, the two opposite poles show themselves in a very clear way: lack of love (infernal ice) versus *Amore* (paradisiacal fire), Giudecca versus Empireo, Judas versus Christ, Satan versus God.

On the other hand, Dite, toponym of the diabolical city, is also, by synecdoche, the name of Lucifer himself (*Inferno,* canto 34, 20). From the Latin *dis* (Dante was inspired by the infernal passages in Virgil's *Aeneid*), it identifies etymologically with *dives, itis* (meaning "rich," just as in Greek *ploutus* means "wealth"), Dite being the god of the treasures hidden deep in the earth. Mallarmé, always aware of the resonance of imperfect languages under the influence of the supreme, original one ("l'immortelle parole" [the immortal word]), registered in "Les dieux antiques" ["The Ancient Gods"]:

> PLUTO: Merely a Greek name for Hades . . . considered the guardian of treasures hidden in the earth! In Latin it was given another name, *Dis*, which has been taken for an abbreviated form of *Dives*, rich, but that is probably linked to *Deus, Divus, Theos* in Greece, and *Dyaus* in India.[10]

Dite, the negative Deus, anti-Deus, Plutonian custodian of the gold from the depth—retained gold, sequestered light, glacial feces—now rules over the frozen swamps of the Cocito ("Lo'mperador del doloroso regno / da mezzo il petto uscia fuor della ghiaccia" [The emperor of the kingdom of despair / Rose up from mid-chest out of the sheer ice]; *Inferno*, canto 34, 28–29).

The rebel angel's ("il primo superbo" [that first proud angel]; *Paradiso*, canto 19, 46) greatest sin was his transgressive attempt to trespass the limits of the sign: "il trapassar del segno," semiological sin (paradigm, later on, of the "original sin" of Adam and Eve; *Paradiso*, canto 26, 117). One should be reminded that Dante accomplishes his transhumanization (*Paradiso*, canto 1, 70) only via divine grace, mediated by Beatrice. He is nevertheless admonished, midway through the voyage, that the *Lumen supreme* [divine light] is but inscrutable: Not "creata vista," not even the beatific Virgin, "the soul that most shines in heaven," nor the Seraphim whose "eye is fixed in God," can penetrate it entirely; less yet the "mortal" mind, who is not allowed to presume, of its own intellective force, that "a tanto segno mover li piedi" [to move his feet toward such goal] (*Paradiso*, canto 21, 91–99).

Aspiring to become equal to or greater than God—pretending in vain to be converted into the *ultimate interpreter* of the Supreme Sign "that itself alone understands and of itself alone is understood" (*Paradiso*, canto 33, 124–25); trying to supersede it with a new Super-Sign ("Non solum autem voluit esse aequalis Deo . . . sed etiam maior voluit esse" [However, not only wanted to be equal to God . . . but also wanted to be even greater], Anselmo, *De casu Diaboli*, as in Scartazzini and Vandelli), Lucifer, before "la somma d'ogni creatura" [the sum of all creatures], the sign of similitude, who once shared the delights of divine paradise ("in deliciis Paradisi Dei"); Lucifer, the "light bearer" who once feigned himself alone capable of the Lumen, has sinned (and fallen) by excess of luminous presumption, by impatience of light: "per non aspettar lume, cadde acerbo" [not waiting for the light, fell unripe] (*Paradiso,* canto 19, 48). Hence the mark of inversion in his oxymoronic name, that claims light and rules darkness.

Translation / Translight

The work of translation aims for, at its limit, the same goal as the one defined by Benjamin: to liberate, in the language of the translation, the pure language veiled in the original, in relation to which the sense of communication (*Bedeutung*) is but a tangential reference. "One can feel only awe at the power of the master who could thus at every moment, realize the inapprehensible in visual images" (T. S. Eliot).[11] A concise and luminous style; a spiritual experience close to *enlightenment;* "the vigor of sunlight in the 'Paradiso,' is unmatched in art"[12]—thus Pound punctuates his reading of the *Paradiso.* Max Bense, at the end of *Aesthetik und Zivilisation* [*Aesthetics and Civilization*], tries to transpose (with ironic distance) the theological notion of God in the "aseptic" lay terms of informational theory: in his model, God would be the "antivisual and nonreflective" theme par excellence that would respond to the supposed aesthetics of improbability, which culminates in the impossibility of perception itself, inscrutability (*Nichtwahrnehmbarkeit*), hence the alternative to transform it in the potential reservoir for a symbolist aesthetic of the highest triviality.* Dante confirms Bense's findings: working at the level of the signifier, he is capable, at each moment, of "verbivocovisualizing" in innovative ways what would be, in principle, antivisual, nonapprehensible.

Dante takes the Italian language to a point where Latin, caught in plain flight of metamorphosis, makes itself transparent in the very moment of naming. Not a dead language any longer, but an active language in live language. "The poem's latitude, as a matter of language, is the most reverberating of our literary language *en masse,* it is—without margin of error—the phenomenon of utmost reach" (Sanguinetti, on the dilatation operated by Dante in the Italian "space of expression"). Dante, inventor and master. There where a word is needed to short-circuit an idea, or in a rhyme position, anything goes: a verb is born of a temporal adverb (*insemprasi,* from *sempre* [always]; *Paradiso,* canto 10, 148); of a personal or possessive pronoun (*inluiarsi, intuarsi, inmiarsi,* from, respectively, *lui, te/tuo, me/mio* [his, you, yours, me, mine]; *Paradiso,* canto 9, 73, 81); from a locative

---

* Max Bense, *Ästhetik und Zivilisation* (Baden-Baden: Aegis Verlag, 1958). —TRANSLATOR

(*insusi,* from *susi* [rise], *Paradiso,* canto 17, 13; *indovarsi,* from *dove* [where], *Paradiso,* canto 33, 138). Plenty of lexical and syntactic mannerisms, of which Gustav René Hocke has already written. The intensification of redundancy, strategically thought out, generates original, surprising information: every time the name of Christ appears in rhyme position, it demands to be repeated two more times, thus breaking the expectation of the terza rima, since Christ is consonant only with Christ (see, for example, the thundering apparition of Christ's cross in the skies of Mars; *Paradiso,* canto 14, 104–8); somewhere else, the terzina's rhythmic scheme can be made to sound strange through the cut of the word in terminal position and the rejection of one of its parts (in this case, the modal adverbial suffix) to the following verse, thus tracing the diagram of the dancing movement (*Paradiso,* canto 24, 16–17: "così quelle carole, differente- / mente danzando . . ."). Alliterations and paronomasia extend the orchestration of rhyme; *parechese,* a variant of paronomasia, gives way to a theological tautology of that which refers only to itself: see the verbal configuration of eternal light that itself alone understands, of itself alone thinks, and by itself alone is understood ("O luce etterna che sola in te sidi / sola t'intendi, e da te intelleta / e intendente"; *Paradiso,* canto 33, 124–26); and finally, anagrammatic dispersions decompose and recompose certain key-words: for example, *Amor(e),* in line 145, is preconstituted by *ROtA* and *MOssA* in key positions in line 144.

All these operations the translator has to transcreate, exceeding the limits of his language, alienating its lexicon, compensating the loss here with an inventive inoculation there, fighting the forced infratranslation with the adventurous hypertranslation, until the ultimate hubris (Luciferian guilt, semiological transgression?) renders him powerless and insane, by transforming the original in the translation of his translation. Like Dante's beatific eye in the divine eye, anything can thus be transilluminated, even if only by a fiery and fleeting lightning. The paradisiacal text inscribes itself (as a mirage?) by a double sparkle, minute as it might be.

Translated by A. S. Bessa

Notes

Except where indicated, all notes have been written by Haroldo de Campos and translated by the volume editors.

Poetry

The Poem: Theory and Practice
In the "Sermão da Sexagésima" ["Sermon of the Sixtieth"] (1655), where he uses the expression "star chess," Father Vieira, while chastising the excesses of "cultismo" ["erudite style"], was "unwittingly describing his own [compositional] style" in the geometric form of a chessboard. (Cf. Antonio J. Saraiva, *O discurso engenhoso* [São Paulo: Perspectiva, 1980].)

The Essence of Omega
This series, originally made up of five poems, carries as subtitle the specification "A phenomenology of composition." It was meant to dialogue with Edgar Allan Poe's "The Philosophy of Composition," an essay on the origin of the poem "The Raven" and also with the sequence of poems *Psicologia da composição* [*Psychology of Composition*] (1947) by João Cabral de Melo Neto. Following the phenomenological method, I attempt here to arrive at the eidos (essence) of language and poetry through the "husking" of words and through phonic fracture.

Hunger of Form
The poems included in this section exemplify concrete poetry in its most rigorous phase: the "mathematics of composition" (sense rationalism). The composer Gilberto Mendes set "nascemorre" ["bornover"] to music, exploring the possibilities of multiple readings. One could even speak here of "minimalism," long before that term came into use, especially in painting and music.

Transient Servitude
[. . .] *Transient Servitude* is composed of two parts: *Proem* and *Poem*. *Proem* contains three pieces, which develop, in a dialectical way, the linguistic and existential play between *poesia pura* (pure poetry) and *poesia para* (committed poetry, poetry for a social purpose, poetry for). The first one is the "fly of blue"; the second, the "fly of flies." Hölderlin: "Und wozu Dichter in dürftger Zeit" [And what for poetry in a time of scarcity?]. And Heidegger on Hölderlin: "Poetry is the foundation of being through the word." These somewhat metaphysical statements are transformed by the poem into a physical matter of facts: hunger in Brazilian underdeveloped regions as a counterweight in the poet's mind in the very act of composing his poem: *nomeio o nome* [I name the noun], *nomeio o homem* [I name

the man], *no meio a fome* [in the middle is hunger]; in Portuguese, by merely cutting the word *nomeio* [I name] one finds *no meio* [in the middle], which introduces "hunger" in the very act of nominating. Feuerbach: "Der Mensch ist was er isst" [Man is what man eats], and Brecht: "Erst kommt das Fressen, denn kommt die Moral" [First comes grub, then comes the moral]. In the circumstance of scarcity, the poet tries to give "un sens plus pure aux mots de la tribu" [a purer sense to the words of the tribe]. A committed poetry without giving up the devices and technical achievements of concrete poetry.

excriptures
1. [The lines "la tua / coscia / distacca / di sull' / altra" (your / thigh / separates / from the / other) is a quote from Giuseppe Ungaretti's *Sentimento del tempo* (*Feeling of Time*), 1931. —EDITORS]

Alea I—Semantic Variations
Billed as "uma epicomédia de bolso" [a mock-pocket-epic] "Alea I" was published in the journal *Invenção, Ano 6, Número 5* [*Invention, Year 6, Number 5*] (1967), published in São Paulo by Décio Pignatari. —EDITORS

Paradisiacal Signifiers
The book *Signância: quase céu* [*Paradisiacal Signifiers*] is divided into three parts, each one corresponding to one of the strata of Dante's topography, but in reverse. It begins through a *quasi coelum,* a quasi paradise, scattered epiphanically on earth and thus hard to recognize (according to the German romantic Novalis who appears here in two poems in the form of an epigraph [*tiereische Natur der Flamme* (savage nature of the flame)] and as an exemplary reading. The second part is "Status viatoris," a transit zone of triviality and the quotidian, equivalent to purgatory, followed by a descent into hell in the third part, "Esboço para uma nékuia"["Sketch for a Nekuia"]. [The last two parts are not reproduced in this volume.]

The Education of the Five Senses
C. S. Peirce: "I can imagine a consciousness whose whole life, alike when wide awake and when drowsy or dreaming, should consist in nothing at all but a violet color or a stink of rotten cabbage." *The Collected Papers of Charles Sanders Peirce— Volume 1* ed. Charles Hartshorne and Paul Weiss (Cambridge, MA: Belknap Press of Harvard University Press, 1965), paragraph 304.

Ode (Explicit) in Defense of Poetry on St. Lukács's Day
This poem, entirely made up of citations, has as point of departure the following excerpt from the conversations between W. Benjamin and B. Brecht, in Svendborg, July 25, 1938 (cf. W. Benjamin, *Essais sur Brecht* [Paris, Maspero, 1969]): "In the afternoon, Brecht found me in the garden reading *Capital.* Brecht: 'I think it's

a good idea to read Marx, especially now that has become so unfashionable among us.' I answered that I often occupy myself with unfashionable books. We begin to speak about Russia's policy on literary matters. 'With those people—I said, referring to Lukács, Gabor, Kurella—it's impossible to create a State.' Brecht: 'Better yet, one can *only* create a State, never a community. They are indeed the enemies of production. Production does not mean a thing to them. One can not trust production. It is by definition unpredictable. One can't tell what will come of it. And they themselves do not want to produce. They want the role of *apparátchiki* and to be in control of others. Each one of their critiques hold a menace.'"

Je est un autre: Ad Augustum

This poem was published in *Código* 5 (Salvador, Bahia), a special number celebrating Augusto de Campos's fiftieth birthday.

Mencius: Theorem of White

Mencius (372–289 B.C.): the most important Chinese moral philosopher after Confucius. Cf. I. A. Richards, *Mencius on the Mind* (London: Kegan Paul, 1932).

Goethean Opuscule

Goethe to Eckermann, 4 February 1829: "The conviction of our survival comes to me from the concept of factivity, because if I, until the end, stay untiringly active, nature, in this way, will be forced to endow me with another form of existence when my present form is unable to sustain my spirit." Goethe to Eckermann, 1 September 1829: "I have no doubts with respect to our survival, for nature cannot dispense with the entelechy. . . ." Cf. Goethe, *Faust* (Munich: Goldman Verlag/Klassiker, 1978).

Goethean Opuscule II

Marianne Jung is the Zuleika of the *West-östlicher Divan*. An aging Goethe, traveling to Frankfurt where he would meet a young Marianne, witnessed a unique meteorological phenomenon—a "white rainbow"—and he interpreted it as a sign of a second erotic youth. *Senesco sed amo:* "I grow old but I love." Probably Anacreon, the Greek lyric poet of the sixth century B.C., quoted by Pound in Latin (Cantos LXXX and LXXXIII). *Saxifrage rose:* allusion to W. Carlos Williams's line "Saxifrage is my flower that spits / the rocks . . ." Sousândrade in "Harpa XLV" ["Harp XLV"]: "and the warm breeze / that my dark hair scented / the tremulous wing of my hair / will whiten . . ."

1984, Anno Orwelli I

This poem was commissioned by the daily *Folha de São Paulo* and was published on the front page of the Sunday edition with a visual arrangement by Wesley Duke Lee on January 1, 1984.

Heraclitus Revisited (1973)

By "transluminations" I mean texts, so to speak, "reimagined" (even more than "transcreated"). In this Heraclitean series I tried to recover the language of the pre-Socratic philosophers from under the patina of conventional prose versions using the techniques of avant-garde poetry, including the spatialization of language. *Pánta rhei* is a mere adaptation of the Joycean "riverrun," already Brazilianized by Augusto de Campos (A. and H. de Campos, *Panaroma de Finnegans Wake* [São Paulo: Perspectiva, 1971]).

Paraphernalia for Hélio Oiticica

Text for Ivan Cardoso's film *H.O.*, dedicated to the career of the visual artist Hélio Oiticica, creator of the "parangolés."

Galaxies

The first text of *Galaxies* (beginning/end: "and here I begin . . .") is from 1963; the last (end/beginning: ". . . I close I conclude"), from 1976. A text imagined in the extreme limits of poetry and prose, bioscriptural pulsation in galactic expansion between these two permutable forms (having as its thematic magnet voyage as a book or the book as a voyage, and for that it is also known as a "book of essays"), I see it now, in hindsight, as an epic insinuation resolved as epiphany.

Finismundo: The Last Voyage

When it was first published as a book (Ouro Preto: Tipografia do Fundo, 1990), under the care of Guilherme Mansur, this poem carried the following explanation:

Homer is silent about Ulysses's end. Tyresias's ambiguous prophecy (*Odyssey,* canto 11) that may contain an allusion to a "death originating from the sea" (*thánatos eks halós*) was the object of much debate throughout the classical and medieval times, finding an echo in Dante (cf. D'Arco Silvio Avalle, "Último viaggio d'Ulisse," *Modelli semiologici nella "Commedia" di Dante* [Milan: Bompiani, 1975]). In the *Inferno* (canto 26, 83–142), Odysseus, transformed into a tongue of fire, answers a question posed by Virgil: "but one of you tell me where / after dying he came to rest." He notes how insatiable curiosity ("l'ardore . . . a divenir del mondo esperto") moved him, in his old age and with few companions ("lo e' compagni eravam vecchi e tardi"), to embark on a "folle volo" (an adventure, the "reckless flight"), that is, to face, once again, the "alto mare aperto" in search of the forbidden island of Purgatory (the "montagna bruna," on top of which, according to Dantesque topography, the Garden of Earthly Delights was located). The old Greek seaman's hubris is punished with a shipwreck: "per voler veder trapassò il segno" ("because he wished to see, he trespassed the sign"), in Boccaccio's words. In that sense, some viewed this episode as analogous to other exemplary cases of the transgression of norms: Lucifer, "the first proud being" (*Paradiso,* canto 19, 46–48),

Adam (*Paradiso*, canto 26, 117), Prometheus. In freely revisiting this topos, I attempted to rework it in two tempos: in the first, with an epic cadence, fusing it to the theme of shipwreck in Mallarmé; in the second, as an ironic paraphrase, projecting it onto a contemporary setting, the search (laughable but always new) of poetry in a trivialized world, "abandoned by the gods."

In 1996, Sette Letras, a Rio publishing house, issued a long statement of mine on the origin of this poem.

Poems for Qohelet

Qohelet, He-Who-Knows, is the Hebrew name of the anonymous book in the Bible also known as the Ecclesiastes. He was a melancholic sage who lived probably in the third century B.C. My transcreation of the poem of wisdom was published by Perspectiva in 1991.

Links for a Renga

I wrote these texts for a multiauthor *renga* ("chained poem," in the Japanese tradition). Cf. R. Bonvicino, ed., *Together* (*um poema, vozes*) (São Paulo: Ateliê Editorial, 1996).

The Left-Winged Angel of History

This poem is a protest against the massacre of the *sem-terra*, i.e., the landless agrarian workers, in Eldorado do Carajás, in the state of Pará, northern Brazil, in April 1996. As yet, the authorities responsible for the massacre (members of the Military Police) have not been punished, and the question is being pursued in a slow legal battle.

Gongorine Tribute to Sá de Miranda

Via Góngora (1561–1627), I pay homage here to Sá de Miranda (1481?–1558), who more than once practiced the "obscure" style. In this text, lines by both poets enter into a dialogue.

Essays

Anthropophagous Reason: Dialogue and Difference in Brazilian Culture

1. Haroldo de Campos, "A poesia concreta e a realidade nacional," *Tendência* (Belo Horizonte) 4 (1962); republished in the review *Anos 60*, no. 1 (Kairos: São Paulo, n.d.): 27–31. See also "Avanguardia e sincronia nella letteratura brasiliana odierna," *Aut-Aut* (Milan) 109–10 (1969).

2. One could also quote this passage from Marx: "It is well known that certain periods of highest development of art stand in no direct connection with the general development of society, nor with the material basis and the skeleton structure

of its organization. Witness the example of the Greeks as compared with the modern nations or even Shakespeare." Karl Marx, *A Contribution to the Critique of Political Economy,* trans. N. I. Stone (Chicago: Charles H. Kerr and Co., 1904), 309.

3. Karl Marx and Friedrich Engels, *The Communist Manifesto,* trans. Paul M. Sweezy (New York: Modern Reader Paperbacks, 1964), 8.

4. I am referring especially to Voloshinov's *Marxism and the Philosophy of Language,* published in Leningrad in 1929 and attributed by some scholars to M. Bakhtin. [In English: trans. Ladislav Matejka and I. R. Titunik (Cambridge: Harvard University Press, 1986). —TRANSLATOR]

5. See, for example, my introductory study to Oswald de Andrade, *Trechos escolhidos* (Rio de Janeiro: Agir, 1967). See also a more recent essay, "Oswald de Andrade," *Europe* 599 (March 1979). [In this volume see "An Oswald de Andrade Triptych," in the section entitled "Reinventing Tradition." —TRANSLATOR]

6. Cf. Hans Robert Jauss, "Geschichte der Kunst und Historie," *Literaturgeschichte als Provokation* (Frankfurt: Suhrkamp, 1970).

7. Theodor Adorno, *Thesen über Tradition.* [In *Insel Almanach auf das Jahr 1966,* 21–33. Quoted by Jauss in "Geschichte de Kunst und Historie." —TRANSLATOR]

8. Here, I would like to make a brief reference in passing to the thesis of a possible pre-Columbian "indigenous baroque," characterized by a "language of signs and symbols, based on myth." This view (which displays some affinity with Eugenio d'Ors's concept of a pan-baroque) was suggested by Prof. Alfredo A. Roggiano (University of Pittsburgh) in a talk presented at the 17th Congress of the Instituto Internacional de Literatura Iberoamericana, Madrid, 1975. Roggiano supported his argument using the case of Mexico and of Paul Westheim's concepts in *Ideas fundamentales del arte prehispánico en México* (Mexico City: Fondo de Cultura Económica, 1967).

9. Mário Faustino, "Evolução da poesia brasileira—Gregório de Matos e Manuel Botelho de Oliveira," *Suplemento dominical do "Jornal do Brasil,"* 14 and 28 August 1958.

10. Augusto de Campos, "Arte final para Gregório," *Bahia/Invenção* (Salvador: Propeg, 1974), an antianthology of Bahian poetry. J. Miguel Wisnik follows this suggestion in his introduction to Gregório de Matos, *Poemas escolhidos* (São Paulo: Cultrix, 1976).

11. Ludwig Pfandl, *Juana Inés de la Cruz, die zehnte Muse von Mexico, ihr Leben, ihre Dichtung, ihre Psyche* (Munich: H. Rinn, 1946).

12. See Haroldo de Campos, "Serafim: um grande não-livro," and "Serafim: análise sintagmática," *Suplemento literário de "O Estado de São Paulo,"* 14 December 1968 and 8 March 1969. Also see my introduction to the reissue of Oswald de Andrade, *Serafim Ponte Grande* (Rio de Janeiro: Civilização Brasileira, 1971). [In English: *Seraphim Grosse Pointe,* trans. K. D. Jackson and Albert Bork (Austin: New

Latin Quarter Editions: 1979). In this volume, see "An Oswald de Andrade Triptych," in the section "Reinventing Tradition." —TRANSLATOR]

13. See my essay, "Structuralism and Semiotics in Brazil: Retrospect/Prospect," *Dispositio* 7–8 (1973): 175–87. There I noted, in reference to Candido's "Dialética da malandragem," that the peculiar narrative structure which he calls the "novel of the rogue" is close, in some way, to Mikhail Bakhtin's thesis on "carnivalesque" literature, as well as to certain of Northrop Frye's typological speculations. Cf. also Severo Sarduy, "Barroco y neobarroco," *América Latina en su literatura,* ed. César Fernández Moreno (Mexico City: UNESCO/Siglo XXI, 1972), 167–84; and the excellent critical summary in Emir Rodríguez-Monegal, "Carnaval/antropofagia/parodia," *Revista iberoamericana* 108–9 (1979): 401–12.

14. I am referring to the sonnet in which Gregório de Matos mocks the pedigree of the Brazilian "new nobility" (the "descendants of armadillo blood") who invoked the privileges of genealogical nobility, tracing their lineage to the Portuguese Captain Diogo Álvares Correia, the *Caramuru* ("son of thunder" or "sea-emerging dragon") who married the daughter of an Indian leader. "Tatuturema" (1868), part of Sousândrade's long epic poem *Guesa,* is a satiric-orgiastic saraband of Indians, missionaries, and colonizers based on the model of the *Walpurgisnacht* in Goethe's first *Faust. Pau brasil* ("Brazilwood," a reference to a type of wood producing a red dye highly prized by Europeans), Oswald de Andrade's first collection of poems (1925), uses excerpts from chronicles and the written reports about Brazil at the time of discovery and the beginning of colonization, in a kind of a montage.

15. Taken from Oswald de Andrade's "Manifesto antropófago." [English translation by Leslie Bary, "Oswald de Andrade's *Cannibalist Manifesto,*" *Latin American Literary Review* 19, no. 38 (1991): 35–47. —TRANSLATOR]

16. Max Bense, "Konkrete Poesie" (Anlässlich des Sonderheftes *noigandres* zum zehnjährigen Bestehen dieser Gruppe für "Konkrete Poesie" in Brasilien), *Sprache im technischen Zeitalter,* vol. 15 (Stuttgart: Kohlhammer, 1965). Also in *Brasilianische Intelligenz* (Wiesbaden: Limes Verlag, 1965).

17. I am referring to Umberto Eco, *Opera aperta* (Milan: Bompiani, 1962). For the preface to the Brazilian edition of this book, Eco wrote the following comment: "It is indeed a curious thing that a few years before I wrote *Opera aperta,* Haroldo de Campos, in one of his articles, anticipates its themes in a surprising way, as if he had reviewed the book I had not yet written and I would later write without having read his article. But this means that certain problems emerge in an urgent way at given historical moments, arising almost automatically from the research in progress."

18. Oswald de Andrade signed articles in his *Revista de antropofagia* (1928–29) with the punning pseudonym "Marxilar."

19. The scattered poetry and sparse prose of Pedro Kilkerry (1885–1917) was collected posthumously and analyzed by Augusto de Campos in *Re/Visão de Kilkerry* (São

Paulo: Fundo Estadual de Cultura, 1971). The study by Octavio Paz to which I refer is "Literatura y literalidad," *El signo y el garabato* (Mexico City: Joaquín Mortiz, 1973).

Disappearance of the Baroque in Brazilian Literature: The Case of Gregório de Matos

1. Lecture given at the Biblioteca Pública Municipal de São Paulo in 1945. Cf. *Boletim bibliográfico* 2, no. 7 (April–June 1945).

2. Antônio Candido and J. Aderaldo Castello, *Presença da literatura brasileira— História e antologia,* vols. 1–3 (São Paulo: Difusão Européia do Livro, 1964).

3. Stuart B. Schwartz, *Sovereignty and Society in Colonial Brazil: The High Court of Bahia and Its Judges, 1609–1751* (Berkeley and Los Angeles: University of California Press, 1973), 324.

4. Fernando da Rocha Peres, *Gregório de Matos e Guerra: uma revisão biográfica* (Bahia: Edições Macunaíma, 1983), 16–17.

5. Walter Benjamin, "Fate and Character," *Reflections: Essays, Aphorisms, Autobiographical Writings,* trans. Edmund Jephcott (New York: Schocken Books, 1978).

The Trans-American Pilgrimage of Sousândrade's *Guesa*

1. Hanno Beck, "Los países tropicales como iconografía natural: Alexander von Humboldt y los comienzos del pensamiento ecologista," *Humboldt* 25, no. 83 (1984): 22–29.

2. "O Sol, de todo desaparecera. / Atahualpa, dos céus desamparado, / Tremeu vendo-se ao meio da cratera / Qual um que se assombra e está petrificado!" [Joaquim de Sousândrade, *O Guesa,* canto 11, ed. Jomar Moraes (São Luís de Maranhão, Brazil: Serviço de Imprensa e Obras Gráficas do Estado, 1979), 295. —EDITORS]

3. "Oh! como é triste da moral primeira / da República ao seio a corrupção! ao seio da pureza—se dissera— / de Cristo o corpo em decomposição." [Sousândrade, *O Guesa,* canto 10, p. 261. —EDITORS]

4. "Oh! o Diamante que, de ser tão puro / foi chama e o mesmo Eterno! Se o contemplo, / nem do fulgor distingo o que é fulguro," [Sousândrade, *O Guesa,* canto 10, p. 198. —EDITORS]

An Oswald de Andrade Triptych

1. "O Modernismo," *Anhembi* (São Paulo) 49, vol. 17 (December 1954): 31–32.

2. See Mário da Silva Brito, *História do modernismo brasileiro* (Saraiva: São Paulo, 1958), 198–215.

3. "The book was of a clear epigonic Parnassianism: Mário, at the time, admired Vicente de Carvalho and lived to collect apt sonnet endings," according to Péricles Eugênio da Silva Ramos in *A literatura no Brasil,* vol. 3, part 1 (Rio de Janeiro: Livraria São José), 496.

4. Oliveira Bastos traced this blueprint in "Esquema, poesia e processo," *Diário de notícias* (Rio de Janeiro), 1 January 1956.

5. João Ribeiro, "Crítica—Os Modernos," *Obras* (Rio de Janeiro: Academia Brasileira de Letras, 1952), 90–98.

6. Ibid., article referring to Oswald de Andrade's *A estrela de absinto.*

7. The title of this poem-novel can be translated freely into Portuguese as *Finnicius revém,* which includes the idea of end and beginning [*fim/início*], of wake or vigil and a new awakening; and, on the other hand, it incorporates the name of Finn, the giant of the Irish legend, whose resurrection, according to the same fictional story, would occur whenever the country would require it. See Augusto and Haroldo de Campos, *Panaroma de "Finnegans Wake"* (São Paulo: Commissão de Literatura, 1962).

8. Mário de Andrade, *Cartas a Manuel Bandeira* (Rio de Janeiro: Simões Editora, 1958), 60. Oswald and Sérgio (Milliet) were in Europe at the time.

9. Oswald de Andrade, *Ponta de lança* (São Paulo: Livraria Martins Editora, n.d.), 55.

10. For W. Y. Tindall, that use of parody in Joyce would express a "comic view of life." Tindall, *James Joyce: His Way of Interpreting the Modern World* (New York: C. Scribner's Sons, 1950), 43–46.

11. Stuart Gilbert, *James Joyce's "Ulysses"* (1930; reprint, London: Faber & Faber, 1952), 41.

12. "Modernism is a diagram of the coffee's bull market, of bankruptcy, and of the Brazilian revolution." Oswald de Andrade, *Ponta de lança,* 120.

13. Antonio Candido, "Estouro e libertação," *Brigada ligeira* (São Paulo: Editora Martins, n.d. [1945]), 21.

14. Oswald de Andrade, *Ponta de lança,* 68.

15. Antonio Candido, "Oswald viajante," *O observador literário* (São Paulo: Commissão Estadual de Literatura, 1959), 91.

16. In this poem, Oswald also achieves a surprising fusion of the lyric "I" with the collective, participatory "I," as I tried to show in "Lirismo e participação," *Suplemento literário de "O Estado de São Paulo,"* 6 July 1963.

17. Philippe Sollers, *Logiques* (Paris: Éditions du Seuil, 1968), 206.

18. On the cover of my copy of *Serafim Ponte Grande,* which I received personally from the author, the term "novel" was crossed out and replaced by the word "invention."

19. See Elisabeth Walther, "Semiotische Analyse," *Mathematik und Dichtung* (Munich: Nymphenburger Verlagshandlung, 1965), 145: "The *index* maintains real relations with its object, it points directly to its object. For instance: the signs on the road, the road itself, proper nouns and, even, all of the indications that determine an object's place, time and number, etc." See also Max Bense, *Semiotik* (Baden-Baden: Agis-Verlag, 1967).

20. This concept of the "estrangement" of Russian formalist theory seems to have inspired the Brechtian "Verfremdungseffekt" in drama theory, which is well known in the West.

21. See Viktor Shklovsky, "Parody in Tristram Shandy," *Theory of Prose* (Moscow, 1925). [In English: "Sterne's *Tristram Shandy:* Stylistic Commentary," in *Russian Formalist Criticism: Four Essays,* trans. and with an introduction by Lee T. Lemon and Marion J. Reis (Lincoln: University of Nebraska Press, 1965), 3–24. A full translation of Shklovsky's *Theory of Prose,* by Benjamin Sher, was published in 1990 by Dalkey Archive Press. —EDITORS]

22. See the article by Prudente de Moraes Neto and Sérgio Buarque de Holanda in *Estética* (Livraria Odeon, Rio de Janeiro) 2 (January–March 1925): 218–22. These critics had already noted that "one of the salient characteristics of this 'novel' by Mr. Oswald de Andrade derives possibly from a certain anthological feature that he imprinted on it. [. . .] The construction is made in the reader's inner spirit. Oswald provides the loose pieces. They can only be combined in a certain way. It's just a matter of combining them and that's it."

23. See Haroldo de Campos, "Estílistica miramarina," *Metalinguagem* (Rio de Janeiro: Editora Vozes, 1967), 87–97. There I perform an analysis based on the language axes identified by Roman Jakobson: (1) the *metaphoric,* which relates things by similarity (paradigmatic axis); (2) the *metonymic,* which relates things by contiguity (syntagmatic axis). See Krystyna Pomorska, *Russian Formalist Theory and Its Poetic Ambience* (The Hague: Mouton, 1968), 82: "[A]ccording to the linguistics of our time, these notions could be applied on every level of language activity," hence the justification for the extension of the concept that I am making here.

24. René Wellek and Austin Warren, *Theory of Literature* (New York: Harcourt, Brace & World, 1956), 236.

25. C. Lévi-Strauss, "La science du concret," *La pensée sauvage* (Paris: Plon, 1962), 3–47. [In English: "The Science of the Concrete," *The Savage Mind* (Chicago: University of Chicago Press, 1966). —EDITORS] See also Paolo Caruso, "Lévi-Strauss e il bricolage," *Almanacco letterario Bompiani* (Milan: Bompiani, 1966), 61–64; Roland Barthes, "Littérature et discontinu" and "L'activité structuraliste," *Essais critiques* (Paris: Éditions du Seuil, 1964), 186 and 214–18, respectively. [In English: "Literature and Discontinuity" and "The Structuralist Activity," *Critical Essays,* trans. Richard Howard (Evanston, IL: Northwestern University Press, 1972), 182 and 214–18. —EDITORS]

26. Antonio Candido, "Estouro e libertação," *Brigada Ligeira* (São Paulo: Editora Martins, [1945]), 11–30. From the two novel-inventions (*Miramar/Serafim*), Candido privileges *Miramar,* which he considers "one of the greatest books in Brazilian literature." We'd rather not choose and confront both as complementary and, in a way, inseparable aspects of the same experiment.

27. The aesthetics of *Serafim* make it an instance of what semiotician Julia Kristeva calls "intertextuality" (dialogue of texts), based on Mikhail Bakhtin's idea of the "polyphonic novel" with a "carnivalesque structure" as opposed to the traditional, "monologic" novel. Furthermore, *Serafim,* thanks to its nature and thematics, lends itself wonderfully to exemplifying the process of "carnivalization" in

literature, a popular and desecrating technique whose origins Bakhtin traces to Greek and Roman antiquity and the Middle Ages. See J. Kristeva, "Le mot, le dialogue, le roman," *Semeiotikè* (Paris: Éditions du Seuil, 1969) [in English: "Word, Dialogue, and Novel," *Desire in Language: A Semiotic Approach to Literature and Art,* ed. Leon S. Roudiez; trans. Thomas Gora, Alice Jardine, and Leon S. Roudiez (New York: Columbia University Press, 1980), 64–91. —TRANSLATOR]; M. Bakhtin, *Rabelais and His World,* trans. Hélène Iswolsky (Cambridge, MA: MIT Press, 1968).

The Open Work of Art

Umberto Eco, in his preface to the Brazilian edition of his work *Opera aperta,* said the following in reference to this essay: "It is indeed a curious thing that a few years before I wrote *Opera aperta,* Haroldo de Campos, in one of his articles, anticipates its themes in a surprising way, as if he had reviewed the book I had not yet written and I would later write without having read his article. But this means that certain problems emerge in an urgent way at given historical moments, arising almost automatically from the research in progress," *Obra aberta* (São Paulo: Editora Perspectiva, 1968), 17.

1. Jean-Paul Sartre, *Situations II* (Paris: Gallimard, 1948), 74–75.

2. Pierre Boulez, "Domaine musical," *Bulletin international de musique contemporaine* (Paris), no. 1 (1954): 124.

3. Or, to use the expression of Adelheid Obradovic: (1) "Nacheinander ohne Durchdringung"—"one part following another without interpenetration" (as in the structure of *Portrait of the Artist as a Young Man*); (2) "Nebeneinander ohne Durchdringung"—"one part juxtaposed to the other without interpenetration" (*Ulysses*); (3) "Durchdringung"—organic "interpenetration" (*Ulysses,* from Molly Bloom's silent monologue, and *Finnegans Wake*), in *Die Behandlung der Räumlichkeit im späteren Werk des James Joyce* (Marburg-Würzburg: Triltsch, 1934), 11.

4. Edmund Husserl, *Ideas: General Introduction to Pure Phenomenology,* trans. W. R. Boyce Gibson (New York: Macmillan, 1952).

5. Michel Fano, "Pouvoirs transmis," *La musique et ses problèmes contemporaines, Cahiers Renauld-Barrault* (Paris), no. 41 (1963): 40.

6. James Blish, "Rituals on Ezra Pound," *Sewanee Review* 53, no. 2 (Spring 1950): 196.

7. Published originally in the newspaper *Diário de São Paulo,* 3 July 1955. Later included in Augusto de Campos, Décio Pignatari, and Haroldo de Campos, *Teoria da poesia concreta* (*Textos críticos e manifestos, 1950–60*) (São Paulo: Edições Invenção, 1965). [Reprints: São Paulo: Duas Cidades, 1975; and São Paulo: Brasiliense, 1987. —EDITORS]

The Informational Temperature of the Text

1. Max Bense, "Klassification in der Literaturtheorie," *Augenblick* 2 (1958).

2. B. Mandelbrot, "Linguistique statistique macroscopique," *Logique, langage et théorie de l'information*, vol. 3 of *Études d'épistemologie génétique* (Paris: Presses Universitaires de France, 1957), 1–78. Subsequent parenthetical page numbers in the text refer to this source.

3. George K. Zipf, *Human Behavior and the Principle of Least Effort* (Cambridge: Addison, 1949).

4. G. A. Miller, *Language and Communication* (New York: McGraw-Hill, 1951).

5. Charles Kay Ogden, *The General Basic English Dictionary* (London: Evans Brothers Limited, 1940).

6. Miller, *Language and Communication*, 115–16.

7. Harry Levin, *James Joyce* (New York: New Directions, 1960).

8. This sense is well emphasized by Max Bense, in "Klassifikation in der Literaturtheorie" and elsewhere.

9. "Verse," Mário Pedrosa wrote, "with its unfolding movement, its cuttings and junctures, has a cultivated nature, unmistakably erudite and discursive." Mário Pedrosa, "Poeta e pintor concretista," *Jornal do Brasil* (Rio de Janeiro), 6 February 1957.

10. Adelheid Obradovic, *Die Behandlung der Räumlichkeit im späteren Werk des James Joyce* (Marburg-Würzburg: Triltsch, 1934).

11. Claude E. Shannon and Warren Weaver, *The Mathematical Theory of Communication* (Urbana: University of Illinois Press, 1964), 56.

12. Levin, *James Joyce*, 196–97.

13. Ibid., 197.

14. Ernest Fenollosa, *The Chinese Written Character as a Medium for Poetry* (New York: Arrow Editions, 1936).

15. Ibid., 5.

16. Pound to Ogden, Rapallo, 28 January 1935, in Ezra Pound, *Letters 1907–1941*, ed. D. D. Paige (London: Faber and Faber, 1951), 266.

17. Ferlinghetti's censure derives from his traditional concept of "oral poetry," not linked with the development of vocal techniques in contemporary music. Pound's text, in a way like Mallarmé's, is a true musical score waiting for performing voices. See Ferlinghetti, *The Pound Newsletter* (San Francisco: Mimeo, 1956), 19.

18. Norbert Wiener, *Cybernetics* (New York: J. Wiley, 1948).

19. Max Bense, *Aesthetica II* (Baden-Baden: Agis-Verlag, 1958).

20. Max Bense, "Das Existenz—Problem der Kunst," *Augenblick* 1 (1958).

21. Max Bense, *Ästhetik und Zivilisation* (Baden-Baden: Aegis Verlag, 1958).

22. Jerome Rothenberg, *The Book of Hours and Constellations: Poems of Eugen Gomringer* (New York: Something Else Press, 1968).

23. Décio Pignatari, "New Poetry: Concrete," in Haroldo de Campos et al., *Teoria da poesia concreta* (São Paulo: Duas Cidades, 1975).

24. Bense here refers to the "eternal objects" of Whitehead, such as "colors or color and form relationships."

25. Max Bense, "Konkrete Malerei," in *Aesthetica III* (Baden-Baden: Agis Verlag, 1958), 88.

Concrete Poetry–Language–Communication

1. Korzybski, quoted by S. I. Hayakawa in "What Is Meant by Aristotelian Structure of Language?" in *Language, Meaning and Maturity: Selections from "Etc. A Review of General Semantics," 1943–1953*, ed. S. I. Hayakawa (New York: Harper & Brothers, 1954), 220.

2. Adelheid Obradovic, "Zeit und Raum und ihre Relationen," chap. 2 of *Die Behandlung der Räumlichkeit im Späteren Werk des James Joyce* (Marburg-Würzburg: Triltsch, 1934), 10.

3. "No individual is free to describe nature with absolute impartiality but is constrained to certain modes of interpretation even while he thinks himself most free. The person most nearly free in such respects would be a linguist familiar with many widely different linguistic systems." —Benjamin Lee Whorf, quoted by Hayakawa ("What is Meant," 222), who comments: "Here Korzybski would feel, I am sure, that a person acquainted with modern mathematics—or at least with the methods of modern mathematics—is already in the situation of 'a linguist familiar with many widely different linguistic systems,' with the advantage, moreover, that these mathematical systems are not the haphazard residue of primitive metaphysical notions and animisms, but are systems of propositional functions, which, being deliberately emptied of content, can be given any content."

4. Trigant Burrow, *The Biology of Human Conflict* (New York: Macmillan, 1937).

5. A crucial point in Fenollosa's essay "The Chinese Written Character as a Medium for Poetry" relates to the ideogram's spatiotemporal character: "One superiority of verbal poetry as an art rests in its getting back to the fundamental reality of *time*. Chinese poetry has the unique advantage of combining both elements. It speaks at once with the vividness of painting, and with the mobility of sounds. It is, in some sense, more objective than either, more dramatic. In reading Chinese we do not seem to be juggling mental counters, but to be watching things work out their own fate." See essay in *The Little Review Anthology*, ed. Margaret Anderson (New York: Hermitage House, 1953), 192.

6. S. I. Hayakawa, "Semantics, General Semantics, and Related Disciplines," in *Language, Meaning and Maturity*, 32.

7. Oliver Bloodstein, "General Semantics and Modern Art," in *Language, Meaning and Maturity*, 289.

8. Hayakawa, "What Is Meant," 221.

9. W. Sluckin, *Minds and Machines* (Harmondsworth, Middlesex: Penguin Books, 1954), 16–18.

10. See *eupoema* (*Ipoem*), by Décio Pignatari: "eu jamais soube ler: meu olhar / de errata a penas deslinda as feias / fauces dos grifos e se refrata / onde se lê leia-se"

("I could never read: my errata / glance painfully interpretties the ugly / fauces of the griffins and refracts: / where it reads should be read." Transl. Soraya Ferreira Alves).

11. Sluckin, *Minds and Machines*, 159–60.

12. "I have mentioned the tyranny of mediaeval logic. According to this European logic thought is a kind of brickyard. It is baked into little hard units or concepts. These are piled in rows according to size and then labeled with words for future use. This use consists in picking out a few bricks, each by its convenient label, and sticking them together into a sort of wall called a sentence by use either of white mortar for the positive copula 'is,' or of black mortar for the negative copula 'is not.' In this way we produce such admirable propositions as 'A ring-tailed baboon is not a constitutional assembly.'" Fenollosa and Pound, "Chinese Written Character," 204.

13. Hiyakawa, "What Is Meant," 223.

14. Fenollosa and Pound, "Chinese Written Character," 206. "By contrast to the method of abstraction, or of defining things in more and still more general terms, Fenollosa emphasizes the method of science, 'which is the method of poetry,' as distinct from that of 'philosophic discussion,' and is the way the Chinese go about it in their ideograph or abbreviated picture writing." Ezra Pound, *ABC of Reading* (New Haven: Yale University Press, 1934), 20. The comparison between Fenollosa and Pound's ideogramic method and Korzybski's non-Aristotelian systems of language would prove a most suggestive study.

15. Adolfo Casais Monteiro, "Palavra, letras e poesia," *O Estado de São Paulo,* 17 February 1957: "The preponderance of the visual over the aural, which is evident in Mallarmé and even more so in Cummings, makes it impossible to listen to poems that are made to be seen, a position taken to its extreme by the concretists, whose poems can't be heard." See, in this regard, Diogo Pacheco's "Musicalidade e verbalização," *Suplemento dominical do "Jornal do Brasil"* (Rio de Janeiro), 17 March 1957.

16. Susanne Langer, *Feeling and Form* (New York: Charles Scribner's Sons, 1953), 277.

17. Oliver Bloodstein, "General Semantics and Modern Art," in *Language, Meaning, and Maturity,* 289.

18. Oliveira Bastos, "Por uma poesia concreta," *Suplemento dominical do "Jornal do Brasil"* (Rio de Janeiro), 24 March 1957.

19. Mário Pedrosa, in his insightful essay "Arte concreta ou a ausencia de ícones," *Jornal do Brasil* (Rio de Janeiro), 15 February 1957, has emphasized the importance of nonverbal communication in concrete poetry.

20. Based on Chang Tung-sun's essay "A Chinese Philosopher's Theory of Knowledge," *Etc. A Review of General Semantics* 9, no. 3 (Spring 1952): 203–26, Ruesch and Kees also note that "Western thought, including scientific logic, has been largely based—or was until recently—upon an Aristotelian approach, which in turn is rooted in the Greek grammar and its subject-predicate language struc-

ture. Within such a structure the subject of discourse has to be stated and the level of abstraction defined. This is not true, for example, in Chinese logic and language, in which the subject-predicate dichotomy is avoided. It is not without interest that the tremendous advances made in Western technology developed only when scientists adopted a language that was not bound by the subject-predicate dichotomy—namely, mathematics." Jürgen Rüsch and Waldo Kees, *Nonverbal Communications—Notes on the Visual Perception of Human Relations* (Berkeley and Los Angeles: University of California Press, 1956), 9.

21. "The orientation recommended by Korzybski to free the individual from the tyranny of words was called by him *extensional*. Roughly speaking, to be extensional is to be aware of things, facts, and operations in the way they are related in nature instead of in the way they are talked about. The extensionally-oriented person differentiates better than the word-minded (intentionally-oriented) one. He is aware of the basic uniqueness of 'things,' 'events,' etc., and so he is more aware of change than the intentionally oriented person, who mistakes the fluid, dynamic world around him for the static, rigid word of labels, 'qualities,' and 'categories' in his head." Anatol Rapoport, "What Is Semantics," in *Language, Meaning, and Maturity*, 13. To which Oliver Bloodstein adds: "The extensional and intentional orientations to art correspond respectively to the perception of form and the perception of content." Bloodstein, "General Semantics and Modern Art," in *Language, Meaning, and Maturity*, 287.

Brazilian and German Avant-Garde Poetry

1. O. M. Carpeaux, "Revelações sobre Rilke," *Correio da manhã* (Rio de Janeiro), 12 January 1956.

2. Previously printed in *Augenblick* 2 (May 1955). The reference to this first publication in the last edition of Gomringer's *Konstellationen* (1963) is inaccurate because the first phase of Max Bense's and Elisabeth Walther's *Augenblick* only began to appear in 1955 (not 1954). I published a Brazilian translation of the manifesto in *Suplemento dominical do "Jornal do Brasil,"* on March 17, 1957. Up until 1950, Gomringer had written Shakespearean sonnets; after two years of silence, he began to produce his first visual poems for the magazine *Spirale* (1953). This is what he himself tells in "The First Years of Concrete Poetry," *Form* (Cambridge) 4 (1967).

3. See Augusto de Campos, Haroldo de Campos, and Décio Pignatari, *Teoria da poesia concreta: Textos críticos e manifestos, 1950–60* (São Paulo: Edições Invenção, 1965). [Second edition under the same title (São Paulo: Duas Cidades, 1975). —EDITORS]

4. Ibid.

5. Note what Gomringer says, in his statement quoted in note 2, about Pignatari's kine-poem "LIFE" (1958): "Since I am inclined to express all thoughts in a short form, and had always taken pleasure in algebraic equations, I found it won-

derful that one could say so much with a single word. I still find sublime, for example, the way in which my friend Décio Pignatari called attention to the word LIFE at a later date. It is the architecture and symbolism of this word that make the poem unique for me." H. Heissenbüttel points out that for Gomringer the ideal concrete poem would be summarized in a single word. See *Über Literatur* (Olten: Walter-Verlag, 1966).

6. Gomringer: "The title that you are proposing, 'concrete poetry,' pleases me very much. Before I named my 'poems' constellations, I had really thought of calling them 'concrete.' As far as I'm concerned, the entire anthology could be named 'concrete poetry.'" (He was talking about the project of an international anthology, only finally published in 1960.)

7. Anatol Rosenfeld, "Balanço da poesia alemã," *Suplemento literário de "O Estado de São Paulo,"* 1 November 1964.

8. In a statement from 1967 (quoted in note 2), Gomringer writes: "Although I had to confess to myself many times that Holz was a strange character, monstrously self-absorbed, in whom I could not place the slightest bit of trust, he exerted a formidable fascination on me. What I could not get off my mind were his grandiloquent verbal creations and his rhythmic directives. He seemed to me somewhat extravagant, from the German point of view, and not sufficiently 'plastic' in his expression. Nonetheless, I still found it impressive that he had had taken the liberty to interfere with the order of language, and that he, more than any other German poet, would concern himself in such a minute way with either the visual layout of the poem or its sound pattern."

9. *Suplemento literário de "O Estado de São Paulo,"* 3 October and 5 December 1962.

10. "One is tempted to affirm, with good reason, that the material and linguistic possibilities of the German language, its visual, metaphoric, acoustic resources and its ambivalence, have never been put to use in a more original and complete way as in Arno Holz's *Phantasus*" (Max Bense, "Textalgebra Arno Holzes").

11. The poem ends in a way that could be equated with the rising of the "constellation" in the Mallarméan sky, issued by thought casting the dice, in an unending struggle against chance:

> My
> dust fluttered;
> rising,
> my memory, like
> a star!

12. [Edited by] Augusto and Haroldo de Campos (São Paulo: Invenção, 1964); includes special contributions by Luiz Costa Lima and Erthos Albino de Sousa. Third, revised and expanded edition published in São Paulo by Perspectiva in 2002.

13. *Suplemento literário de "O Estado de São Paulo,"* 17 November 1962.

14. In *Atta Troll* there is also an aesthetic controversy about *biased (tendentious) poetry* (which we would now term "committed" or "engagé"). In "Heinrich Heine als nationaler Dichter," Lukács tries to characterize the dual goal of the controversy. It was not simply a defense of the autonomy of poetry but rather, an attack against *narrow (tendentious) poetry* "devoid of talent," "stupid" ("die borniette Tendenzpoesie"), narrowly sectarian and unable to view things in a complex and multifaceted movement, in a word, against "prosaically bombastic tendentious poetry," as Heine termed it. [*Deutsche Realisten des 19. Jahrhunderts* (Berlin: Aufbau-Verlag, 1956) (in English: "Heinrich Heine as National Poet," in *German Realists in the Nineteenth Century,* trans. Jeremy Gaines and Paul Keast, ed. Rodney Livingstone [Cambridge, MA: MIT Press, 1993]). —TRANSLATOR] And Lukács concludes: "Heine's struggle against tendentiousness is therefore a thrust in the direction of true, genuine and deep political poetry, where the tendentiousness develops organically out of the subject itself, rather than being plastered over the contents in abstract and prosaic manner" [*German Realists,* 146]. With the same words, we could define the political poetry of Sousândrade, in contrast to overflowing and superficial Brazilian romantic oratory.

15. "His major poem, *Guesa errante,* is one of the most ambitious works ever produced in Latin America; and his life illustrates the archetypal struggle of the Latin American intellectual between 'barbarism' and 'civilization.' . . . If any poem deserves the title of Latin American epic this is it." See "Sousândrade's Stock," *Times Literary Supplement* (London), 24 June 1965, 541.

16. *Suplemento literário de "O Estado de São Paulo,"* 23 December 1961.

17. *Suplemento dominical do "Jornal do Brasil"* (Rio de Janeiro), 28 October and 4 November 1956 [republished in *A arte no horizonte do provável* (São Paulo: Perspectiva, 1969). —EDITORS].

18. Stockhausen, "Sprache und Musik," *Darmstädter Beitrage zur neuen Musik* (Mainz) (1958). In Cologne, in July 1959, I had the opportunity to discuss with the composer the relationships between the new music and the new poetry. In August of that same year, at a lecture given during the Darmstadt summer course, Stockhausen made reference to the new Brazilian concrete-poetry experiments (recently published in Germany by the magazine *nota* 2 [Munich]) and to the new German poetry (Hans G. Helms). He compared them to what was being done in music by him ("Zyklus"); Cornelius Cardew ("Five Books of Study for Pianist," 1958; "Piano Piece," 59); Sylvano Bussoti ("Piano Pieces for David Tudor"); John Cage ("Piano Concerto"); Mauricio Kagel ("Transición II"). See Stockhausen, "Musik und Graphik," Darmstädter Beitrage (Mainz) (1960).

19. "Marco Zero de Andrade," *Suplemento literário de "O Estado de São Paulo,"* 24 October 1964.

20. "Morgenstern, poeta alemão de vanguarda," *Jornal de letras* (Rio de Janeiro), June 1958; "O fabulário lingüístico de Christian Morgenstern," *Página Invenção do "Correio paulistano,"* 4 December 1960.

21. *Página Invenção do "Correio paulistano,"* 15 May 1960.

22. "Reduzierte Sprache / Über einen Text von Gertrude Stein," republished in the work quoted in note 5.

23. Cf. Patrick Bridgwater, ed. and trans., *Twentieth-Century German Verse* (Harmondsworth, Eng.: Penguin, 1963). The comparison between Heissenbüttel and Brecht was done by Walter Jens, *Deutsche Literatur der Gegenwart* (Munich: Piper, 1962). See also Haroldo de Campos, "Três poemas de Helmut Heissenbüttel," *Página Invenção do "Correio paulistano,"* 21 February 1960, and "Breve Antologia de Bertolt Brecht," *Tempo brasileiro* (Rio de Janeiro) 9/10 (1966).

24. Cf. Afterword by the composer Gottfried Michael König.

25. "Voraussetzungen (Aus Anlass einer Lesung von H. G. Helms)," *Akzente* (Munich) 5 (1961).

26. *Die Ideologie der anonymen Gesellschaft* (Cologne: DuMont Schauberg, 1967). Helms seems to have abandoned, at least temporarily, the field of artistic creation.

27. "Premières notes sur la poésie concrète," *Gazette de Lausanne,* 3 June 1961.

28. As Curt Meyer-Classon pointed out to me, this subtitle is ambiguous and can mean: (1) hunt chase of maniacal readers; (2) claws or canines of those avid readers.

29. In 1965, in the Albert Hall of London, before an audience of 6,000 people who were merely expecting to hear Beat poetry (by poets such as Ginsberg, Corso, and Ferlinghetti), Jandl achieved eloquent success, demonstrating the somewhat complex oralization possibilities of concrete poetry. Cf. "Stirring Times," *Times Literary Supplement* (London), 17 June 1965.

30. I quote the introductory remarks of playwright Friedrich Dürrenmatt.

31. See H. M. Enzensberger, *Die Entstehung eines Gedichtes* (Frankfurt: Suhrkamp, 1962); Haroldo de Campos, "Maiakovski em português: Roteiro de uma tradução," *Revista do livro* (Instituto Nacional do Livro, MEC, Rio de Janeiro) 23/24 (1961).

32. In *Bildenschift* (Frankfurt: Suhrkamp, 1965), the experimental trend in Enzensberger's poetry is accentuated.

33. Otto Maria Carpeaux, *A literatura alemã* (São Paulo: Editora Cultrix, 1964). On Schmidt, see also Carpeaux, "A álgebra do caos," *Correio da manhã* (Rio de Janeiro), 17 February 1962.

34. See Walter Widmer, *Fug und Unfug des Übersetzens* (Cologne: Kiepenheuer and Witsch, 1959).

35. The four volumes are bound into a single one, *Aesthetica* (Baden-Baden: Agis Verlag, 1965). Two other important volumes are *Theorie der Texte* (Cologne: Kiepenheuer and Witsch, 1962) and *Semiotik* (Baden-Baden: Agis Verlag, 1967). Bense's work, forerunner of many of the trends of French structuralism, is surprisingly not very well known in France. In the bibliography of issue 4 ("Recherches sémiologiques") of *Communications,* 1964, only *Theorie der Texte* is listed.

36. See especially: Haroldo de Campos, "A nova estética de Max Bense," *Suplemento literário de "O Estado de São Paulo,"* 21 March and 4 April 1959 (republished in *Metalinguagem* [Petrópolis: Editora Vozes, 1967]); "Montagem: Max Bense," *Página Invenção do "Correio paulistano,"* 6 March 1960; "Max Bense: A fantasia racional," *Correio da manhã* (Rio de Janeiro), 9 May 1964; "Max Bense on Brasília" (translation), *Invenção* (São Paulo) 2 (1962).

37. Among E. Walther's most notable works are *Francis Ponge, Eine aesthetische Analyse* (Cologne: Kiepenheuer and Witsch, 1965) and the organization and introduction of the writings of Charles Sanders Peirce, *Die Festigung der Überzeugung* (Baden-Baden: Agis Verlag, 1965).

38. Especially: *Noigandres / Konkrete Texte,* ed. M. Bense and E. Walther, with a preface by H. Heissenbüttel, *Rott* (Stuttgart) 7 (1962); "Poesia concreta" (version of the lecture delivered by M. Bense at the opening of the Brazilian concrete-poetry exhibit at the Latin American Circle of the University of Freiburg, curated by Júlio Medaglia, 1963), *Invenção* 3 (1963); "Konkrete Poesie," *Manuskripte* (Graz, Austria) 11 (1964); *Experimentelle Schreibweisen, Rot* (Stuttgart) 17 (1964); "Konkrete Poesie (Anlässlich des Sonderheftes *noigandres* zum zehnjaehrigen Bestehen dieser Gruppe fur *Konkrete Poesie* in Brasilien)," *Sprache im technischen Zeitalter* (special issue: *Texttheorie und Konkrete Dichtung*) (Stuttgart) 15 (1965). This last piece was republished in *Humboldt* (Hamburg) 13 (1966).

39. Max Bense and Elisabeth Walther published in 1964 Willy Keller's German translation of "O cão sem plumas" by João Cabral de Melo Neto, *Rot* 14.

The Ghost in the Text (Saussure and the Anagrams)

1. André Martinet, *Élements de linguistique générale* (Paris: Colin, 1960), translated by Elisabeth Palmer as *Elements of General Linguistics* (London: Faber and Faber, 1964).

2. Roman Jakobson, "Closing Statement: Linguistics and Poetics," in *Style in Language,* ed. Thomas A. Sebeok (New York: Technology Press of MIT, 1960), 377. Portuguese translation in *Lingüística e comunicação* (São Paulo: Cultrix, 1968).

3. Roman Jakobson, "Der grammatische Bau des Gedichts von B. Brecht 'Wir sind sie,'" in *Beitrage zur Sprachwissenschaft, Volkskunde und Literaturforschung,* eds. A. V. Isacenko, W. Wissmann, and H. Strobach (Berlin: Akademie, 1965). Portuguese translation as "A construção gramatical do poema 'Nós somos ele' de B. Brecht," *Lingüística, poética, cinema* (São Paulo: Perspectiva, 1970).

4. Jakobson, "Der grammatische Bau de Gedichts." [In French as "À la recherche de l'essence du langage," in *Problèmes du langage* (Paris: Gallimard, 1966); in Portuguese in the collection *Lingüística, poética, cinema,* note 3; and in English as "Quest for the Essence of Language," in *Diogenes* 51 (1966), and collected in *Language in Literature* (Cambridge: Belknap, 1987), 413–42. —TRANSLATOR]

5. Giulio C. Lepschy, *La linguistica strutturale* (Turin: Einaudi, 1966). Brazilian publication under the title *A lingüística estrutural* (São Paulo: Perspectiva, 1971). English version as *A Survey of Structural Linguistics* (London: Faber, 1970).

6. Jacques Lacan, "L'instance de la lettre dans l'inconscient, ou la raison depuis Freud," translated as "The Insistence of the Letter in the Unconscious," *Yale French Studies* 36–37 (1966): 122. In the book edition of *Écrits* (Paris: Seuil, 1966), Lacan rewrote the original text in order to revise his judgment on Saussure and poetry in light of Starobinski's work.

7. Jean Starobinski, "Les anagrammes de Ferdinand de Saussure," *Mercure de France* 250 (February 1964): 243–62. Subsequently, Starobinski published four more works on the topic, which were collected in 1971 in the book *Les mots sous les mots* (Paris: Gallimard, 1971). [In Portuguese as *As palavras sob as palavras* (São Paulo: Perspectiva, 1974); and in English as *Words upon Words,* trans. Olivia Emmet (New Haven, CT: Yale University Press, 1979). —TRANSLATOR]

8. *Le récit hunique* (Paris: Editions du Seuil, 1967), 279.

9. Starobinski, "Les anagrammes."

10. Joaquim Mattoso Câmara Jr., *Dicionário de fatos gramaticais* (Rio de Janeiro: Ministério da Educação e Cultura/Casa de Rui Barbosa, 1956), 30.

11. The superb hermeneutic work on the "verbal masks" of Lautréamont, published by Leyla Perrone-Moisés, *Suplemento literário de "O Estado de São Paulo,"* 24 May 1969, focuses above all on the field of the anagram strictly speaking (in this case, a combinatory manipulation of the letters of a personal name).

12. Saussure quoted in Starobinski, *Words upon Words,* 18.

13. Starobinski, *Words upon Words,* 20.

14. In *Fonema e fonologia,* ed. and trans. J. Mattoso Câmara Jr. (Rio de Janeiro: Livaria Acadêmica, 1967).

15. Saussure quoted in Starobinski, *Words upon Words,* 30.

16. Cf. "Retrospecto," in *Fonema e fonologia* (note 14). Jakobson declared that, in his pursuit of the nucleus of the poetic word, in his paronomastic handling of minimal opposed pairs, Khlebnikov promoted the anticipation of the ultimate phonemic units. The poet designated these phenomena as "the internal declension of words." *Note for the first book edition:* This essay of mine was published in 1969. In 1971, in the journal *L'homme,* Jakobson printed the study "La première lettre de Ferdinand de Saussure à Antoine Meillet sur les anagrammes," which confirmed the conjectures developed here about the affinities hinted at between the Saussurian anagram and the Jakobsonian definition of the poetic function (affinities which were made clear only with the discovery of the Genevan master's unpublished manuscripts). Jakobson's piece is now available in *Questions de poétique* (Paris: Seuil, 1973).

17. To see how this problem has today become a trend in the French avant-garde of the 1960s and 1970s, read Jean Louis Houdebine's paper, "L'analyse structurale et la notion du texte comme *espace,*" *Linguistique et littérature,* a special number of the journal *La nouvelle critique* (Paris, Colloque de Cluny, 1968).

18. Already in 1955, at the Teatro de Arena, this and other poems from the series were rendered into oral form by the group Ars Nova, directed by Diogo Pacheco,

simultaneously with a slide projection of its text-score, in a performance that also included the music of Webern. *Note for the first book edition:* In a recent essay on "Un coup de dés," included in *La révolution du langage poétique: l'avant-garde à la fin du XIXe siècle: Lautréamont et Mallarmé* (Paris: Seuil, 1974), Julia Kristeva recognizes the relationship between the "phonic rhythm" of Mallarméan language and the "timbral melody" of Webern, a confirmation of the claims that concrete poetry was making in both the theory and the practice of the poem since the beginning of the 1950s. [See the English translation of Kristeva's essay in *Revolution in Poetic Language,* trans. Margaret Waller (New York: Columbia University Press, 1984). —TRANSLATOR]

19. Starobinski, *Words upon Words,* 96.

20. Ibid., 128. See André Pirro, *L'esthétique de Jean-Sébastien Bach* (Paris: Fischbacher, 1907); *A Translation of the First Nine Chapters of "L'esthétique de Jean-Sébastien Bach" by André Pirro,* trans. Esther Elizabeth Jones (Smith College thesis, 1933). *Note for the first book edition:* Scholars hesitate over the relationship between Meillet and his teacher Saussure. Georges Mounin, *Saussure: ou le structuraliste sans le savoir* (Paris: Seghers, 1968), writes: "One of the chief elements of Saussure's isolation is Meillet's (profound) incomprehension." Tullio de Mauro, in his notes to the Italian edition of the *Corso di linguistica generale* (Bari: Laterza, 1968), comments in the following terms the correspondence exchanged by the teacher and his student about the anagrams: "From Saussure's selected correspondence one can infer that the Parisian student hesitated to reply frankly and must have had a negative opinion about the whole investigation." Jakobson, with good arguments, seeks to demonstrate the opposite in his essay from 1971 quoted in note 16.

21. [De Campos is both paraphrasing and quoting Starobinski, *Words upon Words,* 129. —TRANSLATOR]

22. It would, in any case, be a matter of a phenomenon of "subliminal configuration," like those that Jakobson studies in Slavic folk poetry. Cf. "Configuração verbal subliminar em poesia," in *Lingüística, poética, cinema* [see note 3]—a study significantly headed by an epigraph drawn from Saussure's manuscripts: "Que le critique d'une part, et que le versificateur d'autre part, le veuille ou non" [Whether the critic on the one hand, and the versifier on the other hand, like it or not]. See "Subliminal Verbal Patterning in Poetry," in *Language in Literature,* ed. Krystyna Pomorska and Stephen Rudy (Cambridge: Belknap, 1987), 250–61.

23. Compare with the following: "In poetry, verbal equations are raised to the category of the constitutive principle of the text. . . . A phonological similarity is felt to be a semantic kinship. The play on words, or, to introduce a more erudite and perhaps more precise term, a *paronomasia,* queen of the poetic art" ("Apectos lingüísticos da tradução," in *Lingüística e comunicação* [São Paulo: Cultrix, 1968]; translated as "On Linguistic Aspects of Translation," in *Language in Literature* [Cambridge: Belknap, 1987], 428–35). *Note for the first book edition:* Evidently, the concept of *paronomasia,* in Jakobson, is broad and functional (as are those of metaphor and metonymy), overflowing from the "paronomial" words of the

rhetorical handbooks in order to gather "all the constituents of the verbal code," collated according to the principles studied in Jakobson's "poetry of grammar."

24. *Tel Quel* 29 (1967); translated by Roland-François Lack as "Towards a Semiology of Paragrams," in *The Tel Quel Reader,* ed. Patrick ffrench and Roland-François Lack (London: Routledge, 1998), 25–49. *Note for the first book edition:* Brazilian publication in Julia Kristeva, *Introdução à semanálise* (São Paulo: Perspectiva, 1974). I reproduce here what I wrote in my essay "Umbral para Max Bense," introducing *Pequena estética* (São Paulo: Perspectiva, 1971) by the philosopher from Stuttgart: Kristeva undertakes in "Pour une sémiologie des paragrammes" a productive interpenetration of semiology and logical-mathematical formal diagrams, whose transposition is able to furnish a theoretical model for the explication of signifying systems in natural language, considering any other application a posteriori of those diagrams as a secondary formalization, however not devoid of interest. Umberto Eco regards this "exasperated formalization of poetic discourse" with reservations (*A estrutura ausente* [São Paulo: Perspectiva, 1971]); and Jacques Roubaud and Pierre Lousson dispute it at the level of mathematical correctness (*Action poétique,* no. 41–42, [1969]). Nevertheless, Kristeva's study (even aside from her logico-mathematical pomp, which could be seen in this particular case as a useful "secondary" technique of illustrative diagrammatization), seems to me rich in creative observations and daring provocations, thanks above all to the fascinating elaborations that it makes on the "anagrammatic" postulates of the late Saussure.

25. Kristeva, it would seem, extracts this principle from Saussure's following observation: "I believe I could prove, by a large number of examples, that formal imprecisions, sometimes taken for archaisms, in Saturnian epigraphic poetry, are *deliberate,* and are in accordance with the phonic laws of this poetry."

26. Kristeva, "Towards a Semiology," 25–26.

27. Ibid., 26.

28. *Note for the first book edition:* It is quite true that, from a diachronic angle, the investigations into the "anagrams" (undertaken between 1906 and 1909) are more or less coeval with the lectures that are reproduced in the *Cours* (delivered until 1911). From the synchronic perspective of today's observer, however, these exercises in anagrammatic deciphering, interrupted by unanswered questions and excluded from the knowledge of the readers of the posthumous *Cours* (whose first edition was in 1916)—Jakobson even speaks of the "dissimulation" of the manuscripts for "half a century"—reveal the hidden face of the master, laden with bold premonitions, that only his successors would be capable of recuperating. (Remember that even a specialist like R. Godel, still in 1960, would refer to the anagram notebooks as a "tedious and sterile investigation.")

Poetic Function and Ideogram/The Sinological Argument

1. Saussure attempted to establish a correspondence with Giovanni Pascoli (1855–1912), a "Latinizing" Italian poet. The correspondence was ephemeral, how-

ever, for so far as we know, Pascoli failed to answer the second letter Saussure sent him regarding the occurrence of anagrams and related phenomena in modern Latin poetry. In Starobinski's opinion, it was the Italian poet's silence which, interpreted as a sign of disapproval, caused Saussure to discontinue his research on the subject. [Cf. Jean Starobinski, *Words upon Words,* trans. Olivia Emmet (New Haven, CT: Yale University Press, 1979), 120. —EDITORS] In *La letteratura italiana/ otto-novecento* (1974), Gianfranco Contini opens up new perspectives from which to consider these facts. According to this account, it was his craftsman's "cunning" that lay behind Pascoli's reluctance to furnish any information on the workings of his poetic activity and the "intimate structure of his texts." At the same time, however, Contini considers Pascoli's poems in Italian sufficient to make him, within the existing literature in that language, "the greatest of the innovators of his time" (and the source of important contributions in the field of rhythm and timbre, for example). For the same reason, Croce disapprovingly attributed to him (and to D'Annunzio) the responsibility of being "a forerunner and preparer of futurism." Thus, rather than a denial, Pascoli's silence may represent a voluntarily assumed prohibition.

2. Here it is worth recalling the importance which Robert Greer Cohn confers to *Les mots anglais* in his book *L'oeuvre de Mallarmé: Un coup de dés,* trans. René Arnaud (Paris: Librairie les lettres, 1951). The extremely detailed study of this work gives him a key to genuine deciphering operations of the anagram type (before Starobinski's revelations), and which he performs on Mallarmé's poetry inspired by the poet's own hypothesis that there was a "relation" between "the meaning of words" and their "external pattern."

3. "Car c'est un véritable jeu chinois que le Saturnien, en dehors même de toute chose regardant la métrique" ("For Saturnian verse, quite apart from any metric considerations, is like a Chinese game in its complexity"). Letter from Saussure, July 14, 1906, quoted by Starobinski, *Les mots sous les mots* (Paris: Gallimard, 1971). [English translation by Olivia Emmet, ed., *Words upon Words,* 9. —EDITORS]

4. This essay, "The Poet," is fundamental to an understanding of Fenollosa's thought (in Ralph Waldo Emerson, *Essays and Lectures* [New York: Library of America, 1983], 447–68, quoted passages at 456–57). With regard to Vico, it is worth noting that, in his *Principi di una scienza nuova* (1744), he took the "Chinese model" into account, albeit marginally, in order to highlight the musicality of the Chinese language, related in his view to the "first song of the peoples": "The Chinese, whose vulgar language has no more than three hundred articulate vocables, give them various modifications of pitch and time to match their one hundred and twenty thousand hieroglyphs, and thus speak by singing." [In English: *The New Science of Giambattista Vico,* trans. Thomas Goddard Bergin and Max Harold Fisch (Ithaca, NY: Cornell University Press, 1968), 155. —EDITORS] On the topicality of Vico's poetics, see Alfredo Bosi's invaluable work, "O ser e o tempo da poesia," *Discurso* 3 (1972).

5. According to V. Alleton, the thesis of the "pictographic origins" of writing is "generally accepted"; in the case of Chinese, it is supported, if not exactly demonstrated, by "the significant number of primitive characters which represent objects"—such figurative elements, she holds, survive in the corresponding present-day characters, although in an extremely schematic form. [See Viviane Alleton, *L'écriture chinoise*, 2d ed. (Paris: Presses Universitaires de France, 1976), 8. —EDITORS] Derrida recalls the suggestive psychoanalytic interpretation of Chinese writing developed by Melanie Klein: for her, "(Note [Klein's footnote]: [. . .] earlier picture-script, which underlies our script too, is still active in the phantasies of every individual child, so that the various strokes, dots, etc., of our present script would only be simplifications, achieved as a result of condensation, displacement and other mechanism familiar to us from dreams and neuroses, of the earlier pictures whose traces, however, would be demonstrable in the individual.) The sexual-symbolic meaning of the penholder is apparent in these examples. . . . It can be observed how the sexual symbolic meaning of the penholder merges into the act of writing that the latter discharges." [Jacques Derrida, *Of Grammatology*, trans. Gayatri Chakravorty-Spivak (Baltimore: Johns Hopkins University Press, 1976), 334 n. 37. —EDITORS]

6. Matila C. Ghyka, a mathematician who doubled as a poet-philologist, took a special interest in the phenomena of phonic or "dynamic" suggestion observed in words. In his invaluable *Sortilèges du verbe* (Paris: Gallimard, 1949), he wrote: "Because Chinese ideograms represent visual and not phonetic symbols, Chinese metaphors remain, in general, images in a strict sense. We can say in an approximate way that Chinese people think and express themselves in enumerations, combinations (permutations), and in images; the Semitic peoples in images and parables; "Westerners" in analogies and metaphors (condensed analogies)" (187).

7. In Brazil, D. Pignatari has been concerned, since his pioneering study *Semiótica e literatura* (São Paulo: Perspectiva, 1974), with the problem of the Peircean hypo-icon. He proposes that paronomasia rather than metaphor (the tertiary hypo-icon) should be considered "the figure most suited to the paradigmatic axis of similarities"—at least, "as far as the artistic iconic sign is concerned." Pignatari goes on to assert, referring to Freud and Lacan, that it is not a case of "association of ideas" but rather of "association of forms" (47, 48, 49, 82, 83).

8. V. Alleton points out: "The explanation of the Chinese character as being a kind of etymological rebus has always enjoyed the greatest prestige. . . . It is an effective mnemonic system, often with an etymological basis, although it does not constitute a linguistic analysis" (19–20). She further notes that, although "it does not suffice to look at the characters in order to discover their meaning," this does not mean that "when meeting an unknown ideogram a Chinese reader does not attempt to guess or imagine what word it represents" (by analogy with known characters) "and very often manage to decipher it" (20). This "imaginative" or creative lexicographic tradition, which originates in ancient Chinese practices, was

exhaustively documented and established in the West by the Jesuit L. Wieger in his book *Chinese Characters: Their Origin, Etymology, History, Classification, and Signification; A Thorough Study from Chinese Documents* (1915, English translation, reissued in 1965 by Dover Publications, New York, from the French original of 1899). Some authors, such as R. A. D. Forrest, *The Chinese Language* (London: Faber and Faber, 1948), deplore, from the viewpoint of practical efficacy, the "hyper-refinement" of these scholars, which led to their "beautifying written forms with unnecessary or pleonastic significations." In *Sound and Symbol in Chinese* (London: Oxford University Press, 1923), B. Karlgren speaks of "errors of comprehension" of the ancient characters, of "deliberate substitution" and of "the inventions of careless scribes"; and he refers to the celebrated compilation made by Li Si in about 213 B.C. H. G. Porteus, on the other hand ("Ezra Pound and His Chinese Character: A Radical Examination," 1950), counterargues that this kind of criticism represents "the insensitive solemnity of professional philologists." In this case it would not be appropriate to speak of "errors." Li Si, he asserts, was not a "blind fool"; on the contrary, "there are countless indications that he was a poet of great resourcefulness and imagination"; a poet-etymologist who was often skillful enough to "rehabilitate obsolete characters with the vivacity of new images, and thus preserve the concrete and poetic essence of the language." In this sense, in his *Pound e la Cina* (Milan: Feltrinelli, 1974), G. Mancuso misses the mark, when, in referring to a second compilation, *Shuo-Wen* (a revision and expansion of Li Si's, in about 200 A.D.), he remarks: "The latest studies show that many traditional characters classified as compound ideograms are in reality phonetic compounds"; ancient Chinese literati often committed veritable "ad hoc reconstructions" to justify the etymologies they put forward, striving "very fancifully to interpret the metaphorical meaning of certain compounds which it would be more appropriate to classify as phonetic." If we recall the importance of a dictionary such as the *Littré* had for Mallarmé, we can see how at the poetic level the weight of this centuries-old etymo-fugurative tradition renders the criterion of philologic "truth" irrelevant. . . .

9. Within the framework of Derrida's conception of *archi-écriture*—the movement of *différance*—the oral language is already *writing* in the general sense, regardless of "graphics," strictly speaking. "Arche-writing" involves a trace, which, as an "arche-phenomenon of memory" that precedes the nature/culture opposition, belongs to "the very movement of signification itself," always "written a priori" whether or not it is inscribed in a sensible "external" form. The question of origin ("the myth of the simplicity of origin") is thus shifted. Having stressed that from the viewpoint of linguistic science, both the theory of the precedence of speech over writing ("classical structuralism") and that of the absence of hierarchy in the "substance of expression," be it vocal or graphic (glossemic), seem to be consistent and that "it is hard to decide which is more valid," V. Alleton refers back to Derrida's *Grammatologie* for the philosophical implications of the problem (see

Alleton, *L'écriture chinoise,* 68). It would be appropriate at this point to recapitulate the contribution made by the Prague Linguistic Circle, through Mukařovský, to the aesthetic enhancement of the *graphic plane* (choice of type, arrangement on the page, innovative use of punctuation, capitals and lowercase, etc.), whose importance in the "structure of poetic works" had been neglected, according to the Czech theoretician, in favor of the preponderance of the acoustic viewpoint (cf. "Plan graphique, phonique et poétique," *Travaux du Cercle linguistique de Prague* 4 [1931]; transcribed in *Change* 3, 1969).

10. In his essay on modernist poetics, "A escrava que não é Isaura" (1923), written under the influence of post-Mallarméan European simultaneism (Divoire, Beaudoin), Mário de Andrade focuses on the passage from "melody" (concatenation) to "polyphony" (superimposition), with the aim of obtaining a "final total complex sensation" in the renewed poem. He makes a further distinction between "harmony" ("combination of simultaneous sounds") and "harmonic verse" (made up of loose words without connection): "instead of melody (grammatical phrasing) we have arpeggios, harmony-harmonic verse," and "poetic polyphony" ("loose phrases"): "same feeling of superimposition, no longer of words (notes) but of phrases (melodies)." (Cf. "Prefácio interessantíssimo," 1921 [English version as "Most Interesting Preface" in Mário de Andrade, *Hallucinated City,* trans. Jack E. Tomlins {Nashville: Vanderbilt University Press, 1968} —TRANSLATOR].) The linguist Mitsou Ronat, in "Vers une lecture des 'Anagrammes' par la théorie saussurienne," *Change* 6 (1970), defines the postulate of the "linearity of the signifier" as "music without chords" and the principle of the anagram as "music with chords."

11. With a tactical gesture, Fenollosa places the phonic level of Chinese poetry in parentheses, precisely in order to concentrate on the graphic plane, which provided him with incomparable raw material for reflection. It does not seem justifiable to attribute this attitude to a lack of interest in the acoustic aspects of poetry. This would be inconceivable in someone who for years had studied and practiced the singing and acting methods of Noh theater under Umewaka Minoru and admired in this ancient art of poetic theater the "delicate combination" of "appeals to the eye, the ear and the mind" in order to obtain a "lucid and unified impression." Thus, the legitimate concern expressed by J.Y. Liu when he in turn highlights "the highly complex organic development of sound and sense" (*Art of Chinese Poetry* [Chicago: University of Chicago Press, 1962], 19) in Chinese poetry should not serve as a motive to obscure once again the visual aspects which Fenollosa brought to light, however much they were accompanied by excesses which performed a "shifting" function (in Derrida's sense of the word). It should be noted that since his "terminal note" added in 1935 to his edition of Fenollosa's essay, Pound had recognized the importance of sound as a parameter in Chinese poetry: "Whatever few of us learned from Fenollosa twenty years ago, the whole Occident is still in crass ignorance of the Chinese art of verbal sonority. I now doubt if it was inferior to the Greek" (33). In his intro-

duction to *The Classic Anthology Defined by Confucius* (Cambridge, MA: Harvard University Press, 1954), Achilles Fang recalls another assertion of Pound's: "There can't be any real understanding of a good Chinese poem without knowledge both of the ideogram reaching the eye, and the metrical and melodic form reaching the ear or aural imagination" (xii). David Gordon recalls the poet in the 1950s, during a moment of leisure on the lawn at St. Elizabeths Hospital, "chanting the Chinese sounds" of the Odes he was translating with an "operatic" virtuosity of expression and "tremendous subtlety of intonation" (at a time when Pound was already far advanced in his long-lasting dealings with Chinese poetry) ("'Root/Br./By Product' In Pound's Confucian Ode 166," *Paideuma* 3 [1974]: 13–25).

12. Liu, *Art of Chinese Poetry*, 12.

13. For my interpretation of the ideograms, I have made use of the cited works by the Vaccaris and the Jesuit Wieger.

14. Liu, *Art of Chinese Poetry*, 12. My translation of Li Shang-yin's poem is included in full in my essay "Uma arquitextura do Barroco," in *A operação do texto* (São Paulo: Perspectiva, 1976), where I comment on the "trans-creative" solutions adopted.

15. Porteus, "Pound and his Chinese Character," 205.

16. Ibid., 212.

17. François Cheng, "Le 'langage poétique' chinois," in *La traversée des signes*, [ed. Julia Kristeva et al. (Paris: Éditions du Seuil, 1975) —EDITORS], 45.

18. Ibid.

19. Ibid., 45–46.

20. Ibid., 46.

21. Ibid., 45 n. 4.

22. Ibid., 45.

23. To translate this poem, I went back to the original text with its literal rendering given by Wai-Lim Yip: "The Chinese Poem: A Different Mode of Representation," *Delos* 3 (1969). It was possible to decipher the ideograms by means of the works cited in note 13 above, in addition to *Mathews' Chinese-English Dictionary*, 9th ed. (Cambridge, MA: Harvard University Press, 1963). My translation is published in full in the magazine *Poesia em greve* (1975).

24. It is worth recalling here the conclusions of the "Urbino Colloquium" (1976) on the relations between "text" and "context." These are said to be relations of contiguity, or *metonymic* relations (selection of certain structural features which pass from the latter to the former, where they may even perform a different function) rather than of similitude, or *metaphoric* relations, "from the copy to the original" (see T. Todorov, "L'analyse du récit à Urbino," *Communications* 11 [1968]).

25. Chisolm, *Fenollosa*, 203.

26. Quoted in ibid., 204.

27. *Semiótica e literatura* (São Paulo: Perspectiva, 1974), 56.

1. Albrecht Fabri, "Präliminarien zu einer Theorie der Literatur," *Augenblick* (Stuttgart/Darmstadt) 1 (March 1958).

2. Max Bense, "Das Existenzproblem der Kunst," *Augenblick* (Stuttgart/Darmstadt) 1 (March 1958).

3. Jean-Paul Sartre, "Qu'est-ce que c'est la littérature?" in *Situations II* (Paris: Gallimard, 1951). [In English: *What Is Literature?* trans. Bernard Frechtman (New York: Philosophical Library, 1942), 18. —EDITORS]

4. Paulo Rónai, *Escola de tradutores* (Rio de Janeiro: Livraria São José, 1956).

5. Charles Morris, *Signs, Language and Behavior* (New York: Prentice-Hall, 1950).

6. Ezra Pound, *Literary Essays* (Norfolk: New Directions, 1954), 232.

7. Ibid., 34.

8. Ibid., 34–35.

9. Ibid., 75.

10. T. S. Eliot, "Euripides and Professor Murray," *Selected Essays* (London: Faber and Faber, 1934), 50.

11. "What is remarkable about Pound's Chinese translations is that so often they do contrive to capture the spirit of their originals, even when, as quite often happens, they funk or fumble the letter. [. . .] His pseudo-Sinology releases his latent clairvoyance, just as the pseudo-sciences of the ancients sometimes gave them a supernormal insight." Hugh Gordon Porteus, "Ezra Pound and His Chinese Character: A Radical Examination," in *Ezra Pound,* ed. Peter Russell (London: Peter Nevil Ltd., 1950), 205.

√ 12. Hugh Kenner, introduction to *Translations,* by Ezra Pound (London: Faber and Faber, 1953), 11–12.

13. Boris Pasternak, *Essai d'autobiographie* (Paris: Gallimard, 1958), 55.

14. We thank Professor Boris Schneiderman for his information on Pasternak's translations of Shakespeare.

15. Sílvio Romero, "Manuel Odorico," *História da literatura brasileira,* vol. 1 (Rio de Janeiro: H. Garnier, 1902).

16. Manuel Odorico Mendes, *Odisséia de Homero,* 2d ed. (São Paulo: Atena Editora, 1957).

17. Manuel Odorico Mendes, *A Ilíada de Homero,* 2d ed. (São Paulo: Atena Editora, 1958).

18. Roland Barthes, writing about Michel Butor's *Mobile* in *Essais critiques* [(Paris: Editions du Seuil, 1964) —EDITORS], calls attention to the fact that the Homeric enumeration, true "epic catalogues," as Barthes calls it, may be painted in contemporary colors and so come to give testimony on the "infinite co-possibility of war and power." Odorico Mendes was right, then, in censuring the translators who omitted these lists from their versions.

19. Pound made two adaptations of this line: "imaginary / Audition of the phantasmal sea-surge" (*Mauberley*), and "he lies by the poluphloisboious sea-coast"

(*Moeurs Contemporaines*). "Pelas praias do mar polissonoras" ["Along the poly-sonorous beaches of the sea"] is a possible Portuguese translation of this line.

20. João Ribeiro, "Odorico Mendes—*Odisséia*," in *Crítica*, vol. 1 (Rio de Janeiro: Ed. Academia Brasileira de Letras, 1952).

21. Pound, *Literary Essays*, 249.

22. Ibid., 35.

23. "Rhododáctylos Eos" ["The rosy-fingered Dawn"] is Homer's epithet. Odorico Mendes has this lovely solution: "a dedirrósea Aurora."

24. Augusto de Campos, Décio Pignatari, and Haroldo de Campos, *Cantares de Ezra Pound* (Rio de Janeiro: Ministério da Educação e Cultura, Serviço de Documentação, 1960).

25. Augusto de Campos, *e. e. cummings: 10 poemas* (Rio de Janeiro: Idem, 1960).

26. Augusto de Campos and Haroldo de Campos, *Panaroma do Finnegans Wake* (São Paulo: Comissão Estadual de Literatura, 1962).

27. Porteus, "Pound and His Chinese Character," 205.

Hölderlin's Red Word

1. Quoted in Wolfgang Schadewaldt, "Hölderlin Übersetzung des Sophokles," *Antike und Gegenwart: Über die Tragödie* (Munich: Deutscher Taschenbuch Verlag, 1966), 115. The Portuguese version by Haroldo de Campos of the quoted phrase is "Que se passa? Tua fala se turva de vermelho," which recaptures the turbulence of the original metaphor.

2. Schadewaldt, "Hölderlin Übersetzung des Sophokles," 115.

3. Ibid.

4. It is worth noting that although the so-called *madness* poems must be counted among Hölderlin's most beautiful poetic accomplishments, many still regard them with reserve. Thus, Geneviève Bianquis, in her well-known French translations of Hölderlin's poems, admits having excluded from her selection "the excessively fragmentary hymns and poems of his madness." In addition, Jaspers, upon diagnosing the poet's schizophrenia, objected to the appreciation, which he feared excessive, of the poems of this phase. Otto Maria Carpeaux, *A literatura alemã* (São Paulo: Nova Alexandria, 1994).

5. Ibid., 117.

6. Hölderlin, *Sämtliche Werke*, vol. 5, ed. N. von Hellingrath, Friedrich Seebass, and Ludwig V. Pigenot (Berlin: Propyläen Verlag, 1923), p. XI.

7. Walter Benjamin, "The Task of the Translator," *Illuminations*, ed. Hannah Arendt, trans. Harry Zohn (New York: Harcourt, Brace and World, 1968), 81–82.

8. Bertolt Brecht, *Über Lyrik* (Frankfurt am Main: Suhrkamp Verlag, 1964), 93. In Brecht's *Antigonenmodel*, 1948, there is a "prelude" that relates the play to a current political situation and that takes place in Berlin in April 1945. In the script itself, many of Hölderlin's solutions are preserved, but in a modified form (thus: "du farbst mir / scheint's ein rotes Wort").

9. Schadewaldt, "Hölderlin Übersetzung des Sophokles," 119–20.

10. Ibid., 125.

11. Ibid.

12. Ibid.

13. One of Pound's last translations, published in 1954, was precisely *Women of Trachis,* from a text by Sophocles. In his version, Pound attempted to capture the dynamism of a spoken language, even using slang. However, as in *The Cantos,* the passages of oral fluency contrast with moments of "super-poetry" reserved for the treatment of the "Choruses." It is interesting to compare Pound's elliptical and archaic-like language, the highly worked melopoeia of his "choruses," with that of Hölderlin in his Sophoclean "choruses."

14. Hugh Gordon Porteus, "Ezra Pound and his Chinese Character: A Radical Examination," in *Ezra Pound,* ed. Peter Russell (New York: Haskell House, 1968), 205.

15. [Schadewaldt, "Hölderlin Übersetzung des Sophokles." —EDITORS]

16. Or glimpsing a superb "Lady of azure thought," where the professional Sinologist is able to see only a "quiet girl."

17. Benjamin, *Illuminations,* 80–81.

18. Ibid., 70.

19. Johann Wolfgang von Goethe, *West-östlicher Divan,* ed. Ernst Bauder (Bremen: Carl Schunemann Verlag, 1956), 296.

Eucalypse: The Beautiful Occultation

1. I have numbered each line of the poem to facilitate its analysis. Throughout the essay, I refer to anaphora (in Latin, *repetitio*) in the broadest sense possible. As I use it, the term means not only the repetition of one or more words in the beginning of successive verses but also the reiterative insistence on the same syntactic patterns, even those involving occasional semantic variation. Cf. F. Lázaro Carreter, *Diccionario de términos filológicos* (Madrid: Gredos, 1953); and H. Lausberg, *Elementos de retórica literária* (Lisbon: Gulbenkian, 1966).

2. I have also followed Propp's method to a great extent in *Morfologia de Macunaíma* (São Paulo: Perspectiva, 1973).

3. Although in different ways, Jakobson and Lacan have applied to the dual concept of "metaphor/metonymy" the Freudian terms *Verdichtung* (condensation) and *Verschiebung* (dislocation). In this regard, see N. Ruwet's note to the French translation of "Deux aspects du language et deux types d'aphasie," in Roman Jakobson, *Essais de linguistique générale* (Paris: Minuit, 1963), 66.

4. The image "cántaros de arriba" is of biblical extraction. See Job 38:37, with its reference to "niviê shamáyim."

5. Hugh Kenner has called attention to this etymology in *The Pound Era* (Berkeley and Los Angeles: University of California Press, 1971), 172. In the *Odyssey,* Calypso—whose name derives from the same Greek verb and means "the one that hides"—is the mistress of the island Ogygia. It is she who rescues the ship-

wrecked Ulysses, keeping him for seven years in her remote and paradisiacal island. I must remind the reader that, like the dryad in this poem, agent of the process of *eucalypse,* Calypso is a beautiful and possessive nymph.

6. Endorsing an idea of Blake's, Northrop Frye asserts that the Bible is the "Great Code" of Western literature; see Northrop Frye, *The Great Code/The Bible and Literature* (New York: Harcourt Brace Jovanovich, 1982).

7. Jorge Luis Borges, *Nueve ensayos dantescos* (Madrid: Espasa-Calpe, 1982). [In English: "Nine Dantesque Essays," trans. Esther Allen, in *Selected Non-fictions: Jorge Luis Borges,* ed. Eliot Weinberger (New York: Viking, 1999), 300–301. —EDITORS] See also "Borges/Dante: tradição, tradução, paródia," a panel discussion with Emir Rodríguez Monegal, Haroldo de Campos, Irlemar Chiampi, and Leyla Perrone-Moisés, in *Tradução e comunicação* (São Paulo: Editora Álamo) 1, no. 1 (December 1981).

8. Note that verses 57–63 articulate a network of words ("absence," "echoes," ghosts") reminiscent of Paz's definition of melancholia in *Sor Juana Inés de la Cruz o Las trampas de la fe* (Barcelona: Seix Barral, 1982): "El melancólico no está enamorado de sí mismo sino de un objeto ausente" [The melancholic character is not in love with himself, but with an absent object]. In "Il fantasma di Eros," a chapter in *Stanze* (Turin: Einaudi, 1977), Giorgio Agambem writes of a certain "epiphany of the unseizable" installed in the space left open when "melancholic introspection" turns toward an "unreal object." In Paz's poem, it is the "lover" who, in the face of the "vanishing" of the evasive beloved, feels surrounded by a "puñado de ecos" (a fistful of echoes) and of "sílabas fantasmas" (ghostly syllables), moving toward the "centro de la ausencia" (center of absence).

9. Walter Benjamin, *Ursprung des deutschen Trauerspiels* (Frankfurt: Suhrkamp Verlag, 1972).

10. In Andrew Marvell's "To His Coy Mistress," we find the metaphor of a "vegetable love" slowly growing throughout the centuries, "vaster than empires." Despite the fact that Paz, and, in Brazil, Augusto de Campos have produced admirable translations of this poem, it is João Cabral de Melo Neto, as Francisco Achcar has reminded me, who, in "História natural" (in *Quaderna,* 1960), approaches the passage of the amorous experience through three stages: animal, vegetal, and mineral. He writes:

> (pois os gestos revelam
> o ritmo luminal
> de planta, que se move
> mas no mesmo local).
>
> No fim, já não se sabe
> se ainda é vegetal
> ou se a planta se fez

formação mineral

à força de querer
permanecer tal qual

(for gestures reveal
the luminal rhythm
of a tree that moves
but still in place).

At the end, one doesn't know
if it is still vegetal
or whether the tree has become
mineral formation

by wanting to remain as such

In Marvell's and Cabral's examples, we are faced with metaphor and simile, respectively; in Paz's, the process is metamorphic, Ovidian.

11. G. W. F. Hegel, *Aesthetik I/II (Vorlesungen über die Aesthetik)* (Stuttgart: Reclam, 1980). I am referring here to the topic of *Naturschönes und Kunstschönes* as discussed in the introduction (37–39). Max Bense writes about the modernity of such a concept in "Die Aktualität der Hegelschen Aesthetik," in *Aesthetik und Zivilisation* (Krefeld and Baden-Baden: Agis Verlag, 1958).

Light: Paradisiacal Writing

1. Ezra Pound, "Cavalcanti—Medievalism," in *Literary Essays* (Norfolk: New Directions, 1954), 161.

2. T. S. Eliot, "Dante," in *Selected Essays 1917–1932* (New York: Harcourt, Brace and Company, 1960), 206.

3. Umberto Eco, *Il problema estético in Tommaso d'Aquino* (Milan: Bompiani, 1970).

4. Ibid.

5. Pound, "Cavalcanti—Medievalism," 189–90.

6. Eliot, "Dante," 225.

7. Juri Lotman, "Il problema di una tipologia della cultura," in *I sistemi di signi e lo strutturalismo soviético,* ed. U. Eco and R. Faccani (Milan: Bompiani, 1969), 145.

8. Erich Auerbach, *Dante, Poet of the Secular World,* trans. Ralph Manheim (Chicago: University of Chicago Press, 1979), 130.

9. Norman O. Brown, *Love's Body* (New York: Random House, 1966), 179.

10. Stéphane Mallarmé, "Les dieux antiques," in *Oeuvres complètes,* ed. Henri Mondor and G. Jean-Aubry (Paris: Gallimard, Bibliothèque de la Pléiade, 1945), 1190.

11. Eliot, "Dante," 228.

12. Ezra Pound, *The Spirit of Romance* (Norfolk, CT: J. Laughlin, 1952), 150.

Bibliography of Works by Haroldo de Campos

Poetry

Auto do possesso. São Paulo: Clube de Poesia, 1950. Anthology of poems.

"Antologia de poemas." In *Noigandres* (São Paulo) 5 (1962).

Xadrez de estrelas: Percurso textual, 1949/1974. São Paulo: Perspectiva, 1976. Partially translated into Spanish (*Transideraciones.* Ed. Eduardo Milán and Manuel Ulacia [Mexico: El Tucán de Virginia, 1987]).

Signantia: quasi coelum. São Paulo: Perspectiva, 1979.

Galáxias (1963–1976). São Paulo: Ed. Ex-Libris, 1984. Complete French translation by Inês Oseki-Dépré (1998). Complete English translation by Odile Cisneros and Suzanne Jill Levine (forthcoming).

A educação dos cinco sentidos. São Paulo: Brasiliense, 1985. Spanish translation by Andrés Sánchez Robayna (bilingual edition: *La educación de los cinco sentidos.* Barcelona: Àmbit Serveis Editorials, 1990).

Finismundo: a última viagem. Ouro Preto: Tipografia do Fundo de Ouro Preto, 1990. Reprint, Rio de Janeiro: Sette Letras, 1997. Translated into Spanish (A. S. Robayna), French (I. Oseki-Dépré), and Italian (*Baldus* [Treviso, 1997]).

Os melhores poemas de Haroldo de Campos. São Paulo: Ed. Global, 1992. 2d ed., 1997. 3d ed., 2000.

Yugen: cuaderno japonés. Tenerife, Canarias: Ed. Revista Syntaxis, 1993. Poems translated into Spanish by Andrés Sánchez Robayna.

Gatimanhas e felinuras. With Guilherme Mansur. Tipografia do Fundo de Ouro Preto, 1994. French translation by Inês Oseki-Dépré.

Crisantempo: no espaço curvo nasce um. São Paulo: Perspectiva, 1998.

A máquina do mundo repensada. São Paulo: Ateliê, 2000.

Poetics, Theory, and Criticism

Revisão de Sousândrade. With A. de Campos. São Paulo: Ed. Invenção, 1964. 2d expanded ed., Rio de Janeiro: Nova Fronteira, 1982. 3d ed., São Paulo: Perspectiva, 2002.

Teoria da poesia concreta. With A. de Campos and D. Pignatari. São Paulo: Ed. Invenção, 1965. 2d ed., São Paulo: Duas Cidades, 1975. 3d ed., São Paulo: Brasiliense, 1987.

Metalinguagem. Petrópolis:Vozes, 1967. 3d ed., São Paulo: Cultrix, 1976. Expanded edition: *Metalinguagem e outras metas.* São Paulo: Perspectiva, 1992.

Oswald de Andrade. Rio de Janeiro: Agir/"Nossos Clássicos," 1967.

Sousândrade—Poesia. With Augusto de Campos. Rio de Janeiro: Agir/"Nossos Clássicos," 1967. 3d ed., revised and expanded, 1995.

A arte no horizonte do provável. São Paulo: Perspectiva, 1969. 4th ed., 1977.

Guimarães Rosa em três dimensões. With Pedro Xisto and A. de Campos. São Paulo, Comissão Estadual de Literatura, 1970.

Obras completas de Oswald de Andrade. Rio de Janeiro: Civilização Brasileira, 1971 and 1972.Critical introduction to vols. 2 and 7.

Morfologia do Macunaíma. São Paulo: Perspectiva, 1973.

A operação do texto. São Paulo: Perspectiva, 1976.

Ideograma. São Paulo: Cultrix, 1977. 3d ed: EDUSP, 1994.

Ruptura dos gêneros na literatura latino-americana. São Paulo: Perspectiva, 1977.

Deus e o diabo no "Fausto" de Goethe. São Paulo: Perspectiva, 1981.

O sequestro do barroco na formação da literatura brasileira: O caso Gregório de Matos. Bahia: Fundação "Casa de Jorge Amado," 1989.

Livro de Jó. São Paulo: Giordano/Edições Loyola, 1993. Introduction and critical edition of Elói Ottoni's 1852 translation of the book of Job.

Três (re)inscrições para Severo Sarduy. São Paulo: Memorial da América Latina, 1995.

O arco-íris branco. Rio de Janeiro: Imago, 1997. Essays on literature and culture.

Os sertões—Duas vezes Euclides. With A. de Campos. Rio de Janeiro: Sette Letras, 1997.

Translation

Cantares de Ezra Pound. With A. de Campos and D.Pignatari. Rio de Janeiro: MEC/Serviço de Documentação, 1960. Edition published in Portugal: *Antologia poética de Ezra Pound.* Lisbon: Ulisséia, 1968. Expanded edition including work by Mário Faustino and J. L. Grünewald, São Paulo: Hucitec/Ed. da Univ. de Brasília, 1983. 2d ed. with the title *Ezra Pound: Poesia,* 1985.

Panaroma do Finnegans Wake de James Joyce. With A. de Campos. São Paulo: Perspectiva, 1962. 4th ed., São Paulo: Perspectiva, 2001.

Poemas de Maiakóvski. With A. de Campos and B. Schnaiderman. Rio de Janeiro: Tempo Brasileiro, 1967. Various editions republished by Perspectiva in São Paulo.

Poesia russa moderna. With A. de Campos and B. Schnaiderman. Rio do Janeiro: Civilização Brasileira, 1968. Various editions republished in São Paulo by Brasiliense since 1985.

Traduzir e trovar. With A. de Campos. São Paulo: Papyrus, 1968.

Mallarmé. With A. de Campos and D. Pignatari. São Paulo: Perspectiva, 1974.

Dante: Seis cantos do Paraíso. Rio de Janeiro: Gastão de Holanda, 1976. Limited edition of 100, illustrated by João Câmara. Regular edition: Rio de Janeiro: Fontana/Istituto Italiano di Cultura, 1978.

Transblanco. With Octavio Paz. Rio de Janeiro: Guanabara, 1985. 2d expanded ed., São Paulo: Siciliano, 1994.

Qohélet. São Paulo: Perspectiva, 1990.

Bereshith. São Paulo: Perspectiva, 1993.

Hagoromo de Zeami. Bilingual edition. São Paulo: Estação Liberdade, 1994. Classical Japanese drama.

Mênis: A ira de Aquiles. Bilingual edition. With an essay by Trajano Vieira. São Paulo: Nova Alexandria, 1994.

Escrito sobre jade. Ouro Preto: Tipografia do Fundo de Ouro Preto, 1996. Bilingual edition of 22 classical Chinese poems.

Pedra e luz na poesia de Dante. Bilingual edition. Rio de Janeiro: Imago, 1998.

A Ilíada de Homero. 2 vols. São Paulo: Arx, 2002.

Éden: Um tríptico bíblico. São Paulo: Perspectiva, 2004.

Index of Poem Titles

The group to which a poem belongs is indicated by italic text enclosed in parentheses.

Haroldo de Campos (1929–2003) is renowned worldwide as one of the creators of concrete poetry. He taught literary theory at the Pontifícia Universidade Católica in São Paulo for most of his life and published several volumes of poetry and literary theory. He was a prolific translator who introduced the work of many foreign poets to Brazil, including that of Ezra Pound in the early 1950s.

Antonio Sergio Bessa is director of curatorial and educational programs at the Bronx Museum of the Arts in New York.

Odile Cisneros is an assistant professor in the Department of Modern Languages and Cultural Studies and the Program in Comparative Literature at the University of Alberta in Edmonton, Canada.